TO
SIRRIO
MACCIONI —

FOR INVENTING THO
BEST LOBSTER SALAD
IN THE WORLD, AND
PROVIDING ME WITH A
POLKA-DOT TIE TO
WEAR WHILE
EATING IT.

MANY
THANKS

Dear Sirio,
        You are truly the
master host of the restaurant
world. Both Kathy and I
consider Le Cirque our favorite
eatery in the world.

        Kathy + Rick Hilton

mes compliments aux chef et à Sirio!
                merci,
                Charlie Brinkley

To Cirio —
        Not without you — We will
make your restaurant immortal
on film I hope — Thanks,

Connors   vs.   Nastase   0-6 : 0-6, 1-6 Nastase

A Most Enjoyable Evening —
See you soon!

Amicalement
Nastase

I couldn't
believe
how good
this was
when!
la-la

Dec 10, 1988

The best, the best,
the best there is. Thank you
so much. Thank you

In the Birthday Party
remembrance
Will always treasure
the food + drink! love

Always the
best!
Michael Taylor

This is the best

SIRIO

SIRIO

The Story of My Life and Le Cirque

Sirio Maccioni
and Peter Elliot

WILEY

John Wiley & Sons, Inc.

Published by John Wiley & Sons, Inc., Hoboken, NJ
Published simultaneously in Canada

COVER AND INTERIOR DESIGN: Vertigo Design, NYC
www.vertigodesignnyc.com

Library of Congress Cataloging-in-Publication Data:
Maccioni, Sirio.
Sirio : the story of my life and Le Cirque / by Sirio Maccioni And Peter J. Elliot.
p. cm.
Includes index.
ISBN 0-471-20456-0 (cloth)
1. Le Cirque (Restaurant) 2. Restaurateur—Biography. I. Elliot, Peter J. II. Title.
TX945.5.L39M33 2004
647.95'092—dc22
2004004313

PRINTED IN THE UNITED STATES OF AMERICA
10 9 8 7 6 5 4 3 2 1

IN MEMORY OF MY GRANDMOTHER,
Annunciata Lucarelli

Contents

FOREWORD

Sirio Maccioni is the perfect maestro. He does it all—great food, great entertainment—and always with a room full of the best people.

Le Cirque always has a great feel that I love.

That's the part most people see. The part that is harder to see is really the story of this book: the work that it takes to make it all fun, all seamless, with a room that is always buzzing—and the integrity, the honesty, and, many times, the personal sacrifice that it takes to stay on top.

Sirio is a man who stands by his family and his friends, in good times and in bad. Those are the instincts that have kept him in business all these years, and the instincts that will keep him on the cutting edge.

What more can I say? He's the only person I could ever imagine going into the restaurant business with.

It's the greatest compliment I know.

Bravo Sirio!
See you at dinner tomorrow.

DONALD TRUMP

PREFACE

This biography started with a letter. May 5, 1999: I'd just won a James Beard Award for Best Radio Show on Food for Bloomberg Radio. Instead of feeling elated, I felt deflated and tired. I begged off the after parties and came home to the usual pile of flyers and bills on my doorstep. Among them was a plain white envelope. Had it not looked so naked I might have thrown it out. Inside was a typed note in large block print—from Liz Smith. "Sirio Maccioni is driving us all crazy. He's been talking about writing a book for years—one idea is a modern-day take on Joseph Wechsberg's *Dining at Le Pavillon* but it never seems to happen. Someone else has been contracted to do the book but he's canceling the contract as we speak. He's got a great story to tell. Mort Janklow has been handling. Call him first thing tomorrow morning."

I was dumbfounded—at the letter and the timing. Why hadn't a book been written about him? Sirio isn't just a restaurateur, he's a legend: the Tuscan arbiter of modern café society, endlessly mentioned in gossip columns—photographed with, it seems, every celebrity, every president, and every glamorous woman. A book about Sirio would mean talking with the most important chefs and food writers of the post–world War II period, Bocuse, Vergé, Child, Claiborne, and Soltner—my father's idols all. It would be a history of modern cuisine and an examination of the people who eat it. Paolo Panerai, the editor of *Class*, wrote that what the powerful men and women of the world really had in common wasn't fame or money—it was Sirio. What a subject!

The next day, I called as instructed. Soon I was meeting with Cullen Stanley of the Janklow Nesbit agency, who eyed me with deep suspicion from behind her desk. I was not the first writer to be excited about Sirio and Le Cirque—the food, the women, the social history—and from her demeanor, not likely to be the last. It wasn't just a book about Sirio, it was a book with Sirio. I said I'd at least give it a try.

When I called Sirio to arrange a meeting, I shouldn't have been surprised at his response. "You come for lunch," he said, "and bring some friends." To Sirio's dismay, I arrived tieless and, worse, alone. I suggested we go somewhere quiet to talk. "No, no, no, you sit at the bar, we talk later." A borrowed tie, a Lobster Salad Le Cirque, a few glasses of Veuve Cliquot Grande Dame, *not* the regular label, and a flotilla of waiters later, Sirio came by and gave me one of his famous one-liners. "So the next time you come, you bring a beautiful woman with you for lunch, and I give you the tie!" Was I writing a book? Or just having a long lunch? Any attempt on my part to ask a direct question was rebuffed. The next several attempts all followed the same pattern—although I was pleased to see that each time I came, the time he spent and the stories he told got longer. But Sirio doesn't speak in regular sentences, rather in long, swirling, interconnected anecdotes, in his unique mixture of Italian and English. As he gets more ex-cited telling a story, he sometimes forgets language altogether and sounds like a tape recorder being played backward: "And then I said to her, bah, and she said to me, and I thought, My god, but you know? This is not right!" While I found his manner endearing and his stories layered with subtext, and—if you listened carefully—loaded with juicy nuggets of gossip and his-tory, I wondered how he could inspire such intense personal affection and yet be so apparently dysfunctional. My meetings with Mike Bloomberg were fifteen seconds or less, yet powerful businessmen and women sat with Sirio, bobbing their heads up and down listening to him like they had all the time in the world. Was it possible that people listened simply because they wanted this kind of attention? A corner table? A little flattery from the owner?

Eventually I came up with a plan that he agreed to, but I still wasn't sure how I would get past Sirio's veneer, or absorb the thousands of sto-ries people were telling me about Sirio and Le Cirque. Everyone had a story about Sirio or the restaurant: my florist, Dorothy Wako, who remembered working as an extra for a colleague who was decorating a party at Le Cirque, and getting a crisp $20 bill pressed into her hand for her trouble; a butcher who said Sirio had taught him how to make sausage casings. I had several as well—once when I was nine, with my urbane Uncle Howard, who was hell bent on teaching me proper table manners, and later in my early twenties when I was in love with a North Shore siren, who was determined that I take her to Le Cirque. On both occasions, Sirio seemed to recognize that I was over my head and rescued me—while he cleared my uncle's ashtray, I felt my arm tapped to indicate which glass to pick up, or which fork to use; fifteen years later he arrived tableside with dishes I hadn't ordered and before I could worry about how to pay for them addressed me and said, "This is a gift from Le Cirque for having the intelligence to bring such a beautiful lady to my restaurant."

On my first trip to Sirio's hometown of Montecatini, the method through the maze became clearer. Every year, while he is in residence, he has what he claims will be a small party, "Ten, maybe fifteen at the most— I can't have any more or my wife will leave me," he says every year. In the end, the party usually numbers around one hundred, the staff of the local hotels are brought in to help, and local politicians, movie stars, chefs, and any clients who happen to be summering in the area are all invited. The paparazzi linger. You just never know who might be there—and so it was that I found myself sitting by the pool chatting with Ms. Bette Midler.

"Have you ever written a biography before?" Ms. Midler asked.

"No."

"Have you ever written a book before?"

"No."

"Great. Remind me to call you the next time I want a biography done," she snapped in the scathing tone that has made her famous.

Always a little too serious, I protested I was rather a good choice.

"Maybe," she said cynically, "But I think Sirio has got it wrong this time," and moved to stand up.

What had seemed so amicable sitting by the pool suddenly seemed downright hostile. I lost my temper.

"Excuse me, ma'am. All those years when you were working your way up, didn't someone, somewhere take a chance on you? He has chosen me because it's what he feels is right in his heart. Right or wrong. Some people, you know, still do that."

I was breathless, upset, fighting back a rush of emotion and tears.

Ms. Midler sat down again. This time not the singer, or the actress, but the wife and the mother. She reached across and put her hand on my face.

"Oh-oh-oh," she said softly. "I am sorry. Yes, someone did take a chance on me. Sirio, in his own way, took a chance on me."

She put her hand back in her lap and we sat quietly for a moment, before she said thoughtfully, that living with your heart on your sleeve was a romantic way to live, but not exactly practical, especially in the world of show business. "Of course, he's Italian, and they're better at it than the rest of us!"

I asked her to tell me her Sirio story. "Oh honey," she said, "you just heard it. Listen to your heart."

My heart told me that the reason a book had never been published about Sirio was because everyone went for the glamour and the glitz of Le Cirque and of Sirio. Everyone had a story about Sirio, but Sirio had never really told his own story.

It turns out Sirio is much more than an arbiter of modern day café society, or even a restaurateur. He is also a little Italian boy—who witnessed and survived what no child should ever witness or survive, with immense style. The reason people love him—even though he is, as he would be the first to admit, "A pain in de neck," is because he wears the mark of his survival everywhere—in his words, in his restaurant, in his character. And almost everyone in the world who aspires to be something, someone, gravitates toward it.

Even though they may just call for a reservation.

THANK YOU, MS. MIDLER

I decided that Sirio would tell his story in his own voice, the way he might if he comes by your table, just arranged vocally so you don't have to make the same trip to Montecatini, although I'm sure Sirio would be happy to invite you! To do so, more than 300 hours of my interviews with him were transcribed, wearing out five young men and women who wrote down every word. My job became more one of translating what was difficult to translate, and creating a second voice in the text—Sirio's voice and then mine. I added the chorus, the people who helped confirm, or in some cases deny, Sirio's stories, and in some cases my own observations as well. Is this really the truth about Sirio Maccioni? Yves Montand's biographers, Hervé Hamon and Patrick Rotman, wrote, "In a way, every biography is a work of deception." Sirio, like his mentor Montand, is nothing if not the ultimate *cantastorie*, the storyteller, singing his story to stay out of trouble, keeping people entertained, trying to make everyone feel handsome, beautiful, perfect. Especially himself.

Peter Elliot, June 2004

ACKNOWLEDGMENTS

To everyone who has ever passed through the doors of Le Cirque,
THANK YOU FOR COMING

And to those with whom I didn't always agree,
THANK YOU FOR GIVING ME THE RIGHT TO DISAGREE.

Sirio Maccioni

There are many debts that I will never be able to pay, foremost amongst them Peter Meehan and his partner Hannah Clark. Peter spearheaded the process of translating the Sirio tapes, reviewed the non-Sirio interviews, and collated press clippings and photographs, as well as compiling, testing and writing all of the recipes. My thanks also go to the following people. Mike Bloomberg, for his support and for agreeing that I'd make a far better food critic than a commodities analyst. Also to Mike for introducing me to Liz Smith, who started the whole project—and to her staff, MaryJo McDonough and Denis Ferara. Pam Chirls, my senior editor at Wiley, whose instincts as an editor are second only to her instincts as a mother, parent and nanny, to quite a few overgrown boys. Paul DeAngelis, who took a work of journalism and made it into a biography. Carrie Safron, my colleague who keeps everything going with grace and skill. Michele Connors, Sirio's executive assistant, and Meegan Moszynski before her, who deal with the impossible every day. Fern Berman, for her counsel, advice, and support from start to finish. Dorothy Cann-Hamilton, who guided me toward the right questions. Barbaralee Diamonstein-Spielvogel, for tough—but always accurate—advice. Sheila Lukins, for inspiration, and the best ribs ever! Jean Doumanian, who helped me to see the book as a performance piece as well as a biography. Nancy Cardozo-Cowles, my Aunt, Toni Erlich, and Phyllis Halliday for their fire-side help editing the manuscript and first proposals. My godson Omar Halliday Noujoum, the little boy who helped me see Sirio so clearly. Susan Dooley, for keeping my house and my head together. Ann, Davies, and Jackson Cabot, and Jack, Gwendolyn, Chris, Jennifer, and Molly Rogers. Sirio's family and—in particular—his friends in Tuscany, who were kind enough to trust me with secrets they knew, which in some cases Sirio was unaware of himself. Also in Italy: the mayor of Montecatini, Ettore Severi, Gianni Mercatali, Simone Galligani, Romano Franceschini of Ristorante Romano in Viareggio, and Lorenzo Viani in Forte di Marmi for the best branzino; Paolo Panerai for reading the manuscript at every stage of its creation, in two languages; and a special thank you to Antonella, Egidiana's right hand, who had to take on a fourth son. The crew at Vertigo design: Alison Lew and Renata De Oliveira. Jennifer Mazurkie at Wiley who saw the book through production. Gregory Wegweiser who selected the photos. Milton Glaser for his design advice and drawing for the book. A special thank you to the entire office, wait staff, and cooks of Le Cirque and Circo in New York, Las Vegas, and Mexico. Oligario Vasquez Aldir, Oligario Vasquez Rana, Juan Perez-Gomez, and Benaud Schmidt at Hoteles Camino Real.

To the hundreds of patrons and professionals who spent time telling me their stories, opinions, and remembrances of Sirio, Le Cirque, and the Maccionis—not all of which were able to make it to print, but all of whom form the bedrock of the chorus throughout the book. Amongst them Slim Aarons, Lidia Bastianich, Mario Batali, Bill Boggs, Sissy Biggers, Marian Burros, Cesare Casella, Melissa Clark, Bill Cosby, Bill Cunningham, Rozanne Gold, Amanda Hesser, Bill O'Shaugnessy, Karen Page and Andrew Dornenburg, Julian Niccolini, Drew Nieporent, Nancy Reagan, James and Collette Rossant, Jeffrey Steingarten, Arthur Schwartz, Barbara Taylor-Bradford, Calvin Trillin, Alex Von Bidder, Michael Whiteman, and the family of Frank Zappa.

A special thank you to Cristina Barrios, former assistant to His Majesty, King Juan Carlos of Spain, and now Spain's ambassador to Mexico, for her countless favors to me, to Sirio, and to Créme Brûlée lovers everywhere. The offices of the Kennedy, Nixon, and Clinton libraries. John Gamble, Greg Dale, and Kenton Price, who provided on-demand PC and telecommunications support. To my lawyer, Jodi Peikoff. Lex Fenwick, Brooke Hayward, and Jennifer Rubell. Jamie Walker, for inspiration on the eve of the millennium and Granny's Blend in the nick of time.

And to Drs. Lee Dinwiddie, Al Mitchell, and Rick Margaitis, who had to listen to it all and got me to 285.

I dedicate this book to Robert Hensley Leach: my father, my mentor and my friend.

Peter Elliot

ANGOSCIA

WELCOME TO LE CIRQUE

LOOKING THROUGH THE GLASS DOORS of the imposing nineteenth-century mansion that houses Le Cirque 2000 and up the flight of stairs into its heart, you can see that someone is at home. If the house were still used as a home, you'd expect an obscured and heavy front door, the clang of bells, and a butler in tails. Instead, through the rounded tunnel, like a child's cardboard kaleidoscope, you see what looks unmistakably like a circus show—an explosion of light, movement, color, and energy.

It is rare if Sirio Maccioni, Le Cirque's owner, isn't behind the podium at the very top of the stairs, leaning slightly to the left, a telephone pressed to his ear and one hand scribbling in the reservation book. He has been in this position, at his own restaurant and others, for more than fifty years. A stream of waiters and busboys pass in front of him, rushing between the restaurant's dining rooms balancing giant round trays of glasses and china. As you rise past wooden boxes filled with fresh fruit, jeroboams of champagne, and a collection of ceramic monkeys, it's like looking up at a stage full of dancers doing a group shimmy, moving en masse from stage right to stage left, bodies popping up and down, hands reaching out, and faces turning. You might see a naked table roll by momentarily blocking your view of Sirio—and his of you.

When you do get to the top of the stairs, it looks as if a very opulent modernist circus has left its tents in the middle of the foyer of their robber-baron host. A circular steel frame supports bolts of brightly colored silk, parting to allow a clear view of the nineteenth-century vaulted glass mosaic ceiling and marble walls. The view is so Felliniesque that you half expect Sirio, looking more than ever in his later years like a Tuscan version of John Wayne, his tired eyes protected by almost violet glasses, to step from behind his post and say, arms outstretched, "Welcome to Fantasy Island. I am your host, Sirio Maccioni."

In reality, more often than not, Sirio stays behind the podium, grumbling something in his mixture of Italian and English down the phone, while his aides-de-camp, Benito Sevarin and Mario Wainer, do the meeting and greeting. If they know that Sirio knows you, they will part gently to allow him to move from behind his stand to come out to say hello—depending on Sirio's mood and the guest—in any one of five languages: Italian, French, German, English, or Spanish, with a few choice words in Mandarin. Ladies get a gentle kiss, usually to the hand, and gentlemen either a quick handshake or an imperial nod of the head. Then he steers you firmly, grabbing your arm or shoulder toward Mario, and whispers some ancient code in his ear that conveys exactly where you will be seated.

You may be seated in the dining room immediately to the right, the purple room, the former drawing room of the Villard Mansion. Sirio will sit in here anyone who he senses might be a little more conservative—since as décor goes, the purple room is, comparatively speaking, the most subdued of the lot. Or you may be seated in the red room, the mansion's former dining room, from which emanates a soft, reddish-glowing energy. This relatively narrow, long space, paneled entirely in mahogany, gives off the kind of feeling one imagines on a great art deco ocean liner. The red room is where you'll find Ivana Trump and Henry Kissinger or any number of celebrities or social icons. The bar, its barrel-vaulted ceiling domed twenty feet overhead and intricately paneled in gold, is Le Cirque's wildest and grandest space. Here, champagne bottles pop, cocktails are mixed, and—before what Sirio considers to be draconian antismoking laws were initiated—cigars and cigarettes were selected. On the backlit floating bar rest bowls of Sirio's favorite Italian olives, whole, their stems still attached, stacks of foccacia, and crystal urns full of mixed nuts. These three staples occupy a disproportionate percentage of his diet. The bar is the one area of Le Cirque where Sirio might let a man get away with not wearing a tie—a rule Sirio otherwise refuses to suspend.

Halfway between the bar and the two dining rooms is a landing and the grand staircase. The landing is large enough to house the sommeliers' station and a table for six. At the head of this table is Sirio's salon. From here he can see all the action as it parades in front of him, straight into the most prominent tables in the red room, and still never miss someone who might be coming or going to the two party rooms upstairs. On the wall in the "living hallway" connecting the dining rooms hangs a giant painting that depicts some of the restaurant's more famous guests and a few key employees. Over the years Le Cirque's mercurial owner has had painted in those whom he likes and removed those whom he doesn't.

On any given night more than 500 people or more will walk through Le Cirque and Sirio, either from his position at the podium at the top of the entrance stairs, his seat at the bottom of the grand staircase, or on one of his tours through the restaurant, will try to acknowledge all of them, some more and some less. The difference is considered by many to be your exact spot in the hierarchy of international society.

What Sirio is actually thinking is much more complicated. As you come up the stairs, whether you are known to Sirio or not, you are indeed being inspected for a place in the evening's show.

The decision about where to place you and how you will contribute to the evening is made before you have even arrived at the top of the stairs and has almost nothing to do with who you are. It's a decision that is made up of dozens of factors, but has ultimately less to do with social standing and money, and much more to do with the instinct of a boy who knew at nine who might have food in his pocket, who could be trusted to get you home safely, and who might kill you. The experiences of a lifetime in restaurants have merely honed Sirio Maccioni's skills.

This imperial arbiter of international society is a Tuscan orphan who survived because of his fascination and understanding of people and his fondness for having as many of them in one room as possible. Le Cirque has two meanings in French. The first is "circus," and the second—the one Sirio prefers—is a group of people getting together and having a great time. No other restaurant in the world could fit its name—and the dual meanings—more appropriately and no other restaurant could have a maestro better suited to the task. Sirio's re-creation of the circus, in both senses of the word, does something else—it provides a sense of order for its owner and his family. This outlandish environment was created as a kind of showcase for those qualities of human kindness, sexuality, and taste that he admires. To him, this almost unnatural world of excess, air kissing, and rarefied cuisine is the ultimate test—if you can shine in his circus, no matter who you are, you must have qualities that can shine anywhere in the world.

SIRIO

MY FATHER WAS A VERY GOOD FATHER. In those days there was no bad father, everybody was a good father. We're Italian, it's all in the strength of the family. My family survived war, not just the Second, but the First, and the one before that and the one before that.

Anyway, my father did the best he could. I remember his saying to us not to take sides. Not because we were heroic, but because we'd seen it all already. The black flag of the Fascists, the red flag of the Communists, the flags for the nations that were coming to occupy and kill us, the men who came to take my grandfather away for not wearing the pin or the flag. I remember the stupidity of the Italians, who sent off our soldiers to Ethiopia in clothes for fighting in Russia in the snow, and sent off our soldiers to Russia in linen that was supposed to be used in the desert.

As a child, though, I understood nothing. I just knew I couldn't make any mistakes. When my father died, he said, "Don't lie," which I knew was the same thing. Mistakes are luxuries for other people. No one ever gave me the luxury to make a mistake. Or the luxury to lie. Even though later on I learned that a small lie can save a great situation. I was sitting at Ronald Reagan's table during his first inauguration and he asked me, "So, my boy—did you vote for me?"

Now I didn't know if Reagan would be a good president or not, but his wife came to the restaurant, and he seemed very nice. The voice of my father said, don't lie. And I said to myself, why should I lie?

So I said, "No, Mr. President."

He looked at me and said, "Why, you're not a Republican? You don't like me?"

I said, "Mr. President, of course I like you! You know, I'm Italian, ... ," and then somebody came up to him and he left and I said, "Thank god!"

Then at night at the Kennedy Center I saw him again. Everybody was in line to go to the dance, nobody had enough time to go from one ball to the other, and some people were dancing with their coats on. Reagan was very euphoric. He called me: "You guinea bastard, come here. You come to my party, but you don't vote for me? Tell me why you don't vote for me?"

I said, "Mr. President, I am Italian. In my day Italy only ran well when we didn't have a president...."

He wouldn't let me finish—he only started to laugh. He said to everyone around him—his guards, his staff, his cabinet, "Look, I swear this is the only person in here who can tell me the truth!" And he gave me a big, you know, swing with the hand.

Later on I thought, My god, what have I done? Anyone smart would say, "Of course I voted for you, Mr. President," but I didn't. I always have to be difficult.

I think sometimes that maybe my father would have been like Reagan. He was a very elegant man. He had high, shining boots, boots like rich people wore, and a silver bicycle. He was very well dressed. It's true, he was a little cold. But you didn't go to your father for kisses.

I remember when my father said, "If we go to war, we are going to be dominated by the Germans. They are stronger, and if we lose, it is going to be worse." One time he spanked me very, very hard. I think I took a cigarette in school or something. I was very angry. But another time he built me a radio, a *galena,* the kind you make with a crystal. For me that was paradise. Sometimes I think the problem with me is that I didn't get spanked ever again by anyone! ◄◄►

THE MACCIONIS
OF MONTECATINI

S IRIO'S GRANDFATHER, GIUSEPPE MACCIONI, never tired of telling his sons that they might well be peasants who had no money, but at least they owned their own home—a two-hundred-year-old, two-story stone farmhouse with a gently sloping timbered roof on five hectares of good-quality farmland on the outskirts of the small resort city of Montecatini Terme. Everyone else they knew were tenant farmers, paying rent and usually giving half of the best quality of their harvested produce to their *padrones,* the landowners.

Montecatini was home to two distinct worlds. In town, its glamorous central park, given to the city by the Medicis, was home to eleven spas spouting the slightly sulphorous water that over the centuries had been credited with curing every known ailment, including love. The town's main square, the Piazza del Popolo, was connected to its most famous and elaborate spa, the Tettucio Terme, by a broad, tree-lined avenue named after the composer Giuseppe Verdi, who often summered in Montecatini. Along the avenue were shops, nightclubs, and *gelato* stands, and within walking distance of the park and the spas were the hotels. The most glamorous and regal of these, and the only one with its own adjoining parkland, was the Grand Hotel e La Pace.

Outside of town was traditional Tuscan farmland. Rows of cypress and oleander lined the perimeter of flat fields full of onions, potatoes, or corn. Far in the distance stood the peaks of the hills that protected the valley where the Arno flowed. The people who lived in town thought of their neighbors barely a few kilometers away as country folk, and the people in the country thought of those who lived in town as being almost mercilessly urbane. Given the proximity of the two worlds, most families had a part in both of them.

Giuseppe Maccioni was a religious man who went to church every day, prayed before every meal, and was as strict about the rites of the Catholic church as could be. He wasn't just a believer, he was intimate with the philosophical teachings of the church. He would invite the church's most prominent academics to his humble farm and argue the most intricate points of theology. It was his connections within the church that introduced him to a wider world that he had never seen. Dignitaries from the church, in local business, and occasionally from the government made a habit of stopping at the Maccioni farmhouse just to converse with Giuseppe. Giuseppe was also the local poet. He was classically Tuscan: not educated but intelligent; religious but not servile; proud but not arrogant. Simple, but not stupid.

Giuseppe's father, Serafino Maccioni, bought the house from their *padrones* around 1880 with the help of his eldest son, who had been able to save money cooking in restaurants, first in Montecatini and later, in nearby Florence. The Maccionis were a lucky family. They were known not just for having their own house but for producing the most valuable asset you could have in a rural society: handsome sons, an asset that always seemed to come in threes. Serafino and Giulia had had three boys—Guido, Fernando, and Giuseppe—and soon the Maccioni house was overcrowded with their wives and children. Guido eventually built his own house on the Maccioni land, while Fernando moved to Argentina seeking his own fortune, leaving the house and remaining land to Giuseppe. Giuseppe married Annunciata Lucarelli, the daughter of a local farmer, and they had three sons of their own—Eugenio, Alberto, and another Guido. The now established tradition of having at least one son pursue a career other than farming, which gave the family not only a roof over their heads, but some cash, went to the eldest, Eugenio, who was born in 1906 and usually went by the name Ugo.

The art of hospitality was well ingrained in Tuscans by the time Ugo Maccioni, age twelve, started working in the hotel where his uncle Guido had been a cook—the Grand Hotel Croce di Malta. Ugo's good looks, charm, and natural ability with languages got him to the position of assistant concierge by his midtwenties. Locals still remember Ugo as a young man of quality, not just another hotel worker. He radiated the experience of someone far older than his years and when people called him *Signore,* it was either a compliment or an accusation of presumptuousness, depending on who they were.

Ugo had known Silvia Lenzi for much of their lives. They were cut from the same cloth—children of local farmers who longed for something more. She was not just beautiful, but so striking that she intimidated people. When they were both twenty-four, they were married in Montecatini.

Uncle Fernando returned from Argentina on an Italian liner for the wedding of Ugo and Silvia—tourist class. No one in Montecatini knew anyone who had traveled to the New World in anything other than steerage. And even fewer knew anyone who had come back. Fernando's return though, was temporary: a chance to impress his family with his wealth, to give his favorite nephew his blessing, and to see them all for what he knew would be the last time. After the wedding, Fernando returned to Argentina, where he later died and his family remained. The gesture made a powerful impression on Ugo. His uncle would always represent the Maccioni who dared to pursue his dream.

When Sirio was born on April 6, 1932, he was the third generation of his family to be born in the Maccioni farmhouse. The unusual name was chosen by Eugenio, who dreamed of sailing away on a ship like his uncle Fernando; the *Sirio* was the newest liner in the Italian fleet. Giuseppe, ever the family poet, preferred the original association for his grandson Sirio—with Sirius, the brightest star in the sky.

Like so many Italian families, the Maccionis invested all of their aspirations in their firstborn son.

SIRIO

MY GRANDFATHER WAS A POET. You have to understand, when I was a child, we didn't have television. Even later when we did have television, it was at the local bar, and everyone went to the bar to see the television. We gathered for entertainment, because that's what we were used to. Everyone came to the house. We would arrange the chairs around the fireplace and roast chestnuts and take the ends of the wine to make grappa, or to make *vinella,* a very cold sweet drink for children. Very good.

In Tuscany there's a tradition of the *saltimbanco,* which comes from *saltare,* a word that means literally "to leap onto the table." The men went about the town, picked a table to leap up on, and started telling stories. Another word for them is *cantastorie*—"storytellers." It's a kind of folk story. They sing about where they come from, or about one town against the other, or the tragedy of a woman who married someone she didn't love, and politics, all in rhymes. Really what it was when I was a child was a way for people, smart people, to speak their mind without getting into any trouble. My father played mandolin, a friend played the clarinet, and they knew everything by memory, *Orlando Furioso* and the *Divina commedia.* Do you know how many times I heard my grandfather recite Dante from memory?

During the war my grandfather was held in very good consideration by the local people, especially the women, because he could read. My father and mother could too, but not my grandmother. Few people we knew could read. People would come from all around, mostly women, to have my grandfather read the letters of their boys who were fighting in the war.

AUNT LUIGINA *All of Sirio's best qualities come from his grandparents. Giuseppe was an artist and he wrote absolutely fantastic poetry. He was the best* **cantastorie.** *It wasn't an easy thing to do. It was a kind of a competition. You think of things to sing about, and the second person has to comment on what the first person sang, expand upon it, and make it better! My husband, Guido, did it too; he'd see a beautiful woman walk across the square and he'd write a poem for her on a napkin by the time she reached him. These are the kind of lines Guido wrote:*

> *per far morir quel povero marito*
> *per soddisfar con gli altri il suo appetito*

My grandfather was very generous. Maybe too much. Very religious, always making the sign of the cross in front of a church. He would even tip his hat to the dog warden. It took forever to go anywhere with him, and I cringed every time he stopped. Even then this veneration for the establishment—for the uniform—made me angry inside. If someone came to the house wanting food, he gave them whatever they wanted. My grandmother would say, "If you give it away, what will we eat?" and though we never went hungry, there was very little food and she worried. But he always said, "Tomorrow we will find a way."

Maybe it was a family fault to think too much like Tuscan men. The problem with Tuscans is, every butcher, every shoemaker, every peasant has the mentality to think that there is a straight line from them to da Vinci, Michelangelo, or Brunelleschi. In Tuscany we believe in elite. And this was the problem with my grandfather, he would say, "We are landowners, we don't wash dishes in restaurants." Later, when I started to question, I wondered why in the winter at least, when the hotels were closed, my uncles didn't go to Milan like people from the south to work, to make money, to get a job. They stayed on the farm and sat around the fire and told stories. They were farmers. My father wanted more for me than to be just a farmer. The point was, you didn't go to Milan, or to Florence even, or to Rome. You stayed at home.

One of the poems that we sung around the fire was about the story of Giuseppe's brother, my great uncle Fernando, who went on a ship to Montevideo, Uruguay. In the song Montevideo sounds like it's next door even though he knew it was across the sea. My father remembered Fernando, who had come all the way from Argentina, where he wound up, to be at his wedding: *D'arrivare tanto presto non credeo, da santos passai a Montevideo.*

My father would say the life of most Italians was doomed to poverty and misery. The only way out was education and a profession—not farming or the hotels. He swore that I was never, ever to go into restaurants, or hotels, unless it was with a beautiful woman and I was staying there as a guest. He said he'd kill me first. I didn't understand this attitude at all. I thought that my father had an easy life compared to my uncles and grandfather and my grandmother, who worked as hard as a man. He was a concierge at the hotel, he had elegant clothes, and he had a beautiful wife.

AUNT LUIGINA *Silvia was molta bella, una donna regale—very beautiful. I was what they call frizzante—sparkling, but not beautiful. We would marvel at her, because she looked like a client of the hotel, not just married to someone who worked there. She looked like a woman of luxury. She had very long legs and the most beautiful hands. She seemed out of place in our world. You couldn't imagine her in the fields. It's not that Silvia or Ugo put on airs or graces. They knew who they were, but they were different.*

My mother was very tall, very elegant. I remember my mother with a relative—they were the first women to wear trousers, not just in town but around the house. My grandmother said, "They are beautiful. They can do anything they want." In winter it was very cold. I remember my grandmother putting this special gadget between the sheets in our bed—charcoal in a container that made your bed warm. You know, it was so very nice that it is still the thing I remember most. It wasn't only the warmth of the bed but also the warmth of my mother or my grandmother, of my family. These are the things you remember as a child.

On Sunday my mother would dress up my sister and me to go to church. I could always feel how people looked at us when we came in, and I was very proud to have parents who looked different. Or she'd clean us up after a day on the farm. We would all put on our finest clothes and she would take us to town, to the hotel, to pick up or visit my father. I was jealous, my father was so lucky.

LANDINO LANDINI *[a local photographer] Sirio's mother captivated us all. I was a few years older than Sirio, and she seemed like royalty to me. I was so intimidated by her that when she came into a room, I had to leave. Once Sirio was watching his father and his mother dancing at a local hall and he became so jealous of his father and anybody looking at his mother, that he ran away. Luckily I saw him and knew what was in his mind and was able to bring Sirio back to the dance hall before they had even noticed he was gone.*

My father was the most elegant. I would watch him as he got dressed very early in the morning. To me it was all about clothes. They were a requirement of the job at the Croce di Malta—he had to have them pressed and clean. But for my parents there was also pride in the way our family looked. When he talked to my mother and my grandmother about clothing, about what they were wearing and the lace they made, he was very specific. He always knew about the textures, the weave, the way clothes looked and hung. You know, in those days you didn't buy clothes. You had them made by the tailor, locally or in town. Some of them were very good and some were very bad!

My father was very precise. He was concerned about how I treated my clothes, how I cleaned my room, how I had to have everything just this way. What I remember most about him is the black coat, the crisp white shirt, and the boots. Like all concierges, he wore two golden keys on either side—I asked him all the time if they were real gold. I think he said no, but I always heard yes.

The best thing was the bicycle. I remember my grandfather saying if you work hard, you might get a bicycle of your own by the time you're twenty-one! A bicycle meant power, freedom! It took an hour to walk, but with a bicycle you could go from our house to town in just a few minutes. My father's bicycle was painted nickel, but I thought of it as made of silver. I compared all of this to my uncles who worked on the farm, who got up with the sun and went to sleep with the sun. They worked in the fields and became sweaty and dirty. When it was hot during the day, they came into the house, which was cool because it had big, thick stone walls, and took a siesta. But I thought of my father, at the hotel, and that was much more important.

I didn't think about my father getting up before sunrise to be at the hotel before people got up, and working all day and never coming home until everyone was asleep. No one counted the hours he worked; he only got home when the day was done. I hardly saw him except when he was dressing, Sundays, or if he had a day off. My father hated this kind of life. And the languages! You had to learn the languages of the hotel guests— French, German, English. It was hard. It was hard for me, and my father had even less school than I did. My father was realistic. He had to make money. It was a job. But I didn't know that as a boy. I only saw the coat and the golden keys and the bicycle. The hotel was so clean, with its fresh smell and beautiful people. Wouldn't anyone love working there?

At home was the smell of the farm. The room above the kitchen was warmer than the others, and to stay warm we all slept in the same bed. But my grandfather had a fixation, like some people do now, that eating garlic was healthful, and we lived in a field of wild garlic. And so there was always the smell of garlic in my house. At night I liked to go in the room and sleep with my grandmother, but I couldn't stand the smell of garlic on my grandfather, so I'd go back to my parents' room, or my grandfather would move downstairs, and I'd stay.

After my sister, Clara, was born, I got to stay with my grandparents all the time. I was saved, you know, by the great love of my grandmother. My grandmother had the native intelligence of all great Tuscans. My grandfather was good, but my grandmother was great. She had the strength of ten men. She was like a horse. She made us all survive, I don't know how. ◄◄-

AUNT LUIGINA *Sirio didn't eat anything! His grandmother would always say, "Sirio, mangia"—Sirio, eat! If there was only one apple it was for Sirio. She favored him. If there was a piece of meat it was for Sirio. If there was one egg it was for Sirio. And you know there were all of us in the house then—Giuseppe and Annunciata, Ugo and Silvia, Sirio and Clara, Alberto, me and Guido. Before I married Guido, there were even more relatives there. Sirio doesn't even know how much like his father he is. Even when he was small, he seemed very tough and reserved. Emotional, yet very controlled. Very Tuscan. You know, the more emotional you are, the more reserved you are. Sirio all grown up was the most reserved person I ever knew. And the most emotional.*

FOR THEIR CLASS, THE MACCIONIS WERE PRIVILEGED, yet they lived a life of grinding poverty, a contradiction that would stay with Sirio his whole life. Although they owned the house they lived in, at times it swelled with various members of the family who were temporarily or permanently without someplace to live. The house had no basement and stood next to a little river in an area famous for its high water table. The stone house was cool in the summer but in the wet winter months was so damp that it was often necessary to place boards on the soaked dirt floors. Fighting against the house, trying to stay warm and dry, was a daily battle.

The primary business of the house was farming. Chickens, cows, vegetables, and a wine, which to the tastes of almost anyone seemed a tad salty, like the water that came up in the *bagni* in Montecatini. Its salty nature also made it quickly intoxicating. The mid-1930s were difficult times for the Maccionis, as they were for millions of farmers in Italy and around the world. In general, Italy was less severely affected by the Depression than other industrialized nations. Still, the Italian dictator Benito Mussolini's attempts to revive the economy, through programs that encouraged agricultural production and supported prices, were failing and most were discontinued by 1935.

Dependent as ever on farming at the worst possible time, the only real income in the family came from Eugenio. With his wife, two children, his parents, and two brothers to support, and little income coming in from the farm, a little had to go a long way. Necessities like shoes, clothing, and what Sirio still calls "machine-made" items like soap or salt had to be put off until there was cash to pay for them, usually once a month when Annunciata and Giuseppe took their products to the market.

Light industry—leather, wood, and clothing—were the only sectors that were growing. Meanwhile Mussolini's reforms, among them the first national health system in Europe, did not extend to rural parts of Tuscany. Although the family probably could have received better medical care for free in nearby cities like Pistoia or Florence, the family relied on Dr. Gino Merlini, a man they all knew and respected.

SIRIO

AMERICANS DON'T UNDERSTAND how terrible Italy was then. I mean, yes, as a child, I had a home and bed and a father who had a bicycle, but it was terrible to be my mother and my father and my grandfather and my uncles. Americans—I would die for America, and yet Americans don't know a fraction of what it means for life to be difficult like it was for us then. America is a nation, Germany even then, was a nation, France and England. But Italy had forty million people, each thinking different from the other and proud to do so. We were too independent mentally. My grandfather was just born when Garibaldi united Italy, but there was no real unity! We were all too poor to be united.

At first my grandfather thought Mussolini would do good things because, for the first time since Garibaldi, he really brought Italy together. But by the time I remember anything it was just frightening. My uncles stayed on the farm and kept working. Guido was born only in 1922, so he was too young to marry, which would have given him an exemption from joining the Party. Alberto was older and making sausages. Mussolini was going to tax him for not being married and not making babies. To make real money you had to work in town, like my father, at the hotel. Otherwise there was no cash. You traded a bottle of wine for sugar, or a sausage for some string. One year I got shoes, the next year Clara got them. This is what it was like. You didn't just take an aspirin or go to a doctor.

At first when my mother got sick, she had a simple cold, a throat infection. It all happened very quickly. The local hospital was fifteen miles away in Pistoia, or in Florence. She didn't want to go to either place, and no one was going to take her. My father called Dr. Merlini, whom we knew we could pay with wine, or a meal. I will never forget his coming to the house in a horse and buggy, even though from our house you could see the *autostrada* going to Pistoia and Florence full of cars and trucks. Even then, it seemed stupid. But Dr. Merlini, my family, did what they always did, the old way. There was no medicine, and even if there was, we could not have afforded it. She kept getting worse and I remember I moved into the room with my grandmother and grandfather.

One day my father came to the school with the bicycle to pick me up. "Get up on the handlebars, why don't you? Eh?" he told me, to my delight. We rode all the way home, until we turned the corner into the level yard in front of the house. Right away I knew. Even though the windows were small, I could see through the stone frames that everyone was wearing black.

My mother was dead. It was before the war, 1930-something... you'd have to ask Clara the exact date. It was my first year of school—fall. I think I was five or six. She died of what we'd call pneumonia today. But she really died because of pride, ignorance, and poverty. What a terrible, terrible contradiction.

She was laid out on the bed and my grandmother insisted that I go and say good-bye to her. I didn't want to go in. It was terrible, and I didn't want to go. My father took my hand and pulled me along and I did what I was told. ◄←•

"ALWAYS TELL THE TRUTH"

SIRIO

AFTER MY MOTHER DIED, I just remember it being a very hard time for everyone. I don't think I was special. Italians are funny about death. We don't like to talk about it and we're very superstitious. So I just remember the time, school, what was going on around me. Maybe I concentrated on that more, I don't know. I was like other boys—I went to school, I learned my lessons.

When I first started school, my mother would give me this bread that I loved, semile, a very hard kind of roll for making *panini*. But instead of giving me the sandwich in the morning to take with me on the walk to school, she would bring it to me at school at snack time. When I asked her why I couldn't take it earlier, she said it wouldn't be fresh.

Then when my mother died, my grandmother started to do the same thing. Not long after, I was on a picnic with a cousin of my father's and we were eating the same hard rolls—she went to the same bakery. When I told her that my grandmother brought me sandwiches in the middle of the day so they would be fresh, just like my mother, she smiled. Then, after we had our picnic, we settled on the blanket for a nap, her son was on one side, and I was on the other. I was resting my head on her breast and I could feel it and I could smell her clothes with the odor of heavy wool when it's worn and has gone soft and smells of the earth. I felt very, very sad but I didn't want to cry, not in front of her, not in front of her son.

We lay there for a long time in the sun, and her son fell asleep, but I was still awake. She held me even closer, if there can be such a thing, and told me that my mother had loved me very much. She said that my grandmother was afraid to break the pattern my mother had set, and that in order to be able to buy the roll to bring me at snack time, she always had to sell something first. I didn't say anything, I wasn't angry at my grandmother, and I never told her I knew. I just remember crying a little, smelling how a woman smells, resting my head on her breast and her holding me until I fell asleep. ⫘

SILVIA'S DEATH IN 1938 didn't significantly alter Sirio's day-to-day life, which was at once highly disciplined and highly chaotic. The discipline came from a regular routine at home, where Sirio and his sister seamlessly passed into the care of their grandparents and chorus of supporting aunts and uncles, while his father continued to work at the Croce di Malta. There were chores to do on the farm—learning how to cure ham, or help out at the harvest. Sirio's first year at school added another dimension of order. Under Mussolini, schooling was now compulsory and all children, from aristocratic families to peasant families, came together in one room. Annunciata would pack bundles of Uncle Alberto's homemade mortadella and hard bread, spread with fig jam that came from the tree outside Sirio's window.

Yet chaos was all around him. The same month as Silvia's death, Mussolini introduced the first racial laws, forbidding Jews from marrying Aryans, from holding jobs in the public sector, and from owning more than fifty hectares of land. The invasion of Ethiopia in 1936 had caused the League of Nations to levy economic sanctions, which impeded an already weakened economy—producing in turn increasingly pervasive demands of loyalty to Il Duce and the state. Civil servants were required to wear uniforms, handshaking was forbidden and replaced with the Fascist salute, and *squadristi*—bands of Fascist hooligans—were charged with enforcing personal loyalty to Il Duce at checkpoints throughout the country.

Schools were the most obvious way of instituting Fascist propaganda; a uniform state textbook was introduced using Mussolini's life or the history of the Fascist Party to illustrate almost all subjects. Daily gossip at Sirio's school was peppered with stories of families who had been forced to leave, people they knew who had been tortured or who had been murdered brutally in their sleep.

The Maccioni family were a model example of how one could get through dangerous times with as little impact on one's daily lives as possible. Ugo's boss at the Croce di Malta was its owner, Pacino Pacini. Pacini was influential in Montecatini—not only because he was a hotel owner in a town where hotels were the main source of revenue, but because he was the leader of a local chapter of the PNF, the Fascist Party. Pacini did not insist that Ugo take an active role in the PNF as part of his employment, and some of Pacini's protection rubbed off on Ugo's family, and in particular his brothers, who became adept at staying as far "off the radar" as they could. Guido, then sixteen, stayed mostly hidden, while Alberto pulled his cap down over his eyes and worked as close to the farm as possible.

It was Giuseppe, Sirio's grandfather, who put the family at most risk. In the early days he had thought that Mussolini's reforms might bring positive change. By the time of Silvia's death though, he could no longer stomach the propaganda and, while not militant, he resisted it passively. He had already developed some reputation for not rushing to throw up the black flag of the Fascist Party on occasional spot checks at the family home. Instead, he put up the Italian flag and when the officials came to question him, gave them a brief lecture on the unification of Italy in 1871. Given his age, position in the community, and clear evidence that he wasn't connected to any other power, there was little they could do except make his life difficult.

W E ITALIANS ARE A VERY PRIVATE PEOPLE. When you asked where somebody was, they said, "Oh, he died." You didn't ask why or how. You got smacked if you did. So you didn't ask. But people started to disappear. I remember that around that time my school friend, whose father was a doctor, came to me one day and said: "I'm going away because we are Jewish and we're going over the mountain to Switzerland." I'd never heard of such a thing. To say you were Jewish was like saying you were from Florence, or Rome or Milan. But he said, "We aren't safe."

My attitude today is very much like my father's and my grandfather's then. They went to jail, they were detained, they endured terrible things. They were not heroes. They fought with words, they disagreed, they didn't hurt anyone, and they stayed alive. My grandfather covered for my uncle when my uncle got caught trading something—bread, oil, I can't remember—and they took him away and put him in jail. Other times they came and surrounded our house with their rifles—to make sure that the food we produced went to the army. We knew it didn't go to the army. They just took it for themselves or sold it on. But my grandfather went and talked to the soldiers, young men, about the union of Italy, and Garibaldi. He was brave that way. Or maybe stupid. But he had their respect. ◄◄

WHEN GERMANY INVADED POLAND in September 1939, Sirio was seven years old. Italy was bound to follow suit by the Anti-Comintern Pact, the alliance of Germany, Japan, and Italy, known to Sirio and his school friends as the "Pact of Steel." Realizing the extent to which Italy was unprepared for war, Mussolini was able to hold off formally entering the war until June 1940. Before that formal declaration of war, Ugo had joined the Italian army as a radiographer, a skill, like many others, that he had picked up from his Great Uncle Guido's son Damino. As the eldest son and a widower with two children, Ugo could have taken an exemption. Instead he gambled that the army would not send him to the front and that his brothers, Alberto and Guido, would be given exemptions to stay on the farm. Ugo was right. He was almost immediately sent to a hospital in Bologna and the farm was ordered to produce supplies for the army.

I REMEMBER THE BEGINNING OF THE WAR. I was seven or eight. In every family, somebody had to go to the army. My two uncles were just farmers. My father had two children, he had the right not to go, but what could he do? My father was no hero, but he had courage. And he was smart. He was the one in the family who brought in the money. It's a question of survival. Our house was not safe. There was really no safe. For my father the army was more safe. Safe from the Fascists, safe from the partisans, safe from everyone. The only thing he was not safe from was whoever was coming to kill us and since we didn't know who they were, the army made sense.

In those days we used to go to school and the teacher used to make us pray to God to destroy England and France and America because they were the bad people, the bloodsuckers of our country. They would come and invade Italy, rape our women, kill us, and take things away. Even as a child I knew this was brainwashing. It didn't make sense, because Italians came and beat up my father and my grandfather, an old man. ◄◄

BEFORE HE LEFT FOR BOLOGNA, Ugo constructed a primitive and highly illegal radio, a *galena,* which became Sirio's lifeline. If Ugo couldn't be there, at least Sirio could stay informed about what was happening around them. Food shortages had started around 1941 in the big cities and pressure had increased on the local farmers to produce more. Hoarding was rampant. Farmers like the Maccionis did all they could to adhere to the letter of the law, though not beyond. Unannounced visits from the local militia, usually in search of food stores, increased, as did pressure on his uncles to become active members of the local Fascist organization.

The Italian army suffered a string of military fiascos, including the deadly invasion of Greece (which required the German army to come to salvage the situation), a crushing naval defeat at Cape Matapan, and the loss of its East African empire to British forces in 1941. When Axis forces capitulated at El Alamein in November of 1942, Italy lost its Libyan colony. Less than six months later, Allied forces cut off the Tunisian peninsula, capturing 235,000 Italian and German forces, and were poised to invade the Italian mainland. On July 10, 1943, American and British forces invaded Sicily and met with little opposition. Two weeks later Il Duce was forced to resign and was arrested. Fascism in Italy was over, but the war was not.

What happened that summer of 1943—essentially the collapse of the Italian nation—was the turning point in Sirio's childhood, the moment in which he would tell you his future was laid out for him irrevocably. The already weakened government fell into the hands of Marshal Pietro Badoglio, who neither surrendered to the Allies nor resisted the German occupation of Italy (even on July 25, the day Mussolini resigned, German troops had been pouring through the Brenner Pass). Instead he tried to negotiate an armistice with Germany, hoping to switch to the Allied side in time to prevent Rome from being invaded. The gambit failed—the Germans quickly installed themselves from the tip of Italy's boot to the northern border including Milan, Rome, and, of course, Montecatini. King Victor Emmanuel III and Badoglio fled, while Mussolini was "rescued" by the Germans and installed as the head of a puppet government on the shores of Lake Garda. As for the Allies, they couldn't agree on whether Italy was a friend or foe, or even on how strategically important it was. They did agree that Badoglio was not to be trusted, an attitude that in Sirio's opinion was subsequently applied to the entire Italian race.

The Allied push from Sicily onto the Italian mainland was a slow and painful affair, and the slowness of the Allied advance allowed for the building of an anti-Nazi resistance movement. The first partisan groups appeared in the spring of 1943. Many of them consisted of former soldiers or escaped prisoners of war who took to the hills to escape the Nazis and survived with support of the local peasantry. One of their favorite hiding places in Tuscany was the Padule, a giant flat swamp that started literally behind Sirio's house and stretched to the Arno River, twenty miles to the south. The partisans carried out acts of sabotage and commando raids; but they also settled old scores, which meant that at times the resistance movement seemed to be fighting a civil war as much as a war of liberation.

It was under these conditions of insidious civil war that Sirio—the Maccioni family's "brightest star"—came of age. He was eleven years old.

SIRIO

I N A WAY, when the war started, life was normal. We all had to live. My father would visit sometimes from Bologna and we would go into town to watch whatever remaining tourists dared to come to the spas, and we would watch them eat ice cream. Sometimes he would take Clara and me to see a film, usually American films dubbed into Italian and censored. But my favorite thing to do was to go to the circus, which still came to Montecatini.

So we lived, we farmed, we got arrested! It wasn't until Badoglio left that it all went very bad. Before there were Fascists, now there was nothing: hooligans and partisans and Germans who had come to take over the hotels and the town, and the Allies, the Americans, who started to come up from the south.

I was eleven years old but I knew how to get around. I could walk through the town, I could even go into the Padule, where sometimes my uncles and even my father were hiding. Sometimes I was the only one who knew where they were. The Germans would just come and take you away, or the partisans would just shoot you. I go crazy when people say I look like John Wayne. I hated the idea of John Wayne because, not only did I always side with the Indians, but because we really lived this way—with the violence. It wasn't a movie.

In those films they don't show the bodies that flowed down the river past our house. When Clara and I were still going to school, we sometimes had to step over the body of someone we knew and just keep going. The worst was at night. You just never knew. The Nazis came looking for Jews, or my father, or my uncles, or partisans. They would raid the house and take everything. And then you just tried to go back to sleep. Or you never slept.

One time I had to go bring food to my uncles in the swamp. I crawled to the place where I was supposed to leave the food and ran into some Germans in a truck. They told me to stop, but I started to run, and I heard a shot and I thought I was dead, but realized quickly that the bullet had just hit my leg and it wasn't so bad. So I just lay down and listened while the soldiers searched. At first I thought they were after me, but I was only ten or eleven, and when I heard them in the distance find what they were looking for, I realized they didn't want me. They shot everybody. I could hear them. It was raining very soft and I just lay there listening in the grass, trying not to scream from the pain in my leg. I listened while the people they had shot lay dying. I found out later that eight men had been killed. At the moment I was lying there, I thought they might have been my uncles. When it was over, and I knew my uncles were not with the dead, I crawled out of the Padule and went home and my grandmother cleaned out the wound with vinegar while my grandfather held me down. ◄◄-

SIRIO'S FATHER WAS STILL STATIONED in Bologna when the government collapsed. He worried about his children desperately, but had little choice except to trust that his parents would protect them and keep him informed as best they could. As the situation in Italy deteriorated, it became more and more difficult to get leave to visit Montecatini. The Germans had constructed a fortified wall, known as the Gothic line, designed to prevent an Allied advance across the Apennines and on to Bologna and Milan. Montecatini was designated a safe city: a comfortable and convenient base of operations for the German troops, with its wide avenues, ample rooms, and excellent food. The hotels became hospitals, with the white crosses of the Red Cross marked on their roofs.

The Allies captured Rome on June 4, 1944, and were making rapid progress north. It was only a matter of time before they reached Ugo's home in the flat fields just a few miles beneath where the Gothic line passed Montecatini. At the rate the Allies were advancing, Ugo's family were likely to be in direct contact with an invading force as well as the retreating Germans. The question for Ugo was whether to stay in Bologna and risk being captured by the retreating German army—or to make a run to the south to protect his family, hopefully bypassing the German retreat.

By late August the Allied Fifth Army had reached Pisa, but stopped—waiting for the Eighth Army to deliver the "first punch" on the Gothic line from the Adriatic Side. On August 25, the Eighth Army began its assault, breaking through the line on September 1, 1944. Within hours, the "Second Punch," had begun. Ugo knew that if he intended to get home, he would have to move before the Allied advance got bogged down at the Gothic line. It was now or never. On the evening of September 7, risking capture by German soldiers who were already scouring the occupied territories for able-bodied young men to use as slave labor or just shooting them on suspicion they were partisans, Ugo Maccioni set off on foot heading south across the mountains and the Gothic line.

SIRIO

WE DIDN'T HAVE A TELEPHONE, or any way of knowing that my father was coming home, but there he was. I looked up and he was standing there. Everyone was very happy to see him, but we didn't make a lot of noise or fuss. It was dangerous to do so—we could hear the armies and the bombs and we knew a little of what was going on around us. It was both exciting and very bad.

My grandmother made a special lunch. She even went out to the chicken house to get fresh eggs. To have an egg was a big thing! She went to the fields to forage for fresh onions, wild garlic, fennel, and artichokes. She sautéed the onions in olive oil to make *alietti,* a kind of omelette.

While she cooked he asked me to get the radio, which had been dug into a concrete hole, protected with a plastic ring and covered in dirt. I used to love knowing which plant was really the *galena*! My father and my grandfather listened to the radio very quietly—the Allies had begun the bombing of Bologna that morning and ground forces were attacking positions all along the front. The Germans had started their retreat from Montecatini. After lunch he told me to go find my uncles and tell them to come home as quickly and safely as possible.

There were three rooms upstairs. Clara and I had the room where my parents used to be, which we sometimes shared with Alberto. My grandmother and grandfather had the room in the middle above the kitchen, because it was warm. Guido, Luigina, and the baby, Katia, had the room at the end. But when my father came home he slept in my grandparents' room because the room had an armoire with a hidden compartment. It also hid a door that went to the chimney and you could climb up it and out a hole onto the roof and if he needed to escape he could jump from the roof to the river behind the house and then out into the fields.

The next day German soldiers came to the house. They were looking for food to take with them, they searched the house, and even looked in my grandparents' room, went outside again, and decided the only thing worth taking was the cow. Even though my father was in the house, my grandmother made a big fight. She tried to explain that we had permission to keep one cow because there was a newborn child in the house. But the Germans were leaving and they didn't care. When they went to take the cow, she lunged at both soldiers with a wooden board. I thought they might just shoot her, but I think they were amazed that anyone would fight so hard for a cow. Then they just left. ◄◄

BY THE MORNING OF SEPTEMBER 11 the Germans had made an almost complete withdrawal and Ugo risked going into Montecatini on his bicycle. They had already abandoned the Grand Hotel Croce di Malta, where Ugo had worked before the war. At the spa's most famous hotel, the Grand Hotel e la Pace, only the shells of the tents that had been built out into its private park as army barracks were still standing. The cavernous main building, used by the highest-ranking German officers as it was once used as a seasonal residence for the world's highest-ranking royalty, looked as luxurious and regal as always. As Ugo secretly watched the final retreat, the skies whistled with the peculiar sound of bombs slicing through the air. The German retreat was being covered by their forces still lodged in the mountains high above Montecatini—some in the ancient hill town of Montecatini Alta—and they continued to lob shells over the city and into the Padule.

Ugo went to the crowded marketplace on the Via Bicchierai. Right near the railway station, at the point where the road for the market meets the Corso Matteotti, the main road into Montecatini, is a small open-sided piazza. A bomb, intended for the Padule several miles away, exploded there instead. Three people were killed instantly. Ugo was rushed to the local emergency room where he clung to life—chunks of shrapnel protruding from his chest and legs.

The hospital had neither medicine, nor blood.

SIRIO

I WAS DOWN IN THE OPEN COUNTRY. I don't remember who came. He said you must come right away. Four people have been hurt and one is a Maccioni, but no one was sure. He was pulling on my arm.

We went to town. Montecatini was supposed to be safe—we'd put up with everything else, but the bombs weren't supposed to fall on the city. People thought it might have been a sniper. It was in the area where the market is. Everyone was hysterical and all the women were crying, the buildings were burning. And we didn't know who or what it was. But I knew my father was hurt. And I knew then, I guess in my mind, that it was a bomb. But this wasn't supposed to be happening. It wasn't supposed to happen.

We went to the small hospital, the *pronto soccorso,* that's still there. Nonna, my grandmother, was there already. It was very bad. They decided not to bring my sister inside, but I was able to speak to him. But he was not... I knew he was not. ...

He had lost a lot of blood. And there was no blood to be had. My god—none at all. One of my uncles tried to go on a bicycle to a larger hospital in Livorno to get blood. Livorno is fifty miles away, in a war, on a bicycle, can you imagine? I tried to talk with my father, but it was very hard. My father was always very correct, you know? Very elegant and to see him there struggling to take a breath. ... He was holding my hand and trying to talk to me. I looked at my grandmother to help me, but she was behind the screen. And I was alone with him and he said to stay with Nonna, and to take care of my sister. And always to tell the truth. He tried to say other things, but he was going in and out, he was very weak. Eventually, my grandmother came in and took me away from there.

They told me he would live, but I knew he would not survive. For two days the bombs fell, while everyone stayed in the house. The Allies were trying to hit the *autostrada* that ran nearby, and the house kept shaking.

My mother's sisters and my grandmother's sisters were praying for my father. I don't mean to be unkind, but I thought they were fools. I could hear their voices in my head even when they weren't talking. They talked about my mother, who was dead, they said that I looked like my father and Clara looked like my mother and that I was a poor, unfortunate boy. Worse, that I was unlucky. "Poor poor boy, poor little orphan boy," they said, "God spare the children from being orphans."

After a couple of days, I left the house and I went to sit at the grave of my mother for a long time. I knew my family was out looking for me, to tell me what I already knew—that my father was dead and that what they had been saying was true, that I was an orphan farm boy.

It was September 14, 1944. My father was dead. I went to town and I sat on the white marble steps of the Tettucio Terme. From there I saw the Allied armies moving in. The Germans had now gone. The Americans? Well, they looked like the circus coming to town. ◄◄

IT'S ALWAYS ABOUT LEAVING

SIRIO

I DIDN'T CRY WHEN MY FATHER DIED. I knew I was going to have a difficult life. I knew I would have to be very strong, and never make a mistake and never lie, like my father told me. But I didn't cry. I was just one of millions who were going through this and when that happens, you don't talk about it, you just do it.

"Doing it" meant I worked. I washed the jeeps of the American soldiers and they gave me chocolate, or a little change. In the movies you see them bringing us chocolate and bread. Well, I worked for that chocolate. And when you see pictures of the liberation, the celebrating, you maybe think it was over in one day. But it wasn't like that. Yes, we celebrated… but we were still occupied. I've seen occupation by the Germans. And I've seen occupation by the Allies. And believe me, it was a difficult occupation. It may have been a liberation, but it was a liberty we were forced to accept. Everyone was afraid.

The Allies brought things, supplies, sugar, medicine—but they also did many bad things. The Allied troops could be very friendly, or very nasty, and in one way it was worse than the Germans because we didn't know why or what to expect. They broke into shops, took things, beat up people, scared old ladies. They seemed very nice, but when they were called to the front and they didn't want to go, they became dangerous. They would drink whatever they could get their hands on, grappa, grain alcohol—even gasoline. It was terrible. I would listen to the women the troops ran into when they were drunk…we just learned to put our hands over our ears. There's a town very near to Montecatini where there are big pine forests…the Allies came and used the women like whores. To this day there are families that come from those women. When I saw that, I came to believe that no one—not the Americans, not the Germans, not the Italians—no one was right.

Today when people ask me, "How did you feel as a child?" it just makes me angry. Who had time then to know about feelings? I didn't have feelings—I lived, I survived. I was angry. When you're poor you're angry and I'm still angry. But it made me focused. Disciplined.

The hardest thing was losing hope. At first with Mussolini there had been hope. The only thing he really did right was to say that we Italians were not slaves, that the women were not whores and the men were not Latin lovers. We felt like it was true. But then it was not true, and we were distrusted, looked down on. I could feel that feeling in the way the French used to look at me. It was the same way even when I first came to New York. Italians were people others didn't trust, who lost the war, who tried to make it good when it was bad. Even then I knew what that meant: that I didn't have any room to be stupid.

Mussolini tried to do some good, but he almost destroyed Italy, and for what? For nothing. The most important thing is, we didn't have the right to disagree. I believe in only one thing—the right to disagree. If the Americans need me I am ready to go and fight for America. But I also want the right to disagree.

No one wants to look to the past five hundred years. They all have guilty consciences. It's history. What's the point to have gone through all of this, war, devastation, countries ruined, women ruined, to lose the history? When I was a boy, the *squadristi* would tie up men in the square and give them castor oil to make them shit on themselves. Do we go back to that? Or my grandfather dragged across the piazza and his arm almost broken with the *manganello* because he wouldn't wear the black flag on his chest?

And so the easy solution is the bombs. They weren't supposed to bomb Montecatini, because it was protected by the Red Cross and because there were hospitals, but the area all around was constantly being bombed. I kept the photos of Eisenhower and the American generals on my wall, but later on I took them all down and I burned them. And Badoglio, why would anyone keep a picture of him?

I'm a man against bombs. I'm a good Catholic in my way, and I'm devoted to the Pope. But if tomorrow the Pope says that to solve the problem we have to use bombs, then I'm against the Pope. Through what small intelligence I have, I know that through all history, bombing has never been the solution to something. It does not work. There is no such a thing as an intelligent bomb. It was an intelligent bomb that killed my father.

You know, many times in my life people have said to me that, with the things I've seen, I should go talk with a psychoanalyst. I will never go because I'm afraid they will put me in a mental hospital and I'll never come out. It's not that I think I am great, that I'm the savior of the world, but I always find that I automatically have to go against the stronger. It comes from my father, from my grandfather. It makes no difference whether it's a small thing or a big thing. You have to be what you are, to do what has to be done with a pure conscience.

Don't think I'm doing it for the good of my heart. I think its revenge for the way I grew up. A gift from the land, from Tuscany, from being Tuscan. And I don't want to give that up to any doctor. It is not for sale. It belongs to me. It's what we lived and fought for. It's *angoscia*—anguish— and it is terrible. ◄◄-

WHEN THE WAR IN EUROPE ENDED in May 1945, Italy was the oddity among European states: it had neither won nor lost. The victorious Allies were still not sure to what degree Italy should get its support. Internally, the nation was crippled by massive unemployment, runaway inflation, and the costs of reconstruction. Montecatini, along with the rest of Italy, remained occupied by Allied forces, but the town had advantages others didn't. Except for the bombing that had killed Sirio's father, the town itself was remarkably untouched. The successive hordes of foreign troops had treated the hotels that had doubled as barracks with the respect they might have accorded them had they been paying guests.

Tourism was essential to rebuilding the economy and, fortunately, it was the quickest local industry to rebound. Even before the war, the concept of spending a month at a spa to cure physical ailments was being replaced by more modern ideas about medicine. Only habit protected the particular world of European spas like Montecatini. Hoteliers saw to it that Montecatini capitalized on its reputation for "the cure," but emphasized the curative nature of rest, relaxation, and in particular, losing weight. In the 1920s Mussolini had pushed to revive the spas by making them look more like backlot stage sets of faraway Hollywood than crumbling shrines to aristocracy. The intervening war years had merely given the shining new structures the refined patina of age. A stunning modernist train station completed in 1935 and its location along the quickly rebuilt *autostrada* made Montecatini attractive, particularly to the most important postwar clientele: Americans, as well as those known throughout the world as café society, the people who spent their lives on the road, traveling from one chic destination to the other. In the shadow of the most deadly war in world history, Montecatini had the right mix of Old World class, Italian charm, modern convenience, and *arriviste* ambition. While the rest of Italy struggled, Montecatini seemed like a relative oasis.

Sirio was one of an army of local boys who took part scrubbing, mopping, and vacuuming the hotels that summer of 1945, before the first guests arrived in the fall. Sirio was dazzled. The people Sirio had seen only in dubbed and censored films were now walking along the Viale Verdi—Gary Cooper, Cary Grant, and Grace Kelly (the future Princess Grace of Monaco); the Agnellis, Churchills, and Windsors. Sirio was already aware of who most of these people were, but their celebrity or fame didn't impress him nearly as much as their clothes, the amount of chatter generated by their presence, and their freedom.

M ONTECATINI WAS MAYBE A LITTLE BETTER OFF than other places in Italy. Everything started again very quickly: the hotels, the spas, even the restaurants. I tried to start again too, but it was not so easy. I was technically still in school, but during the war, school was interrupted all the time (and after 1943 there really had been no school). One day someone was not there because they were harvesting, or someone died, or the bombs shut it all down.

When it started again after the war, I could do only one more year free. And I really didn't want to go back. After the war, I was no longer the son of a man who worked at the hotel, a concierge, but the orphan son of farmers. Now girls would say to me, "My family doesn't want me to see you," and that sort of thing. They wouldn't even speak to me. But my grandmother and grandfather made me finish primary school.

I wanted to go to school but I couldn't. When we were very young everyone—farmers and children of the *padrones*—were all in one room, but to go on to the next level you had to have money. I couldn't go to my uncles or my grandmother and ask for money to go to school. Even though as a war orphan I would probably have been given the money to go. The school was in Pistoia, which was too far away from my family. I didn't want to leave home. In my head I heard my father say that the life of an Italian who doesn't get an education is doomed to poverty and misery, but I also heard him say to take care of my family.

After the war things were also worse for my family. The Communists in Tuscany were becoming very big and my family was seen as being anti-Red and the Reds made things very hard, especially on my uncles. My grandfather was tired and getting older and my grandmother was already sixty-five years old and was working to keep the house and run the farm with my uncles. It was almost impossible to live. I don't know how they did it.

I think mostly I just didn't want to leave home, and so I decided not to go to high school. I tried to learn how to be a mechanic, but I didn't like to be dirty. I was supposed to change the oil in the car and didn't know it was very hot, and I burned myself and I said to myself, "This is really not what I want to do."

I had to make a very difficult decision. It would have been very, very easy to be on the wrong side [of the law]. People smuggled, cheated, lied, everyone changed sides to do what was convenient at the end of the war, but from my father and my grandfather I had a different idea in my head.

In Montecatini, maybe in all of Italy, only the hotel school and the hotels were functioning, and as a war orphan I had the right to attend. I knew this was not what my father would have wanted, or my grandfather. My grandfather was always saying: "We are landowners, we don't wash dishes in restaurants." And my father had always wanted more for me than to be a waiter. But I had no choice. We were so poor, and all I could think of was not to be poor. In the hotels I could make money.

Besides, everyone around me worked in the hotels in some way—as a waiter, as a cook—and they always thought that it would make them rich, or anyway, successful. But there was a hierarchy and it was very strong. If you worked hard, twenty or thirty years later maybe you became the manager of a small hotel, not very good, or if you were very lucky you would land somewhere like La Pace and you could become an assistant manager. It was not very glamorous at all. But I didn't know any of this then, I just knew that I was angry, that I wanted to make money, and that I would have to be smarter and quicker than my father and not make any mistakes and then maybe I could do well.

The hotel school in Montecatini was really a source for labor for the hotels. You worked during the season at the hotel and then you sat in a classroom and learned the things you needed. My first job was at the Croce di Malta. When I went to work there—it's where my father and my great-uncle had worked—they told me I needed black shoes. I didn't have black shoes. We would have to wait a year to buy that kind of thing—when the harvest came in—or else sell something of value. So my grandmother took a pair of my father's shoes, which were too large for me, and painted them black. Very badly, so that when they dried, the brown color came back. And my sister, Clara, who was already learning to sew for other people, made me a white shirt from my mother's linen. It was all we had.

The hotels were run with a provincial mentality. You had to speak a minimum of two languages. If you wanted to be a little better, you had to speak three: your own language and French and English. French because it was the classical mentality and French because the restaurants in the big hotels, even in Italy, were run in the French manner—they even spoke in French! And English because it was what you had to do whether you liked it or not. I am not talking about managers, but waiters.

But we also learned the things that no one ever teaches anymore, the things that make a waiter who is Italian different from everyone else. A waiter in Tuscany was not a cook, but he had to think with the mentality of a cook. If there were mushrooms—porcini or ovoli that only come in once or twice a year, for a very short time—the chef didn't prepare them in the kitchen and put them on a plate for you. All they did in the kitchen was clean them. The waiter had to prepare them at the table: cut them into thin slices, perfectly, dress them with olive oil and maybe a touch of lemon, salt, and pepper. One extra drop of oil and I could ruin these delicate mushrooms, and be ruined myself! I had to learn things like how to hold the spoon and the fork in order to serve, how to prepare pasta at the table, or how to slice a steak. Most important we had to fillet the fish. In Tuscany the whole fish was brought to the table with the plates all around, and we would have to debone, fillet, and serve the fish perfectly for each guest, presenting their piece to them without spilling the oil or getting bits of the fish on them. These are things waiters don't do today.

I learned very quickly that the real key to success in the hotels, besides being very good at working at the table, was to listen to what the customers wanted and to respond without offending the people I worked with. I was good at that. It was very important to know which of the people you worked with were the smart ones and which were the stupid ones, but never to offend either.

You went to the school during the hotel's off-season, in a classroom. There you learned the classic things I've been talking about—how to serve, where to place silverware, how to carve, that sort of thing. But if you were good you could continue to work in other restaurants. I went to work, first at a very good restaurant in Florence called Otello. I could work out everything that I had to do for the restaurant, but I could not work out how to sleep. They put fifteen people in a room on mats with a bathroom down the hall. The stink was unbearable. Maybe the only smart thing I did was never go into that room to sleep. When everyone else got off work they either went out drinking or went to sleep in that room, but I stayed at the restaurant and became good friends with the managers and the owners who stayed up to go through the books or check the wines or just to get ready for the next day. I don't think I slept at all six days a week. On Sunday I would take the train back to Montecatini and sleep there and come back on Monday.

During these late nights I learned things. I started to learn about good Italian wines, and I really started to notice how inefficiently restaurants were run. The mentality of the restaurant was more like a family. They opened when they felt like it, closed when they felt like it, and cooked what they wanted. This made for a very good restaurant, but you could see they never really made more money than what it took for them to live, which now I think was a good thing.

AUNT LUIGINA *Maybe it came from his father and mother, or maybe it was just smart, but Sirio was always very good at knowing who was going to be a success and who wasn't. You just never saw him with the bad boys in town.*

It wasn't that I was so good. I wasn't. I just knew I couldn't afford to make a mistake. It was very clear that success in the business depended on who you knew. In the hotel business all the best people knew one another. You got the jobs because you were good and they trusted you to not make them look like an idiot. They hired one person because he was the best in the dining room, another because he was best at the door, and a third because he was best at organizing the housekeeping crew. It's how it worked. Everyone moved together. If a job opened up in another hotel or a restaurant you didn't give it to the person with the bad reputation. Maybe the people with the bad reputations had more fun! You heard the stories: they stole something or they got a girl in trouble and that was the end of them. I couldn't do that. What I learned very quickly was that in this world there is good and there is best. The world gets lulled into thinking something is good, when good is just mediocre. The Croce di Malta was a good hotel, but La Pace was La Pace. Everyone wanted to work at La Pace, because once you were there, you could go anywhere. La Pace was like having a passport to go work at any hotel in the world.

At the Croce di Malta I had been under the wing of Sandro Giovanetti, who was the maître d'hôtel. Aldo Bindi was the head of the dining room at La Pace and the important people from La Pace could really have the best of anyone they wanted. He had long had his eye on Giovanetti, but Giovanetti couldn't leave the Croce di Malta at first, or something, so Bindi took me. My family had worked at the Croce di Malta for a long time, but Pacino Pacini, who owned the hotel, knew this was a good move for me. Because of this support I learned that you never leave in a bad way: you leave, but you keep the relationship. So I started at La Pace under Gino, and, later, Vittorio Mariatini, who was the general manager, very tough, and Giovanetti came the season after.

At La Pace we didn't pretend to be the best, we had to *be* the best. Everyone understood what to do, and if you didn't, no one was afraid to ask. If you were afraid to ask, you didn't belong. There was less bickering between this person and that person because everyone knew that the goal was to get everything about the service just right, a perfect balance, respectful, professional, not this slobbering you see these days, but not too servile either. The secret, the thing we were always trying to get right, was to be there and not to be there all at the same time. You serve, but you are not servile. You are not, never, an equal—that's a disaster—but people prefer someone they respect over someone they can step on.

Right away I saw a difference in the people I was serving. There was this princess or that princess, more international guests, and the Americans. I must have served Mrs. Rose Kennedy, the mother, one thousand times. The whole family came for a month and the husband and sons went all over Europe and left the women at La Pace so they could travel. The Duke and Duchess of Windsor, Onassis from Greece, lots of Germans, and some English. It was a very regular circuit. St. Tropez, Montecatini in spring and summer, St. Moritz or Sestriere in winter, London, New York, or Paris in between.

The aim for all of us in the school was to reach London, because that was the best place to learn English and still be connected to the hotels in Europe and the hotel school. My father knew French. He read in French and I was learning French as best I could in school with a teacher in Montecatini, but I spent the whole time looking at her tits and didn't learn anything at all. So, it was London, but there were few places in London and they didn't take just anyone—certainly not anyone Italian, and you were competing with people from Spain, and Germany, and France too. So I kept applying through the school but nothing ever happened.

My second year at La Pace, I met a lady from a very important family. Her name was Adrian Kaiser. She was very beautiful and very rich and she kept calling me to her room. It was, you know, very obvious what she wanted. But then, I couldn't make a mistake. You didn't mix with the people in the hotel if you didn't want to lose your job, and this lady was very, very wealthy. And even though I was very skinny, she kept talking to me. I would tell her things about my family and about my dreams. And then she offered me a job as her companion. She wanted to take me to Salzburg with her. She said she would pay for my education, for my clothes, for everything. All I had to do was to be her companion.

It was even a joke in the hotel about whether I would go with her—my boss, Bindi, even said to me that if she went out with me, he would give me the night off! [But] I had to say no. And she got upset and went to the hotel to ask if she could take me with her. They said yes, but still I said no. How could I go to my grandmother and say I was going to be a gigolo? In the end, Mrs. Kaiser left a check for me with the hotel, for my grandmother, but we never cashed it. I don't think she ever knew how hard it was for me to make that decision. I dreamed about those ships, trains, and planes. I thought she might be right. She was a very nice lady. Maybe it was my first really big mistake: I probably would have done much better to be a kept man.

One winter, I went to work in Abetone, in the mountains, at another of Pacini's hotels. There I was working in a restaurant called La Selleta when I met Zeno Colo. He was a local skiing champion, and he was from a town not very far from me in Montecatini. He was very Tuscan—very tall. We talked and had fun and I didn't think very much of it except that he was a nice man. He skied on homemade wooden skies!

The next winter season I went to work at the Hotel Principe di Piedmonte in Sestriere, which is owned by the Agnelli family. From one day to the next Zeno Colo went from being a poor Tuscan ski instructor to, you know, the most famous skier in the world. He had won the World Championship in 1950, the first one held after the war. And there he was in Sestriere, among all these people making a big fuss over him. When he saw a face he knew, he screamed at me: "Bimbo! What are we doing here with all these people, they are all *crazy*!" Later in the season when it was a little quieter, the manager decided he wanted to stage a race among the staffs of the hotels in Sestriere. He came to me and said he had heard I was a very good skier, and that I had to practice very hard so that we could win the race. I had never skied before in my life. I suspected Zeno, so I went to him and said: "What have you done?" He said not to worry and that he would give me lessons. We practiced very hard. He took me to the top of Mount Sises, I think it's 2600 meters straight down to the village. But I was young and unafraid. And soon I got to be pretty good.

The day of the race they gave me half a bottle of grappa to boost my courage and I went down the mountain and when it came to the turn I fell, but just a little and I noticed as I went along the rest of the way that my foot was a bit wobbly, but it wasn't until later that I realized I had broken my ankle! I came in second or third, but best of all, I got almost three months off in the hotel while it healed. No work—and these girls came to massage me. The manager felt bad, and everyone agreed never to tell my grandmother that I wasn't working. Sestriere was also when people started to compare me to John Wayne, since I walked funny on account of the ankle. Other than that, it was the best time of my life!

In April I went back to work at La Pace. That season I met the Fiores, a nice couple and a very attractive daughter, named Giusetta. The Fiores owned a restaurant in Paris. I talked to them the way you talk to people at a resort, and they said that if I was in Paris I should come see them and they would give me a job working in their restaurant. I didn't think too much of it. But later on the school told me about a program at the Hôtel Plaza-Athénée in Paris. The idea was, you went and worked in the hotel, they gave you a room, and you learned French. I was already more or less at the top of the list in Italian hotels. What could I do in Italy? Go to Milan or Rome and wait twenty-five or thirty years to become general manager of one of their big hotels? This may sound arrogant, but all you needed was just to be there and not be stupid. It was already clear that I was not going to London. So I concentrated on doing what I could to get this job in Paris, and I did it. I wrote the letters by hand in French and composed

them and typed them, letter by letter, on the typewriters at the school—
and I could not type. ◄┼

SIRIO'S FATHER AND MOTHER HAD WISHED for more than
farm life for their son, and Sirio was delivering. Like other young
men he was cocky: he entered into relationships with girls he
probably shouldn't have, and though he meant to give all of the
money he earned to his family, much of it instead wound up going
into his wardrobe. If he was going to dream of traveling the
world, he would need the clothes to go with it. This did not mean
a lot of clothing: just properly tailored suits and a handsome,
large-patterned houndstooth overcoat—his pride and joy. He
looked as well turned out as his dashing father, right down to the
tall black leather boots.

Where Sirio differed from his father was in his ambition and
his social agility. Hard work and the changing social makeup of the
postwar world afforded him the ability to mingle with people his
parents would never have dared to. Consciously or not, he was
part of the aspiring class, a class that naturally sought out that
other class that Sirio would come to know best, café society. The
Agnellis were in a class by themselves. Not only did he work for
the family at their hotel, but he studied their business, Fiat, then
one of the few modern, industrialized organizations in Italy that
was developing rapidly enough to keep pace with the rest of
Europe. Almost every other part of the Italian economy, and its
politics, remained a shambles. Postwar modernization was con-
fined almost solely to the northwest of the country, Turin and
Milan, and elsewhere a quarter of all Italians were classified as
poor. Over 90 percent of all Italians had no electricity, running
water, or toilets. Sirio was lucky to have a job at all, although he
was still essentially an itinerant worker, going from hotel to hotel,
restaurant to restaurant, whenever there was work. The older he
got, the fewer opportunities there would be. When he put on the
sparkling white tuxedo jacket of his uniform at the hotel, he knew

that it wasn't his. The borrowed clothes, the warm rooms, the regular meals were fun, but it was painfully clear in 1950 that if he wanted to succeed, it would probably have to be outside Italy.

Leaving home, for any young man, is bound to be life altering. For Sirio it was fraught with an even deeper level of emotional anxiety. Without his mother and father, Sirio's attachment to Tuscany and to his family home became amplified, almost compulsive, which was only compounded by the fact that his family treated him as the lord of the manor, their brightest star. He had grown up doted on by his uncles and raised by his grandmother—in a country where women didn't have the right to vote until after World War II and wouldn't gain the right to divorce until 1974. He learned from an early age that, as a man—and an orphan—in Tuscan society, he could ask for and receive almost anything he wanted. If the fruit from his beloved fig tree was picked too early or too late, he would have a tantrum. If the family was going to a local fair and Sirio didn't want to go, he would stamp about until someone agreed to stay with him. He couldn't stand to be alone, but he wanted the company of women on his own terms. Sirio had become the Prince of Montecatini.

Outwardly, the Prince leaped at the chance to travel far from the house that contained the family's poverty and his worst memories to rescue their fortunes abroad. Yet it was also pure anguish to even think about leaving home: it was not just the home of his mother and father and the family that coddled and rescued him, but the very bedrock of his character.

SIRIO

M Y GRANDMOTHER WAS ALWAYS PUSHING ME to get out, to work, to leave. Sometimes, you know, I just wanted to be at home. She was particularly pleased about the opportunity in Paris because we all knew the story of the Livis, our neighbors, who were socialists. They lived in Monsummano, which is really the closest village to our house in Montecatini. The father, who made brooms, was a friend of my grandfather. The family had been forced to leave by the Fascists and the father escaped across the mountains to Marseilles.

The Livis' son, Ivo, was already a legend to us—an Italian who was doing very well as a singer in France. He had left before I was born, but in our day, when we didn't know anyone who'd ever *been* to Paris, it meant I would know someone when I got there. So we got a letter of introduction from one of his aunts and I got a passport.

I wanted to go and I didn't want to go. There was really no future for me in Montecatini. I knew it in my stomach. I had to leave. I had to learn languages. I had to try to be the best I could be. But still I wasn't sure, even when the letter came back from the Plaza-Athénée saying to come. Maybe what really made me get on the train was I was in trouble with a girl. Her father and brother were saying they would kill me if they ever saw me near her ever again, and I believed them!

I went to the station with three bags, everything I owned, and no money. No money, because the hotel had said they'd have some *argent de poche*, spending money, for me when I arrived. Everyone in the family came to see me off. They were all crying. "Why are you going, why are you going?" I was crying too. It was the hardest moment of my life. It was all I had and it felt like a tragedy, like I was abandoning them forever. And even today it still goes on. It's always about leaving. Every time when I leave home I close my eyes and make sure I can picture it in my head. I always look back and make sure it is all clear, because I don't know that I'll ever come back.

My grandmother, though, did not cry. Her face was so strong, like she'd have tied me to the train to make sure I left—that I did not give in to them. I thought if I stepped down from the train one more time she would have hit me.

AUNT LUIGINA *Our lives were really like a novel, a book. We were so poor, but in poverty there is so much love. All these endings and beginnings. We hoped so much for Sirio to be happy, to be success-ful, to be rich. But we felt guilty. He was really our symbol, the symbol of the Maccioni family, the family I had married into, and he was leaving. He was so, so young. It was painful to see someone so young trying so hard to be so old.*

KATIA *[Luigina and Guido's daughter] I was just six years old, but you always remember people leaving, especially because we were afraid he would never come back. I just remember thinking how big and how handsome he looked—and he couldn't have been more than seventeen or eighteen.*

CLARA *It wasn't romantic at all. It was a little like my father leaving for the army. Here we were again, someone in the family leaving, maybe never to come back, and now Sirio was leaving too.*

Years and years later when my grandmother was dead, I was telling the story about my leaving home at a family dinner and saying how Nonna, my grandmother, was such a strong Tuscan woman that she would not wave at my train, that she would never behave like they did in cheap films, and when I finished the story my sister, who is very shy, called me away from the table and told me that I should be ashamed of myself. She said Nonna was inconsolable for weeks after I left, and that the only reason she didn't lift up her arm to wave good-bye to me was because she thought if she did she would die.

I never told the story again.

I was saved by the big love of my grandmother. She knew I had to leave. It was my own personal war against the world, and I had to win it. I remember thinking about that as the train was leaving, as it went past the place where my father was killed, past the hippodrome where we went to the circus, and out to the seacoast. I would always have the resentment. But I swore I would win the war—and that I would never open up, and not kill anyone along the way. ◄◄

Chicken Liver Crostini

When Sirio eats at home, either in New York or in Montecatini, hardly a meal goes by where Egidiana doesn't make chicken livers sautéed with onions for Sirio, who eats them right out of the pan, standing in the kitchen. For everyone else at the table, or in the restaurants, it is served as presented here. Either way, the secret is to get the freshest, firmest chicken livers you can find and not to overcook them.

⅓ tablespoon olive oil

¾ cup chopped onion

6 fresh sage leaves, finely chopped

1 clove garlic, peeled and finely chopped

1 cup chicken livers (about 1 pound), coarsely chopped

3 tablespoons white wine

1 teaspoon tomato paste, diluted in ¼ cup water

2 tablespoons butter, at room temperature

2 tablespoons anchovy filets, coarsely chopped

2 tablespoons salt-packed capers, rinsed and coarsely chopped

Salt and black pepper

Red pepper flakes (optional)

8 slices Tuscan bread or baguette, toasted

Heat the oil in a sauté pan over medium-high heat, add the onion and sage, and sauté for about 3 minutes, until the onion just begins to color. Add the garlic and cook for 1 minute, until fragrant and lightly colored. Add the chicken livers and cook for 2 to 3 minutes.

Add the wine and diluted tomato paste and simmer over high heat until the liquid evaporates. Off the heat, stir in the butter, anchovies, and capers. Season with salt, black pepper, and optional red pepper flakes. Serve warm on toasts.

Frittata di Cipolle serves 4

AMONG THE MEMORIES that send Sirio into raptures about the food of Italy are: the smell of roasted chestnuts; the Tuscan holy grail of olive oil, salt, and pepper; and "maybe, maybe," says Sirio, "a sprig of rosemary or thyme on a piece of meat or fish."

Of all of them, the classic onion frittata—made by Nonna Annunciata with wild onions picked from the fields around his family farm, eggs from chickens his uncles tended, and oil from their own olive trees— is closest to Sirio's heart. If you have or can find wild onions, you can substitute them for the white onion and zucchini used in this recipe.

6 eggs

2 tablespoons grated Parmesan

2 sprigs fresh parsley, finely chopped (about 1 teaspoon)

Salt and pepper

Olive oil

1 large white onion, peeled and thinly sliced

4 small zucchini, thinly sliced

In a large bowl, combine the eggs, Parmesan, and parsley. Season with salt and pepper to taste. Beat well, then set aside.

In a 9- or 10-inch heavy nonstick sauté pan, heat the olive oil over medium-high heat. Add the onion and zucchini and cook until they begin to soften, 4 to 5 minutes.

Spread the vegetables evenly over the bottom of the sauté pan. Pour the egg mixture on top of the vegetables, spreading it evenly. Reduce the heat to medium, and cook, without stirring, until the eggs are firm on top. Carefully flip the frittata, using a large lid or plate to help you, and cook the other side for 1 to 2 minutes. Serve immediately, or refrigerate and serve cold.

From The Maccioni Family Cookbook: Recipes and Memories from an Italian-American Kitchen *(Stewart, Tabori & Chang, 2003) by Egi Maccioni with Peter Kaminsky.*

Bollito Misto SERVES 8

SERVING PEASANT FOOD to restaurant customers is a Maccioni hall-mark. Sirio grew up with his Uncle Alberto, a butcher who would hang pigs from the rafters of the family farmhouse and make sausage. "Not a bit of the pig would go to waste. Nothing, not beef if you could get it, or chicken, would ever go to waste." At the slaughter, there would be a big party for the whole family and the dish they would make would be bollito misto. No one has ever been able to assuage Sirio's longing for these parties like his wife, who over the years modified this recipe for the restaurant as well as at home.

Chicken Sausage

2 *pounds ground chicken (or 3 whole chicken breasts, skinned, deboned, and very finely chopped)*

3 *eggs*

⅔ *cup mortadella, thinly sliced and ripped into small pieces*

½ *cup grated Parmesan*

¼ *cup coarsely chopped flat-leaf parsley*

1 *clove garlic, finely chopped*

1 *teaspoon salt*

½ *teaspoon pepper*

¼ *teaspoon grated nutmeg*

Broth, Meat, and Vegetables

1 *quart chicken broth*

2 *pounds beef shank*

2 *pounds beef short ribs*

1 *red onion, peeled*

1 *white onion, peeled*

3 *stalks celery*

1 *ripe tomato, halved*

2 *bay leaves*

3 *sprigs parsley*

Salt

4 *black peppercorns*

4 *carrots, peeled and cut into 2-inch pieces*

4 *potatoes, peeled and cut into 2-inch pieces*

4   leeks, ends trimmed of, cut in half, and well cleaned

Pepper

Minestra di Semolina

3   eggs, lightly beaten

½   cup Cream of Wheat

¼   cup grated Parmesan

1   tablespoon whole milk, plus additional as needed

1   tablespoon butter, softened

1   teaspoon salt

½   teaspoon pepper

Condiments

½   cup green sauce (recipe follows)

½   cup Tuscan red sauce (recipe follows)

Chicken Sausage

In a large bowl, combine all of the ingredients and mix well. Shape the mixture into a log about 3 to 4 inches in diameter. Wrap the log securely in cheesecloth and tie it well with kitchen twine. Refrigerate until needed.

Broth, Meat, and Vegetables

Place 6 cups cold water, the chicken broth, beef shank and ribs, red and white onions, celery, tomato, bay leaves, parsley, 1 teaspoon salt, and the peppercorns in a very large soup pot. Bring to a boil. Reduce the heat and simmer, covered, for 45 minutes. Add prepared chicken sausage and simmer for another 45 minutes. Add the carrots, potatoes, and leeks, and simmer for 30 minutes more.

Carefully transfer the carrots, potatoes, leeks, shank, ribs, and chicken sausage from the broth to a large, warm platter. Drizzle a few large spoonfuls of broth on top of the vegetables and meat to keep them moist. Cover and let sit in a warm place until ready to serve.

Strain the remaining broth, discarding the contents of the strainer. Skim off any visible fat from the broth. Return the broth to boil on medium-high and let it boil for about 10 minutes. Add salt and pepper to taste.

From The Maccioni Family Cookbook: Recipes and Memories from an Italian-American Kitchen *(Stewart, Tabori & Chang, 2003) by Egi Maccioni with Peter Kaminsky.*

In a medium bowl, whisk the eggs and Cream of Wheat together. Add the Parmesan, milk, butter, salt, and pepper and whisk well to combine. The mixture should be the consistency of thick pancake batter. Add more milk, a bit at a time, if the mixture is too thick.

Heat a medium nonstick sauté pan over medium heat. Pour the batter into the preheated sauté pan, making one even layer. Cook for 1 minute, reduce the heat to low, and continue cooking for 4 minutes, until the pancake has become firm throughout. Gently flip the pancake and cook for 3 minutes. Remove the pancake from the skillet and let cool. Cut into ¼-inch pieces.

TO SERVE Serve the broth garnished with the minestra di semolina as a first course. Then serve the reserved meats and vegetables with the green sauce and Tuscan red sauce.

GREEN SAUCE MAKES ABOUT ½ CUP

½ small red onion, peeled and finely chopped

⅓ cup packed parsley, finely chopped

2 small cornichon pickles

1 clove garlic, peeled

1 tablespoon finely chopped green bell pepper

2 tablespoons capers

Black pepper

Crushed red pepper

Olive oil

Red wine vinegar

Combine the onion, parsley, cornichons, garlic, bell pepper, and capers in a food processor and pulse just until everything is well chopped but not puréed. Add small amounts of black pepper, crushed red pepper, olive oil, and vinegar to taste, pulsing to incorporate them well.

NOTE This recipe can be doubled or tripled to make as much green sauce as you need.

Tuscan Red Sauce   MAKES ABOUT 1 CUP

- 2 cloves garlic
- 2 cups flat-leaf parsley leaves
- ¼ cup olive oil
- ¼ cup tomato paste dissolved in 1 cup water
- Salt and pepper

Mince the garlic and parsley together. In a medium saucepan, heat the oil on high heat until very hot but not smoking. Add the garlic-parsley mixture and cook, tossing occasionally, for about 1 minute. Add the dissolved tomato paste. Stir the sauce constantly until it begins to thicken. Remove from the heat. Season to taste with salt and pepper.

Pig's Feet with Black Truffle

"I WANT TO EAT NOW all the things I didn't want so much when I was young," Sirio says. The peasant foods that his grandmother made for him remain Sirio's favorites, and all are invariably fried: fried zucchini flowers, fried fish, fried rabbit, and fried pig's feet—the skin of which fries like nothing else. It's like a perfect French fry, the notes of salt, fat, and texture multiplied tenfold. With the addition of the black truffles, it is a sublime study in simplicity.

Note that the dish is prepared over 2 days. Deboning the feet may be intimidating, but the first foot is the hardest. Serve with crushed herb potatoes and sautéed spinach.

- 4 pig's feet, scrubbed
- 1 onion, halved
- 1 leek, cleaned and chopped
- Handful of parsley stems
- ¼ cup unseasoned bread crumbs, made from day-old bread
- ½ ounce black truffle, finely chopped
- Oil for frying
- Salt

Wrap each foot in cheesecloth, fastening the bundles with string. Set the feet in a large pot, add the onion, leek, and parsley stems, and cover with cold water. Bring to a boil and cook at a simmer for 3½ hours, replenishing the water as necessary. Discard the vegetables and cooking liquid.

Bone the feet while they're still warm: discard the cheesecloth, set them claw side down on a cutting board, and begin by removing the larger bones that would have led up into the legs. Continue picking (thinking about the way the bones in your feet are arranged may help you approach this task more systematically) until you've removed 32 bones from each foot. Try to keep the skin in one piece. When you have cleaned all 4 feet, carefully inspect the interdigital areas and trim away any remaining patches of bristled skin.

Arrange the boned feet skin side down on a baking sheet and form each into a loose rectangular shape. Sprinkle each with a few teaspoons of bread crumbs and a pinch of black truffle, then carefully flip and repeat. Set another baking sheet on top of the feet, weight it, and refrigerate overnight. After the gelatin in the feet has set, trim them into a neat and even shape. They can be held at this stage for up to 3 days in the refrigerator.

Heat enough oil to come ¼ inch up the sides of a large nonstick sauté pan over high heat. When the oil is hot but not smoking slide the pig's feet in skin side down. Have a piece of aluminum foil ready to tent the pan—the oil will sputter violently and continue to do so for the first few minutes. Fry for about 8 minutes, until crisped and deeply browned, then flip and cook 3 minutes more.

Transfer the pig's feet to a rack to drain for a moment, salt well, and serve.

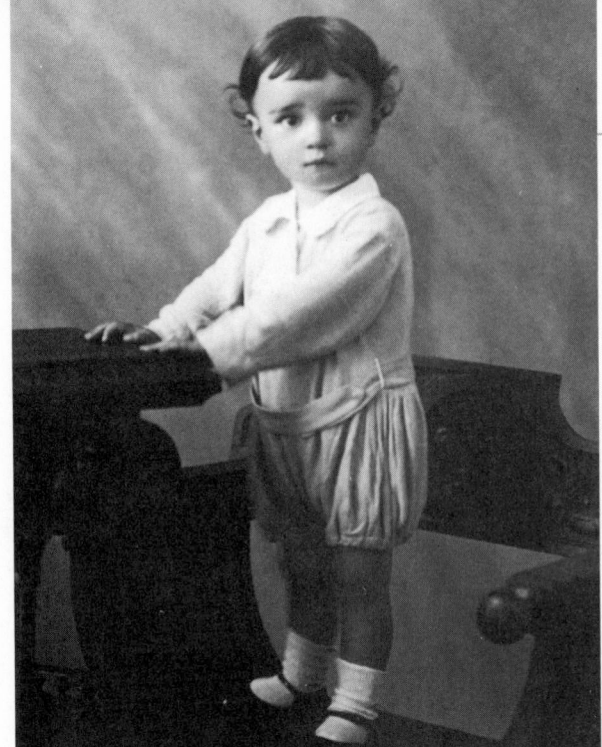

THIS PAGE
TOP:
Sirio, age 2,
Montecatini

BOTTOM:
The Maccioni Family
celebrates the
75th birthday of
Serafino.
FROM LEFT TO RIGHT,
STARTING AT THE
BOTTOM: Ferdinando,
Damino, Gino.
MIDDLE ROW:
Great Uncle Guido,
Great Grandmother,
Giulia, Great
Grandfather, Serafino,
Annuniciata, Guido,
Giuseppe.
BACK ROW:
Cousin Guino, Uncle
Alberto, Eugenio.

FACING PAGE
TOP:
Giulia and Sirio's
Great Uncle
Fernando in Buenos
Aires, Argentina,
shortly before
he arrived for the
wedding of Eugenio
and Silvia.

BOTTOM:
Sirio on his way to
school, Spring 1941.
It would be his last
year of regular
schooling.

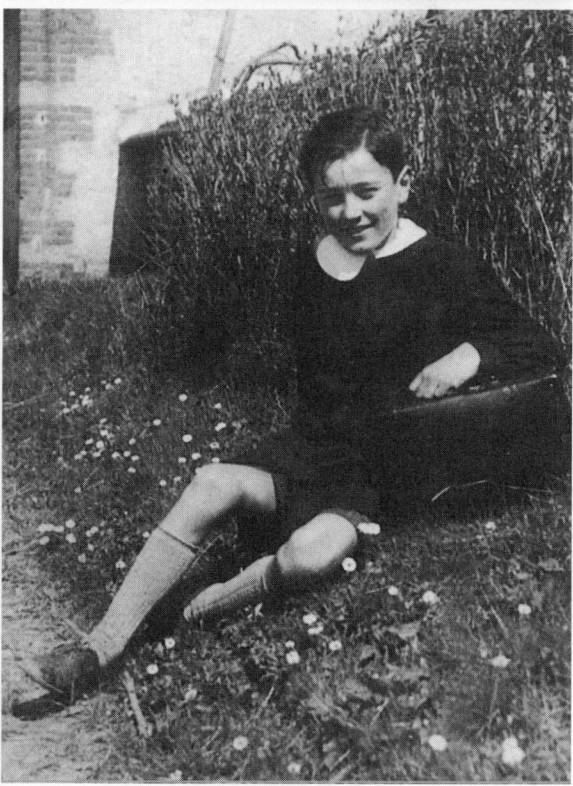

THIS PAGE:
The family of
Eugenio Maccioni:
Silvia, Eugenio,
Clara, and Sirio,
1937.

FACING PAGE
TOP:
Sirio working a party
for the hotel school
in Montecatini,
Spring 1950.

BOTTOM:
Sirio hits the slopes
at Sestriere; Principe
di Piemonte in the
background.

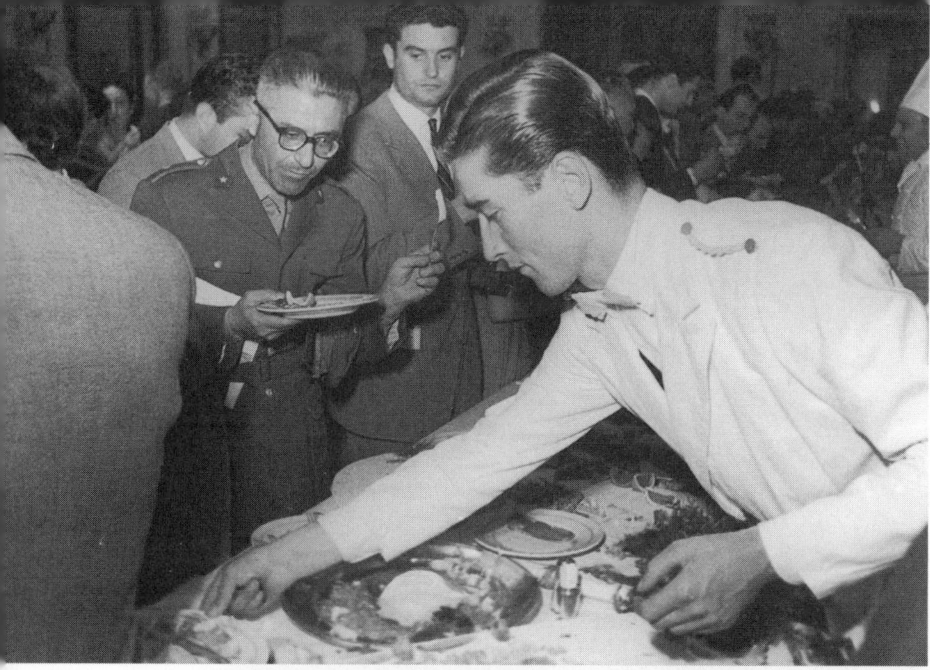

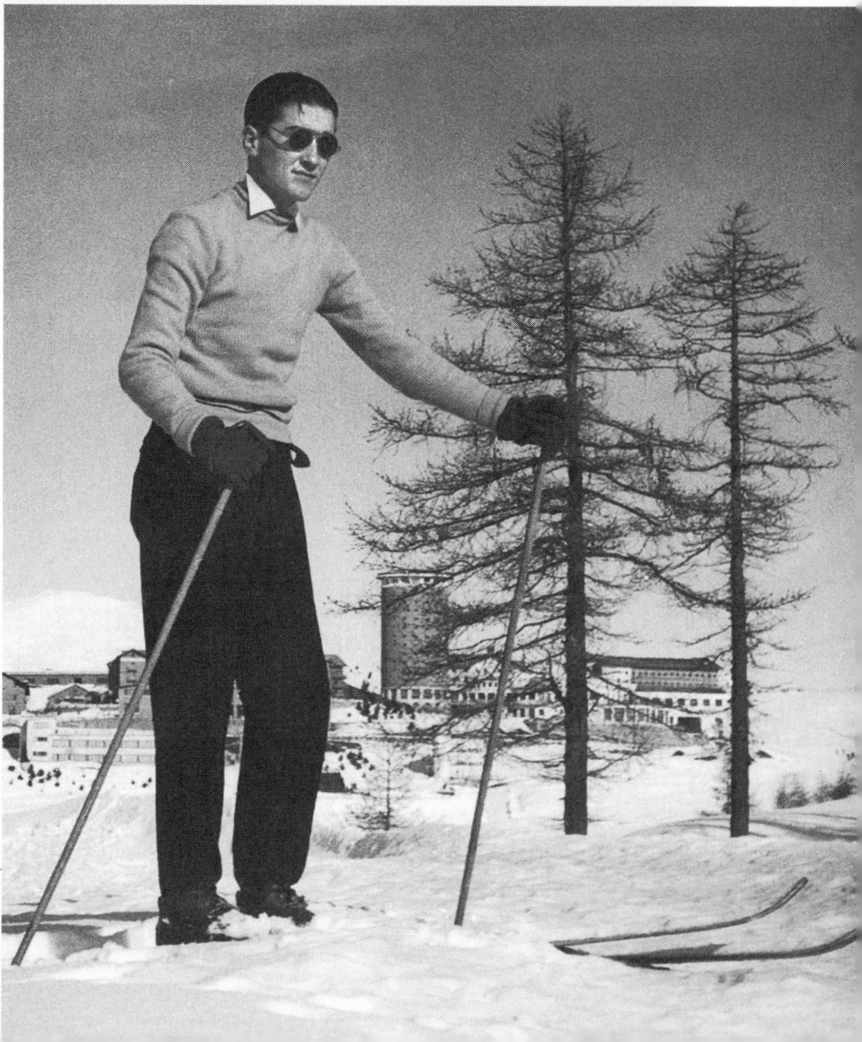

LEAVING HOME

GETTING STARTED
IN PARIS

SIRIO

W HEN I ARRIVED AT THE STATION IN PARIS, I didn't know how to get to the hotel and I had no money. I remember thinking that it was a good moment to turn around and go back home. An Italian man came up and asked where I was going—it was like a divine intervention. I told him the Plaza-Athénée. I was a little presumptuous and I saw that he was wondering if I was a guest so I told him about my job. He said it was too far to walk to the hotel. I insisted—too proud to admit I had no money. Who goes to a foreign city without money? He kept talking with me until I finally confessed. This man, whose name was Thomas Cairati, worked at the Restaurant Pocardi on the Boulevard des Italiens. He brought me to the hotel in a taxi and gave me what would now be fifty francs to get through my first week in Paris. That was a lot of money! But he said that any boy my age who had a job at the Plaza-Athénée would be sure to pay him back. And I did.

When I arrived at the Plaza-Athénée, I went to the servants' entrance. I didn't dare go through the front door. I saw a man and I told him I was there for my room and to start my training. But I didn't really speak any French. The staff looked at me with faces like I was ... a thing! It was horrible. I was trying to understand what they were yelling. They said, "Yes they had a job, and yes this and yes that," but that the job was on the condition I spoke French. I couldn't speak French, so I couldn't have the job.

I did the best I could to explain that I couldn't go back, I had to stay. I asked if they knew Ivo Livi the Italian singer, and they said no, they did not. Eventually they told me that I could leave my bags while I found somewhere else to stay, and that if I could learn French in three months, I could try again to join the program. Maybe.

I kept asking people about Ivo Livi, even people on the street, but no one knew who I was talking about. So I went to the Fiores, the people who had come to Montecatini and offered me a job if I ever came to Paris. The restaurant was called Florence, 19 Rue Pointhie, so I walked there. When I arrived they looked at me, shocked. They had no job and no place for me. Even if they could have offered me a job, they had nowhere for me to sleep.

In a way, I was lucky. It wasn't like I could walk back to Montecatini. I had gone to France to learn French and I wasn't going anywhere now that I was here. The Fiores and I did what all Italians do: we argued until everyone was hungry from arguing and then we went to the kitchen and ate and kept arguing until finally they agreed that I could work for them for three months, until I learned enough French to go back to the Plaza-Athénée. They found me a room, down the street at an old hotel, really a boarding-house called the Hôtel de Paris, and that's where I stayed. And so I worked at the Florence. I did everything—busboy, cook, waiter, everything.

I still don't know really why they finally gave in. Maybe Giusetta had something to do with it. I remembered her from Montecatini. She was fifteen years older, and in Paris she did everything for me. She became my mentor. In every sense. I always think she did it out of pity, because I was skinny. I was always dreaming. She taught me the reality of life. She was a very attractive person. I thought only, my god, I am so young, with this woman, and I can't believe it—but she gave me everything.

And then there was another miracle. All the most famous Italians came to the Florence—Lino Ventura, Serge Reggiani, Carlos Cardero, Vito Condutti—and their pictures were up on the wall. And there was also a picture of Yves Montand, who I thought was French. One day Montand, who was really just then beginning to be the most famous person in France, came in with his ex-girlfriend, Edith Piaf. Edith Piaf was not a very attractive woman, but when she sang she transformed herself. Even I would look at her and say, "Yes, I can see why they were together...."

There I was, bussing this table or that and I heard Yves Montand speaking to Mr. Fiore in perfect Italian. And it wasn't just perfect Italian; it was Tuscan, the very same language that I spoke, from the same area! So when Mr. Fiore came back from the table, I asked him how it could be that Yves Montand spoke Italian like someone from Monsummano? And Mrs. Fiore looked at me like I was stupid and told me that was because he was *from* Monsummano!

So then I told her about my letter from an aunt of Ivo Livi, and we put it all together: Ivo Livi was Yves Montand! When the family escaped to France he had been very young. He grew up in a totally Italian house and his mother never really learned to speak French properly. She would mix up the words. When she called him to come upstairs she would scream across the rooftops, *"Ivo, monta!"* which was a combination of the French and the Italian for "come up here!" Later when he was choosing a French name for the stage, he remembered this and decided to call himself Yves Montand. And no one in Italy or in France knew this. I couldn't believe it, but it was true.

Mrs. Fiore let me run back to my room to get the letter from his aunt and much later, at the end of his meal, she let me give it to him. He did not respond right away, and I didn't want to interfere or be presumptuous. Instead he left me a note telling me to come to his show the next night, and that there would be two tickets waiting for me and who to talk to so I could come backstage to talk with him.

I went to the Olympia—a very famous music hall—the next night and I sat there in shock. I had seen him in a film, but in person he was different, magnetic. When I went backstage he was very loose, very happy, There were other people in the room and everyone was laughing. He spoke to them in French, but kept coming back to me in Italian. I could tell the others were asking who I was and he kept saying, "He's a waiter, but we'll soon change that!" He was amazed that I wanted to be what he called a waiter. In those days a waiter, especially in France but even in Italy, was this unhappy person with a stupid face and a napkin over his arm who walked like Charlie Chaplin. He just couldn't understand why I wanted to be a waiter. I told him I wanted more than just that.

That night he invited me to come out with him and his group. Later I would find out that before the show you couldn't talk to him. He had terrible stage fright. But afterward he was another person. We would go out to eat, or go to a club, usually both! There were beautiful girls, people fawning over him. It was fun to be with him, to meet interesting, beautiful people. He would always say, "Come on, you're young, you're in Paris, and you're with me." You know how many times he told me that? "Look at where we come from, and where we are. You could have all this too." I don't think I really understood what he meant until much later.

People always say to me, "Why do you always talk about Montand? Why did you like him so much?" And unless you come from where we came from, maybe it's hard to understand. Even later, when he became passionate about socialism, I admired him most for being straightforward and willing to admit mistakes, to talk about them and still be exactly who he was. Yves Montand became more than my mentor; he became like a father. We shared the same feeling, the *angoscia*. You know why I'm good, if I can be so presumptuous to say so? It's because I always have something bitter here in my stomach—*angoscia*. Montand had it too.

But he was Yves Montand, and I was still a waiter. Not even a waiter! I had no money, so I didn't go out so much, unless it was with him or with someone who invited me out. There weren't so many men in Paris after the war, and one way to make money was to go to a place on the Champs Élysées, a dance hall with a restaurant attached to it. You could go there in the afternoon on a Sunday and you stood and girls would come with a little ticket and give it to you and you had to dance with them. It was mostly the tango! I think for four tickets you could get a *choucroute*. The girls in the afternoon were working girls, from the factories, nice but a little sad, and the ones later at night were more beautiful and fun.

I also went to a club called Scheherazade, which was owned by an Italian so sometimes I could go there for free. It was the first time I ever ate in a restaurant I didn't work in. The food was so different from what I knew in Tuscany, but I liked it very much. I had my first chicken Kiev and "red soup"—borscht—and there were gypsy violins.

For a moment, Montand made me believe that I could be something else. He thought I would make a better performer than a waiter, so he brought me to be in the chorus of the Folies Bergère. The first thing they asked me to do was to take off my clothes; the boys didn't wear much more than the girls. I was standing there, so skinny that they pointed and laughed and decided I should wear a tunic. In my head I was thinking, "How am I going to tell my grandmother I've changed my mind and want to be a singer like Ivo Livi?" But I did it anyway because it made him happy. And the girls! My god, thirty of them rushing by with almost no clothes on … and I had to change with them. I don't like to change even in a room with other men, so I piled my things in a corner and dressed outside in the dark. And of course I was terrible! I just stood there and didn't know what to do.

I don't know if they called Montand but later he asked me, "Maybe you don't like girls?" Finally I had to confess that it was quite the opposite—I was getting too excited, you know?!

I think I was there maybe ten days and thank god, the show closed and I knew they weren't going to ask me to stay on for the next one. The last night, the star of the show was Carmencito Del Rio, "Miss Cuba 1950." I don't know what that really meant. They said she was Miss Cuba for the movies, Miss Cuba for the elegance—I think she was Miss Cuba for the tits. Anyway, she saw that I was unhappy. *"Que pasa, Italianito?"* she asked. I told her and she said, "Let's go out on the town!" I was bragging and said we would go meet Montand at the Place des Ternes, a very chic bistro. What I really hoped was that he would be there so that he would pay for dinner! When we walked in I could tell that everyone in the room looked at us with their jaws down, this little skinny nobody with the most beautiful woman in Paris. We sat down to eat and we ordered, but I didn't see Montand, and I really didn't have enough money! I kept looking at my watch because I knew the Metro would stop soon and I wouldn't be able to get home. But she was very intelligent and worked out the problem, and said she would pay for dinner and that I would come home with her. She was so beautiful—but my god, the *angoscia*! I was so nervous worrying about the money and about going home with her that I could feel the sweat collecting in my shoes.

When we got there, she had a little refrigerator and a bottle of very sweet German white wine—not bad. She left me while she went to change, which took forever, with the makeup and the eyelashes and everything. While I waited I sat and I drank this wine, almost the whole bottle to give myself courage. And since I really don't drink, when she was finally ready, I had fallen asleep! When I woke up in the morning, there was Miss Cuba 1950, lying on her satin sheets, and I had never touched her. I left her a note apologizing and asked her to call me again—which of course she never did.

After the Folies Bergère, Montand brought me over to the Plaza-Athénée, and we walked through the front door! He took me straight to the man who ran it, whom he knew, and that was that. My French was much better, of course, but still not perfect, but by that afternoon I was in the program at the Plaza-Athénée. Three months earlier I had been everything the French say about the Italians—skinny, stupid, spaghetti boy—and now I was the protégé of Yves Montand, one of the most famous men in France. I was at the top of the world, for maybe one or two minutes. ◄◄

SIRIO'S GLEE at having so successfully beaten the system lasted barely an hour. He had built up in his mind a fantasy of what his experience at one of the world's most famous hotels would be like: besides an aura of luxury that in his head surpassed even that of La Pace or the hotels in Sestriere, there would be kind-faced older professors who guided him in the ways of hotel management. A knowledge of the basics of the kitchen was as important for trainees as performance in the dining room, and Sirio imagined chefs with tall white toques teaching him the essentials of cuisine. For a time he even fancied that his true calling might be in the kitchen and that with some supportive instruction his career might take a different turn. Then there would be the beautiful women who would teach him French, and Sundays off reading and eating in Parisian pastry shops, spending the *argent de poche* the hotel had promised him.

The reality was a Darwinian training regime, a cramped garret space with walls so thin that he might as well have had no privacy at all, and a bathroom shared with everyone else on staff. After a week he decided to keep his room at the Hôtel de Paris. At the Plaza-Athénée, he was taken directly to the kitchen, not for his first lessons in the culinary arts or to meet his professors, but to be handed a mop and a bucket and told to get to work. His lessons in French would happen at the Berlitz school after his daily shift, and the *argent de poche* didn't exist at all. Sirio would receive the training he had been promised — on the job.

Nonetheless, the Plaza-Athénée remained a key stop on the road to a perfect resume, its restaurant, Le Relais, under Chef Lucien Diat a breeding ground for all the important French chefs of the period. Lucien's brother, Louis, the chef at the Ritz-Carlton in New York City and a columnist for *Gourmet* magazine in America, was credited with the invention of vichyssoise, among other feats. On both sides of the Atlantic, the brothers were considered the direct descendants of Escoffier.

Sirio's real job in the kitchen, and later in the dining room, was cleaning, fetching, and helping where he could. Fairly soon, he was allowed to observe, and in some cases participate in, the activities of the kitchen. As in Italy, there was no set schedule. Staff worked from before breakfast until well after dinner, with few breaks in between, six days a week. They worked hard, kept their mouths shut, did what they were told, and hoped that nothing bad happened. The system had worked for centuries, although Sirio, along with many of his contemporaries in the kitchen, was already questioning if it really worked at all.

HERE WERE THREE STAGES to my training at the Plaza-Athénée: kitchen, dining room, and hotel management. The difference between then and now is that then a waiter had to know how long it took to cook a *sole meunière*. The fish, the butter, it's all very delicate, a minute too much and it's ruined—but if the waiter asked two minutes too early he might have something thrown at him. It happened, and people were often physically hurt. I might walk by the line of cooks and the nice ones would throw whatever was left after they chopped something—some parsley, or some onion. The mean ones would throw a glass of water, soup, or consommé. I don't say this to complain; it is just the way it was.

Besides, I had no right to complain. It was during the reconstruction, right after the war, and everyone had to work. I worked six nights a week, morning to night. I was lucky if I got to the Berlitz school, where I was supposed to learn French, once a week. They talked to me about verbs, conjugations. I didn't know anything and I was ashamed to ask. I felt lost. I started to react, but couldn't react. I nearly cried out of rage. But I knew how to read, and I had a feeling for it, so I tried to read as much as I could. Books in Italian or in French. I liked books about history and society, and biographies, anything I could find. I read all the books on French cuisine— Escoffier, Carême, and Brillat-Savarin—until I could recite them from memory, like the *Divina Commedia*. I was determined to speak French better than the French, to know more about food than the French, and to live better than the French.

ROGER VERGÉ *[Le Relais colleague] He was always reading. Anytime there was a break you'd see him in the corner reading a book. All the others stood on the street smoking or looking at women. In a way it was impudent: he wanted us all to see he was studying while we were playing.*

It wasn't that I wanted to know so much about the food. I did it because I didn't want to be condescended to. I knew good food could be produced in a kitchen. I had seen it already in Italy…but they looked down so much on Italian food, Italian cooking, Italian people. Like stupid people all over world, more outside the kitchen than inside, they kept telling me, "Oh, you're a Fascist, you're a Nazi." I knew there were people I could talk to, intelligent people, but I couldn't say anything, and I didn't have the language yet to fight back intelligently. So I just kept my mouth shut and watched everything.

Today people say, "Ah Diat, he was a god," but he wasn't. It was very difficult to be a chef. In the French system the manager was a god. If he passed through the dining room and he smiled at you, you felt good for a month. The chef was a god only in the kitchen. Diat himself was treated like an animal, so that's how he treated everyone in the kitchen. Every chef should say thank you to Paul Bocuse. He was a true star! He and a few others were the first to treat the people they worked with with respect.

In those days all the great chefs worked in hotels. The hotels were the only places that could afford the people it took to support that system of cooking: the peeling, the saucemaking, and the variety of items on the menu. There were only a few restaurants outside of that system: Taillevent, Tour d'Argent, Maxim's, La Serre, and maybe a few others. And let me point out that all these were owned by restaurateurs. You did not have chef-owned restaurants. There was no such thing. Otherwise, all the restaurants were bistros—honest food, the husband and wife in the kitchen doing whatever they wanted, and very often great wine.

The big chefs were tied to the hotels, and they didn't have the power chefs have now. It was how it worked. You couldn't get out. Diat was always angry, I guess because of that. The French system was very hard on young people. When I finally got to be part of the team, the first three months Diat never talked to me. In the morning, he came in, counted all the people, and ignored me. I didn't exist. Later, I only knew I existed when he smacked me in the head because I had stopped cleaning a moment to look at what they were doing—which they didn't do so well. I saw Diat himself come by, taste a sauce, and add flour—which you don't do. The only decent person working in the kitchen was Roger Vergé, who was the chef garde-manger.

ROGER VERGÉ *Sirio was so skinny. He was thin, and you could see the hunger in his eyes. We worked in this kitchen where we were all poor, all hungry, all abused. You felt like a mutiny might happen any minute, but I would try to send him the message with my eyes that it was just a phase, that he would live through it, that we would all live through it.*

It was a very difficult time. Montand had married Simone Signoret, and was becoming more and more famous so I didn't see him so much. And I was infatuated with Giusetta. She was my whole world. I had always thought I was skinny and ugly. She said the opposite. But when she realized that I was becoming jealous, she put me straight: "If you need money, if you need me, whatever, I am here. But you cannot fall in love with me." And of course because she said I couldn't, I did. So then she put an end to it.

I was devastated. And then, I was not. Like that. I didn't sit by the Seine crying. It was something in the way she handled it, something about how she said to me, "Separate the part of you that is physical from the part that is mental." I remember her saying, "I can be the physical, sometimes, and the mental too, but I can't be all that you need. There will be someone else for you who does that." And I knew she was right. She complimented me on not being stupid and making a drama. She made it so that I felt more like a naïve young man with a future, not a lovesick dog. I realized I had to overcome it. And when I did, I saw a different world. ◄◄-

SIRIO'S FAMILY WROTE HIM LETTERS filled with news from the farm: the grapes had been picked, they had missed him at the annual crush, and there had been a street fair in a neighboring village. Alberto was trying to revive his business as a butcher. Guido had opened a stall at the market to sell odds and ends; he and Luigina were contemplating building an extension onto the house. Clara was growing into a fine young woman and various aunts were helping guide her toward becoming a seamstress.

Every six months, representatives of the hotel school would visit to assess their students' performance. Sirio was preparing for his next such examination in the fall of 1951 when the switch-board operator passed a message onto Sirio that his grandfather had died of a stroke and that he should get home immediately. He tried to find out how he could get back to Italy most quickly. It would have cost any money he had saved. He could have done it. It was more that he did not have the desire: he could hope to change the world, but he could not bear to see another dead body of somebody he loved. The hotel switchboard operator let him call his family to tell them that he could not come to the funeral. In his misery, he made a vow that the next and only funeral he would ever attend would be his own.

SIRIO

I T WASN'T ALL BAD. It was more that it was a bad time to be in Paris if you were an Italian who was poor and insecure. It was the hardest part of my life: I couldn't get home—even if I wanted to, even if I had to—and I did have to when my grandfather died, but let's not talk about that. To not be able to afford to go back home was bad enough. What was worse was that I was always thinking about when I would be going back home.

I believe home is deep in everybody. The concept of home is not only where you go to sleep—where you live is important—but home is every-thing. It's your family; it's where you were born, the beginning of your life, the sound, the color, the smell of your home. And from Paris those things were so much stronger. When I was hungry I pictured in my head the fig tree in front of my window. I remembered the first street I walked along with my parents, my grandparents, when I was very small, going to town, to church, to school. Home is more than that. Home, in a sense, brings you back to the time when you were protected, when you were a child and you had somebody making decisions for you. Looking for home is very important in everybody's life. Most of the time we lose too much time working to be successful, but I believe all this is to re-create home.

Very often I thought about having to go back to Montecatini, about having failed. But then I thought that, even though it was hard, I was working and getting to know the most important people in the restaurants, in the hotels. I still saw Giusetta and I received packages and letters. My grandmother sent me fig jam and I read the letters from my grandfather and I cried over them, alone, in private. My grandmother couldn't write, so when he died, I didn't get the letters anymore. I didn't want anyone to see. I didn't want them to see me weak. ◄←

THE NEXT GENERATION
OF CHEFS

FTER SIRIO'S STAGE IN THE KITCHEN came one in the dining room. Here, what he had learned in Italy was complemented by more advanced lessons. His instructors would stand over him with a stopwatch and have him debone and slice a chicken. This ritual was performed once a month until it could be done in less than a minute without even a speck of *jus* landing on his crisply starched white shirt. There were lessons on how to prepare a crepe suzette, and dishes that needed to be flambéed at the table. Knife skills were particularly important, such as peeling a whole orange so that the rind came off in one, almost mechanically precise strip. The sommelier spent weeks teaching which glasses were to go with which wines. The basic skills of *couper, recomposer,* and *présenter* were reinforced over and over again, with their ultimate test happening in the dining room. Sirio also spent time at the hotel's front desk, although he would still be expected in the dining room or the kitchen in the evening.

Sirio's induction into the French caste of kitchen and dining room laborers was only a touch more difficult because he was a foreigner and not yet as fluent in the language as his colleagues. An entire new generation of chefs was in Paris after the war. While working through the classic and traditional systems embodied by the Diats, they began plotting their own paths for overthrowing the entrenched behavior of the French professional kitchen. Many dared to dream about having their own restaurants someday, where they could prepare food the way they wanted to, and where they would treat their staff better. Through his own experience in the kitchen, Sirio, after a few more trials and tribulations, became a part of this milieu of chefs who, in late-night meetings in smoky bistros or cramped rooms, developed what later came to be known as nouvelle cuisine. Sirio was a witness to the beginning of the revolution, and in many ways a part of it.

Roger Vergé became one of Sirio's mentors in Paris, although they were in fact contemporaries. Fear in the kitchen of Le Relais was so intense that in his first few months Vergé dared not speak to the young Italian. One of the worst things that could happen was to be caught in a compromising position of any kind. The worst thing of all was to be caught eating the food.

SIRIO

ORTOLANS ARE THESE LITTLE ROASTED BIRDS that come only from France—very rare, even then. When they were prepared in the kitchen everyone was very reverent. They told stories about the things you put on your head and the special things you did before you ate them. To me they looked like the baby quail we eat in Tuscany all the time. One night when I was given responsibility to carry a tray of them to the dining room, one of them fell off the tray. No one was looking and I was hungry, so I put it in my mouth and ate it whole, like you're supposed to, and went on to the dining room. To me, it tasted just like any small roasted bird.

Within seconds, I swear, everyone knew—it was as if there had been an alarm inside that bird. Someone counted the birds every night, so they knew one was missing. The floor manager made everyone come into the kitchen, and it was like the inquisition. I knew I was going to admit what I'd done and right away I also knew that I would be fired. So I went to Vergé and confessed. He swore at me. But then he went to the manager and said that he was responsible—that he had dropped the bird and thrown it away. I don't think they believed him, but they let it pass.

ROGER VERGÉ **Sirio makes me sound so heroic. But it really was easy. I knew he would be fired and I wouldn't.**

Maybe it was a good thing, because that was really the first time I got to speak to Vergé seriously. I waited for him outside until he was finished for the night and I thanked him again. We walked along and he asked me if I was still hungry, and I said, yes of course, so we went toward his apartment and stopped on the way for eggs and herbs and vegetables. His apartment was very small and only had a little electric hot plate—and to use one thing you had to turn the other off, but still he made the best omelette for me. It was the best meal I had in Paris.

ROGER VERGÉ **What really got me was that I'd never eaten an ortolan before and he had and he dared to say he didn't think it was so good! And later on when I asked him if he was still hungry, he had the nerve to say yes! He could have gone on eating all day. He was ravenous. He ate like a poor person eats, as if every meal might be his last. I remember him scraping the bottom of a cup of cappuccino so hard with his spoon that I thought he'd scrape the enamel off.**

After that, Vergé and I became best friends and that made a big difference in my life in Paris, since he was the first person I could really talk to. Not just because of the language, but because we were trained not to, and because I don't fit in so easily. I like to meet new people, but maybe because I am from Tuscany where we are more reserved, or maybe because

I really only trust my family, it takes time, and it's work for me. People don't believe it, but I'm a little shy. And I only like who I like. It's a contradiction, but true. So it took a while before I really started to feel comfortable and had the courage to meet more people, get into the life of Paris, go to restaurants and clubs. It was then I started to see better who was good and who was bad. I also worked more in the dining room and met more clients, and then I saw them again out in the clubs, and on the streets. That's where I first met Frank Sinatra, and where I met Juan Carlos again, who had grown up in Italy when his family were exiled from Spain. None of us, not even him, I think, thought he would be the king of Spain. We shared the language and had fun in Paris. In every country you learn to find the good people. Oh, I also found the less good and the most pretentious.

FLORENCE FABRICANT *[author] Sirio is not a natural glad-hander. He doesn't have the easy conviviality of other restaurateurs. He works at it, and he's more polished. He has a natural talent for knowing who is truly important and who is not. What makes Sirio unique in the food world is that he has a flawless instinct for spotting cycles and trends in food.*

Everyone wanted change. The system for making food in France was very rigid, very formal. It was probably still the best system but had become almost militaristic. To cook in a great restaurant even now, you have to have these techniques. Everyone came to Paris. They came from the north, from the south, from the east and west, where each place has its own definable cuisine. When Vergé made me his omelette, he made it the way he learned as a child in the hills of Provence, and with the same ingredients. Such a thing would never be considered "food" in a French restaurant under Diat.

Bocuse cooked the cuisine of Lyon, a cuisine I particularly like, but some felt was too rough. But it was a legitimate cuisine. The point is that they came from these different places but, while they were under Diat or some other schizophrenic chef, they were taught only to make a white sauce, a brown sauce, and some other sauce, and that killed creativity, it killed the soul of the food. And I understand it: there were a certain number of people who had to do the work, the prep work, and a certain number of people to be served. It became a factory. There needed to be less prep work but the inclination was to make more—we were so many and we cost them nothing. Maybe they didn't mean to kill the creativity, but they did, and the same thing happens today.

Creativity in the kitchen has to be encouraged! It is the heart of Italian cooking: you see a bit of wild asparagus, you see a mushroom, you see an egg, and you use them! That is why Italians never need refrigerators—you buy only from the market. The great food of France is really the same, but this system had been killed in the place where it was supposed to be the best—in the big city restaurants.

This was the contradiction that needed to be put right. The nouvelle cuisine chefs never thought they were creating a new cuisine. There is nothing new in food. It's just that each chef from each area wanted do his food in a personal manner, with more feeling.

> COLMAN ANDREWS *[editor,* **Saveur** *magazine] The fathers of the movement were really Fernand Point of La Pyramide in Vienne and Alexandre Dumaine of La Côte d'Or in Saulieu, who were among the first influential French chef-restaurateurs to encourage creativity in the kitchen and to integrate regional products and dishes into a more formal culinary idiom.*

> PAUL BOCUSE *What Sirio and I shared was a philosophy about the generosity of cuisine—and the generosity of life. There was nothing generous about where Sirio and I learned about food. It was very hard, very rigid, and severe. We all came to know the ortolan story. It's more than a story about birds. Good comes from helping people. Sirio is first of all a friend. If I need something, in the restaurant or in life, he is there. And I am there for him.*

All of the chefs of the next generation came from this period: Bocuse, Vergé, Senderens, the Troisgros brothers—we all knew each other. We talked and we planned, it was like a revolution. They wanted to allow creativity into the kitchen, but without losing the technique. And they refused to treat people badly. These were the principles that became the foundation for what would later be called nouvelle cuisine. In fact we never knew that phrase. It was Gault Millau who came up with that, twenty years later. All we wanted was the courage to break free, and that was the moment we were all just developing the courage. We knew Fernand Point and Alexandre Dumaine. They were like the leaders of the revolution, but they were in the country, far away. We were too poor and working too hard to go see them. Paris was still ruled by the hotel mentality. It took Michel Guérard, who along with the Troisgros brothers became the most famous for nouvelle cuisine, another fifteen years before he opened his first restaurant. At the time he was a pastry chef or something at the Hôtel Crillon. It took Bocuse and Vergé time as well. None of us had the courage to just leave and go out on our own. If I had known then what I know now, yes, I would have probably done many things sooner. But maybe it was better I didn't. ◄◄

COLMAN ANDREWS *Michel Guérard opened Le Pot au Feu in Asnières, a Paris suburb, in 1965. He was making pot-au-feu and some other traditional fare. Still they were dishes that were emblematic of a turning point in French cuisine. Along with other young French chefs of the period, including Paul Bocuse, Alain Chapel, Fredy Girardet, Jean Delaveyne, Alain Senderens, and Pierre and Jean Troisgros. It wasn't really until the revolts of 1968 that it took off. In their own version of self-determination, many young chefs sought for the first time to take control of their own kitchens, to cast themselves not as indentured cooks, but as "author-composers," creators.*

AFTER TWO YEARS at the Plaza-Athénée, Sirio's period of indentured servitude was over, and the hotel school in Montecatini gave him its blessing. He had the option to either stay on at the hotel and pursue a career there, or to leave and pursue other opportunities. Sirio's French was fluent and he felt he had learned everything he was going to learn at the hotel. With the arrogance of youth, he felt that the changes his friends were going to make in their kitchens should be applied to the front of the house as well as the back. It was time to make a move, and Sirio knew exactly where he wanted to go: Maxim's, one of the few restaurants outside of a hotel that was successful for being a restaurant, not just a bistro, and that had a genuinely world-class clientele.

SIRIO

I T WAS CLEAR TO ME by the time I left the Plaza-Athénée that I really wanted to run a restaurant, or a hotel, but I couldn't do anything until I knew that I was better. What I learned at the Plaza-Athénée was that I already knew a lot.

The only place in Paris that really held any interest for me was Maxim's. It was the only other place where you could find café society in Paris. So I applied for a position, but I never got anywhere. Then Montand took me there and introduced me to Louis Vaudables. I talked with him, and he looked at me. I could speak French very well now. I liked him, and I thought he liked me, but he said there was really nothing for me to do there except maybe bus tables. I wanted much more than this—but I wanted to work there so even though I was disappointed I said, "Yes, Thank you," thinking I would be able to work up to a higher position quickly.

Montand thought it was terrible that I had agreed! "At least before you were a waiter! Now you're going to be a busboy?" So he went over to talk with Vaudables himself. For as long as I live I will never forget what I overheard. Vaudables said, "Monsieur Montand, he's good, but he's Italian." Clearly, Vaudables thought it would be bad to have an Italian working in Maxim's as a waiter.

Then Montand said, "*Moi aussi!*"—So am I."

You would have thought Vaudables was going to die on the spot. Just as I had not known that Ivo Livi was Yves Montand, neither did Monsieur Vaudables.

And right there, maybe because of this, I started to work at Maxim's. First it was as a private waiter for Monsieur Vaudables, then as a fill-in when the place was busy. The work was tough, the waiters were very good, very professional, but they would kill you if you got in their way. It was a good change, and I got through it okay. It was also an important break because now there were four places—La Pace, Sestriere, the Plaza-Athénée, and now Maxim's—where I'd seen many of the same people. And they now saw me in different places, doing different things. Sometimes the most important thing about running a restaurant is just being there.

I didn't work at Maxim's very long, just long enough to learn the most important thing about the restaurant business. Monsieur Vaudables used to say, *"Jamais un table à Maxim's, toujours un table à Maxim's!"*—Never a table at Maxim's, *always* a table at Maxim's! The trick is, you think of the restaurant space as a whole and you put in tables when you need to, and take them out when there aren't so many people. You always want your restaurant to look full. It's an illusion but it is the way it has to be.

I learned many important things at Maxim's. To me Vaudables was a true restaurateur and the person I think of when I say that, if a restaurateur was smart, he wouldn't be a restaurateur. It's just common sense. Give the people what they want. If they want a whole fish, grilled, then give it to them. Don't give away the best table, so that it's there when you need it. Give the early people the center tables, so they think they are important. Never have an empty table in the room. Do the impossible. Never say no: if people come in and there's no table, you make a table—put the table in the bar, put the table in the kitchen, find space! Make people feel wanted. This is not genius; this is just not being stupid.

At the Plaza-Athénée things were sometimes done poorly because people didn't cost anything. If one person couldn't do the job, you put on two people to do it. The Plaza-Athénée was all about "no!"—about what you couldn't do. I knew there were people in France who were all about "yes!"—about the possible. I had met them. I wanted to find more people who would say "yes!" not "no!"

HAMBURG

WHILE SIRIO WAS IN PARIS he did not forget his connections back home in the Italian restaurant and hotel community and they did not forget him. His personal connections with anyone significant in the hotel and restaurant world would become a hallmark of Sirio's rise in the industry. He never forgot a name, a face, or a résumé. Fifty years later he never says a name without automatically attaching to it the exact connection, usually reciting the person's address. Sirio was still attached technically to the hotel school in Montecatini, although it had come to be more of an elaborate employment agency. He continued to press them for a posting to London; instead, while he was at Maxim's a position at the Hotel Atlantic in Hamburg became available. Besides the hotel's glamorous prewar past, he was attracted by the number of his Italian colleagues who were accepting positions there, and he agreed to a similar post as the one he'd had at the Plaza-Athénée, this time learning German and working in the hotel.

W HEN I GOT THE MESSAGE about a position at the Hotel Atlantic, I didn't think about it. I just took it! It could have been anywhere. Mostly I cared about going home for a bit. But it didn't work like that. They gave me a train ticket from Paris to Hamburg. I asked if I could redo the ticket as Paris–Milan–Hamburg, but they said that was out of the question. And I didn't have the money to buy my own. So I had to face going to Germany for maybe another two or three years without going home.

When I realized I couldn't fight this, I used the money I had to buy books. I bought two books. Can you imagine? An Italian in Paris trying to find books in Italian teaching me how to speak German! But I did it. And I got another book—I think it was the first analysis about what had gone on inside Germany during the war, about von Stauffenberg and his attempt to eliminate Hitler. I never forgot reading about what the Nazis did to him and the other people who were caught with him. They made them take off their belts so that their pants fell to the ground—humiliating them and then murdering them. If someone could write about this, only eight years later, it made me think that the Germans were willing to look at themselves after all to see what had made Hitler happen, to look at both sides of their own story.

It was a long trip on the train and I had a lot of time to think. When you're in the restaurant business you don't have a lot of time to sit, let alone sit and think. And when I do sit down—not in a restaurant—it all comes up, everything, this giant feeling and my brain goes very fast. Leaving places, any place, always does this to me. Even now if I go to a hotel for a few days, wherever it is, I get this feeling that is always just like leaving home for the first time.

So I am on the train thinking too much. A part of me still felt forced to go and another part of me was glad to go. I was trying to think about my career, what I would do, how I would behave, but all I could think of was that I was going to this country, to these people, who I could have said, had killed my father. I remember at the end of the war my grandfather took in two deserters from the German army. We tried to tell them they were safe in our house, but you could see the fear in their eyes. They stayed one night, and in the morning, the army came down the road to our house, and the soldiers started to run, and they were shot by their own troops in the fields around my house. It was terrible. But I'd seen Italians do it too. This proved to me that the Germans were no more responsible for Hitler than we were for Mussolini. If there are good Germans, good French, and good Italians, then how could I blame an entire nation for killing my father?

Then I got mad. When I thought about the real reason I was going to Germany, it was because there was nothing for me at home. After the war, the left became very powerful in Italy, especially in Tuscany. There are these giant swings in history, the right, the left, then back again. People get some political idea in their heads and whoever is strongest takes it out on whoever is weaker. The rise of the Reds in Italy made it difficult for anyone in our business to get ahead there. It was very tough for my family, and that's why I think my grandmother was always pushing me to leave, to stay away. I could have done it on my own—I could have, but it would have taken so much longer, and I wanted to move fast. There was more hope for me outside of Italy than inside of it, even though it really, really broke my heart.

What was happening was the reverse version of what had happened to the Livis and many other families in the 1920s under Mussolini. To tell the truth, I was very angry at Montand at this time. He was going to Moscow and very publicly supporting the Communists. From what I saw and heard, they didn't sound to me very different from the Fascists before.

When I arrived in Hamburg it was a sea of cranes. Allied bombing had flattened the whole city and they were rebuilding it very quickly. It was not very attractive. I had some money this time, so I asked the taxi to take me to the Hotel Atlantic. Hamburg has this big lake in the middle, Lake Alster. I knew the Hotel was on the lake, but it seemed we kept driving around and around the lake.

It was a bad thing I didn't know enough German to tell the taxi driver to stop, but a good thing that I was able to see most of the city the first day. When we got to the Atlantic, I searched and searched for the staff entrance but couldn't find it. So finally the taxi decided to pull right up to the front door. I immediately apologized for arriving this way. I walked up through the center of the hotel and met the general manager, who showed me to a room inside the hotel, up in the attic but clean, and renovated, like a real hotel room with a bathroom.

I couldn't believe it. He told me to stay in the room and the head housekeeper, Frau Pauline, would come to look after me in five minutes. So I stayed, and five minutes later this beautiful woman comes in. Her breasts arrived five minutes before her. I was young. It was like a piece of chocolate to a kid. She explained to me that for one week I would sleep here, in the staff quarters, and then they would find me a rented room with some other people who worked at the hotel. The idea was that they paid for my room and fed me and I was to take my German lessons and after a while, if I behaved, on my day off, they would give me a little pocket money to spend. Then Frau Pauline closed the door behind her and, you know, lifted up her dress. It was paradise.

Going to work the next day amazed me! Unlike the guests at the Plaza-Athénée, or any place I had worked, the Germans enjoyed breakfast—a large cooked breakfast, with sausages and eggs and fresh fruits I had never seen. As an Italian I thought fruit came only after dinner, and eggs were eaten at lunch or dinner and were a luxury. And then I worked the lunch and everyone was very nice and smiled at me. I didn't understand anything, but it was all very modern and very organized, and I knew I liked it.

Then at 3:00 P.M. the manager came over in a very upright German way and told me to leave. I didn't understand enough German and his face was so stern, so I just stood there until finally he smacked my back and pushed me out the dining room and I thought, "Oh my God, what did I do? I went with Frau Pauline and got fired on my first day!" I was practicing in my head what to tell my grandmother. And then the hotel director came over to me and again as I began to offer explanations, he looked at me with a kind, open face and explained that in Germany the staff worked in shifts. And that mine had just ended. They wanted to make sure that I had time to study. Study! I had never heard of such a thing: in Italy and in France we worked until they were done with us. To finish work at three o'clock in the afternoon! I thought I was in paradise: no work, time to study, and Frau Pauline.

I wanted to work extra shifts to learn and to make money, but they were very strict about the amount of hours you worked. Even that was very organized. If you wanted to work beyond your shift, they let you work two nights a week for the banquets and receptions. You could make a lot of money and learn a lot about the banquet business and how to take care of the big parties. With all the rebuilding going on, there was a lot of business coming in to Hamburg from all over the world, and the hotel was used for receptions, parties, seminars, all that sort of thing.

The other nights I studied, and studied hard. It was really the first time I'd ever been to a modern school. They were very encouraging, they wanted you to learn, to eat well, to rest, to be happy. It was very different from what I felt in France, or Italy. Maybe it was because in Germany they wanted to be better, and so did I. So I learned more.

I started to save enough money that I could buy decent clothes and not feel like a pauper. Later on I shared an apartment with Pino Ciaceri, whose family owned the Eden Hotel in Rome, and we became good friends. We went out a lot. There were almost no men, and many of the men were crippled. And there were lots of women.

After a while I started to see more clearly how the hotel operated: it was like nothing I'd ever seen. There was a union, and the union protected you. But they only protected you if you were good. If you did your job well, the hotel respected you and you were fine with the union. They worked together, not against each other. If you didn't do a good job, union or not, you got thrown out. If they said, "You don't speak the language well, you have to go to school more this week," I went.

Of course, being who I am, I had to make things difficult. Two of the biggest receptions were for the Shah of Iran and the Queen of England. For these two events I worked out a quicker way to get from the reception room to the kitchen, through a door nobody used. The floor manager found out what I was doing and got very angry. He wanted people to go his way, for his own reasons. I thought his reasons were stupid. Normally I would have fought it—I think sometimes that if I were a revolutionary I'd be worse than Che Guevara—but I liked him and I could see that he was a smart, good man and so I did what he said. I learned that if you're honest and you respect the people you work for—even if it's not so smart all the time—you can do it. You choose your battles in the restaurant— you don't always have to be Che Guevara for a door! **◄╋**

AFTER WORLD WAR II, the newly created West Germany was trying to make the city of Hamburg a showpiece for the revival of the German economy. Many of the same cast of characters Sirio had seen in Italy and in France began appearing at the Hotel Atlantic. This time the primary purpose of those Niarchoses, Rockefellers, and Onassises he met and served was not pleasure, but business. Sirio had to fine-tune his dining room behavior accordingly. The men who were doing deals over breakfast at the Atlantic were most concerned that their food come out precisely on time, and hot. They didn't care about the culinary experience, as they had in Italy or France. Sirio was quick to discover, however, that for all their seriousness, the people who had seen him in Sestriere, or at La Pace or at Maxim's were visibly happy to see him again in Hamburg. Sirio, an Italian in Germany, was a comforting sign of home for the growing international jet set.

In Hamburg, Sirio was fast becoming established in a set of his own. As soon as Germany was up and running again after the war, hotel owners had been quick to capitalize on a pool of beautifully trained Italians in the hospitality business. Sirio was one of several young men, largely from Tuscany, who would come to dominate the front-of-house operations of the best hotels and restaurants in Europe and America. It was almost a kind of Italian cartel.

For a time, the Italian cartel was focused on Hamburg. While Sirio was at the Hotel Atlantic, two Genoan businessman created a Swiss-German-Italian cruise line called the Home Lines, a passenger operation that bought the *Atlantic*. They refitted this old ship to fill the gap on the Hamburg–New York–Caribbean run until the company was able to construct newer ships. The idea was to re-create the link between the old prewar hotels like the Hotel Atlantic and the transatlantic ocean liners. Although the *Atlantic* was in no way comparable to the great prewar liners, or even the later Italian ones, she had one distinct advantage: she was literally the only passenger liner after the war servicing the North Atlantic from Bremerhaven, northern Europe's largest port. She couldn't compete with Cunard's *Queen Elizabeth* and *Queen Mary,* or the French Lines' restored *Île de France*—but she could provide Italian cuisine and flair. The Home Lines secured the services of Ferrucio Castoldi, the manager of the Hotel Royale in San Remo, to gather a crew of mostly Italian staff.

Castoldi, whom Sirio had met during his days at La Pace, convinced Sirio and a few other Italian colleagues, including his sister Clara's soon-to-be husband, Piero Pieri, to join the new venture. Sirio knew that working on board the transatlantic liners was a time-honored way of gaining a great deal of professional experience very quickly.

The Home Lines called the trilingual crop of young Italian men "the Chosen"—a reference to their special status as translators and service staff for the super-chic passengers in first-class. At each port—New York, Nassau, Port-au-Prince, Santa Domingo, and the ultimate attraction, Havana—"the Chosen" were supposed to be given special leaves to explore more or less at will.

New Year's Eve 1954 found Sirio on board the *Atlantic,* the hotel's partner ship, preparing for his first trip on board an ocean liner and headed for the Americas. As soon as the gangplanks had been lifted, the ship's purser, an Italian named Giuseppe Grandi, collected the passports of all "the Chosen." Sirio was suspicious, but handed his over like the rest of his colleagues. They were all handed uniforms, told to change into them, and report to the deck.

Their first job turned out not to be translation, but to scrape off the thick ice covering the porthole windows. It was soon apparent that "the Chosen" had been naïve: They were to be cheap ship labor. Sirio might as well have been back at the Croce di Malta mopping floors.

There was no turning back. The ship was nudged out of its slip and pushed out toward the North Sea to Hamburg, then across the Atlantic to New York.

THE
HOME LINES

SIRIO

THEY CALLED US "THE CHOSEN," though later on I realized they chose us because we were the most gullible. The real problem— maybe the problem with my whole life—was sleep. Our quarters were down in the bottom of the ship at the back, next to the propellers. The ship had been reconstructed, but only partially, and it was still an old ship. You can't imagine what it was like to be down there. The vibration of the propellers alone would keep anyone awake. We were also sharing with "the crew"—not trained service staff, but sailors—and though some of them were nice, they were all very rough. There weren't even really beds, more like hammocks, and the ones that were by the wall of the ship were wet and cold. There were four of us to a very small cabin.

The schedule of the ship was very different from a hotel or a restaurant. A ship isn't like a dining room on land where you open at 5:30 and maybe 400 people come over the course of the night for one hour, 7:30 or 8:00 being very bad because more people like to come then. On the boat it's all done in seatings. One thousand people all sit down more or less at the same time for breakfast, for lunch and for dinner. And there's nothing else for the passengers to do, so in between, you have to do tea or cocktails or dessert or nightcaps. There really wasn't time to sleep. And I admit, I did it to myself—I still do. I liked to work longer—a lunch and a dinner together, so that I could get more time off later. It was easier—at least easier for me—to just go behind a sofa in the lounge at night when it finally got a little quiet and try to get some sleep. But sometimes I snored and I would get caught. We weren't supposed to sleep like that, but on a ship they couldn't fire us, so they would punish me—make me work in the tourist-class dining rooms or make me cover more shifts or not let me ashore.

PIERO PIERI *[Sirio's brother-in-law] Most of us who traveled on the boat wanted to see the world. Sirio wanted to see the world too, but he was very serious about working. We'd get in trouble for missing a shift or fooling around. Sirio got into trouble for doing too much! He wanted to work all the time. He'd work service in the different parts of the ship after he was already done in another part of the ship, or take over someone's shift in first class so they could sleep or play or do something. Sirio had a problem with the purser, a man called Grandi, who didn't like him. I think it was jealousy.*

Grandi was just mean. He was connected in some way to the Italian prime minister or something, but if he was so smart, what was he doing here? In those days, there were fewer people in first class. And it was really the only line that could get people from Germany and northern Europe to America, so the people in first class were very often German and American businessmen, and some Italians. Again, I saw many of the same people in Montecatini.

When I came on board, the first thing I had to do was to get used to the sea. I'd never been on a boat in my whole life, let alone on the ocean. Once I no longer got so sick, it still took me a long time to learn how to serve with the ship going up and down and side to side. I learned not to stare at the plate or whatever I was carrying, but to look straight ahead.

After that I was fine. I even liked being at sea, especially when the weather got bad because it meant that the passengers stayed in their rooms. Except one group—some German businessmen—who always insisted on being served in the dining room. We would tie down the tables and chairs and they'd sit there, eating and smoking cigars. To this day, the smell of cigars and sea air makes me sick. Once when it was really bad we decided it would be funny to unlash the table. The men came for lunch as usual, and with the first lurch of the boat they and the entire table were blown clear across the dining room. They didn't return until the waters calmed!

Mario Ratto was the chef on board. He had been the cook for the Italian royal family. Cooking on a boat is not the same thing as cooking on land. Not only because of the numbers of people you have to serve all at once, but also because the kitchen is limited in what can be cooked. At Bremerhaven they took on board sides of beef, crates of fish, and mountains of potatoes. You have to remember, this was after the war, rationing had just ended. The only time people saw this kind of food was in a hotel or on a ship. In the kitchen there were these enormous storage rooms with lobster and foie gras and caviar—things that could stay fresh for a whole voyage. We did buffets at midnight, all pasta, and for a ship very good. The only real problem was there was nothing green and what was green was frozen. That was the first time I saw in large quantity frozen peas and corn and carrots. I don't remember any lettuce.

Every Italian I worked with complained that the food was bad. Honestly, I didn't think the food was bad. It was simple food, what people call continental food—which is really the food of hotels. If you have frozen, you work with frozen. The stupidity is to try to make it something it isn't. Ratto did the best he could with very little professional help. It was not like he could just turn to someone and say, "I need a little sauce" or "I just need a little tomato concassée for this pasta." If he'd had help, the help would not have known the difference between a tomato concassée and a potato. I watched and learned a lot about how food was made and how it came out of the kitchen. He was very disciplined—that was the key. I knew you could make good food in big numbers. It was just a matter of organization.

JAMES VILLAS *[author]* *Sirio was sailing during a golden era for the ships. Planes hadn't yet taken over, and it was still the only way for most people to travel across the ocean. It was terribly glamorous. In particular, the competition after the war was intense, and all that competition made for a great traveling experience. Without attention to details like food, a ship could go bankrupt overnight. And there wasn't much else to do except eat! So there were midnight buffets, teas, brunches, all the time, always beautifully presented.*

We first arrived at Halifax—not New York—and when we did finally get to New York we were working, so I could not go up on deck and say, "Ah, look at the Statue of Liberty!" All those things people who come to America talk about—coming up the river and seeing the skyscrapers for the first time—I never saw. Besides, if I hadn't been working and had gone up to see, I'd have been frozen to death. It was cold! We came to the piers on the West Side, which then still had many, many ships, the French Line and the English ships and the American ones too. I do remember thinking it was incredible to come in on this big ship and walk out through the door straight into the city. We ran to Times Square and went into the first movie house we could find to stay warm. I think I saw five films that day—we went from one to the other just for the heat!

The first restaurant I saw—well, I wouldn't have called it a restaurant, even then—was a Chock Full o'Nuts. I was amazed. The food was not good food, but it wasn't pretentious. We asked for what we wanted, and they gave it to us. It was clean and efficient. We'd never seen anything like it! We sat at the bar—it was all new and modern. The girls had big tits and kept bringing us coffee. We didn't have much money, so when they saw that we were cold, they kept filling up our coffee cups. I put my hand over the cup because I thought I would have to pay, and the lady just removed my hand! You know, when you're a server you don't touch people so I thought maybe she liked me! The coffee was bad, but it was hot, and as long as it was hot, it didn't seem to matter. The food was covered in sauce, but the next day we went in and asked for no sauce and they did just that. And if we didn't like something, it wasn't a drama like with the French or even the Italians. They just looked at us funny and threw it away, like that, and made it again the way we asked for. All these people would say: I want my egg like this or like that. I thought it was the best eating place I'd ever been in, because they knew who they were and what they did. They were honest.

I had saved a little money and had decided back in Germany that what I wanted to get in New York was a radio, a shortwave Grundig radio, which was very expensive in Europe. I knew exactly what I wanted and how much I wanted to pay for it. It's always very important to know what is going on in the world and here I was on a ship and we had no idea what was happening in the world. With the radio I would know more than even the captain, and I could start to listen in other languages and stay connected.

PIERO PIERI *Sirio wanted to buy not just any radio—it had to be one that could pick up signals from around the world. He could have bought a coat or a sweater—or even had a drink in a bar— but he thought all of that was a waste of money.*

In New York, the ship changed from a transatlantic liner to a cruise ship for the route south. What that really meant was that it went from being separated by classes—first, second, and third—to being an open ship where the people who paid more for their rooms got better service. On the cruises, the ship had many more Americans, some English, and lots of Canadians. The ship got new food, and I had one of my first lessons in how food is different in America. There was iceberg lettuce, which looked to me like ice and didn't taste much better. They picked up some American cooks. The one who spoke some Italian said to me: "Everyone knows that salad is all about the dressing!"—one of the strangest things I'd ever heard, since in Montecatini when we went out into the fields behind our house we knew every leaf by its different flavor. I also remember their bringing caskets on the ship! I was a little shocked, but then we had everything on board: a doctor, a priest, something to bury people in. Given what went on most of the time, I began to realize why all three were necessary.

The boat took us to Nassau, Port-au-Prince, Tobago, and then to Cuba. I had wired an old friend from Montecatini, Vasco Cecchi, who was major domo at the Presidential Palace for Batista. There was another Italian family, the Barlettas, and they controlled the importing of foreign cars, the newspaper *Diario,* and several hotels. When we got to Havana we were greeted by a police escort and red carpets and the whole deal—not for the passengers, but for us! It certainly didn't help with Grandi. Cecchi showed us around—the best places, the best clubs and restaurants. We went dancing and it was all very beautiful, like paradise, but I could tell something was wrong.

This first time in Cuba I was a little naïve. I like having a good time, and I like beautiful women. Havana had all of that, and I didn't really want to see the rest. There was an undercurrent of violence everywhere. I saw immediately that in Cuba there was nothing to do but cut sugarcane and make cigars, work in the hotels, or be a prostitute. I went to a woman's house and there was a crucifix over the bed and a man opening the door for me. My first night there, a woman just waved her hand and said, "Don't worry, he's just my husband." ◄◄

SIRIO WORKED SEVERAL MORE round trips between Hamburg, New York, and Cuba in the spring of 1955, returning to Hamburg to work at the Hotel Atlantic in April. That summer a German colleague planned a driving trip to Italy with his mother, with a featured stop in Montecatini. They asked Sirio if he would like to join them and perhaps show them around Tuscany.

SIRIO

►►

M Y FRIEND'S FATHER had run a very nice hotel called the Esplanade. The father died in the war, the mother was now running the hotel, and the son worked with me for a bit at the Hotel Atlantic. They represented the good side of Germany to me. They ran their hotel with perfection. They had a new Mercedes and a house they had just built in the suburbs of Hamburg. They worked very hard, but they lived too. I sat in the back of the car all the way home to Italy, and I thought how strange it was that I should be taken home in a German car, by Germans, to my house.

CLARA *When Sirio sent a message us to tell us that he was coming home and being brought by two Germans, all I could think of was the time when two Germans came to the house to try to take away Father. We didn't know what to expect.*

My grandfather never believed that anyone was bad. I had yet to meet a German who had not been very nice to me and my experience in Hamburg—education, friendship, food ... well, maybe not the food, but at least it was honest. They fought hard to be a success. What is wrong with that?

I felt enormous pride. I had been around the world, I had seen things no one in my family had seen. But inside I still felt ashamed. When we got to the house, I asked my friends to sit in the car for a moment, even though it was hot. I went in and said hello and then asked my family to go outside and help with my bags while I made sure that everything looked okay. I could not believe I was really bringing my rich friends to my poor house, you know? It was a farm, the chickens ran wild, and my uncles' sausages were hanging down from the ceiling and dripping fat onto the dirt floors.

AUNT LUIGINA *Sirio came into the house and went right for the closets and shelves, like a storm. He found his mother's best linen and covered up everything, the bed, the old scratched table, like he was covering up the poverty. In Tuscany that's what the mother does—makes the house nice when friends come by—and Sirio's mother was gone and Annunicata was a peasant woman who didn't care about such things. So Sirio did it. The house looked like a dress shop when he was done!*

RICCARDO PUCCI *[former general manager, La Pace] When he came home from Germany he fussed and fussed about his guests. But then he fussed and fussed about the hotel too. His guests had to have everything the way he wanted it. Nothing could go wrong, and if it did, I was to send a message. It was a little too much, but at the same time it is what makes him great. He notices everything.*

When I got home I felt excited and disappointed at the same time. I would have cried but I didn't know how to anymore. I went to look from my window to see the figs. I saw that the tree was much smaller.... I know I wasn't the first person to come home after a long time and say, "it's all smaller." I thought of the people who had brought me home, who were so nice to me. They had also gone through a war, including the destruction of their city. She had lost a husband and much more, but still she had a hotel, a business, the power of money, and she was doing new things and moving to a new house. And there was my family, as always, in Montecatini. And we never moved, never changed. I wanted to be a magician and change it all.

And then, of course, I just got angry. I opened my eyes and my ears and my nose and smelled the farm. Some people like that smell: it is what it is. For me that smell, and the mosquitoes biting, was like Adam and Eve noticing they were naked. Suddenly I realized again that I too came from a farm, where my grandmother worked like a man night and day. Uncle Alberto continued to try to make sausages and run a butcher shop, but he made ten thousand lire and threw away nine. I told him I would get him a car, a Fiat 600, and he said no. My uncle Guido was still at the track playing at this and that. My grandmother still rolled out the pasta by hand. I told her I would buy her a machine. She said no! It killed me that my sister repaired clothes for rich people. I wanted her to have a Vespa instead of a rusty old bicycle. Italy was waking up! And I thought, I am not going back to Hamburg. I will stay in Montecatini and make all this better. I will fix it all.

When I went into town things were very different. Montecatini was at the height of the boom, and it still had the right people. The first thing I noticed was that I was no longer the guy who wanted to learn how to be a waiter—that now I was the guy who had been to Cuba. I was walking on the Viale Verdi with my very correct, very beautifully dressed German friend and his mother. I looked at the girls and, excuse the expression, but I could see that now these women were interested in me—to talk, to socialize, and maybe more. I was free, I was available, it was summer, why not? But I didn't. I didn't, not because I was so great, but because I got much more pleasure to say to them, "Oh, you're the one who said to me before...you're just a farmer...."

I did some jobs, I went to talk to the people who owned the hotels, to my friends at La Pace, and I made calls to other places in Italy, and I thought, I'll be at the top of the hotel business and I'll make all this money and I'll make it so my family doesn't have to live like this anymore.

RICCARDO PUCCI *Sirio was so ambitious. I had stayed on a more traditional course and was at La Pace and I told him, the hotel chains are never going to let a twenty-three-year-old run the hotel! But he thought that he should run the hotel. There were plenty of positions for him—they would have taken him—but they would have taken him down a level or two. He was already way above them. He could have done it, and they probably should have let him. I didn't tell him that. You didn't give advice to Sirio Maccioni. There was nothing for him to do but to own or manage a hotel and that wasn't going to happen—not in Montecatini, not in Italy.*

EGIDIANA PALMIERI *I didn't meet Sirio when he first came back from his travels. I really met him again later. But we had all heard. We all saw him in the town. We had known each other when we were children, I knew his sister, Clara. But he was from the country, and I was from the city of Montecatini. All of three kilometers, but that's how it was. I remember seeing him and telling my girlfriends that he had the body of a boy—tall, thin, and very handsome, but like a boy, not quite like a man—and the soul of someone very, very old.*

When my friends came back from Rome to pick me up to go back to Hamburg, I remember standing in the space between the front of the house and where the chickens were kept. I saw the face of my sister, the face of my grandmother, my uncles. All these people who were so kind, so generous, who gave their lives for me and for Clara. And I was a pig to be so... so ashamed of them. My uncles packed the car and I just stood there and I realized that I didn't hate home, that I loved it. At home I slept, at home I was loved, at home I ate.... Everything else was a nothing. I felt this for a moment, and then I remember my grandmother leading me to the back of the Mercedes, and before I knew it I was inside, and she gave me a bag that had food in it for all of us for the journey. And I understood everything. ◄◄◄

SIRIO'S EXPERIENCES IN PARIS, in Germany, and on the *Atlantic* had given him a solid foundation. It was his trip home to Montecatini that transformed him from naïve student to driven adult. He did a brief stint at the Hotel Dolder in Zurich and returned to Hamburg before deciding to return for another round of cruises with the Home Lines, this time with a different intent—to explore if there could be a future for him in any of the ports on the route, in particular Havana. New Year's Eve 1956 found him aboard the *Homeric,* the second of the Home Line ships.

SIRIO

WHEN WE GOT TO PORT-AU-PRINCE, a group of us went ashore and there were these people at the dock who told us, "Come for drinks, a little music, some local food, and meet the local girls." We knew what we were doing but we were stupid. We got into a car and drove up into the mountains and you could see everything for miles—the sea, even the stacks of the ship. But we were very far away. The place had chickens running around, vines growing everywhere, and a shack where there was a bar. In a corner a speaker was playing music and crackling very bad and they gave us warm Coca-Cola with too much rum. And then the girls came out. It's not just that they were ugly—they were just so unhappy. They weren't interested in us, and we weren't interested in them, and so we said, "Let's go."

But we were up in the mountains, far away, and we had no idea how to get back. We were trapped. And so they took everything—my Tissot watch from Zurich, my camera, everything. By the time we went through this confrontation, it was very late. And finally they drove us back, but as we came into the port we could see that the ship was leaving without us.

Somehow we commandeered a police boat and we chased down the ship. Everyone was standing on the side of the boat to see what was going on and they were cheering and yelling and we pulled up alongside and climbed onto the boat. It was very, very funny. Except of course, Grandi then took away our shore leave for the rest of the trip.

Except that in Havana there was nothing Grandi could do. Cecchi had arranged for me to work while I was there and since this was part of the deal when I decided to go on the *Homeric,* Grandi couldn't interfere. I went into Havana and I stayed there.

This time I saw Havana with my eyes open. To be there felt like being drunk the whole time. The dancing was fun, the women were beautiful, working in the clubs was fun. But it was very decadent. There was a whole other side—people lying in the gutters bleeding, beaten up for gambling debts. J. Edgar Hoover on vacation with Lucky Luciano, the American gangster! Hoover with the young boys. Even then I didn't know much, but there was Frank Costello, Bugsy Siegel, and Meyer Lansky, all these gangsters, and they were with the director of the FBI.

There was something very exciting and very cruel about the power and the money, the women, the gambling. More than Monaco, more than the Folies Bergère, it was very raw. Very attractive, but very scary.

When the ship came back I had to leave. Everywhere in Havana people were saying to me: "Sirio, you could run this, Sirio, you do that." Cecchi in fact opened a restaurant he called Montecatini, which he wanted me to run with him. It was a world of possibility, but somehow I knew it was not possible for me. I had telegrammed friends in New York City, the Moschinis, who were from Montecatini, and who owned the Hotel Stanford, at 43 West Thirty-Second Street—it's still there—to say I was coming. But I wasn't sure I meant it. I could have gone back to Hamburg. I could have gone anywhere then. My head was full of things.

I got back on the boat and maybe because my head was in this place I was worse than ever about the rules. I wanted to be better, but I couldn't do it, and every day the rebellion grew stronger. The more they said I could not do, the more I wanted to do. So I went back to no shore leave, and the fights with Grandi got worse. It was like a fury inside me. I always tried to do the right thing, but the business about holding our passports was illegal! And after I talked to enough people, I knew that I could get a new passport.

When we got to New York it was my birthday, April 6. I put my sweater and my radio in a bag and I gave everything else to my shipmates. When you leave ship you are in uniform, and the customs people don't ask for your passport anyway. I told them I had to go and get my radio fixed; I patted the bag and showed them. The minute I was around the corner I put my sweater on and went to the Stanford. They were very nice to me. I stayed there, thinking I would go to the Italian embassy in the morning and get my new passport and go home to Italy. I stayed very quiet, and my shipmates brought me a few of my things and I remember going to the roof of the Stanford and watching the ship pull away, without my feeling anything at all.

It wasn't that I had "jumped ship," or that my dream had always been to come to New York. It was just that I was there, I didn't want to go back to the ship, I was angry, and I stayed. Also I was happy. Happy and angry. I think I've been happy and a little angry ever since. ◄◄

FIG JAM WITH BAY LEAF

SIRIO REMINISCES, "When I was in Paris working, away from home for the first time, I would imagine in my head the fig tree that grew outside my window in Montecatini. My grandmother would make jam from the figs and send it to me. It gave me courage when I was sad and lonely." This version, from Sirio's colleague Roger Vergé, is as close as anyone has come to duplicating the jam.

2¼ pounds figs
2¼ pounds sugar
6 bay leaves

Wash, dry, and cut the figs into pieces. In a large saucepan, bring 1 cup of water and the sugar to a soft boil. Add the figs and cook for 35 to 40 minutes. Test for doneness by dropping a bit of the jam on a plate. It should congeal as it cools, forming a drop that is not very runny. At that point, remove immediately from the heat. Skim and pour into canning jars, putting one leaf in each jar.

NOTE If you wish to can these preserves for long-term storage, you should add 2 tablespoons lemon juice per quart of jam, and process the bottled preserves in a hot-water bath for 85 minutes for pint bottles and 90 minutes for quart bottles.

From Roger Vergé's Cooking with Fruit *(Harry N. Abrams, 1998) Roger Vergé, Adeline Brousse, Jean-Pierre Dieterlen, Molly Stevens.*

Pastry Cream

SIRIO'S ADDICTION to cream and sugar mixed together, in any form, has kept Le Cirque's pastry chefs busy for thirty years. This version from Jacques Torres, used for the bomboloni and the Napoloean Le Cirque, is Sirio's favorite.

> 2 tablespoons cornstarch
>
> ½ cup sugar
>
> 4 large egg yolks
>
> 2 cups whole milk
>
> 1 vanilla bean
>
> 1 tablespoon unsalted butter (optional)

Sift together the cornstarch and half of the sugar in a medium mixing bowl. Add the egg yolks and whisk until well combined. The egg mixture should be thick, smooth, and homogenous.

Pour the milk and the remaining ¼ cup sugar into a nonreactive 2-quart heavy-bottomed saucepan and place the saucepan over medium-high heat. Use a large saucepan because the pastry cream gains volume as it cooks and room is needed to vigorously whisk without spilling. While the milk is heating, use a sharp knife to slice the vanilla bean in half lengthwise. Separate the seeds from the skin by scraping the blade of the knife along the inside of the bean. Add the seeds and the skin to the heating milk and bring to a boil.

Temper the egg mixture with the hot milk by carefully pouring about half of the milk into the egg mixture. Immediately whisk to prevent the eggs from scrambling. Pour the tempered egg mixture back into the saucepan and continue to whisk, remembering to whisk the edge of the saucepan where the pastry cream can stick and burn. As the temperature rises, the mixture will slowly start to thicken. The pastry cream will become very thick very quickly just before it boils. (The eggs and starch cause it to thicken.) Continuously whisk to ensure that the mixture cooks evenly. Once the pastry cream has come to a boil, continue to whisk and cook for another 2 minutes to fully develop the flavor of the pastry cream and to cook out the flavor of the starch.

Remove the pan from the heat. Strain the pastry cream through a fine-mesh sieve to remove any pieces of cooked egg and the vanilla bean.

If you would like to add butter, this is the time to add it. Cut the butter into small chunks and stir it in until it is well incorporated. Pour the pastry cream into a clean, airtight container and place a piece of plastic wrap directly on top of the pastry cream to prevent a skin from forming. Let cool at room temperature, then store in the refrigerator for up to 3 days, until ready to use.

VARIATIONS

It is very easy to flavor pastry cream to complement the dessert you are making. With a whisk or spatula, fold about 1 tablespoon of any flavored liqueur into the pastry cream at any point in the recipe. It is best to add it right before using the pastry cream; you can flavor only the amount needed for a specific dessert. Be sure to add the liqueur slowly and to taste often. If you add too much, the pastry cream will become runny and lose its ability to hold its shape.

If you prefer to add flavor without alcohol, you will need to do so at the beginning of the recipe. Place the grated zest of 2 oranges in the heating milk to infuse it with the flavor of the orange.

From Dessert Circus at Home: Fun, Fanciful, and Easy-to-Make Desserts *(William Morrow and Company, New York, 1999) by Jacques Torres with Christina Wright and Kris Kruid.*

BOMBOLONI   <small>MAKES 4½ DOZEN</small>

BESIDES ITS COMBINATION of all the things Sirio loves in food—salty and sweet—they remind him of two other things he loves: Italy and women. "On the beaches in Italy a vendor walks amongst the colorful pavilions selling bomboloni—and they have to be the perfect size so that you can pop one into the mouth of a beautiful woman."

> Scant ¼ cup loosely packed fresh compressed yeast
> 3½ cups bread flour, plus additional as needed
> 4 large eggs
> ⅓ cup sugar, plus extra for coating
> 1½ teaspoons salt
> ¾ cup plus 2 tablespoons unsalted butter, cubed
> Vegetable or canola oil, for frying
> Raspberry jam (optional)

Dissolve the yeast in a small bowl with ¼ cup cold water. Place the flour, eggs, sugar, and salt in the bowl of a stand mixer fitted with the paddle attachment and beat on medium speed until the ingredients are dispersed, about 5 seconds. Add the dissolved yeast and beat for about 2 minutes on medium-high speed, until the dough is well combined and holds together. Add the cubed butter and mix for another 5 to 7 minutes, until the dough no longer sticks to the side of the mixing bowl. If the dough is overly sticky, you may need to add about 1 tablespoon of flour. It is usually necessary to scrape down the side of the bowl with a rubber spatula to encourage the dough to form a ball and come away from the side. Remove the paddle and pat the dough into a ball at the bottom of the bowl. Cover the mixing bowl with plastic wrap and let the dough rest at room temperature for about 20 minutes. The dough will rise slightly.

Remove the dough from the mixing bowl and punch it down to remove the air. Spread it onto a lightly floured baking sheet with your fingers and flatten the dough until it is about ¾-inch thick. Cover with plastic wrap and let it rest in the refrigerator for a minimum of 2 hours or overnight. It will slightly proof.

Remove the dough from the refrigerator and place on a lightly floured work surface. Flatten it slightly with your hands. Cut the dough into circles with a 1½-inch diameter cutter, keeping the cuts as close together as possible. Pat any leftover dough into a rectangle and cut more circles out of it. (At this stage, the bomboloni can be frozen for up to 1 week if well wrapped in plastic wrap. Allow the bomboloni to defrost in the refrigerator before proofing.)

Place the bomboloni on a parchment-covered baking sheet lightly sprayed with vegetable cooking spray. Space them 2 inches apart. Loosely cover the baking sheet with plastic wrap. Allow the bomboloni to proof at room temperature for about 2 hours, until they have doubled in size and appear light and full of air.

Heat the oil about 15 minutes in an electric fryer or in a 4-quart heavy-bottomed saucepan over medium-high heat to 320°F. If using a saucepan, check the temperature with a candy thermometer. Fry 5 to 7 bomboloni at one time—any more than that and the oil temperature will dip down too much and they will not fry evenly. Fry for 3 to 5 minutes, until they are golden brown. While the bomboloni are cooking, turn to evenly fry each side. As they fry, they will increase in size. Remove the bomboloni with a large slotted spoon and set on a paper towel to drain the excess oil.

TO SERVE While the bomboloni are still warm, roll them in a bowl filled with sugar until evenly coated.

If desired, fill the bomboloni with raspberry jam. Put the jam in a pastry bag fitted with a ¼-inch plain tip. Use a sharp paring knife to make a small hole on the bottom of each bomboloni. Place the tip of the pastry bag in the hole and squeeze until the bomboloni feels heavy. It is best to fill the bomboloni while they are still warm and the dough soft and pliable. Serve immediately.

THIS PAGE

TOP LEFT:
Sirio in Paris, 1951, wearing his favorite coat. A coat was more important than food.

TOP RIGHT:
Sirio posing on someone else's motoguzzi, Montecatini, 1955. He swore that, the next time he came home, he'd own one of his own.

BOTTOM:
From left to right, Sirio, Gian-Piero Flori, and Mark Egerman in the dining room of the Hotel Atlantic in Hamburg, 1954.

FACING PAGE
TOP:
Sirio on a passage through the Panama Canal, 1955.

BOTTOM:
The "Chosen." The multilingual crew of the Atlantic, visiting Chef Vasco Cecchi at the Presidential Palace of Fulgencio Battista, Cuba, 1955.

ARRIVING

"HE'S GOOD, BUT HE'S ITALIAN"

SIRIO

I AM IN LOVE WITH MY SONS. Maybe it isn't normal, but I come from Italy. I don't talk to my boys so much about my childhood in Italy, but I insist they understand what it was like to be an Italian in America. It was very hard, but at least I made money. Of course they always complain: "Papa, please don't tell us again how you suffered." The truth is, I don't tell these stories to them because I want the pity, or because I wish them to be poor, I tell them because I want them to make it better.

When the ship left, I found out that I had to wait until I could get a new Italian passport. The Moschinis were happy for me to stay, there was plenty of work, and I liked New York. In my head I thought I might stay a few months. I had always wanted to learn English. I found out very quickly that Hunter College had courses that were not very expensive, but more important I found courses in English for Germans. I took those because I knew German so well. At the Stanford I did everything: I painted hallways, I waited on rooms, I worked with the mechanics. I had a room where you had to move the bed to open the door. But it had a little hot plate and a window. It was nice, quiet, and I could cook. I also started to make some money. ◄←

THE MONTECATINI CONNECTION started to work for Sirio as it had worked in Europe and on the ships. Besides giving him a room at the Stanford, the Moschinis helped plug him into the network of Italians who had come to America to work in the restaurant business. Sirio's first restaurant job in America was in Glen Cove, Long Island, at a restaurant called The Villa Pierre. The Villa Pierre was run by Piero Sacco, whom Sirio knew because his aunt had been the comptroller at La Pace. Sacco was even more interesting and important to Sirio because he was one of the few Italians who actually had made it to London. He had worked at the Grill Room at the Savoy, a restaurant that was a favorite of the international establishment. In New York in 1956, Sacco's status in the world of waiters and restaurateurs meant nothing to American restaurant-goers. Italian restaurants like Sacco's had to masquerade as French restaurants in order to gain acceptance from the public. Sirio found out quickly that being Italian in America was going to be as difficult as, if not more so than, being Italian in France.

SIRIO

→→

IF YOU WERE ITALIAN you had to stick with the Italians. It could be very hard to get a job, because all the jobs were controlled by the union and I wasn't part of the union, or the mob! The Waldorf-Astoria had the biggest party rooms and events. I didn't want to work there in the restaurant because the money wasn't good and, as an Italian, I couldn't get a position there anyway, but I did want to work for the parties. Was very good experience. Very quick. But at first to get even a job for a night, I stood in a line, you know, on the street.

GEORGE LANG *[owner, Café des Artistes] I was working at the Waldorf-Astoria then, and we hired armies of part-time workers. We selected certain staff for certain jobs and we chose people we knew or we had worked with for the important jobs. If they worked hard and were smart, they could get to the head of the line very quickly. Sirio was always there! His name always came up on the list and so eventually he didn't have to deal with the humiliation of standing on line to get a one-night job. He was always the first choice.*

While you were on the line, people would try to stop you; they'd harass you, say terrible things, threaten you. They didn't want you to muscle in on positions. But as long as you got in to see the man who was selecting workers, they usually took you. I learned very quickly that it was always much easier and safer to stick with people I knew—that's how it worked. If an Italian was the banquet manager at a job, then he put the word out and all the Italians would come. It was much less dangerous that way. But I still had to be very careful, and mostly I had to keep my mouth shut. One stupid word and I could be fired.

RUDY GIULIANI *It's very hard for people nowadays to believe how extreme the discrimination against Italians was. I remember the last stages of it—Italians couldn't get jobs, and if they did, they'd be discriminated against. When I had to deal with discrimination, my mother would just say, "They are uneducated." Sirio was really in the worst time for this kind of discrimination.*

I came to the country of liberty or democracy expecting it would be better than France. Well, it wasn't like the French, who might call someone a Fascist or a traitor. It was just stupidity. People didn't want to use Italian words. Italian restaurants did not even dare to have a name that was Italian. There were Italian restaurants that served Neapolitan food—pasta, red sauce, whatever—and it would have a name like Johnny's or Susie's, or no name at all. And there were really no restaurants that served Tuscan food—if they existed, I didn't know them and they would not have had

Italian names either. That really bothered me: a French name was okay, but an Italian was not.

And it wasn't so easy with other Italians. The Sicilians and the Neapolitans hated me because I was a Tuscan, but when their friends weren't looking they'd run up to ask me if Italy had television yet, if we had this, if we had that, how well we ate, if I knew if their families were okay. I'd tell them, Italy is great, people are moving to the cities, they have Vespas and Fiats and television and everything. It was a boom time then in Italy. ◄◄

RUDY GIULIANI *There was competition between Italians too. It was natural. My parents had never been to Italy and they were fascinated by it. My father was Tuscan—his father came from Montecatini like Sirio. But my mother was from Naples ... and you'd think it was the civil war! The people from Tuscany have the additional pride of being pure Italian. They will tell you, "We speak the Italian of the books, the Italian of the church, the real Italian." I bet that was a huge source of comfort for Sirio.*

WHEN SIRIO ARRIVED IN NEW YORK in 1956, the restaurant scene was divided into a few very distinct categories. There were the coffee shops like Chock Full o'Nuts and more casual neighborhood eating places that served the American diner food that had impressed Sirio and his comrades so much on their first visit. There were the former clubs or speakeasies that had turned into restaurants, like the "21" Club and the Colony, which catered almost exclusively to an uptown, upper-class clientele. Then there were the restaurants that served particular communities, such as Delmonico's, which served the Wall Street crowd, and Sardi's, which fed theatergoers and Broadway celebrities. There were a few restaurants that appealed to gourmands, but Le Pavillon, the bastion of French cuisine run by the city's most famous maître d'hôtel and owner, Henri Soulé, dominated the category. Then there were hotel restaurants and the nightclubs. Restaurants of the kind of quality espoused by Le Pavillon, the Colony, or "21" were almost the exclusive patronage of café society—people whose social lives existed outside of their homes and who could afford to dine out. One thing was sure: Mr. and Mrs. America had never set foot through the doors of any of these establishments.

To be involved in the New York restaurant industry in any serious way, you had to have experience both on the party circuit—mostly in the hotels, but also in some restaurants—and you had to have experience working in one of the four most important restaurants, "21," Delmonico's, the Colony, or Le Pavillon. You also had to be a member of the union.

I JOINED THE UNION so I could work in the hotels. It was before I even had a green card: October 3, 1956. But it was hard to really make money in the hotels, and certainly hard in hotel restaurants. Since I wanted to make money I had to work in a real restaurant, and those four were the only ones I could take seriously. The French Pavillon was not a place where I could go to work even if I had wanted to, and I didn't. Soulé would not hire an Italian. There were "21" and the Colony, but there it didn't work to show up at the door and say, "I want a job," though I tried it! They had to know you, see how you worked, see if you could handle their particular clientele. Since there were no jobs unless someone died or quit, the only way for them to see you was to fill in or be an extra at a party or banquet. You worked hard and hoped they noticed you while you kept your ears close to the ground for when someone quit or died. I didn't know anyone at "21" or the Colony then, so if there were parties there, I didn't get asked. That left Delmonico's. I approached Oscar Tucci, who was Italian, and he took me on, first as a waiter, then later for everything else!

Everything about Delmonico's was big—even the chef. Big lunch—usually two seatings of up to 500 people, almost all international financiers—lots of waiters, big kitchen. The food was okay. They were intelligent enough to offer a good roast beef, steak, good liver, a breast of chicken, very good seafood, smoked salmon, chowders, some kind of minestrone, and limited desserts—chocolate cake, cheesecake, ice cream. And it was very efficient. The salads I didn't understand, and still don't. They all liked using iceberg lettuce, which looked to me like an iceberg and tasted worse, and then they poured a thick sauce over it they called "bleu cheese" dressing, which wasn't even made with cheese. But it was honest food. I worked the Roman Room, a part of the restaurant where they seated the important people. Again I saw Onassis, all three Rockefeller brothers, Niarchos, Agnelli—more the crowd in Hamburg, the business people, and they liked me. They asked for me, which made Tucci a little nervous, but he was too smart not to give them what they wanted, so I started to work those tables only. But the secret was that I never, ever pushed it in the faces of my colleagues, or my boss.

I learned the hard way, early on, that knowing these people does not make you their best friend and it alienates the people you work with. There is no one more stupid than the waiter who thinks that just because a rich person smiles at you, you are set for life. Usually it's the opposite. They use you when they need you and then don't remember you when you have a problem. This is a very important lesson. Young people in the business think it's funny, or glamorous to know these people and to talk about it. The secret is never to talk about it, not with your colleagues, not with other guests, not with anyone—only family. Otherwise it comes back and gets you. Every time. Reveal nothing, not even what they eat. If a table said to me, "What is Mr. Rockefeller having?" I always said, "I'm not sure, let me send over Mr. Tucci."

The way you really shine is being the best. Eventually it does get noticed. If you ask to be noticed, if you get presumptuous, you get killed. I bet you, da Vinci would not have hesitated to do what I do. It's the people who think that just because you are great or rich or talented or you own something, you don't have to pick up a napkin or an ashtray who are wrong. They may look successful, but they are not.

Are not.

DAVID ROCKEFELLER *Sirio was unique. In those days service was just something in the background and waiters were fairly obsequious. You expected that. What you didn't expect was a sparkle and an intelligence, and Sirio had that. He also knew more about food, and back then people just didn't. You trusted him because he knew, and you didn't think you were being sold. Half the time, if he selected it, it didn't wind up on the bill. It wasn't that I was going to invite him to dinner or anything, it's that somehow he got the line just right between servant and professional. You could identify with the professional and were grateful for the service.*

I did very well at Delmonico's and I got on well with Tucci and my English got better, but not that much. One day he left me at the door and these people came in and flashed their badges at me. I was so shocked that I didn't really speak. The men said they needed to go to the kitchens, so I took them there. They searched through the whole place checking for illegal aliens. They were looking at everyone's papers. I never opened my mouth, and they never asked me. I showed them out and I thought, "I am going to get in trouble."

The next day I called the secretary of a man named William O'Shaughnessy, who was in the immigration department and who came in for lunch every day. I went to his office, we talked, and he was very nice. And finally he asked me what I was doing there. And I explained to him what had happened at the restaurant, and he laughed and got up to show me to the door. He said, "Thank you for telling me this. I'll see you tomorrow at the restaurant."

Finally I just yelled, "I'm an alien, I'm an alien," and he slammed the door like I had said something very bad. He got very cross at me and told me to shut up and never to say that again. He wasn't supposed to know this. He told me to just go away and pretend none of this ever happened. But I said I had to be legal. He said I had to prove why there was a reason to hire a foreigner for a job an American could do—and anybody could be a waiter! This was the thinking then. I wouldn't let it go and, finally, he said he would see what he could do as long as I never mentioned it again.

His secretary had family in Sicily. She was a very nice lady, very beautiful, but with a tiny mustache. Very attractive. Her name was Cecilia and she helped me with all the paperwork. She would try to practice her Italian with me but she had such a thick dialect, I didn't understand what she was saying. She kept saying, "This has never happened, everyone can understand me!" but I couldn't. She started to give me a complex, and finally I had to ask her to stop!

I liked Cecilia and we had good relations. First I met her brother, who was very big, very serious, and the next thing she wanted me to meet her parents. You know, she could have made my life very difficult, but I knew that this relationship was not going anywhere. I decided it was better to tell the truth, even though it meant I could be dead or deported! Probably both. So I told her. Instead of getting angry she was grateful because, she said, no man had ever respected her enough not to lie to her.

To get my green card, I had to go back to Italy. I asked Tucci if I could do so, in order to be legal, and he agreed to let me go and give me back my job when I returned. I flew on an airplane for the first time, KLM, via Amsterdam to Milan, and then took the train home.

I had other ideas in mind as well. I wanted my green card, but I also thought it might be a good time to return to Italy for good. So I arranged these meetings. I had met the head of Ciga—then the most important Italian hotel chain—a man named Michelangeli Lamberto, and he had promised me a meeting. So I arranged the appointment, but when I arrived, I was met by an assistant. I told him I spoke four languages fluently, I had started to know people, I had the education and the experience, and I was running the dining room at Delmonico's. He said he liked what I did, but that if I were to join them they would start me in the basement. I told him I wanted to run a hotel, or a dining room, and I wasn't going to settle for less. But I was very nice and just said, "Tell Mr. Lamberto I stopped in to see him," and left.

In Montecatini, there were some other possible deals too. A man offered me an entire hotel on Viale Verdi, but the deal wasn't good and I was beginning to think that Montecatini probably wasn't going to be a great place to build my career. It was at the peak of the postwar boom, but already you could see that it couldn't last. The fun was now happening along the coast in Liguria, in Forte di Marmi and Viareggio—new resorts, new hotels, new people. That was really when I met Egidiana again. We had known each other from Montecatini, like everyone knows each other, but we'd never really talked. She was singing at Gambrinus in Montecatini, which was really the best club in town, just off the main piazza, and she was the most beautiful woman. A real woman, not a girl, with these eyes and amazing legs and I thought, "My god, she is very, very attractive." She was also singing in Viareggio and in Forte di Marmi, and I went there a lot and she would be there too. We started talking and I asked her to dinner and we had fun. We would go dancing all the time. I loved to dance and am very good at it. The girls would all wait to dance with me, but I liked to dance with Egidiana best.

EGIDIANA *He was a funny boy. He'd watch me all the time from the tables, trying to look like he wasn't looking. He actually got into a bit of trouble at Gambrinus because he kept coming every night, every performance, and he would come alone, so the people who ran the club asked him to stop—if you came to the club you really had to be with someone. So then he started coming with Clara, his sister, who was my friend. He would dance with her but spend the whole time looking at me, so finally she didn't want to come with him anymore!*

She says that I chased her, but she chased me! She was much more serious than me. In those days you separated the women you went to bed with and the women you wanted to marry. I found out, thank god, that she was good at both. But I didn't want to get married. I saw all my friends ... castrated. I looked at so many of the young women in the park who had said to me, "You're just a farmer," and their husbands with their stupid faces and the babies crying, and I thought, "I don't want this."

If I wanted to marry, I had to be free to come and go as I please. I was honest with Egidiana. I didn't know what I was doing, whether I would stay in America or come back to Italy. I had to get my papers, I had to travel. I had no money, but most important I had a taste to see the world. And Egidiana is the most intelligent woman in the world. She knew how to deal with a stupid man. She didn't put any pressure on me at all—maybe the opposite, which made me insane, I wanted her even more. But she said, "No, no, the man I want needs to be successful and has to feel he is successful," and that man was not me, not yet. So the idea, mine and hers, was that at the beginning we would see which way we wanted to go.

> EGIDIANA *He was handsome, but very different from the other boys. Very insecure, and so serious. I knew right away that the problem with him was that life had made him become too old too fast. When you're young you want a boy who's fun to play with, you don't want so much to take care of him, and Sirio I so much wanted to take care of. He needed it. He craved it—but didn't want it. I knew if I wanted him that it would just take time.*

I went back to New York, first class, on the *Giulio Cesare,* as a passenger, just to do it, and when I got back to New York in the summer of 1957, I was now a legal worker, and eventually I started the process of applying for citizenship. It was a happy time. I talked to Egidiana a lot. We wrote letters and talked on the phone and sent telegrams. Mostly I worked and I built a reputation. Since I started working, my aim was to work in the right place and meet the right people, not really to make money. I was alone, I didn't have a family to support. I just needed enough to survive and it was extremely important to me, maybe it still is, that I could move quickly. That doesn't mean, though, that I didn't want to make money!

At Delmonico's I worked for three more years for almost nothing. They were making me pay for the green card and my time away. In restaurants, certainly in those days, there is this cake and each one in the restaurant has his piece, the owner, the chef, the maître d'hôtel. If you wait long enough, you get a piece of the cake. I just didn't know if I could wait for the cake. Part of the reason I started to look around was that I needed to make more money. And there were new things happening in food, new restaurants opening—at last there was some choice! When Oscar Tucci heard I was looking around, he came over to me and asked why I was leaving. I told him—money and experience—and he said, "But you've always had the key! The key!" Meaning I was supposed to steal. They expected you to do that. But I could not!

HARRY POKALOPOLOUS *[restaurateur] Really, he was a pro, before there were pros in the business. Still, even with all his experience, he was an immigrant like me, from the old country, lucky to have a job, happy to be in America.*

It was a good time. I liked Delmonico's and I liked Oscar Tucci. He was good to me in many ways. He always gave me the best tables and didn't get jealous. I would take care of the Rockefellers and Senator [Herbert] Lehman, all the big people. Eventually I become in charge of the Roman Room. There were a lot of people from the government—the Kennedys again, Governor [Thomas] Dewey, and a lot of the judges from the courts nearby. One time we did a reception for King Umberto, the exiled king of Italy, and Tucci made sure I was there to take care of the party. The King and I had a little talk, he asked where I came from and was very gracious.

I didn't really have friends outside of the restaurant and the business then. I would write to Egidiana and go back to work. I was living a very simple life at the Stanford. In those days New York was very quiet on the weekends; everything was closed. By Friday if you didn't buy your milk and bread it was very difficult to eat unless you went to a restaurant. And even many restaurants closed on Sunday. I still went to the cafeteria in Times Square. They had a Virginia ham steak with fried eggs and boiled potato. All week I dreamed about having that. Then I became more sophisticated and I went to the Oyster Bar. I would have six oysters and six shrimp and then go back to my ham steak.

FROM DELMONICO'S TO THE COLONY

THERE WAS A SEA CHANGE in American restaurants between the time of Sirio's arrival in 1956 and John F. Kennedy's moving into the White House in 1961. Restaurants were opening in New York City that were in many ways a tad less formal than those of old, but more deeply sophisticated: La Caravelle, Lutèce, La Côte Basque (the less formal twin to Le Pavillon), and La Grenouille. They were in many ways the first regular restaurants to concentrate on the quality of cuisine and service as a profession and as a destination, not just a stop on the way to the theater or to a club. The nation's new first lady, Jacqueline Kennedy, had been one of the first and most prominent of guests at these restaurants—a clear signal, well before her husband's election, that the future president was very much like the new style of restaurant—chic, a little informal, and supremely tasteful. She even installed a French chef at the White House the minute they unpacked. The arrival of the Kennedys and the era of

Camelot only solidified Americans' interest in all things French, from fine French furniture to fine French food. For a nation at the peak of its newfound global power, French was classy.

Over the course of his career, Sirio's idea of how a perfect restaurant would function bubbled in the back of his brain. His next career move would have to reflect the direction he intended to pursue should he ever wish to open a hotel or a restaurant of his own. Henri Soulé's Le Pavillon remained the pinnacle of the French style in America. Although Sirio had never been to Le Pavillon, to him Soulé and Soulé's cooks were like Louis Diat performing what Sirio cynically calls "the French culinary act," an expression he parodies by mincing the words and pronouncing "act" with the guttural echo of a German "*Achtung!*" The idea that such a pretentious restaurant should be the standard by which all other serious restaurants were judged seemed illogical. Sirio far preferred the ad-hoc style of his native cuisine, but Italian food in America was impossibly down-market.

The new wave of French restaurants, Lutèce in particular, appealed to Sirio far more than Soulé's two restaurants, but none was looking for an employee of Sirio's caliber. This left the Colony, an old restaurant, but one that Sirio felt had established the right combination of class, service, and a less rigid French cuisine. Also, it was owned by Italians.

The Colony, on East Sixty-first Street and Madison Avenue, was underneath a building that contained, on its second floor, a gambling den and, above that, a fashionable private hospital that specialized in accommodating patients who required a certain amount of tact, since drying out, face lifts, enforced diets, and abortions were its main stock in trade. Like "21," the Colony had started its life as a speakeasy. The restaurant provided food and drink to the gentlemen and their molls who shot crap upstairs as well as to the hospital. In the days of Prohibition, the elevator in the building had been used as a moving wine cellar. Prohibition might have ended decades earlier, but it left an allure of something sexy and faintly illegal. Legend had it that in the late 1920s, Mrs. William

K. Vanderbilt, society's leading arbiter, came to the restaurant after finding out that her husband was spending time there, declared it acceptable, and from then on, the Colony became a bastion for America's upper class. From the brass name embedded in concrete on the sidewalk under the awning to a lobby that contained not only a concession booth from jewelers Van Cleef and Arpels and separate smoking lounges for ladies and gentlemen but a kennel to occupy poodles while their owners dined, the Colony felt more like a resort than a restaurant. The bar area was draped in festive blue and white stripes and a canopy hung over the bar itself. Tradition throughout the Colony's first thirty years dictated that clients gather at the bar, have their first of many drinks, then proceed back into the more formal, plush-red-velvet dining room.

Crystal chandeliers hung down the length of the long Red Room, lending it the atmosphere of an ocean liner. The tables were placed along the sides of the room, effectively in three tiers, the last section being the least desirable, and the first two forming a kind of social gauntlet for the dowager society ladies of New York on their way to sit down. The Colony's success, in particular after the war, depended largely on an almost casual relationship with its famous or wealthy clientele and an adherence to seasonality in cuisine. Hamburger wasn't on the menu at the Colony, but there were shad roe and asparagus in spring, raspberries in high summer, and the first pheasant in early September—all relatively simply prepared and, perhaps more important, reasonably priced. And if you insisted on a hamburger, you had but to ask and it would appear.

SIRIO

I T IS VERY IMPORTANT, when you leave, to leave on good terms. Everyone has to move on, but you don't need to be stupid about it. I talked to Tucci and we become really very good friends. He understood that I needed to move on and he helped me to do it. The thing is to do it in a smart way, so that you become part of a network, and the person from the past wants to know you in the future.

I spoke to Henri Surmain at Lutèce, which had just opened. To me it was the perfect, least pretentious restaurant in town. I liked the chef, André Soltner, but the restaurant was very small: Surmain did the door, even Soltner did the door! So there was no place for me, but we became very good friends.

Le Pavillon was at the Ritz Tower, but my god, it was very formal, very rigid—I didn't want to go back to that. It was what New York needed in the 1940s and '50s but, by the '60s, it was old. There was La Côte Basque, Soulé's other restaurant, but there you had to deal with Madame Henriette, who ran it for him. She was something else, a real character, and we never knew if she was his girlfriend or not, but later on she bought La Côte Basque from his wife and ran it until she died. There was Joe Baum, who was a very interesting man doing amazing things for Restaurant Associates, the new Four Seasons, and the Forum of the Twelve Caesars, with its forks the size of your arm. Each of Restaurant Associates' restaurants had its own gimmick, but they were all too ridiculous. I can be stupid, but I can't be vulgar. Also, Restaurant Associates was already a big company. To go work for them would have been like going to Ciga—they would have looked at me and said, "Fine, you do the dishes for a few years, and then we'll talk."

La Grenouille and La Caravelle had opened too, but each was run by a family, so there was no place for me there either. And "21" was not what I wanted. It was like Delmonico's, only uptown, and I was trying to leave that.

There was also El Morocco. Angelo, who ran the door, was a friend of mine, and it would have been no problem for me to work there, but it was a nightclub. I had been once to El Morocco with Oscar Tucci and his wife. At that kind of place, friends from the restaurant business would be treated well. El Morocco's table number 1 was where the most important people were seated, and when I went with Oscar Tucci, Angelo sat us opposite it. I looked to my right and there was Lauren Bacall. I don't really know why—maybe because she didn't know I was there—but she was sitting with her legs open. And you know, I could see everything. So I just stared and stared. I think I could have stared forever really, and finally I heard a voice in my head saying, "Are you finished? Are you done?" and I looked up and, my god, she was looking right at me, and she said "Like it?" I just nodded my head and she repeated, "Are you done?" Then, "May I close them now?" Years later when I answered the phone at Le Cirque and heard that same voice saying, "Are you done?" I would laugh and know it was her. My god, what legs!

Anyway, it would have been the wrong move to work at a club. For a start, I would never have survived Lauren Bacall! So that left the Colony, which really was the home of café society. By then I had worked a few parties there, so I knew I liked it. They had only the best people, but it wasn't snobby. What people said was that no matter who you were, you could not be sure you'd be treated nice at Le Pavillon, but at the Colony everyone was treated nice—well, most of the time. I had met the owner, Gene Cavallero, but it was really Oscar Tucci who introduced me to him. Otherwise, they probably would never have let me in the door.

I think, though, there was another reason Cavallero let me come to the Colony. It was very successful, but by the time I got there it was already forty years old. Restaurants have cycles. Every twenty years there is a big change, and for New York the change came in 1960. Cavallero had a son, Gene Jr., he had a restaurant, he knew he wasn't going to move, or change the design, but he had to make it different, a little more exciting. He would never have told me, and I didn't presume, but I do think that he let me come in because he wanted someone a little younger, a little presumptuous, a little sexier. In some ways Gene, the father, was more like me than his own son. He said, "I understand you, I come from the same routine, I also worked hard. My son hasn't suffered enough, you'll have troubles with him." But he said it in a way that I knew meant to reassure me, to say, "It's up to you to make this work—to make a space for yourself. You have to show my son that you know what you're talking about."

CELESTINA WALLACE *[socialite] Oh, it would have been quite a big risk for Cavallero. The waiters there had been there since before I was born and they didn't just let in a newcomer so fast. To put a young man on the main floor was very threatening, not just to the people who worked there, I suppose, but to us. You're used to seeing the same person and we would go there, four or five times a week! But Gene was a smart man. He'd just hired a waiter, but I think he intended to groom a champion.*

My first big party was for Mr. William Zeckendorf Sr. He was a big man, very impatient, and when he came in, Mr. Cavallero said I would be in charge of his party. Then Zeckendorf looked at me, very surprised, and said in a way that I knew was a little bit more than a challenge, "Let's just hope you don't fuck it up."

I managed the table. It was a big table, ten or twelve people, and everything was going well. Mr. Zeckendorf ordered the *dindonneau grillé,* a roasted baby turkey. It was a good dish, clean, served half, and very real. It was from a farm in upstate New York and in those days almost no matter what you did to it, it was going to taste good.

I don't want to say it was malicious, I'll never know, though such a thing had never happened before. When I went to serve the turkey, something caught my arm and the turkey fell off and under the table. I looked up very quickly to see if anyone had noticed it. I remembered my training at Maxim's—a mistake is fine as long as you repair it elegantly and quickly. So I invented a ruse—I told Mr. Zeckendorf that he had a phone call. He told me not to bother him. I walked away and came back. I couldn't change the story now! Finally I got him to go to the phone to take the call that didn't exist and I slipped the turkey back into the kitchen. There was no way to cook another one in time, so they just dressed it up again. When he was back at the table, Zeckendorf was screaming, "There was no one on the phone at all. Don't bother me again!" I poured him some wine. He always had very important wines. He calmed down and by the time his end of the table was served, the turkey was re-presented to him and I thought, I am a hero. When the dinner was over and the guests were leaving, Mr. Zeckendorf was the last to leave. He shook my hand and pulled me close to him and whispered in my ear, "I at least hope you had the decency to clean off my turkey before you served it to me again." And then he walked straight over to Mr. Cavallero, who was standing at the door.

I knew that it was the end of my career at the Colony and I could see them both looking my way. When Mr. Zeckendorf left, Cavallero called me over and I got ready to say I would leave. He said to me, "You young Italians, you think you can do everything and you can't." I told him I had only tried to do my best, and he yelled back at me, "Well, this time your best wasn't good enough."

But he didn't fire me!

When I started at the Colony, it was all about people who thought they owned everything. They owned the chair, they owned the table, they owned the napkin, and they liked to think they owned me. And for a long time everyone—the waiters and the owners—treated them this way. I think if I brought anything to the restaurant, it was to introduce, slowly, the idea that you didn't have to be a mincing slave. They were just people. Maybe, being from Italy, I didn't think these people were so important. Money itself doesn't impress me so much. Character does. I couldn't be rude to the people who had no character—and there were lots, believe me—but by doing things in a different way, I think I made it a better place to eat.

I had to do it without offending the guests or the owner. There is nothing worse than a presumptuous waiter. I was burning up with anger, but I controlled it by putting it in a different place. It was all part of the war in my head, the one I had to win. I kept going, smiled at the customer, made sure they got what they wanted, that the owner got what he wanted, that my colleagues didn't kill me. I was a perfect robot with a smile.

Cavallero was right. The first few years at the Colony were very, very hard. The same people who came to Delmonico's to have a martini or three at lunch were much more demanding uptown with their wives, or sometimes their girls. You can't know how careful I had to be. Maybe as an Italian I knew better than others that anyone—woman or man—has a right to a private life. I never presumed anything, and never got too cute. The day you get too cute is the day you lose your job. That's not to say I didn't get into trouble. Once, early on, I poured a glass of cognac to the height we had been told to pour it, the customer said, "I'm not a baby, I'm not sick," and prodded me to fill up the glass to the rim. Cavallero called me over and said if I filled a glass like that again, he'd take the cost of the drink out of my pay.

Another time Cavallero heard me ask a table if everything was okay. He went into a rage, pulled me aside, and ordered me never to ask such a thing. "They are at the Colony, of course they are okay! They should be glad that we let them through the door. At the Colony we never ask. We just assume they are happy." I thought this was the height of presumptuousness, but it became very important to me, because I learned that he was both right and wrong. The mistake was not in asking the question, the mistake was in how to phrase it. He was right never to ask, "Is everything okay?" because most of the time it is not okay. The waiter does not really want to know the answer and the client is not really going to tell him. The most intelligent thing a waiter can do is to offer his services. Not "Is your meal okay?" or "Is everything fine?" but an open-ended invitation, "Is there anything I can do for you?" That is very different. So I started asking that question. Mr. Cavallero never minded and I could see it changed the faces of the customers. They didn't have to pretend everything was okay, it allowed them to say, "Well yes, in fact, I would like another this, or maybe a little of that." Or they asked a question, and from that question I learned something.

ROGER YASEEN *[investment banker/gourmet] Right from the beginning there was something very different about Sirio. A good diplomat makes it easy for you to do something his way. Americans were used to having pushy waiters or never really getting what they wanted. Sirio never pushed and always got you what you wanted. Very unlike Soulé. With Sirio you felt like everyone was part of a wonderful, delicious secret.*

The truth was, restaurants didn't want to give the customers what they wanted. The kitchen was always waging a war against the customer. If you went into the kitchen to say that a customer didn't like a sauce, or the way a piece of meat was cooked, you might as well pack your bags. I went in and made friends in the kitchen the same way I made friends in the dining room. I got on their side in a way that the cooks didn't see it as an attack. A *sous*-chef would have killed me if I had said, "I know how to do that better, I learned it with Diat, the heir to Escoffier." I had to prove I knew what I was talking about. I think I was the only one brave enough to even talk to people in the kitchen about food. But once they knew me, they talked with me and I developed a rapport. I'm not saying they ever really listened—they probably didn't—but when I needed something in the dining room I could usually get it, and other waiters could not.

Sometimes people wanted something very simple and sometimes they wanted something more complex. It was never the same people: the fancy people wanted the simple food and the simple people the fancy food. So I went to the kitchen and I knew how to ask. What I really was, was the diners' ambassador to the kitchen. I knew how to ask for what they wanted, when most of the time they didn't know themselves. I always knew.

MICHAEL BATTERBERRY *[founder / editor,* **Food Arts***] Sirio has always had an exquisite sense of fashionable food for two distinct groups: those who wear it on their backs, and those who want it on their plates. They're not usually the same, since fashionable people often don't understand fashionable food. He would very slowly, very patiently introduce not just food—that came later—but a sense of style, a demeanor. He was the teacher, teaching those who thought they had already been taught. It was all about style, mixed with a sense of exclusivity.*

The Colony was not haute cuisine. The Colony was café society and what that society wanted was a good restaurant with good food in a space that was attractive, but not stuffy. The French were really not able to do it. The English were better at it, but in 1960 it was the Americans who knew how to get it just right. The Colony had a broiled fish, a paillard of veal, good beef, capon; it was food people wanted. They had pasta; it was probably the only important restaurant in New York that would serve pasta with pride, and it was quite good. This was what I learned at Maxim's, and Cavallero did it well too: don't think so much about who you are or what you are, just give the people what they want to eat. In a so-called haute cuisine restaurant, it was unacceptable even to prepare a broiled fish. The Pavillon and all those places were not for café society, but for masochists willing to submit to the French culinary act. I'd seen it and done it and hated it.

I was still learning a lot about food in America. It wasn't that Americans did not have good food, it's that they did not have the years of tradition and experience and they did not travel as much. People didn't know what a grilled piece of fish was. In most restaurants if you asked for a grilled fish, they would take the fish, cook it in the oven, then put black marks on the side! I think Americans had picked up more influences from the Chinese restaurants than from the French. It was during those days that I heard for the first time people asking for "roast duck, very crispy"— like you get in a Chinese restaurant, not like we would roast a duck in Italy or in France. At the Colony they made a *sauce d'orange* for the "roast duck, very crispy" which was sometime very nice, and sometimes like marmalade. But they also had things that I had never seen before: soft-shell crabs in season, which you couldn't find in Europe, except maybe Venice, and beautiful bay scallops.

Everyone said that the very rich didn't know anything about food. They did, they traveled and they knew what they liked. It had to be the best. It was also very important that it not be too much about the food, or too little. They had busy social lives and the Colony was just one stop in the day. You had to get it just right. ◄◄◄

MICHAEL THOMAS *[author, columnist] The Colony was very grown-up, with fancy people, like Sinatra. In those days the Duke and Duchess of Windsor were the patron saints of café society. There weren't that many places to go. When you did, it wasn't really for the food, it was a moving social scene. You went to the St. Regis for drinks, moved on to the Colony or "21" for dinner, then out to El Morocco or the Stork Club. On any night you were bound to meet at least twenty people you knew. That was café society. I bet it was no more than the old New York 400, the people that filled Mrs. Vanderbilt's ballroom. By 1961 there were still 400 people, but different people.*

MAÎTRE D'!

I N APRIL 1961, about a year after Sirio arrived at the Colony, the restaurant's long-time and very popular maître d'hôtel, Albert Torino, died. On a temporary basis, and only for the bar area, Sirio was assigned to meet, greet, and arrange the seating of the restaurant's clients. The outside world calls this a "maître d'hôtel," or "maître d" for short, but Sirio knew it just as "doing the door." Monday morning Sirio showed up early for his first day "to do the door" at the front of the house at one of the world's most famous restaurants.

W HEN ALBERTO TORINO DIED everyone wanted to know who was going to fill his shoes. Mr. Cavallero called me to his office and offered me the job and even I was a little surprised. He made a big deal about how everyone had been waiting twenty years to get this job. And I said to him, "Well, if they've been waiting this long then they're probably tired of all that waiting."

So then he said I was arrogant, which maybe I was. I said to Mr. Cavallero that I was happy to take the job but that I needed his help to talk to the other waiters and staff to smooth things out and he said, "Since when did you care about what the staff thinks?" I said, "What I think and what I do, Mr. Cavallero, are two different things." Anyway, he said, "Do the door for a few weeks," and I did the door for ten years.

I really just took over the bar at first. Of the two parts of the restaurant, the bar had the blue and white canopy while the Red Room was very red…oh my god, was it red: red carpets, red curtains, red walls, red, red, red! The bar was where the elite of the elite wanted to be, along with the people from Hollywood, Ava Gardner and Elizabeth Taylor with Richard Burton—they came, but just to fight! They would arrive at 2:30 and stay until dinner, screaming at one another.

MICHAEL THOMAS *The Colony wasn't so much about money—it was about recognition. People may have thought there was a Siberia, but there really wasn't. You were recognized or you weren't recognized. Favored more, or favored less.*

CELESTINA WALLACE *The bar was for the international set, Hollywood people, the nouveau riche, men with very expensive girls. Fun. And of course, that's where I wanted to be. But when my grandmother took me to the Colony, we always sat in the Red Room. My first memory of Sirio was when I came in once without my grandmother and he cleared the way for me to sit in the bar. It was like being upgraded to first class!*

My first day at the door, I went to the book and I saw the names— Windsor, Niarchos, Sinatra, Onassis, Billy Baldwin, the decorator—and I noticed that beside each name, where there was supposed to be a table number, was written "the usual table." Without giving it too much thought, I went upstairs to meet with the waiters who were now my "lieutenants." I asked for their support and they stared at me blankly. I had thought I would make them respect me by asking, but in fact they didn't care. All they saw was some Italian guy who, if he did good, would make them money and, if he did bad, would cost them money. It was that simple.

So then I went about my business and just before lunch I asked Mr. Cavallero to explain to me which table was "the usual table" for each customer so I could seat them. He just lifted his hand and pointed over at the table in the corner of the bar, "That is the usual table." It was one and the same table—they all thought it was theirs!

I didn't have time to think about what to do because they all started to come in. So I decided to use a policy of first come, first served. And the first person to arrive was Sinatra, which was very unusual for him. I had known Mr. Sinatra now a long time from the restaurant and from Paris, and he went to the bar to have a drink and started to tell me that he and his friends had ganged up on Cavallero to get me my new assignment, and he was congratulating me, but I had to tell him to please go to his table and not have his drink at the bar. And you know, he went very quickly from congratulations to being not very happy. He said, "Listen, kid, let's not have a fight on our first day!"

But once I explained the problem to him, he went to sit at the table. While Sinatra sat and fumed, I ran to the kitchen and sent a plate heaped high with thinly sliced Italian prosciutto.

The next person to come in was Aristotle Onassis. He never wore an overcoat, not even in the coldest weather, only a gray flannel suit, and a dark suit at night, always with a matching tie. Riveting. You could see in five minutes why women, men, everyone was seduced by him, why he was so powerful. He had amazing energy. He went to every lunch, every dinner, every party. He was at the height of his relationship with Maria Callas, but they always came in separately. She was insecure, where he was secure, but she threw off the same intense energy. You could see why they had wound up together. Whatever she did to lose all that weight ruined her, she looked like she had the skin of a chicken, but still she was electric and together they were like a jolt into your face.

So Onassis came in and immediately saw who was at his table. "So, you give Sinatra my table because he's your *paesan,* eh? You Italians always stick together...." Still, the comment seemed more tongue-in-cheek than threatening.

Next to come in were the Duke and Duchess of Windsor. He was far too elegant to make a fuss about the table, but as we walked by Sinatra there was a slight look as I brought them to a banquette. I seated them beside each other and explained to the Duke that I thought this new seating arrangement would be more comfortable. He looked at me with a face like a mean puppy and said, "I don't ask you to think—I just want my table." But I kept going. I had known them from Montecatini and I knew he liked very simple dishes—what they now call "spa food." I asked the kitchen to put some crabmeat—the closest thing they had in America to *granseuola*—along with lemon and pignoli over slices of thin potato with lettuce and egg. I brought it to the table, and I made a quick dressing at the table with olive oil from Italy that I kept hidden, and then I went back to work. After he had the first bite, he called me over, remembering me from Montecatini, and went on about the olive oil and how he too had to smuggle in olive oil from Tuscany.

Niarchos was the most difficult. He got very upset and demanded to speak to Alberto. He kept insisting, until finally Mr. Cavallero had to come out and tell him very gently that Mr. Torino was dead and he would have to be a little forgiving of me. I don't think he was, but he did go sit at another table and never again fussed over which table was his or someone else's.

Billy Baldwin came in with Cary Grant, and by then the room was full so I asked if they could sit in the Red Room, at a table that was behind a big velvet curtain. We called it the "mystery table," for people who wanted to be alone, and also because at that table you had the option to go through the kitchen and out the back door, and believe me, we had to do that a lot! So I asked if they wanted to sit there, and they said yes. We had a waiter then at the Colony named Franco, who was very handsome, almost pretty, and everyone called him Sabrina, like Audrey Hepburn in the movie. At about 1:30, 1:45, at the height of lunch, I heard a scream and Franco came running out, "They're touching me! They're touching me!" I felt a little bad, because I knew they probably *were* touching him, but I just said, "Let them touch, I don't have another table!" ◄◄

SERENDIPITY IS THE ART of making your own luck. To New York society, it was as if a new, young stallion had suddenly appeared at the door of the Colony, when in fact, Sirio had been there for a year already. After a lifetime of doing much but saying very little, suddenly he was the gatekeeper at the most socially prominent restaurant, in the most important town, in the most important country in the world. Practically speaking, the job meant arranging the room with its client roster of the world's wealthy and powerful, but it also meant directing or suggesting their meals, taking their orders, overseeing the staff assigned to their tables, frequently carving or cutting or preparing foods at the table, and, in particular, discreetly dealing with money. In an age where credit cards did not exist, most patrons kept regular tabs. Restaurants like the Colony and Le Pavillon functioned sometimes almost as much as banks as they did restaurants.

What made Sirio unique as he assumed his new position was that he could accommodate all of these tasks seamlessly, and apparently at the same time. His skill at getting from the kitchen to the table and at negotiating the dining room—pouring, plating, cutting, presenting, and answering the phone—was as solid and etched in his physical body as a dancer. The comparison to a dancer would stick with him the rest of his career. He oozed not just a Tuscan charm, but his own style of flirtation. Café society was mesmerized. Within weeks of his becoming maître d' at the bar of the Colony, no less than an authority than Henry Luce declared in *Life* magazine, "Our beloved Colony has a new maître d. He's young, he's elegant, he's smart. If he spoke English, he'd be even better." Sirio Maccioni had metamorphosed into the sexiest man in town.

SIRIO

PEOPLE TALKED ABOUT SEX and maybe, yes, I had an attitude, a physical bearing. I was skinny, I was elegant—I knew how to look at people. I looked at a woman and the woman understood it, but it never offended the man. This is the number-one point—to be a real diplomat. Otherwise I could have ruined the whole thing. It was a tightrope. The perfect restaurateur, like the perfect entrepreneur, has to be insecure. He has to play it by ear, but mostly he has to know to keep his mouth shut and open it at exactly the right time, every time. The point is that a big percentage of these ladies came to the Colony. For me, it was very difficult to resist because, for me in those days—a man, a normal man, a Latin man—what does he want?

But for some of them I was just a thing, and if they wanted me, they expected me to serve them. The women that came in and asked for it—forget it. The women who didn't push for it—I loved to give.

ELAINE KAUFMAN *[owner of Elaine's] All you need to know about Sirio was that he was the hottest-looking man in New York. He was a mover. Now, I'm not saying that he did it with every one of them, but that it was important that they all thought he did. And he knew how to control that better than anyone in New York.*

At the Colony, one of the first things I did at the door was make a new system for the tips. The old way, people would try to squeeze a dollar or five dollars into my hand. Instead of that, now I left envelopes with the cashier. I don't know why, but in the envelopes they always left more—ten or twenty. It was a lot of money back then! Later I was told it was a kind of competition: "How much did you leave Sirio?" Of course, the other person always wanted to say they left more.

Competition with the ladies was also very important. And knowing how to play the game. It was important to be friendly with the person in charge of the Colony, in charge of the French Pavillon or El Morocco—Angelo did the door at what we called Elmo's. He was tall, with white hair, and elegant. We were, maybe, the two most elegant men in New York, and women would come after us. Often there were telephone numbers and messages as well as tips in the white envelopes. But you had to be careful. My god, I wondered, do they think they're *buying* me? Fifty percent wanted to do it that way, but they didn't all want it for that reason—some actually wanted to be friendly. One time I went to the Pierre to make arrangements for a private party a lady wanted to have at the restaurant, and she insisted I come to her suite. She opened the door in her dressing gown and said simply, "This is the party," and that was that. I mean, I wasn't stupid, I enjoyed planning this particular party. But the payback came quickly when she came into the restaurant and said, "I want that table, or … no, no, no, no, I don't want to sit here anymore, give me this, give me that."

I learned fast that I couldn't do this, that it meant losing my independence. Like not taking money for tables. The minute you take money, you cannot move. Men would come up to me and say, "What's the matter with you? I try to give you fifty dollars and you still make me wait?"

CELESTINA WALLACE *He was a flirt, there's no doubt about it. It was about allure. It was so much more sexual than sex. I would never have considered sex with Sirio. He was so much smarter than that and so was I. He was straight and he understood jewels, clothes, how I smelled, how I looked. He appreciated every part. He never took it too far and yet you spent the evening in a swoon, imagining what could be, which is so much better than actually having sex.*

Some of ladies and men were just mean. There was a Mrs. "Bet" Leary, some relation to the Queen of England, who wouldn't give a person a glass of water if he were dying in the desert, or Joan Crawford, who was maybe a little crazy. And Callas, who was so difficult. Pamela Harriman, the wife of Churchill, and then [Leland] Hayward, and then the governor—always very crisp, very controlling. We got along. We had an understanding. I did things for her, she did things for me. I wanted to say to the people who expected me to do just what they wanted, whatever it was: "Where do you think Dante came from, and Leonardo da Vinci?" But of course, I did nothing of the sort. I could never do anything or get back at them. I just did what I had to do.

But some of the women and men were much better than that, and made me feel good. I talked to Mrs. Paley maybe every day for ten years. She was perhaps the most beautiful of them all, not so much because of her looks—which were much better than any of the pictures show—but because she was very kind, proper, direct. You knew what she wanted, and you knew exactly where you stood. And Marella Agnelli. Very classic. I had great respect for her husband. These women were criticized a lot and maybe that too is why I liked them. I knew I was nothing, I came from a farm, but they were always very correct with me. I bet that when some of the other women went home, they just said, "Oh, that waiter," but that when Mrs. Paley or Mrs. Agnelli went home, she would say, "Ah, Sirio, he was so kind today, I must remember to call and say thank you." And they did. That was what made them the most beautiful women.

Mrs. Kennedy—Jackie—was maybe my favorite. I waited on all the Kennedys, they came two or three times a week. Joseph, the father, would come for lunch and then come at dinner with his wife, Rose, whom I had taken care of in Montecatini. She liked the bar. He preferred the Red Room. I had a relationship with both of them, but I never mixed with them. Another rule: never be too familiar. Never say to the gentlemen you saw last night with someone else, "Do you want to have the same drink as last night?" Don't be too anything, otherwise he may look at you and say, "Idiot, last night I was in Chicago." Then you will never see them again, and you'll have a bad reputation as well.

But I served them all: Ted, and Patricia, the sister who married Peter Lawford—she would call out to me on the street, "Sirio, Sirio!!!" Robert was very tough, very hard, I would see him yell; they were not always very nice, but they were always very respectful to me. And the President. The day he was shot I was at the Colony. Egidiana cried for three days. She kept saying, "How could they kill the President?" For me it was really the first time I lost a little bit of faith in America. I remembered seeing Lucky Luciano and Frank Costello with J. Edgar Hoover in Cuba, and I remembered Hoover's boyfriends and how much Hoover and the mob hated the Kennedys and how much the Kennedys hated them. And I got to thinking that this poor Oswald could not really have done it alone, that it must be something much bigger.

After Kennedy was killed, everyone talked about what they think happened, but even knowing what I knew, I never talked about it. Not because I am so discreet, but because except for Kennedy dying and for Mrs. Kennedy, I didn't really care. People who talked too much were not going to be successful in the business, and I knew I was going to be. I liked my job. I was too busy to listen. I was much more attracted to providing service than in listening to the gossip. It was okay to listen, but not to tell.

You have to know your clients. I had all the presidents, the daughters and sons of presidents, kings, governors, Rockefeller, Harriman, Bernard Baruch. I talked to them. I'm not saying that they came to me because I was so smart or that I knew anything about solving the world's problems, but I made it easy for them, and they liked someone to talk to who wouldn't call the newspaper or tell their wife. Still, I had to know what they were talking about! I read all the time and I watched the papers closely for local gossip. All the newspapers, every day. And I read a book a week, rotating languages. One week English, the next French, German, Spanish, and Italian.

I started to develop a personal mailing list, and I spent mornings on the phone, calling clients to find out when they were planning to come into the restaurant, making reservations for them. ◄◄

GEORGE LANG *The most significant aspect of Sirio was his encyclopedic memory for the minutiae of his clients' lives. He knew everything and everybody, where they went, who they were married to, who they'd been married to before, where their money came from, what they liked, when they liked it. It was endless. He just knew more than they knew.*

SIRIO HAD ALREADY SPENT A LIFETIME observing the fine line between the servers and the served and, despite his success, he was exceedingly careful never to cross it. What could appear perfectly amicable in one moment could turn ugly the next. One had to give a client everything he or she wanted, yet never cross over the line, although in many cases the line was growing increasingly fuzzy. One of these was Juan Carlos, heir to the throne of Spain, though few expected he would ever claim it while the dictator Francisco Franco held power. Since the two had both been raised in Italy, if in different circumstances, and had cavorted in Paris in their twenties, Sirio was more able to accept himself in the role of friend. Sirio helped arrange Juan Carlos's American engagement party to Sophia of Greece at the Colony.

It was also in Paris that Sirio first met Frank Sinatra. Since Sirio didn't speak much English at the time and didn't understand Sinatra's Italian, there wasn't much more rapport beyond Sinatra's clear preference to be served by a young Italian. Later, Sirio saw and occasionally served Sinatra in all of the places where their paths crossed, but most frequently at the Colony.

At the Colony Sinatra took the young Italian under his wing. He made a bet on this young stallion he'd already known for a decade, frequently steering his young charge toward restaurant or club deals that were happening across the country where he thought he (or they) might benefit. Or he would discuss the possibility of the two going into business together. Sirio was smart enough not to take it too seriously, although he was sure never to miss a name, a contact, or a resource. Sinatra was also a gossip—happy to provide Sirio with little nuggets of information on many of the Colony's illustrious clientele. To Sirio's knowledge, Sinatra never got into any scraps inside or outside the Colony, but his entourage, which included Pat De Cicco, Chuck Broccoli, and Peter Lawford, frequently did. It was clear, if unwritten, that in return for Sirio's discretion, Sirio would reap Sinatra's favor. It became the unwritten rule of Sirio's career.

And then there was the line that had to be tread most carefully—the women, in many cases part of author Truman Capote's coterie of "Swans": Marella Agnelli, Gloria Guiness, C. Z. Guest, Lee Radziwell (Jackie Kennedy's sister), and Princess Luciana Pignatelli, all of whom Sirio knew from different stages in their lives and their marriages.

As glamorous, famous, and well connected as he appeared, Sirio never made the mistake of thinking he was anything other than a paid employee of the Cavalleros. He knew that most of his vaunted clientele thought of him as merely an attractive stop on the way to their favorite tables. He was, as he always says, nothing more than a "presumptuous waiter."

For a presumptuous waiter, he was earning a lot of money. By his thirtieth birthday, he purchased not one, but two apartments in Montecatini, a supreme sign of his newly found security. He purchased a new car for his uncles (even though they didn't want it) and had enough money put away to support his family in Italy. The rest went to a growing collection of tailor-made, mostly Italian, clothes and a fascination for the gadgets of the age—the most expensive audio equipment, the newest, most modern furniture. He even had his maître d' uniform made in Rome, by Caraceni.

A few years after he started at the Colony Sirio moved to a sixth-floor walkup, a door down from Lutèce on East Fiftieth Street. He still jokes that he was so close to his friend André Soltner's restaurant that when he was hungry he could lean out the window with a slice of bread and soak up the flavors pouring from the kitchen. Sirio became a late-night regular at Lutèce, where the two would spend their postwork hours eating, tasting, and drinking.

The Colony closed in July, allowing its staff to have a month off. Continuing his habit of working more than anyone else so he could accumulate more time off later, Sirio was able to spend almost the entire summer in Italy. His relationship with Egidiana had taken on a new dimension. Her singing career in Italy had continued to boom, but Sirio thought the key to her success, like his own, would be international. He didn't hesitate to interfere and direct his chanteuse's career. Through the restaurant he had met Erberto Landi, a New York–based talent agent who specialized in Italian singers. Landi had scored a deal with Capitol Records to promote "Italy's exciting baritone" Luciano Virgili and his band of singers—which included Egi. Sirio hardly knew Virgili. All he cared about was that Egi would be coming to America—though, of course, he didn't say that to her. The troupe toured the United States, ending their "Singing Tour of Italy" with an engagement at Carnegie Hall on Saturday, January 12, 1963. When Egi came out for her solos, she tripped over a microphone cable and nearly landed in the orchestra pit. She recovered, sang

"Quando, Quando," and "Summertime," and received the only standing ovation of the evening.

The tour had been a sellout and established Egi as a talent in her own right. After the tour she was able to reunite with some of her own family who had settled in Brooklyn in the late 1950s, and to spend time with Sirio. Still, six years after their courtship began, she went back to Montecatini without a promise of marriage. She left the wedding dress that she had prepared in a box in her uncle's house in Bensonhurst.

The tour's ultimate success happened when she got home. A talent scout from RCA brought her to Rome, where she was offered an unusually lush contract: money, singing lessons in the capital, promotion, travel, all expenses paid, and three records, guaranteed. RCA's aim, as Sirio later told the story, was to transform Egi into Italy's Julie London—a suave, multilingual bombshell, one part seductress, one part girl-next-door. Sirio's protégée was on her way to stardom.

Egi was still her own boss. She wrote to her parents on March 24, from Rome, to say that she had refused to sign the contract. Her relationship with Sirio, she wrote, was worth more than her career. She loved him too much, even though she still wasn't sure that he felt the same way. She hoped she wouldn't regret the decision, she wrote, but felt confident about making it.

Although Egi did not go with RCA, she continued to sing professionally throughout Italy, and in the spring of 1964 she went on another U.S. tour with Virgili and Landi, returning for her second appearance at Carnegie Hall on April 11. After she returned to Brooklyn from a performance in Albany late that month, Sirio finally proposed to her.

SIRIO

WHEN I GOT MARRIED I was quite old. In those days thirty-two was old to get married, but it was time. Her name is Egi—for Egidiana, a very unusual name. Her great uncle was a great man, an archbishop who could have been the pope, except something went wrong. His name was Egidio, and the niece is named after him. The Palmieris lived in a smart town house in the center of Montecatini. I was just a poor farmer from the fields. It was the war that brought us all together in many ways.

EGIDIANA *The war made everyone the same. Sirio's people came from the land, and we lived in town. During the war food was a big issue. In the city it was very hard to get it, and growing up hungry is something you never forget. It seemed that soldiers—Germans, then Americans—were always banging the door of our house down, marching through with guns, and grabbing whatever they could.*

When the American soldiers left Montecatini, they came and were banging on the door and my mother, my grandmother, and me were all in this big bed hoping they would go away. My aunt had unraveled the sweaters the Americans had given us and she rolled them into these big balls of yarn. So there I was this little girl, with these two old ladies, in this bed on top of all these balls of wool, thinking that the Americans had come back because they wanted their wool! It sounds funny, but that's what it was like. They would take anything.

We all lived through these things together. People who disap-peared, soldiers who didn't come back, lives changed forever. My uncle and brother spent the whole war upstairs in the eaves of the house playing cards, so he wouldn't get captured. I would go door to door after the war with my grandmother to make pasta to trade for food or sometimes to pay off my father's gambling debts. This was not the life of a grand family! And yes, maybe when I saw Sirio again later on, I saw him differently than other girls saw him.

Our relationship had begun with the affair we had when I went back for my visa in 1957. My wife always complained that I took too long to make up my mind. Maybe I did. I was alone, and she was not. Even in America, she had family and I did not. When you are alone you get nervous, and I was very nervous. I had my sister, Clara, who got married to Piero, but still there was my grandmother, my two uncles, and I needed to make sure they were safe. I was making some real money and I could do something, but still I didn't get married. Okay? I'm a person with weaknesses, and for me it was not so easy. I was cautious. I was looking for a girl I could bring home—and how could I take Egidiana Palmieri home to my farm? I had to do something, be somebody, be someone ... and I was still a waiter. My god, she was already singing at Carnegie Hall and I was just a waiter.

Like every Tuscan I am sometimes ashamed to show affection, to say "I love you." It's more likely I could say I love my grandmother than to say that to a woman who could be my wife. The women I really had relationships with, my sister and my grandmother, our conversation was not like what you have with your wife, and I didn't know how. Luckily, I have a great wife who is more intelligent than me, and she overlooked all these things.

Then again, she give up a great career, and married a waiter, so maybe she's not so intelligent. She came to sing at Carnegie Hall and went back and gave up a big contract, $25,000, then! With everything—Rome, lessons, a three-record deal. They wanted to make her the Julie London of Italy. And I wanted that for her, but she gave it up.

EGIDIANA *I wanted to be a housewife and a mother. Really, that was the most I ever wanted. For a time I would model fur coats and my girlfriends would say that's what they wanted—furs, cars, diamonds, cigarettes. I didn't want fur coats. I just wanted a family. I loved to sing, but it became a career by accident. I couldn't read music. I sang in English, Spanish, even Greek. I had good pronunciation, nobody seemed to notice or care, but I didn't know what I was talking about. So that was scary, but really, I just didn't have the ambition. I knew what I wanted and it was not that. I think it meant more to Sirio than to me.*

Egidiana is a special case. I want to do lots of things. Change lots of things. She just wants one thing. She keeps coming back the day after and the day after. She is so sure of herself, so focused, that you believe anything she says.

I knew I couldn't have anything I wanted without a future and I knew, in the end, that a family of my own was going to be my real future.

Maybe, finally, it got into my head that my grandmother, my uncles, my sister, were okay. It just took time.

If I had married another woman, I would have been in prison, because I don't divorce, I kill. It had to be someone who could put up with me. I knew I would stay in restaurants. When you go into restaurants you make a choice about your lifestyle. You give up nights and weekends and holidays and all the things normal people have. Marrying that is worse than marrying a doctor or the president.

We had the wedding at the church at the United Nations on July 17, 1964, and then a reception at Oscar Tucci's, my old boss and very good friend at 1165 Park Avenue, the penthouse. It was very nice. We couldn't go on a honeymoon because I had to work. So we went to the movies and then she moved into the apartment next to Lutèce with me. Right away it was a nightmare. I thought I was finished. It was a sixth-floor walk-up. I wouldn't even get to the top of the stairs and she'd smell the perfume or the cigarette smoke or see the mark of red lips on my cheek and she'd scream and we'd fight until finally I said, "This has to stop. I do what I do. I won't go through this stupidity every night." It was really something not to be free. To have to answer to her and to the questions. But I liked her. We liked each other and in time things got calm. At least in an Italian way. People would come knocking on the door because they thought we were going to kill each other, but it's the same way now. I think I shout louder, so I always win. She inspires me because she takes all the nonsense of me, of life, of the restaurant, and filters it and raises a family and makes beautiful food and loves a madman. In me everything is amplified, like a loudspeaker—she is very good at turning down the volume.

My wife is the best thing I have. ◄◄

WITHIN A YEAR, the little apartment by Lutèce had three occupants: Sirio, Egi, and their first child, Mario. It was a fitting first birth for a restaurant family. Sirio was at the door of the Colony while Egi was in labor at the Polyclinic, a hospital on the West Side of Manhattan popular with immigrant Italians and gangsters and the newborn's first visitor wasn't his father, but Frank Sinatra, bearing a silver brush from Cartier. Once home, Egi kept in constant contact with the Italian-American community in New York, through her family in Brooklyn, and set about being the perfect mother to her son and the best wife she could be to her largely absent husband. Sirio had been made an official part of the Colony's management, with a salary plus tips and control of operations in the dining room, which to a large extent allowed him to influence decisions in the kitchen. Henri Soulé died in his restaurant in 1966, and although his restaurant lived on for another four years, its clientele decamped largely to the Colony. Without Soulé, Le Pavillon ceased to be fashionable. The focus of fashion turned to the Colony and to Sirio.

SIRIO

THE PEOPLE MADE THE RESTAURANT. The trick for me was to get the food and the people right. And it was not my restaurant. I had to win by doing, I had to be different. And I was. I don't think I was so smart. I just did everything. It was fun. The people were fun, sophisticated, very attractive. Not always easy, but maybe it was the first time I really liked what I was doing. They were very, very happy times. If Mrs. Paley didn't come, I would just call her, "Why you not come for lunch?" Or any of them. Leonard Lyons was a very influential gossip columnist. He would stop by all the time, sometimes just for a coffee, and I would find out a lot from him, and sometimes he would learn something from me, but he was very decent, very respectful of me and of the clients. And there were the photographers, like Slim Aarons, and the fashion people, who came to see what people were wearing.

After a while, people stopped saying, "We're going to the Colony," and said instead, "We're going to Sirio's." Cavallero didn't like that, and I had to be careful, respectful, but it was true. I took the people, placed them, and treated them in just the right way and worked with the kitchen to give them what they wanted. It took me three or four years but it worked and, not to be presumptuous, I think Cavallero was happy.

Some very funny and some not so funny things happened all the time. There was a waiter, a man we called Rosso because of his red hair, who was from Piemonte. He would eat anything. He'd take scraps of meat from the kitchen, from plates, and make a kind of meat loaf. He'd take a bottle from the cellar, and just eat. Quite good actually.

J. Edgar Hoover and his gang would eat at the Colony all the time. He stayed at the Plaza when he was in New York and the hotel let him call us to come over and bring him dessert, often very late at night. One time I came up to his room, it was 1 o'clock in the morning and the door was open. I walked in and there he was with all these young men! I went to leave, but he just motioned for me to stay and to serve the desserts to all of them. He really didn't care.

The Colony was under the hospital and sometimes people died there, so sometimes we would go into the elevator and there'd be a dead body. We'd be carrying trays of food, or be coming from the office or the wine cellar and we would see someone's feet with a tag on the toes! Once, a man was in the middle of cutting his steak at table 31, and he died. Of course he wound up in the elevator and while he was there his shoes disappeared. Everyone got hysterical over the shoes: "Where are they? Why would someone take his shoes?" although we all knew it was Rosso. But of course no one said anything. He'd have taken the suit too, but he couldn't get it off.

Then there was Sinatra and Mia Farrow. Like clockwork, they would come in at 8:45, he would go to the bar, have a drink, and at 9:00 they would go to the table. At 9:15 they would start an argument, and at 9:17 she would get hysterical or throw the drink in his face and he would slap her, and at 9:19 she would leave. He always stayed. He'd say, "Now let's have dinner."

Then there were the really difficult people, like Charles Revson. He always had to have his steak Diane made at the table in an unused saucepan—he insisted on a new one every time. He would fuss and fuss over how it was being made. Eventually I learned how to get most of it ready in the kitchen first, so he just thought that it was all done tableside. I never understood why he fussed so much anyway, because after we made it the way he wanted, he just poured ketchup over the whole thing and mashed it up. Of course, they didn't really give him a new pan every time. They just brought it to the back and took a metal scrubbing brush to it.

I didn't get all the difficult people; Joseph Garni got some of them too. He was my first assistant in the dining room. He had an incredible memory and spoke very elegantly. He had a following, especially among some of the older ladies. He would always take care of Mrs. Sulzberger, the mother of Punch, the matriarch of the family that owns *The New York Times*. The mother Sulzberger was intelligent but difficult, and only Joseph had the courage enough to deal with her. He used to say: "Mrs. Sulzberger, when you come in, the sun is shining and you look wonderful" and that kind of thing. That was too much sugar for me. I prefer to look at a person, be pleasant without talking so much. I remember that one day, after Mrs. Sulzberger had been sick, she came in from the hospital and he said, "Oh, Mrs. Sulzberger, you look so wonderful" She got upset and said, "Don't make fun of me—I'm dying! Now give me a table!" just like that. ◄◄

MICHAEL LOMONACO *[chef] I was best friends with the Palmieri kids in Brooklyn—we grew up together, and Egi would come out to see her family. But when Sirio came out, it was like the King arrived. You have to imagine, it's Brooklyn, 1967, we're reading about Capote's Black and White Ball and all these famous people over there in Manhattan, and Sirio is the man who has met them all! Sirio got Egi's Uncle Renato and everyone else jobs at the Colony and when they were out of their uniforms they'd sit around bitching. But when Sirio was around, they were all much more timid and he'd scowl at them if they talked too much about work or the clients.*

SIRIO WATCHED as many of the Colony's most illustrious clients married and divorced one another, yet still used the restaurant as their meeting place of choice, if at different tables. The men usually kept their tables in the divorces, but the women would move to new tables, or in some cases better ones. Broadway producer Leland Hayward always had a table in the dining room to the right, which he kept through his marriage to Hollywood acolyte Slim Keith. When he divorced her to marry Pamela Digby

Churchill, Slim moved to Babe Paley's regular table a few feet away. For her part, Pamela Hayward eventually married Governor Averell Harriman, and moved to his table, just to the left as you came into the dining room. When she was First Lady, Jacqueline Kennedy generally preferred a table in the dining room, but when she started to date Aristotle Onassis she moved to his table in the bar. When the two announced their marriage, they told Sirio first at the Colony, honoring in some small way his role as a hand-maiden to their relationship. Marriages, divorces, affairs, business deals, movies, plays, gay people, straight people, royalty, and riffraff—Sirio was learning to see it all, and work out where each person fit into the makeup of a room.

As Sirio's skill in the dining room and his reputation contin-ued to soar, the world around him was changing rapidly. The war in Vietnam, the assassination of Robert Kennedy, student riots in the United States, France, and Italy, were having a profound effect on the restaurant business in New York. The restaurant's clientele was exchanging Savile Row suits and Balenciaga gowns for turtle-necks and miniskirts. High-profile restaurants had to hire restaurant union staff, increasing labor costs. Rents soared and even garbage, laundry, and food costs increased dramatically. Meanwhile, a recession was choking most restaurants' income.

Somehow, the Colony soldiered on.

SIRIO

THE REASONS CITED for a restaurant's success are always the same as the ones blamed for its failure. Everything was changing very fast, but we still did very well at the Colony. Things were getting bad at the Colony, but nothing that couldn't be fixed. The owners just didn't want to spend the money. I remember pointing out to Mr. Cavallero that there was a hole in the canopy. They patched it instead of replacing it. The carpets were worn; less worn bits of carpet from other parts of the restaurant were glued into their place. The busboys would make extra strong coffee so that captains could use it to stain the dulled finish on their dinner jackets. They kept saying to me, "Sirio, you don't know. It's just a phase, it will all come back," but I knew I was seeing a permanent change in the industry.

Restaurants get a lot of abuse. They have to stay ahead of the times, not behind them. People had started to read about restaurants; for a time the newspapers and magazines had a lot of power. For the Colony, the worst came when Gael Greene wrote a very bad article for *New York* magazine ("Colony Waxworks" 1/4/71). Greene used to come in with a group of younger 1968 type of flower people, with these hats. She was fun, vibrant, and she had a certain look—I liked her, but the article was very bad. She was making a name for herself like they all do. It was the kind of article that can destroy any restaurant—mostly true, but so unnecessary. She knew that there were rats downstairs because people from inside were talking to her. It was true that they had closed off a room near the pastry kitchen where they made the soufflés and the chocolate beignet.

For a time, the article actually helped. People came back to protect the restaurant. But things were getting very bad in the world economically, and by then it was too late. Gene Jr. was actually ahead of his time in trying to work with the unions, alter menus, and get wine costs down. But what really happened was real estate. The landlords wanted the Colony gone, so they could sell the land to build a skyscraper. They didn't just raise the rent, they raised it ten times. There was no way to pay it.

The Cavalleros offered me a partnership, but even that was crazy— they wanted $250,000 from me to buy into the restaurant. It wasn't even that I didn't have the money, though my god, I didn't. It was that I still would have had no control. So when I said no to the offer, I said thank you very much, and made my decision to leave. The restaurant closed on December 4, 1971. Gene Cavallero Sr. died six months later.

PLANNING
A RESTAURANT

ECIDING TO LEAVE THE COLONY was the first decision Sirio Maccioni made as a future restaurateur. It was easy to blame the closing of the Colony—and a long roster of restaurants whose names started with Le, La, or Les—on rising costs and a stagnant economy. But the clearing of the decks was in no way limited to French or haute cuisine restaurants. The empire built by Joe Baum and Restaurant Associates was collapsing—while the Four Seasons survived, the rest of the group, including the Forum of the Twelve Caesars, all closed or were sold. Ocean liners were being put into dry dock and hotels were empty. Even the restaurants at the lower end of the scale were in full retreat. New York classics like Schrafft's, Horn and Hardart, and Chock Full o'Nuts, where Sirio had his first ham steak, were shutting their doors. Clearly the change was as much cultural as economic. The prevailing order of café society—drinks, dinner, and dancing—no longer held. As dramatic a sign of change as the vanishing of white gloves and hats in favor of miniskirts and bell-bottoms was the fact that in the food world James Beard and Julia Child had replaced Escoffier and Carême as reigning culinary authorities. The restaurant world was in free fall, but people hadn't stopped eating. The world that appeared to be coming to an end gave someone with Sirio's skills a distinct advantage.

One solution for the redefined culinary experience was to combine all three aspects of society life—drinks, dinner, dancing—but gear them to a more egalitarian audience, in one restaurant space. This was the direction taken by Maxwell's Plum—a singles bar, restaurant, and club all under a giant Tiffany glass ceiling located on a forlorn stretch of First Avenue, near Sixty-fourth Street. Maxwell's Plum was the creation of Warner LeRoy, the son of Hollywood director Mervyn LeRoy and Doris Warner, herself the daughter of Harry M. Warner, a cofounder of Warner Bros. At Plum's, stewardesses mingled with sheiks and the American establishment. It wasn't so much about being recognized or which table you got as about whom you took home. It proved you could have fun, wear miniskirts, and eat hamburgers, all at the same time. It was as significant socially to the children of café society as the Colony and El Morocco had been for their parents.

Egidiana had their second child—another boy, named Marco—in 1968 and the couple moved to a rent-stabilized apartment on East Sixty-second Street to be closer to the Colony. Sirio considered a move back to Italy, but now, though plenty of people there wanted his services, none could afford him. New York may have been going through a bad patch, but it still offered him and his young family the best opportunity for success. Sirio didn't have any cash of his own to put into a deal, and the money that was offered him from various businessmen and -women willing to invest in New York's most famous maître d'hôtel usually came with too many strings or complications.

Sirio admired the concept of Plum's, but couldn't envision himself working there. Why couldn't the people of his own generation, or even the generation that had enjoyed the Colony, have a version of the same thing? One of his first phone calls had been to Louis Vaudables, his old boss at Maxim's in Paris. Vaudables had sold Maxim's to Pierre Cardin and planned to open Maxim's in

New York, at the Pierre Hotel on Fifth Avenue. Vaudables and Cardin agreed that Sirio would be the perfect front-of-house man. At the last minute, however, the deal fell through and the Pierre was still vacant. Sirio and several of Cardin's partners patched together a different idea for the same space: a lounge, restaurant, and nightclub under one roof, to be called La Forêt.

SIRIO

WHEN THE DEAL WITH THE PIERRE fell apart for Pierre Cardin—who is really Italian, Piero Cardini—I still had nothing to do and here was an idea I could do without having to come up with any money. Elegant people, attractive people, all coming to a place where there was music, fun, good food; that was both a place to just have a drink, smoke, eat if you wanted, and then stay late for dancing and music. We started the first part of the night with Peter Duchin and his band, which was perfect. He used to play at the St. Regis, so he attracted all those people who wanted to come to see him. Then later, during dinner, there were gypsy violins. That was because Serge Sememenko, who was a partner and Russian, liked them. After came the disco music. It was the first real discothèque in New York, before Steve Rubell, before Studio 54 and all that. We stayed open very late, until three, four in the morning and sometimes until dawn on the weekends.

The opening was incredible. Everyone came. Mrs. Onassis, even the Duke and Duchess, who were then very old, came (and they did the first dance). They didn't come because of the Pierre, they came because I said, "please do me a favor." It was fun. People came and drank and ate and danced. I loved it.

At La Forêt I was the whole operation: I took the reservations, I arranged the floor, I made sure the music was going, I took orders at the table, I did the tableside service. I was the owner, the maître d'hôtel, the chef, and the busboy. I worked all the time but it was maybe the first time I didn't complain. It was fun. I had Caraceni make me a new tuxedo with four buttons, very modern, but more in the English style than the French or even

Italian. I started to wear things I could never have at the Colony—different ties, waistcoats, colors…a little more sexy, if I can be presumptuous.

> BILL BLASS *[designer] I rather wish Sirio had stayed a club man … food only complicates things. People still smoked and danced and had fun, and they did a lot of other things too, but somehow that was still, at least for our set, illicit. Everyone knew it was happening but part of it was that on the outside it didn't look like it. What I liked was that the clothes opened up before the people. Sirio started to wear tighter clothes and had sideburns!*

I really admired Warner. He had a very different crowd. The people I knew, of my generation and maybe older, wanted to have fun. The world was loosening up, but not as loose as that. We still wanted to dress, still wanted to eat good food, still wanted to look at beautiful women, without its being so obvious. A part of that was really very international. Italy was very wild in the 1960s and '70s, but part of the sex appeal was in not giving too much of it away. Part of being attractive, especially in Europe, is that it doesn't always have to do with money. Not everyone had to be a millionaire or a socialite. In fact, I preferred the people who weren't. I liked the people who wanted to be something or someone and weren't presumptuous.

> PETER DUCHIN *I knew Sirio at the Colony. But our crowd really didn't go there. It wasn't until La Forêt that I really got to know and like him. Before he was the gatekeeper, but at La Forêt we could talk. And he was good to the band. You'd be amazed at how many people treated them bad. I also remember that—as social as I am and as social as Sirio is—we actually were kind of uncomfortable with all these high society people. He was much more comfortable hanging out with me and the band or the security people of the fancy people who'd come. He knew where he was at, what he was doing and why. That takes courage and skill. He knew it was just a gig.*

La Forêt was at the Pierre and really, I hadn't been at a hotel—working in a hotel—since the Plaza-Athénée in the early 1950s. I had to learn very quick how to work with the hotel union and how to do things I didn't do at the Colony or anywhere else; manage lots of different kinds of people, wait staff, kitchen staff, musicians; how to do all the back of the house business and still be at the door to meet customers. I think La Forêt was a very interesting concept, maybe ahead of its time. When the hotel was sold to a British company, Trusthouse Forte, it all fell apart very quickly. Times were bad. The hotel was doing badly. When things are going well at a hotel, they are always very happy to give away space that they don't use—maybe someone would come to stay at the Pierre because they wanted to go to La Forêt, and maybe not. But when things start to go bad, no hotel puts up with something that may or may not be making money for them. They have two choices—they either make more money from the space by renting it, or they get you to give them more of the money you make, or both. So they came in and made us raise the prices and started altering the concept. I knew they would ruin the idea and they did. They wanted to change everything but mostly they wanted more money. Up to then the rent was almost nothing. It was a basement space, I don't think they ever used it again. We were the only people who could get anyone to come downstairs! I left in 1972, before it was closed. ◄◄

FOR THE SECOND TIME in two years, Sirio was without a job. As always, however, he had a million tricks up his sleeve, and several leads. Egi had just given birth to their third boy, Mauro, and the possibility of a return to Europe was perhaps more real than at any time since he'd obtained his green card. With Mario seven and Marco five, it would have been a perfect moment to return to Italy—if Italy weren't embroiled in turmoil of its own that was a little too close to Sirio's own history for comfort. The same tide of student demonstrations and political change that had produced a pronounced leaning to the left in the United States, France, and the United Kingdom had led to a surge in neo-fascism in Italy, which was met by a corresponding response in left-wing terror- ism. Just when it seemed that a position running a major hotel chain or restaurant in Italy was most possible, it became the least attractive option for him and his family. Instead, Sirio called his contacts in France, Switzerland, and Germany, but kept returning to the same idea—that it was time to create something of his own.

The idea, as always, started with the real estate. Sirio had discussions with a number of landlords—among them the Zeckendorfs, the New York real estate dynasty. Peter Duchin had introduced Sirio to William Zeckendorf Jr., a food and wine connoisseur, and the son of the man whose turkey had gone missing ten years before.

The family were the managing partners in a private residential hotel on Sixty-fifth Street between Park and Madison Avenues on the Upper East Side called The Mayfair. The hotel had been built by one of the most prominent and expensive apartment-house designers of the post–World War I period, J. E. R. Carpenter. His original design included an intimately proportioned European-style lobby, a private party space, and a small restaurant on the ground floor.

The stumbling blocks to pursuing any kind of deal were that the majority of the building was owned by the East River Savings Bank and that the hotel had a number of very demanding permanent residents who were all sitting tenants. The Zeckendorfs wanted Sirio to be a part owner and general manager of the hotel, protecting the Zeckendorfs' interest and creating one for Sirio. The buy-in price was $750,000 for 10 percent of the hotel, with a possible option to acquire another 15 percent and with the Zeckendorfs backing the loans. For a farmer from Montecatini who had just turned down a three-bedroom coop apartment at 625 Park Avenue for $49,000, such figures were out of the question. Sirio wanted only the restaurant space and the ability to run his own restaurant, in his own name, within the hotel—something that had never been done in New York.

There were other offers too, including one to run his own hotel backed by Gianni Agnelli. The hotel would have been called either the Hotel Sirio, or just "515," for its address on Park Avenue at the corner of Sixtieth Street. When the deal fell through in late 1972, Sirio went back to looking at restaurant and hotel space both in New York and in Europe.

Meanwhile, the Zeckendorfs had not found a buyer for the Mayfair and Sirio's offer for the restaurant space alone was suddenly more attractive. The hotel was losing $500,000 a year in food and beverage and Bill Zeckendorf Jr. agreed to spin off the restaurant space, lease it to Sirio separately, and find someone else to run the hotel. He bet that Sirio's expertise and lineage would virtually guarantee a successful restaurant and that in turn would put the Mayfair back on the map, add prestige to the Zeckendorf brand name in the real estate business, and stop the tide of losses at the hotel. Sirio's financial commitment would be minimal—about $200,000.

The first thing Sirio needed to do was find a chef for the restaurant. It had to be someone who could accommodate Sirio's culinary and service philosophy, someone who was already a recognized commodity, and, in particular, someone who had money. He picked up the phone and called Jean Vergnes, a former colleague from his early days at the Colony, who was then at Maxwell's Plum.

Vergnes had been the chef at the Colony from 1951 to 1962, and in that time he had become almost a father figure to a generation of young French chefs making their way in the new world. After he left the Colony, early in Sirio's reign, he took a series of jobs, including food director of the supermarket chain Stop and Shop, and of a rural hotel, before ending up at Plum's. Sirio took it as a good sign that Vergnes had become more famous for making hamburgers for girls in hot pants than he ever had been for making soufflés for the more appropriately dressed. Sirio knew Vergnes's heart was in the carriage trade, not the hamburger trade.

Vergnes, at fifty, wasn't quite who Sirio had imagined would help him execute his culinary philosophy—or indeed become his business partner. He had imagined someone more his own age or younger and more Mediterranean in his approach to food. Nevertheless, they shared the same culinary language, if not the same philosophy. It wasn't likely that Sirio would find a thirty-year-old French chef, with Vergnes's pedigree, who also happened to have $100,000 in the bank. The facts that he and Vergnes had worked together extensively and that Vergnes was at least sensitive to Sirio's Italian culinary leanings counted for a lot. It was Vergnes who had rescued Sirio on his first day "at the door" at the Colony when Sirio needed to tame Frank Sinatra with a plate of prosciutto.

More important to Sirio—who was never one to miss an opportunity to court public, or private, opinion—he knew that Vergnes was very well connected to the New York food intelligentsia. Vergnes would bring with him an enormous amount of goodwill, a tradable commodity when you're opening a new restaurant. Taking Vergnes was a no-risk proposition.

Sirio was aiming for the younger side of the Colony crowd, but with a feeling more resembling Forte di Marmi, the fashionable Italian seaside resort. It was to be the casual culture of the Kennedys, the tanned toes of Marella Agnelli kicking up sand in Gucci sandals—a canteen for the new generation who worked hard and played hard. Sirio and Vergnes tentatively named the new restaurant Le Cirque.

Another consideration was the physical space: before the deal was even signed he had met, on Bill Zeckendorf Jr.'s advice, society decorator Ellen Lehman McCluskey. Zeckendorf and Sirio felt that she would design a room that would not overpower the cast Sirio intended to assemble. However, Sirio's insistence that the restaurant have its own separate street entrance, with the Zeckendorfs paying for its construction, nearly caused the deal to fall apart. But Sirio was adamant.

Finally Zeckendorf offered him the space in the bottom of the hotel practically rent-free for twenty-five years. The hotel would take care of the building costs, refurbish the kitchen, and create the separate street entrance that Sirio insisted upon. In an unusual twist, Sirio and Vergnes purchased a part of the Zeckendorf family's—mostly burgundy—private wine cellar for $5000. The partners would have to pay for everything inside the space—tables, chairs, linen, and staff—plus operate the hotel's in-house catering department. John McGrath, the president of the East River Bank, remained skeptical; an unorthodox hotel deal in what was then considered impossibly far uptown didn't seem like a good risk. Luckily, McGrath was a former Colony client and a friend of the Zeckendorfs and he finally agreed that the deal, although sweet, was the best they could hope for under the circumstances.

William Zeckendorf Jr. went with Sirio to Chase Manhattan Bank and undersigned a loan of $100,000. With Jean Vergnes's $100,000, the partnership of Maccioni and Vergnes officially went into business when they were handed their New York City liquor license on May 15, 1973.

SIRIO

OSTLY IT WAS A CONCEPTION. A mentality. Work hard. Make the place attractive, make the place warm, and do not kill people with the price. When I was at the Pierre there was a girl who traveled to Paris all the time. She'd always come back and describe the nightlife: "*C'était comme en cirque.*" It's an expression in French that I liked. *Le cirque* in French means "circus," but it also means "to have a good time," and I liked the two meanings. I also liked that it wasn't the name of a dish or a place, which I think is pretentious. I wanted a place to eat good food, but with the feeling of the circus, not the church. I like the church but I don't want to eat there. Maybe it's because I'm Italian. During the war I would go to the circus with my father and my uncles, then we went on our own. The circus wasn't about the rides, or the animals—which smelled. To me the circus was about the clown. He made it fun. During a terrible time he could make fun. And you know, times were not so good in 1973! And this was the point—I didn't see why you couldn't dress up, have fun, and eat well. Attractive people, important people. It was that simple. This philosophy never changed.

RICCARDO PUCCI *One of the reasons for Sirio's success is that he knew the right people. Not always the successful people, but the right people. At La Pace, and then in Paris, and in New York. When he started his own business he already knew who the people were who counted. That's the key to Sirio. It's important because if you don't put people in the right place with other right people in the dining room, you have just another restaurant.*

I understood how these hotels work. Putting a restaurant into a hotel should be a logical thing, but it never worked because the hotel insisted on running the restaurant—always badly. In New York it hadn't been done and Europe it had been done badly. But I knew it could work if the restaurant had its own identity and its own entrance. I was scared ... and not scared. I knew what kind of a restaurant I wanted, but the thought of the money they wanted made me sick. The money I borrowed made me sick enough. I couldn't believe I had done it. I think I just did it because I had to and that from then on I would spend the rest of my life in fear that one day I would wake up and not be able to pay back the $100,000. But what I had done with Zeckendorf worked very well for me. It probably would not have worked for anyone else.

WILLIAM LIE ZECKENDORF *[Son of William Zeckendorf Jr.] People can say what they like, but it had never been done. Hotels always thought they could run restaurants and failed. Restaurants within hotels were always just hotel restaurants. Le Cirque was the first restaurant to operate within a hotel but to have essentially nothing to do with its operation or management. It just happened that it worked for my father, and it was perfect for Sirio.*

If I'd had the courage, I'd have started ten years before, because all the things about restaurants were the same everywhere in the world and I knew exactly what I wanted to do in food and in service, exactly. It's a philosophy.

I talked with my partner about the food and how food that comes from the kitchen has to be what people want, not what the chef wants to prepare. This was always the problem with restaurants. The chef did what he wanted in the kitchen and the person at the front did what he wanted in the dining room and the customer suffered. My philosophy was "Tonight, Le Cirque prepares for you," not, "Tonight, the chef has prepared for you." I come from a country of forty million people where each person thinks different from the other. In a restaurant this cannot be, everyone has to be together, from the kitchen to the wait staff; there can be no wall between the two.

Both the kitchen and dining room staff had to learn to do things differently. I don't care what the chef says, or the presumptuous waiter—each has to work with the other. You cannot separate or divide them.

So the first thing I wanted to do was teach the wait staff to say yes, all the time, not no. I told Jean I would fire anyone who I saw arguing with a customer. If a customer wanted scrambled eggs on toast, the waiter was to say yes, and to go to the kitchen and ask, and they would do it. It shouldn't have to depend on a special relationship between the waiter and the man in the kitchen. It shouldn't mean the waiter has to ask the headwaiter who has to ask the manager who has to call the owner. Anyone who worked at Le Cirque should be able to do this. But of course doing this made the chef crazy.

JEAN VERGNES *A kitchen works in a very specific way. You prepare the food items you need beforehand, you have a certain number of items on the menu, you expect a certain number of people, and you cook to accommodate them. What Sirio didn't understand, and I assume still doesn't understand, is that when he or a waiter walks in to the kitchen during service and asks for something different it throws off the whole kitchen. But that is Sirio.*

I knew that at first we had to have the dining room like everyone else—captains and subcaptains and the next waiter and all that nonsense, which I hated. The busboy should know as much about what is going on as the chef. But when we started, we had to do things the way people were used to. You have to ease in slowly.

Another big change in the philosophy was the tables. Before we even opened, I came in one day and the ladies who lived in the hotel—Mrs. Lipton, Mrs. Doubleday, Mrs. Ruskin—were all standing by the tables they wanted! I said to them, "Ladies, ladies, I will make space for you, but you must call for a reservation when we are open." They got very angry:

"But we always had our own tables!" I said, "Let me take your reservation now, come for a glass of champagne, and you'll see how we do things differently, and that you'll like the table where you sit. I promise."

And that's how I did it with everyone. It was harder to change the mentality that such and such a table was someone's table for the whole night. At the Colony, someone important, or not so important even, would call to say they wanted a table for dinner. That was it. You were expected to hold the table for whenever they came in. If they came in and saw that there was someone at "their" table, they would turn around and leave, and you didn't have the business.

I didn't want this in my restaurant. What I had learned from La Forêt was that you don't have to change the music three times a night, you have to change the people! And this meant you broke the evening into three parts—5:30, 7:30, and 9:30, more or less. You "turned" the tables. That way a restaurant that serves only 80 people can serve 240. I also knew that this would change things in the kitchen. It's not that they had to work longer, which is what they would tell you. They just had to work differently.

Then there was the food itself. The system to make food in a restaurant kitchen is a great thing. It allows you to make the 240 or so meals a night. But systems get old and people get old and tired and they get lazy. These are the things I learned at the Plaza-Athénée and all over the world. Kitchens were really held hostage by the schizophrenic *sauciers*, a band of lunatics who went from restaurant to restaurant. That was the tragedy. People didn't talk about the chef going from here over to there, but about the *saucier* from La Côte Basque who went to La Grenouille and was now at La Caravelle. The *saucier* would come in when no one else was working, at five or six in the morning, make a sauce for the fish, a sauce for the meat, a sauce for the chicken, and leave. The sauces would sit in the bain-marie for the rest of the day. It was disgusting. You had a good fish or something drowned in a sauce, salmon that was too pink, coated in aspic. I don't think anyone really liked it, but that's what people had been trained to expect from restaurant food. Americans thought it was "haute cuisine," which it wasn't. People can say what they like, but I was the protector of these customers—it becomes so easy to accept that what is mediocre is really the best.

PROFESSOR THOMAS KELLY *[Cornell School of Hotel Management]* *From the very beginning, Sirio set out to change our standards of acceptance on every level. He was committed to doing everything right, from the best quality ingredients to professional delivery systems. People say it existed, but it really didn't. Sirio really started that. He made it okay to be a waiter, okay to be a customer, and okay to be a purveyor.*

I knew what the best was and how to get it done. The system said, a waiter couldn't talk to the chef. But now I was the owner. Just because I was not a chef did not mean I wasn't going to say what went on in the kitchen.

Jean was a very good man. What was great about him was that he was not so much like the others. He knew you could take the way French food is cooked and make it in big numbers. Maybe he didn't always like to do it in this way, but he did know how to do it, at least while we were planning the menu.

Let's be very clear. To me the way Italian food works, in the kitchen, on the plate, is the best. Salt, olive oil, pepper, that's it. A grilled piece of fish, or meat, a little thyme or rosemary. Wild garlic roasted until it is sweet. Even when we opened Le Cirque, there was no way to present that kind of food in a restaurant. I mean you could not do it. Who needs a chef? I could go back into the kitchen, put a little olive oil in a pan, sauté a fish, bring it out on a plate, and lay it in front of Mrs. Colgate. She would have had a heart attack. Right or wrong, the way of restaurants in America was French. I love the trattorias in Italy, but America was not yet ready for this kind of cooking. They still aren't. People who pay lots of money want a presentation— they want food that is plated. No one eats at home like that. But when people go to a restaurant, they don't want food they could have at home— they want to be entertained. That was my philosophy then and it never has changed. The menu had to be 80 percent reality and 20 percent fantasy. The "reality" food had to look familiar but be the best—the best flounder, the best paillard of veal or minute steak, and not covered in some sauce. If they wanted sauce, the sauce was served on the side, the vegetables on the side.

We wrote the menu in French for Jean and because then that's what people expected. But I really fought with Jean to make sure that there was everything on it. I believe in big menus. The chef may say, "This is too much prep," but if you don't have the one thing a customer wants she does not come back. I had been to Chinese restaurants. The food was disgusting—I mean really, out of the container—but the menus amazed me. You could have anything. And if you could speak Chinese and talk to the cook, you could get the best of anything you wanted. Why should choice like that be limited to Chinese restaurants?

This is how we made the first menu for Le Cirque. I listed the daily specials "from the broiler"—*côte de veau,* an *entrecôte,* the half turkey *le dindonneau au bacon.* Jean wanted a cold buffet, arranged in the dining room, of *bouef à la mode, contrefilet rôti, homard, saumon.* But then I wanted to put the food I liked, from Italy and from France, which we put under "specialités de la Maison": *carpaccio Toscana, côte de veau milanais,* and *gourgonette de sole frites.*

The approach has not really changed at Le Cirque. The menu should cover everything. I love the tower of oysters and clams like we did at Delmonico's and the egg dishes like omelettes and soufflés at the Colony. I wanted a bistro menu raised to my standards.

I don't think my partner liked any of this. We made many compromises, some of which maybe now I wouldn't do, but it worked fine for then. It was an ambitious menu, he was a good man and a good chef, and while there was much I didn't like, my concern was really to run the dining room by my philosophy, and there he didn't interfere so much.

Opening Le Cirque was natural. People would say that to open a restaurant you either had to know gangsters and Mafia, or be more stupid than a taxi driver. This is silly. If I were smart, I'd have been a taxi driver, and a good one too. And the first is much less common than people think. It's too hard to get money from a restaurant and gangsters are too intelligent. But my point is, I saw opening a restaurant as serious business—a profession that is respectable if you are stupid enough to do it. I wanted the people who were important to see that the restaurant business is a real business. You know, when I die I hope that is all they say about me: that I made it respectable to be a waiter. ⤛

THE PARTNERSHIP OF MACCIONI AND VERGNES was tested out with two parties that represented two very carefully selected groups.

The first was a party for Sirio's lawyer, Victor Jacobs, who was also the most influential lawyer in the restaurant business. In fact, he provides the only true link between Sirio and Henri Soulé—they both shared Jacobs's services. Jacobs—a German Jewish émigré, had escaped before the war and had made a name for himself representing the interests of other émigrés and in particular, using legal means to secure the safety of other Jews and later on, recovering their assets. By the 1970s though, he lived the life of a man of leisure, eating and drinking only the best, surrounding himself with beautiful women, acquiring art, and providing legal services only to the very few he considered worthy. Not surprisingly, he was also well connected socially, providing a bridge between the culinary world and the social world that he dominated. Until his death in 1992, he remained Sirio's closest advisor and best friend. It was Jacobs who received the late-night telephone calls, listened to Sirio's tirades on perfection, and advised his young charge to accept the deal from the Zeckendorfs. After his preview party, Jacobs reported to the scions of finance, fashion, and art that Le Cirque was about to be the most important restaurant of the century.

The second party was for Roger Yaseen, an influential investment banker and the president of the American chapter of the Societé des Tastevins, a group founded on the sole premise of consuming the best food and wine. In a nation where food was considered mostly just fuel, the partners knew they had to make a bridge to a collective of gourmands, who just happened to include members like Julia Child and Craig Claiborne.

Everyone at the parties reported that "*c'etait comme en cirque.*" Three years before, Bill Paley's CBS had recorded the opening party for La Forêt and produced an accompanying TV documentary on its seemingly omnipresent and handsome maître d'hôtel. This time around, no television crews were necessary. Before its doors had even officially opened to the public on March 24, 1974, Le Cirque had perhaps the best social connections of any restaurant in the world.

OPENING
LE CIRQUE

SIRIO

WHEN WE OPENED ... IT WAS CRAZY! From day one we were overbooked and I had almost no help. I did the door, did my best to take orders at the table, answered the phones, and tried to work with the kitchen. I drove poor Jean crazy and he drove me crazy too.

I try to go back in my head now but all I remember is not sleeping. Why, when I finally had my own restaurant, did I wind up sleeping on the banquette worried that someone was going to come run me over with the vacuum? In the first months we had to supply the food for the hotel guests. But we didn't have a night staff, so I stayed, worked on the books, and ordered everything and most of the time it got so late that I just slept on the banquette so I could let the morning crew in to do the breakfast. Then I went around the corner and went to sleep until ten o'clock. Every restaurateur should live very close to where they work, it gives you a big advantage.

Jean Vergnes really worked because there was a mix, a diversity of the Colony set and by that I mean the ladies, and some men, who were the old society of New York. The crowd was changing very fast. I encouraged beautiful people, interesting people, people of different races and colors. I liked that. Mostly I liked people my age. They were the people doing things, making the world, changing the world. So many people, but they were all very interesting, very exciting people. ◄◄-

ROGER YASEEN *Sirio was smart enough to tap me, practically beg me, to be the first group to open the restaurant. A respect for fine food was a more important signal to send out to the world than a love of society. In fact, he knew and I think I knew, that he was in fact doing both. The evening was an unusual success, not because the food was good, not because everyone was someone. It was and they were. But mostly because everyone had a genuinely good time.*

THE LE CIRQUE SPACE was roughly L-shaped. The larger part of the L was the main dining area. It was scarcely larger than the living room of a Park Avenue apartment, albeit with three columns down the center of the room. Taking her cue from the restaurant's name, Ellen McCluskey had made it into a playfully mock version of the Singerie Room at Versailles, with painted latticework and eight murals of aristocratic monkeys amorously at play. The color scheme was soft pink and the banquettes that lined the L were a muted gray. Clever placement of mirrors to make the tiny space look larger and giant protruding sconces completed the overall look of the new enterprise.

The space was designed to accommodate twenty tables, with rows of Louis XV chairs, their backs striped in a more shocking shade of orange, their carved wooden legs positioned corner to corner, a pinky from the chair next to it. Toni Cimino, who had done the flowers at the Colony and had followed Sirio to La Forêt, was in charge of the flowers and the overall presentation of the tables. What Sirio could not have in a grand space he made up in very grand details. He insisted on higher-than-restaurant-quality linen for the tables, and the folds of every corner had to hang in a reverse fold without a dimple. In lieu of lavish flower arrangements, Toni made extravagant, if minuscule, vases for every table. Sirio ordered and fussed endlessly over the custom-designed Limoges china. The plates continued the monkey theme, with the restaurant's logo imprinted into the design and with two-inch borders in an array of vibrant colors: orange, green, yellow, and red.

Any of the individual elements could appear tacky, but the overall effect was not. Legions of writers, critics, designers, and gourmands have tried to assess what made the room work when by all rights it shouldn't have. What McCluskey had created was a space that registered just enough—like an elaborate frame on an abstract painting.

SIRIO

R IGHT AWAY THERE WAS THE CRITICISM from everyone, the press mostly, that I was not democratic with the tables, but I was too tired to get into that. It was a perfect setup for me, because from my position at the door I could see everybody at the bar, everybody in the whole room. I run a restaurant—it's a business, not a popularity contest—and people like to see people. Beautiful people, famous people, important people. And yes, if I liked to, I put them at the most visible or requested tables. Did some people get into those tables more often? Yes. In my head though, I never thought that those tables belonged to those people, or that I wouldn't give the same tables to someone from the street who I liked— if I could have, if I wasn't always booked. And very often, just to stop all the criticism I'd put people nobody knew at those tables.

BRYAN MILLER *[author] Whoever said restaurants were democratic institutions? They aren't. It's not like some people were treated badly at Le Cirque, it's just that other people were treated better. That's life. You try to make it level, and if anyone tried, it was Sirio. If a regular customer walks in, you should expect they would be treated better. If you buy a car from the same dealership year after year, don't you expect to get a better deal? Why is this so surprising?*

People who tell you they like everybody? They lie. I like who I like. And I don't lie. People say I am snob. I am not. I believe in the elite. In Tuscany, we believe in the elite in every sense of the word. What is so wrong with elite? Elite means to do better. We grow up, we look up to the top of the hill and aspire to be like that person in the villa. But that person got to the villa by being smart, intelligent, rich, or many things. America is full of people who aspire to get to the top by being smart, by being better. If they get there by being bad, I have no interest in them—they are the worst. Actually, it's the phonies I hate the most. They come up and say, "Do you know who I am?" Nothing makes me madder. Let me do my job and the restaurant looks perfect. You have to sit everyone in just the right way, but not fuss about it too much. Maybe in those years it would have been more honest just to show some people to the door—but we didn't do that. Some people should not have come to a restaurant like Le Cirque.

BILL BLASS *[the late designer] Sirio is the only person, still, who knows how to seat a room. He's a designer that way. Like I hang a piece of fabric, he knows how to look at a room and seat it, which is a very difficult thing to do.*

We had the best people. Right away. Very important people, but also curious people. And what I liked best—neighborhood people. I liked people who just walked in, like a very good local bistro. Of course the local people were maybe different from other parts of New York. ...

BRYAN MILLER *Never before or since has there been a room with that electricity. Business, arts, society, classy New York, were all together and there were no gawkers. It was just magic. Even the monkeys, the ugly sconces, the bad lights. And Sirio's real magic is that all these people are not easy. None of them. He made them all relaxed. He tamed them. It was more relaxed than any other fine restaurant in the world.*

There's this saying, "The customer is always right." Not true. Not always. The customer is not always right. The customer always gets what he wants. Very different. All I do is try to understand what they want. It's not so hard. The customers, they are not restaurateurs, they are not chefs ... in fact, my job is to protect them from the chef! You come here and you don't want to know who prepared the food as long as it's prepared in the right way and served properly. The chefs think they are the most important element in the restaurant. The important thing is that when you go into the restaurant you must have somebody who isn't pompous and who makes you feel at home. I wish everyone understood the difference between good and great food, but I settle for knowing they are happy and will come back.

CINDY ADAMS *[gossip columnist] He was always bringing the chef out to the table to meet us. It did convey a nice message across the dining room—that we were important enough to have a visit from the chef. But in truth, I didn't care, since I only cared that the food was there, that I recognized it, that it was hot, and that there was lots of it! Sirio knows that's all that most people really want.*

Despite everything I say, I love French food and the French system to make food is the best. But the food snobs they would say, "Ah, this restaurant isn't really French" or, "This restaurant really isn't Italian," or they complain about the tables, though most of the time it was the press that complained about the tables. They want to make it so that the only reason for the restaurant to be a success is because of the ladies—and I have a lot of the ladies who come to lunch who want to ... you know. Why can't anyone say, "This is a good restaurant"? ◄◄

JULIA CHILD *There's all this talk about whether Sirio is democratic or not democratic, about the girls, about whether Le Cirque is a French or an Italian restaurant. I didn't see Sirio as a sex symbol, I saw him as Sirio. It's Sirio's restaurant, Sirio's food. He is always at the door, always helpful, and it's always **fun** there, and those are really the only things that matter.*

TWO ELEMENTS WERE KEY to Le Cirque's success: Sirio's management of his clientele, and his management of the media. They were the most conspicuously engineered part of the show and could be summed up in one word: "aspiration." It really did not matter whether the clients were young or old, or what "set" they may or may not have belonged to. As long as they aspired to something, and had a decent jacket, they fit into Sirio's room. That was the long-term plan. In the short term, Sirio knew that his core business was going to have to be based on old debts that needed paying. There was the former Colony crowd—in Sirio's opinion, by no means washed up or tired. Sirio knew that part of aspiration was that the new crowd, whether they liked it or not, aspired to improve on the old. Then there were the old-guard Wasps who lived at the hotel.

The crowd that Sirio specifically targeted was the new elite—the heads of art, fashion, business, finance, and politics. The old crowd gave him entrée to the new crowd and, as he had perfected at the Colony and La Forêt, judicious phone calls and notes would be dispatched. The maestro was sure that, once invited, they would never leave.

Like the relationship between the kitchen and the dining room, Sirio knew instinctively (he'd call any other interpretation presumptuous) that carefully managing his clientele also went hand in hand with managing the media. Early on in his days at the Colony, he had made the most of what is often referred to as the "other media." It was all well and good for a restaurant to get accolades from food critics, but a mention of someone famous leaving the restaurant in a gossip column, or a photograph in a fashion magazine of a fabulous-looking woman entering it, was worth much more. Sirio knew to cultivate both the professional food critics and these "other media" outlets.

The most influential restaurant critics when Sirio opened Le Cirque were James Beard, who wrote books and articles for a number of magazines, and Craig Claiborne, who almost single-handedly had created a food section at *The New York Times*. Beard was the arbiter of American cuisine and restaurants, while

Claiborne favored European cuisines. Beard, an Oregonian by birth, and Claiborne, a Southerner, both operated in a late-nineteenth-century American way, as if Manhattan's French restaurants and Italian maîtres d'hôtel were nice men who came to collect your sister for an evening stroll through the square. You didn't really get to know them until they asked for her hand in marriage. In the same way, Claiborne or Beard would come to a restaurant tens of times, but wouldn't write about the restaurant critically until they had been to the home of the chef or the restaurateur to try to understand what the chef and restaurateur were trying to create. It was assumed that a restaurant was an imperfect means of expressing a concept. If the concept of the restaurateur or chef matched as closely as possible what he was able to execute in the restaurant, then the review was favorable. The game could therefore take years to play. No one played it better than Sirio, who leaned naturally toward Claiborne, while still keeping Beard friendly and feeding him lavishly. Claiborne became as close as one could call to being a personal friend of Sirio's—talking with him on the phone almost daily and spending time at each other's homes—while still maintaining his journalistic integrity. Sirio also became as friendly with Claiborne's partner at *The New York Times,* Pierre Franey, who had been the chef at Le Pavillon.

Then there were the magazines, like *Gourmet,* and the guidebooks, like the Mobil Guide and Gault Millau, whose editors and publishers were frequently invited and entertained at Le Cirque, often under the pretext of introducing a new ingredient, or a fête thrown for a visiting chef, such as Paul Bocuse, Fredy Girardet, or Roger Vergé.

It was with the "other media" that Sirio excelled. Most frequently it was photographers from *Women's Wear Daily,* but also paparazzi from newspapers around the world, who made the bushes outside Le Cirque their second home. They were never allowed inside. Those who were—syndicated gossip columnists like Liz Smith, Cindy Adams, and Aihleen Mehle—were held to an almost imperial code of honor. Nothing heard within its walls could be attributed without the subject's consent. Printing a list of who was at the restaurant on any given night was considered acceptable. Quoting overheard conversations was not. This was basically the same rule that held at the "best" private homes or salons. No one would dare raise the ire of Sirio or, more important, interfere with others' enjoyment. Le Cirque was at one moment the safest place to hold a conversation and the most public.

New York magazine and to a certain extent *Town and Country* and *W,* the glossy offshoot of *Women's Wear Daily*, fulfilled both roles—as sources of legitimate and celebrity journalism. In many ways the periodicals were more powerful indicators of Sirio's success than any other media source.

Still, it was *The New York Times* that was the first to review the restaurant. Published on June 21, 1974, John Canaday's piece addressed all the hooks on which other critics would hang their reviews. Canaday immediately identified the clubby nature of the restaurant, which he attributed to a "clientele inherited to a large extent from the defunct Colony." He, as an outsider, felt treated accordingly. He did not mention Sirio by name but wrote that, while waiting anonymously, he felt "barely tolerated, while a lot of fancy looking people, exiting, exchanged vows of love with the maître d'hôtel." He was given a side table, where he could not see what he described as possibly the most attractive restaurant interior in New York, had relatively mediocre service and food that went from an "ordinary" veal scaloppine to a grilled saddle of lamb "that was the best either my wife or I had ever tasted anywhere." On a second visit with a guest not known to the house, but dressed like "royalty traveling incognito," he was treated to a better table, given better service but experienced similar inconsistencies in food. He ate "something called 'carpaccio,'" and had asparagus and hollandaise. He gave Le Cirque a "dim and begrudged" two stars.

In Sirio's view the first major review was a success because it captured the element that was most important to Sirio—Canaday had broadcast to the world, in the paper of record, that Le Cirque was clearly the place to be and that its food was more bistro than "FFF," slang in those days for "Fine French Food." He also knew that one of his most staunch and earliest supporters was Mrs. Arthur Ochs Sulzberger, the wife of the publisher of the *Times.*

In later years, a review like Canaday's would have sent Sirio into a tailspin of rage. The review was written from the perspective of someone who didn't know or understand the sociology around him and was happy not to, but at the same time was not critical of it. It was so self-deprecating that Sirio could forgive its author his good grace and humor.

As for the kitchen, Sirio was as happy as Sirio gets. He did his best to tolerate what he considered certain compromises. He had known from the beginning that his food philosophy differed from Vergnes's, but right now his primary concerns were that food came out of the kitchen hot and on time—even though it was the maître d' who often prevented both—and that it be respectably delicious and simple enough to keep them coming back for more. In that regard, Sirio and Vergnes's white tablecloth bistro was succeeding in spades. The maestro exacted no more from his chef and partner. Yet.

SIRIO

J EAN AND I FOUGHT ALL THE TIME, but it was a good fight. It's normal in this business, healthy. When I don't fight, I worry. But he was a good man and a good chef. I always wanted more specials, more changes, things in season, and he was always saying no. To follow the seasons is expensive too. To get the first truffles, the oil, the caviar, the porcini mushrooms flown in first-class was expensive. And he hated that. But I didn't take a salary, and I knew it would work. I discovered that not only did it get our clients excited, but it worked more in the kitchen. You do the same thing day after day, it gets dull. You add new things and it creates a spark.

Maybe the biggest food issue that came up after the business with the *saucier*, was making pasta and risottos and soufflés. The stupidity of this amazed me. Chefs would automatically say you couldn't make risotto in a restaurant. Of course you can make risotto. And soufflés! A soufflé is the easiest thing in the world to prepare. Jean wanted to make money, and this was a good way, and easy, but it was always, "No, no, you can't do that!" But we did it and later on he said, "We make the best risotto in the world at Le Cirque!"

I knew how to get the fashion people to try white truffles, or a really great consommé. I would send out a little something from the kitchen. Olive oil was still rare, mushrooms, radicchio from Treviso—now people take all these sort of things for granted, but in those days they were very foreign. I did some things by the table, simple things people liked. Once I served a salad, tossed it with the oil, and when people asked me what virgin oil was, I said—maybe I shouldn't have—"They are olives that have never been with a man." And when I brought over the first white truffles and sent some of them over with a little baked potato to a man who was a very good customer, he called over the waiter and said, "You better tell the boss that these potatoes smell." Most kitchens would laugh and say he was an idiot, but I went over to him and explained to this very important, educated man about truffles, and you know what? He became one of our best clients, and for his whole life an expert on truffles.

MARTHA STEWART *My first visit to Le Cirque was in September, and I gave my daughter a luncheon to celebrate her 21st birthday—we went to Le Cirque for fettucine con tartuffo bianchi—the white truffles were plump and generously grated over the top. I watched in horrified amazement as Alexis' beautiful girlfriends pushed the truffles off to the sides of their plates. Sirio observed and, in his inimitable way, flirted with the girls, coaxing them to be adventuresome. But, unable to persuade them, he whisked away the plates and brought out a tableful of desserts that were immediately devoured!*

This is how to think in this business: if someone is waiting at the bar, you send over a glass of champagne and they'll be happy to wait. But my partner would scream at me, "Ah, before we make any money you spend it all by giving everything away." I wanted to make money too, but I knew these things were more important. You have to build a business, and in food that means you have to build the culture.

> BRYAN MILLER *Pierre [Franey] would tell me that Jean was livid about the amount of free food and drink that Sirio would give away. But that was Sirio. If it was cold and someone was waiting in the bar, Sirio would rush out a cup of consommé. Or he'd give away desserts almost as a matter of policy. And then there was the champagne! If even the slightest thing went wrong, there was a glass of champagne. People just didn't do that then. All Jean could see was his investment going down the drain.*

> MICHAEL BATTERBERRY *What caught so many people off guard about Sirio is that he is so diametrically opposite the tradition of the imposing Frenchman at the front door of every French restaurant. He dares to have fun. He is the quintessential dashing Italian. But behind all the bravura, he's in a perpetual state of high hysteria. And all his best customers are a part of it. He involves you in some kind of ancient Italian agony that is far beyond the dashing maître' d'.*

We were a success. Crazy. But a success. When I look back at it now, though, it wasn't that we were so smart, just that everyone else was so stupid. ◄◄

ALMOST ONE YEAR INTO ITS RUN, in March 1975, Gael Greene listed Le Cirque thirteenth in her ranking of *New York*'s Top Restaurants, making the comment that the restaurant was a "soup kitchen for the anguished orphans of the late Colony." Not only did Sirio find the comment wickedly amusing, he knew that the magazine didn't hesitate to chronicle much of what happened at Le Cirque in its pages and that Greene herself was at the restaurant as frequently as other members of the food media establishment. The Le Cirque New York media juggernaut rolled on.

What turned Le Cirque, ostensibly a New York–based French restaurant, into a national media phenomenon was a dish that sounded distinctly Italian—pasta primavera. The recipe was introduced in *The New York Times* by Craig Claiborne, who originally called it "Spaghetti Le Cirque." Shortly after, the dish, now called pasta primavera, was featured on the cover of the inaugural issue of a new food magazine, *Food & Wine,* described in cookbooks, and cooked live on talk shows. A dish of spaghetti, cream sauce, and fresh vegetables suddenly became the paradigm of the new age of cooking. In an era when Americans were already tossing their unused woks and fondue sets into the spare room for next year's tag sale, pasta primavera was accessible, didn't require extra equipment, and had the faint touch of sophistication—after all, its original incarnation was served exclusively at what by 1977 was arguably the most famous restaurant in New York.

Some of the nastiest fights in the food industry have been over recipes for which one chef claims to be the sole inventor. Until pasta primavera, there had never been a case where a restaurateur claimed to have invented the dish over the assertions of his own chef.

SIRIO

WHEN THINGS STARTED TO CALM DOWN a bit at the restaurant, we were all invited to the Nova Scotia estate of an Italian man called Barone Amato. The house was called Shangri-la. It was lovely, and it felt very nice to be away.

We all went together—Egidiana, me, Craig Claiborne, Pierre Franey, and Jean and his wife, Pauline, a very nice lady. It was spring, but in Nova Scotia it was still cold. We had a very nice time but all we ate was meat—boar, venison—and after a few days we all wanted something simpler. We were far away from anywhere and could not buy things, so we used what was in the house. My wife scavenged through the cupboards, found spaghetti, frozen peas, a few usable vegetables, some mushrooms, a tomato and some garlic that we made into a concassée. There was no olive oil, so we made a sauce of cream and parmesan, tossed it together very quickly, and that was it. When I came back to New York, we worked on the recipe a bit, but not very much, and we served it in the restaurant as a special. People liked it and it took off. It was really the biggest thing. Everyone wanted this dish. They all had to have it. ◄◄-

IN HIS 1986 AUTOBIOGRAPHY, Jean Vergnes says he created the dish at the home of artist and influential food enthusiast Ed Giobbi, at his home in Westchester County, where Franey and Claiborne and the great chefs of the period often gathered. He says he and chef de cuisine Jean-Louis Todeschini played with the dish back at Le Cirque's kitchens, Sirio offered his opinions, and that's how the dish was created. Claiborne, who was a close friend of both Vergnes and Sirio, never sanctioned one version or the other—in his original 1977 piece, he says it was created at *his* house. Like all great recipes, a little of each version is true. Sirio did go to Nova Scotia, Vergnes and Giobbi and Todeschini did play around with the formula, and they all cooked it at Claiborne's house, but the dish was Sirio's. There is no clearer evidence than the fact that Vergnes, Todeschini, and every chef or cook that would follow would not allow pasta primavera to be made in the kitchens of Le Cirque.

SIRIO

-→→

W⁹HEN I BROUGHT PASTA PRIMAVERA they said, "No, no, no, it's too complicated, we can't do that. I'm sorry. … "They didn't want spaghetti to contaminate "their" kitchen. It was a war. So we put a pan of hot water in the corridor and cooked the pasta there and finished it in the dining room. The first time Bocuse came to Le Cirque, he came with Vergé and Pierre Troisgros and said, "We hear that you have good pasta. We would like to have pasta." So I prepared the pasta at the table. I was very honored, you know. When my partner came out and said, "And now let's get to the serious stuff, what can I prepare for you?" Bocuse said, "I'm sorry, but we'd like to have more pasta."

MICHAEL LOMONACO *Pasta primavera is so Sirio it amazes me that anyone questions it, but I suppose that's what it was about then. Chefs made food, maître d's did what they did, and the two were not supposed to cross. It became so famous that they weren't going to allow Sirio to claim it, but it reeks of his spontaneity and drama.*

What makes me mad is the mentality. Chefs are the only ones who can do anything in a restaurant. Here's what they teach: "This is my dish, my butter, my whatever." It's not true. It's the butter of Le Cirque, it's the dish of Le Cirque, it's the pasta of Le Cirque.

Pasta is Italian, not French, but everything had to be French, so when people would ask for pasta I'd go to him and say we need pasta on the menu, it would be good for the restaurant. He'd say, "No." And I would say, "But when we were at the Colony, and Mr. Cavallero asked you to make pasta you'd do it, you'd do anything he wanted, and my partner would say, "Oh, Sirio, this is a different restaurant. This is a French restaurant." Finally I just said, "This is what the people want, and we must have it: One pasta special every day." And I got what I wished for. Each one was more awful than the next. It was like beating a dead horse.

So I stopped asking for pasta and we just had pasta primavera, which we did in the dining room, but we didn't put it on the menu out of respect to Jean, which in the end was a better thing. The fact we prepared it in the dining room made it even more special, because people thought we made it just for them—which in a way, we did. It's still not on the menu—but always there for a client.

GEOFFREY ZAKARIAN *[chef, Town] The whole issue is ridiculous. The chefs—Vergnes and, later on, Sailhac—hated it. It was like the evil stepchild. We had to prep it in this dingy back part of that awful kitchen, and then it was all put together in the dining room. Boulud hated it too, but he was the first French chef who cooked in an American way. At least he understood why the dish was so important for Le Cirque. But still, we had to prepare it away from him!*

DANIEL BOULUD *[chef, Daniel] We prepped it for Sirio and then it was made elsewhere. It was a little alien to me at first, I didn't understand it, but later I saw it was an Italian dish, made in a distinctly French way, and that is Sirio's genius.*

Please, you have to understand, I have great respect for Jean, who is a very nice man. Maybe as we got more and more into the business, our philosophies separated. I wanted things to go more and more one way and he wanted to make money. I wanted to make money too and we were making lots of money, but I thought that as more and more people were added to the kitchen, we also needed to add more people to service. I used my wife's Uncle Renato at the door. Even my sons started to come in to help. I got a few more people, but we added much more in the kitchen, and the food was still the same. We went on like this for a long time, but I started to think that maybe we were in trouble. ◄◄

VERGNES' FOOD WAS SOME OF THE BEST in the city. Still, critics were lukewarm, and with the exception of pasta primavera, no one was really going to Le Cirque for the food. Sirio wanted more.

Sirio eventually got more help, including from a man who would become his most trusted colleague, Frank Dilia. In Le Cirque's early years, Frank ran the restaurant's entire back-of-house operation. He controlled the money, the payroll, the wine cellar, and, most important to Sirio, the supplies of olive oil, truffles, and caviar. Sirio maintains that without Frank Le Cirque would never have been the same.

Frank, a few more wait staff, and, for all of Sirio's grumbling, a smoothly operating kitchen meant that Sirio was able to have a semblance of normal life, or at least the normal life of a restaurateur. He even managed to sneak away with the family on Sundays and Mondays. They bought a house at Hunter Mountain, a ski resort in the Catskills, where other chefs, including André Soltner, had chalets. The few moments he was home often had a professional aspect: Sirio might come home with a client of the restaurant, one of the Zeckendorfs, a food writer, or a celebrity, and ask Egidiana to whip up some fantastic Italian specialty or another. Any time left over was sacred, when Sirio slept and his children and wife did their best not to rouse him.

Sundays were reserved for the family, although Sirio would occasionally repair to the home of Pierre and Betty Franey on the eastern end of Long Island. Two years into Le Cirque's run, Pierre and Betty's daughter was married at Craig Claiborne's house on Gardiner's Bay. The invited guests represented a who's who of the food world, including Sirio and Vergnes, who had brought along Todeschini. Also at the party was Gael Greene, the writer who had trashed the Colony and who wasn't positive in her initial assessment of Le Cirque. Sirio's strategy with all food writers was to seduce them with his charms, then offer them a kind of honorary partnership role, as he had learned to do with Claiborne.

As Greene would recount in her next review of Le Cirque, the wedding was a happy affair, a marvelous excuse for the most important foodies in America to do what they do best—cook, eat, and drink. After the party, Greene caught a ride back to New York City with Jean-Louis Todeschini. A few months later, on January 31, 1977, she wrote her first flattering review of Le Cirque. The review was daring, titled "I Love Le Cirque, but Can I Be Trusted?" she admitted right away that her judgment was clouded by the fact that she was more than a little involved with the restaurant's chef de cuisine whom, she told her readers, she'd met at the Franey wedding. The piece was deliciously sensual and disarmingly honest. She was prepared to bare her soul to explain that a restaurant wasn't always just about the food. Sirio loved it. Greene's relationship with Todeschini came to an end but she became one of Sirio's best, if occasionally harshest, critics.

Sirio is prone to volunteer without prompting that most restaurant reviewers know nothing about the restaurant business and even less about food (with exception made for Craig Claiborne and, by association, his protégé Bryan Miller), then just as quickly deny he's ever uttered such a remark and go on to say that reviewers are a necessary part of the business because they keep you on your toes.

Nonetheless, he can recount the exact date of a review from any magazine or newspaper of note, the author, and the author's history. And if the review is bad, he can always remember the exact hour where he first read it.

SIRIO

I WILL NEVER FORGET. Egidiana and I had gone back to Montecatini, and she had to return to New York before me to take the boys to back to school. It was August 26, 1977. I landed at Kennedy. From there I always took a taxi back to our apartment. But when I got through customs, I saw Egidiana standing there waiting for me.

At first I thought nothing was wrong, that she was just being nice, but then she did not move her mouth and I started to panic. *"Che cosa è questo, Egidiana?"* What is it? I begged her. I thought—my god, what could it be? I asked her if the boys were okay and she said yes. Then what could be worse than the death of my sons or someone in my family? Only one thing could come close. "Let me see," I said, and she gave me the review from Mimi Sheraton in the *Times*. She had taken the two stars from Canaday and dropped one. But it wasn't the stars. It was the review.

Sheraton said I pulled a chair away from the table and that I threw her purse at her—or something stupid like that. She said that first I called her "madame," and then later on *"signora,"* then finally "What do you want, lady?" As if I don't know the difference between a madame and a *signora*, or talk that way. Never. And then all the tired things about the tables and how they were too close and she didn't get special treatment. The critics say they don't want a special table, and when you don't give it to them, they crucify you. All reporters, especially from *The New York Times,* can't understand Le Cirque. They thought it had to be Old World and old style when in fact that was the problem. What I hated the most was that this supposedly democratic paper was so elitist, but masquerading as democratic. They were only upset because they didn't give permission for Le Cirque to be the place of the elite. *The New York Times* likes to make people and then they like to take them down. They thought all restaurants have to be French, have to have the stupid waiter that walks like Charlie Chaplin. That is not Le Cirque. ◄◄

SIRIO NEVER RECOVERED from that first Sheraton review. Where Gael Greene's review, only seven months earlier, had talked about "a fatal impulse to please, the shortcuts, the wonderfully stubborn ambition, the innocence," Sheraton saw neither innocence nor an impulse to please. She saw only chaos. In aiming to please everyone, Sirio had failed to please the critic. And in directing at least some of the attack at Sirio personally, Sheraton had got right through to his soft underbelly. Sheraton denies that she did it intentionally, reviewing only as she saw the restaurant function and as objectively as she could. Years later, she still denies her criticism was too harsh. "Reviewers review as objectively as they can," she said. "We're journalists, expressing measured opinion. It's a job. That's all."

Sirio went to the restaurant that night to cheer up the staff, but spent most of the evening on the phone. He called everyone he could think of, following a routine that he still performs like a ritual when something upsets him, calling, complaining, whining like a wounded boy. In the morning, he couldn't get up. Egi, as always, came to her husband's rescue, making him espresso and getting him to the front door of the restaurant.

That Saturday after the *Times* review is now part of Le Cirque legend. The restaurant did a record lunch business, 146 covers instead of the usual 40 or 50, even though it was summer. Many customers had delayed their Friday night sojourns to their weekend houses to show support for Le Cirque. Some patrons came in and slapped the review on a stake.

While the fury at Sheraton never did subside, something else was going on in the maestro's head. If he took himself out of the equation, Sirio could see that Sheraton had mostly attacked the food. He didn't agree that the food was as bad as she said, but he knew that the time was ripe to move on with his own food philosophy and with his own restaurant.

A few weeks later, Sirio approached Vergnes and asked to dissolve their partnership.

I HAVE OVERWORKED ALL MY LIFE because I don't like being criticized. I decided that night: Either we move the restaurant toward my philosophy and become the best restaurant in the world, or I would give up then and there.

So I went to Jean. We had had a good partnership. Like some marriages, they are good, and then they are not. I liked and valued Jean, but he was not right for the Le Cirque I wanted to run. Since we were partners, that meant I wanted out, even if he got Le Cirque and I went off and did something else. And that's what I said to him. It was like a divorce.

We had the same lawyer, Victor Jacobs. He suggested that we have the restaurant valued, and whoever wanted the space would pay the other. After a while Jean came back and said he wanted out. I could have the space and the restaurant. That was the easy part. The hard part was that in three years the restaurant had risen to a value of one million dollars.

I talked to my family and we agreed to pay Jean his half a million. Right away I gave him the $150,000 and I promised to pay the remaining $350,000 within three years.

We met at "21" in May 1978 to sign the papers. Jean and his wife Pauline, me, Egidiana, and Victor Jacobs. We signed and that was it. It was fun, we had champagne. I like Pauline and Jean. I learned many things from him. And I'm a bit jealous because he's a wealthy man and I'm still a waiter. I said to myself, How will I ever pay back all this money? Now I will have to shoot myself.

I didn't sleep for months. I hated that feeling, but within two and a half years, I paid him back. And Le Cirque, Le Cirque went *boom!*

When I left that night after we signed at "21," I thought my father would be very proud. ◄◄

SIRIO'S BAKED EGGS   SERVES 1

SIRIO SAYS, "In truth, people who work in restaurants are happy with the simplest food—scrambled eggs, toast, something a little savory...." And more often than not, when Sirio is hungry, it is late, or the party is over, someone in the kitchen will make this deceptively simple egg and tomato recipe for their tired maestro. With a fresh salad, a loaf of warm bread, and some sausage, you have a perfect, elegant meal.

2   tablespoons extra-virgin olive oil

1   small clove garlic, thinly sliced

1   cup crushed plum tomatoes or canned San Marzano tomatoes
    Salt

2   slices thick-cut bacon, cut into 2-inch matchsticks

2   eggs

Preheat the oven to 400°F.

To make the tomato sauce, add the olive oil and garlic to a small saucepan and cook over medium-low heat until the garlic is softened and fragrant, about 3 to 5 minutes. Add the tomatoes and cook, stirring occasionally, until the oil floats free from the tomatoes and the sauce is slightly reduced, about 25 minutes. Salt to taste and reserve.

Meanwhile, put the bacon in a cold frying pan and heat at medium-low. Fry until crisp, then transfer to paper towels to drain.

Put a layer of tomato sauce in the bottom of a shallow crème brûlée ramekin or an 8-ounce cocotte. Break the eggs directly into the ramekin and put it in the oven; bake just until the whites have set, approximately 8 to 10 minutes. Garnish with the crisped lardons and eat immediately.

Chestnut Farfalle with Soft Chicken Quenelles and White Truffles SERVES 4

At The Colony and at Le Cirque, swells who didn't necessarily know anything about food were thrilled to eat quenelles, something that sounded fancy, but tasted like improved mashed potatoes. Sirio never tires of complaining to his chefs that quenelles—a mixture of anything from chicken to fish that look like large dumplings—may be a cliché of haute cuisine, but when done correctly they are delicious and, most important, recognizable. This version, a gift to Sirio from Alain Ducasse, pays homage to Sirio's fondness for the much maligned quenelle, as well as his love for chestnuts, truffles, and pasta.

Chestnut Farfalle

- 1 cup chestnut flour
- ⅔ cup all-purpose flour, plus additional for dusting
- 2 eggs, beaten

Quenelles

- ½ skinless chicken breast
- ⅔ cup heavy cream
- Salt
- 1 quart chicken stock
- 2 tablespoons rendered foie gras fat or duck fat
- 1 cup dark chicken stock
- 1 teaspoon grapeseed oil
- 1 clove garlic, unpeeled
- 6 ounces pancetta, sliced
- 3 tablespoons fleur de sel butter or salted butter
- 12 slivers porcini mushroom
- 1½ ounces white truffles

Chestnut Farfalle

Sift the flours together onto a clean work surface. Form a mound with the flour and hollow out a well in the center with your fingers. Pour the beaten eggs into the well and stir them with a fork (or your fingers), slowly incorporating the flour from the sides of the well until the dough is workable, if sticky. Dust your hands and knead the dough, adding additional flour only to keep the dough from sticking to your hands or the counter, until firm and smooth. Wrap in plastic and rest for at least 15 minutes and up to 1 hour.

Roll the dough out with a pasta machine until it's just less than ¼-inch thick (the machine's second-to-last setting). Cut out rounds with a 2-inch fluted cookie cutter, then pinch the center of each disk to form a butterfly shape. Knead the scraps together, reroll through the pasta machine, and continue to make farfalle until you've used all the dough.

Quenelles

Bring a large pot of water to simmer on the stove.

Coarsely chop the chicken breast (it should yield about ⅔ to ¾ cup chopped meat). Place the chopped chicken, the cream, and a pinch of salt in the work bowl of a food processor and purée for about 2 minutes, until it has a consistent texture—it does not need to be a homogenized purée, just a workable batter.

Place a bowl of clean cold water nearby as you begin to form the quenelles. Using a teaspoon, scoop out a heaping spoonful of the chicken mixture; then, with the inverted bowl of a second teaspoon, press down on it to create a slightly oblong, rounded shape. Nudge the quenelle off the first spoon into the simmering water with the second spoon. Rinse off the spoons in the bowl of cold water. Repeat until you've made 16 quenelles, working in batches as necessary so the quenelles don't overcook. They are cooked when they can be easily flipped with a slotted spoon, about 5 to 7 minutes. Remove from the water with a slotted spoon and reserve.

To Finish and Serve

Bring the quart of chicken stock to a boil in a pan large enough to accommodate the farfalle.

Melt the goose or duck fat in a small saucepan; add the dark chicken stock and reduce by half over high heat.

Heat the grapeseed oil over medium heat in a sauté pan large enough to accommodate the pancetta and farfalle. Add the garlic and pancetta slices and cook until they've rendered some of their fat and crisped slightly, about 4 to 8 minutes. Discard the garlic, drain the fat from the pan, and add the reduced dark chicken stock.

Drop the farfalle into the boiling chicken stock and cook until al dente, about 3 to 4 minutes. At that time, taste a farfalle to make sure the thick middle section is cooked.

Add the drained pasta to the pan with the pancetta. Add the butter, turn off the heat, and toss the pasta to coat it thoroughly with the sauce. Add the quenelles and gently toss to warm.

Lay slices of pancetta in the bottom of each of four warmed pasta plates, then portion out pasta and four quenelles per plate. Spoon any remaining juices from the pan over the pasta, garnish with the slivers of raw porcini mushrooms, and grate the white truffles onto each plate at the table, in the presence of your guests.

PASTA PRIMAVERA   SERVES 4 TO 6

PASTA PRIMAVERA IS A STUDY in Italian spontaneity—which accounts for the millions of versions that came after the original recipe. Here's how it's made at the restaurant, with instructions for tableside service included. At home, Sirio blanches all the vegetables in one pot of boiling, salted water, then cooks the pasta in it as well.

6 tablespoons olive oil

1½ cups plum tomatoes, chopped, peeled, and seeded, or whole canned San Marzano tomatoes, chopped, seeded, and drained

2 cloves garlic, minced

Salt

2 cups porcini or button mushrooms, roughly chopped

Pepper

1 cup asparagus tips, blanched in boiling salted water for 4 minutes

1 cup broccoli florets, blanched in boiling salted water for 4 minutes

1 medium zucchini, quartered, cut into 1-inch lengths and blanched in boiling salted water for 4 minutes

½ up frozen peas, thawed in boiling salted water

1   cup heavy cream

⅔   cup Parmigiano-Reggiano, plus additional for garnish

2   tablespoons butter

1   pound spaghetti

½   cup pignoli, lightly toasted

2   tablespoons basil, cut into a chiffonade

Heat 2 tablespoons of the olive oil in a medium sauté pan over high heat. Add the tomatoes, half the garlic, and a pinch of salt and cook until the tomatoes have rendered most their juice and begun to color, stirring or tossing occasionally, about 4 to 8 minutes. Set aside and keep warm.

Heat 2 tablespoons olive oil in a medium sauté pan over high heat and sauté the mushrooms with the remaining garlic and a pinch of salt until they've given off most of their water and are nicely browned, about 8 to 10 minutes. Set aside, season to taste, and keep warm.

Heat the remaining 2 tablespoons olive oil over medium-high heat in a large sauté pan, add the remaining garlic, and cook the blanched vegetables until they've taken on a little color but are still firm, about 5 minutes. Set aside, season to taste, and keep warm.

Bring a large pot of salted water to a boil. Meanwhile, reduce the cream by half in a pan large enough to hold the cooked spaghetti, stir in the Parmesan and butter, and turn the heat to low. Cook the spaghetti. When the spaghetti is 1 or 2 minutes shy of al dente, strain and transfer it to the pan with the reduced cream to finish cooking.

TO SERVE Transfer the spaghetti and cream to a warmed bowl large enough to hold all the ingredients and bring it to the table with the reserved tomato sauce, mushrooms, and sautéed vegetables, and the pignoli, each in separate bowls. Toss the spaghetti first with the mushrooms, then the vegetables and then portion it onto warmed pasta plates. Garnish each plate with toasted pignoli, 2 spoonfuls of the tomato sauce, a pinch of the chiffonade of basil, and freshly grated Parmesan, salt, and pepper to taste.

Lobster Salad Le Cirque

"At lunch, people want the luxury of lobster, the texture—not the mess!" A staple of the "Ladies who lunch," and quite a few of the men, this salad remains a hallmark of Sirio's theory about how food should be presented in the dining room: composed on the plate, but not too formal, and its elements kept separate and distinct. More than 100 are served daily. Over the years Sirio's chefs have won the battle to dress the salad in the kitchen. Sirio still prefers to dress it himself—and you may prefer to do the same.

1 large tomato, peeled and quartered

$\frac{1}{4}$ shallot, minced

Pinch fresh thyme leaves

1 tablespoon olive oil

4 outside leaves Boston lettuce

3 Maine lobsters ($1\frac{1}{2}$-pounds each), cooked in salted water and shelled, tails cut into $\frac{1}{4}$-inch slices

6 asparagus tips (the top two inches or so of the asparagus), blanched in boiling salted water for 4 minutes

$\frac{1}{4}$ pound haricots verts, blanched in boiling salted water for 4 minutes

2 fingerling or other small potatoes, blanched in boiling salted water until tender and thinly sliced

$\frac{1}{2}$ avocado, pitted, peeled, and sliced as thinly as possible

Black Truffle Dressing

2 tablespoons sherry vinegar

2 tablespoons olive oil

2 tablespoons canola oil

2 tablespoons black truffle oil

1 tablespoon canned black truffle jus

1 teaspoon truffle peelings, finely minced

Salt and pepper

Combine the tomato pieces with the shallot, thyme, and olive oil. Let marinate at least 20 minutes or as long as overnight (if overnight, covered in the refrigerator).

When you're almost ready to finish the salad, put two large plates in the refrigerator to chill.

To make the dressing, whisk all the ingredients together. Taste, adding more vinegar, salt, or pepper if needed.

TO SERVE Nestle 2 Boston lettuce leaves together in the center of each plate to form a bowl, then fill each with meat from 1 claw and 1½ tails. (Reserve extra meat for another purpose.) Then, using the face of a clock as a reference, arrange three asparagus at 12 o'clock on the plate, two of the marinated tomato quarters at 3, half of the blanched haricots verts at 6, and a fan of half the sliced avocado at 9. Repeat for the second plate. Dress the entire plate with the dressing and serve at once.

FLOUNDER LE CIRQUE SERVES 2

SIRIO PROUDLY ADMITS that this is the dish that has sustained Le Cirque since it first opened its doors. Like quenelles, Flounder Le Cirque is a very grand name for something that is actually quite simple. "Why shouldn't a great chef make something, perfectly fried, very light, with the peas served on the side, the sauce, served on the side, the way people like it?" he asks. "They should be proud to do so." And any chef who works for Sirio has to be! Herb crushed potatoes and sautéed spinach are great side dishes for this entrée as well.

>   2 flounder filets, 12 ounces each
>   1 cup clarified butter
> 1½ cups unseasoned bread crumbs, made from day-old bread
>   ½ cup olive oil
>   Salt
>   Mustard hollandaise, for garnish

Dip each filet in clarified butter, let any excess drain off, then dredge in the bread crumbs, mounding them over the top to ensure it's fully coated. Stack the breaded filets on top of each other between sheets of parchment paper and chill for at least 15 minutes and up to 4 hours.

Set your broiler pan 5 inches from the heating element and pre-heat the broiler. Brush 2 stainless-steel cooling racks (the type used for cooling cakes or cookies) with olive oil. Brush the filets with olive oil, taking care to coat both sides thoroughly—any bread crumbs that haven't been brushed with oil will burn under the broiler.

Set the filets on one of the cooling racks and transfer it to the broiler. Cook until golden brown, about 7 to 8 minutes. If the filets still are firm enough, flip them very gently with a fish spatula and cook 3 minutes more. However, if they flake with even the slightest prodding, take the cooling rack out of the broiler, invert the other oiled rack on top of it (and the filets), and quickly flip the two, so that the second side of the flounder is now face up on the second cooling rack. Remove the first rack carefully, return to the broiler, and cook 3 minutes more.

TO SERVE Be very careful when retrieving the fish from the broiler and transferring them to serving plates—they can be extremely delicate and break easily. Season with salt and serve immediately with mustard hollandaise.

NAVARIN LE CIRQUE SERVES 4

FOR ALL SIRIO'S AFFECTION for bistro food raised to Le Cirque standards, he doesn't like to eat steak—and there has never been one on the menu. He feels the same way about lamb, "I love lamb, but people don't want to see it lying on their plate like a steak." This recipe helped introduce Americans to the taste of lamb without offending their sensibilities. Besides his beloved lamb chops, this is also his favorite way to eat lamb at home.

> 4 pounds boneless lamb shoulder, cut into 2-inch cubes
>
> Salt and pepper
>
> Flour, for dredging
>
> 3 tablespoons olive oil
>
> 1 cup chopped onion
>
> ½ cup chopped carrot
>
> ½ cup chopped celery
>
> 1 orange, zested and juiced
>
> 1 head garlic, cut in half
>
> 1 or 2 sprigs thyme
>
> 2 quarts veal or dark chicken stock
>
> ½ cup peas, blanched if fresh
>
> 4 new potatoes, boiled and quartered
>
> 4 Thumbelina or other small carrots, blanched
>
> Additional orange zest, to garnish

Season the lamb liberally with salt and pepper, then dredge the lamb lightly in the flour. Heat 2 tablespoons of the olive oil in a pan large enough to accommodate all the recipe's ingredients over high heat. When the oil is shimmering, add the lamb (working in batches, if necessary) and brown the meat evenly on all sides, 10 to 15 minutes. Remove the meat from the pan and discard the fat.

Preheat the oven to 375°F.

Return the pan to the stove and add the remaining 1 tablespoon olive oil. Add the onion, carrot, and celery and cook over medium heat, until the vegetables have softened and just begun to color, about 10 minutes.

Deglaze with the orange juice, scraping to get all the browned bits off the bottom of the pan, then add the browned meat, garlic, orange zest (reserving a pinch for service), and thyme. Add stock to barely cover. Bring to a boil, then lower the heat and reduce to a simmer. Cover and transfer to the oven.

Check the pan after 10 minutes to make sure the liquid isn't boiling; if it is, lower the heat to 300°F. Cook for 1 hour or more, as necessary, until the meat is tender and the liquid in the pan has reduced slightly.

Remove the pan from the oven and transfer the braised meat to a platter or cutting board to rest. Strain the sauce, pressing on the vegetables to extract as much liquid as possible, discarding the solids. Then put the sauce in a pan on the stove and reduce it over high heat until thickened considerably.

TO SERVE Warm the peas, potatoes, and baby carrots in the sauce briefly, then divide them and the lamb among four serving plates. Pour the sauce through a strainer over each of the four portions and garnish with a pinch of orange zest. Serve immediately.

VEAL MILANESE SERVES 2

LE CIRQUE 2000 has its own full-time butcher, so it's easy for the restaurant to use the frenched and pounded-out veal chop called for in the recipe. Unless you have a butcher who'll prepare them for you, or you're confident in your butchering skills, you may have better results pounding out a lesser cut.

While you're cooking the chops, gently shake the pan and move the chop around to make sure it's not sticking to the bottom of the pan. Keep the heat on the low side of medium—it's okay for the butter to sizzle, but if it shows the slightest sign of coloring, pull the pan off the burner and swirl to cool it down.

At home, Sirio uses three parts olive oil and one part butter—"it gives it the softness that makes it a great dish." He also takes it off the bone for a quicker preparation, "but then it's a cutlet, not a chop!" Kitchen nomenclature is important to Sirio. A small chopped arugula and tomato salad is the perfect accompaniment.

1   cup all-purpose flour

2   eggs, beaten

3   cups unseasoned bread crumbs, made from day-old bread

2   veal chops, on the bone, frenched and pounded out as thin as pos-
    sible (about ⅛-inch thick)

½   cup clarified butter

    Salt

    Lemon wedges

Set up a station to bread the veal: from left to right, have a large plate with the flour on it, then a wide, shallow bowl (a pie plate works) holding the beaten eggs, then another wide, shallow bowl with the bread crumbs. Coat each chop first with egg, then flour (tapping off the excess), then egg again; then bury it in the bread crumbs, mounding the crumbs over the top of the chop to ensure it's fully coated. Stack the breaded chops on top of each other between sheets of parchment paper and chill for at least 15 minutes and up to 4 hours.

Preheat the oven to 200°F and set a cooling rack on a cookie sheet in the oven.

Warm half the butter over medium-low heat in a 12-inch sauté pan and slide in the first chop. Cook for 3 minutes on each side, basting the thicker section with butter where the bone meets the chop to cook it through. Cook each side for 1 or 2 more minutes, until lightly browned and crisped. Salt the chop and transfer to the rack in the oven to keep it warm. Drain the pan and repeat with the second chop.

TO SERVE Serve with the lemon wedges.

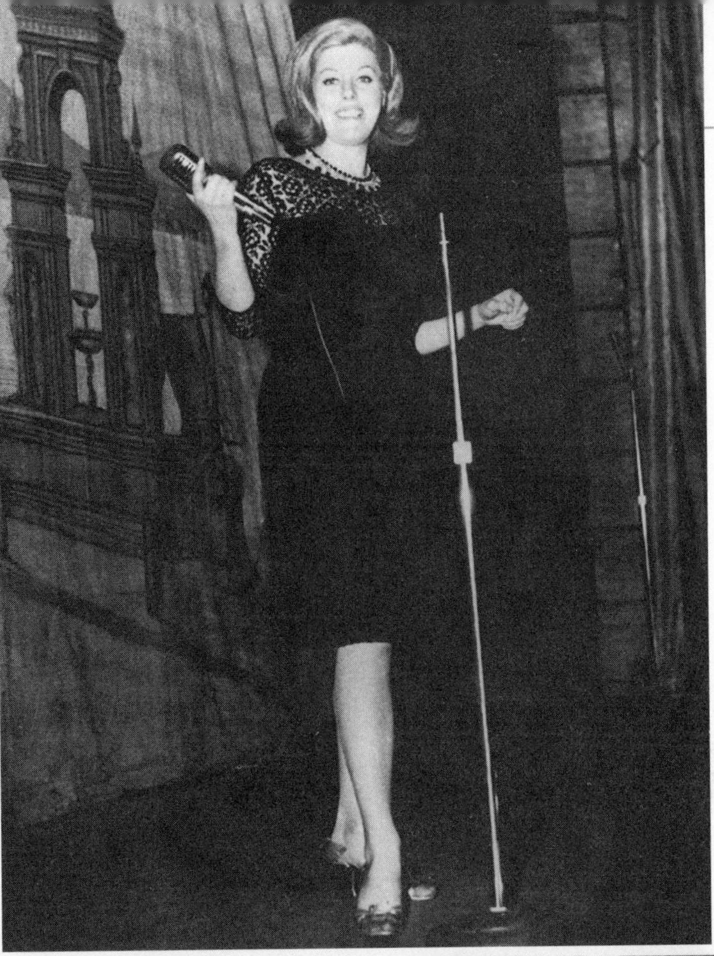

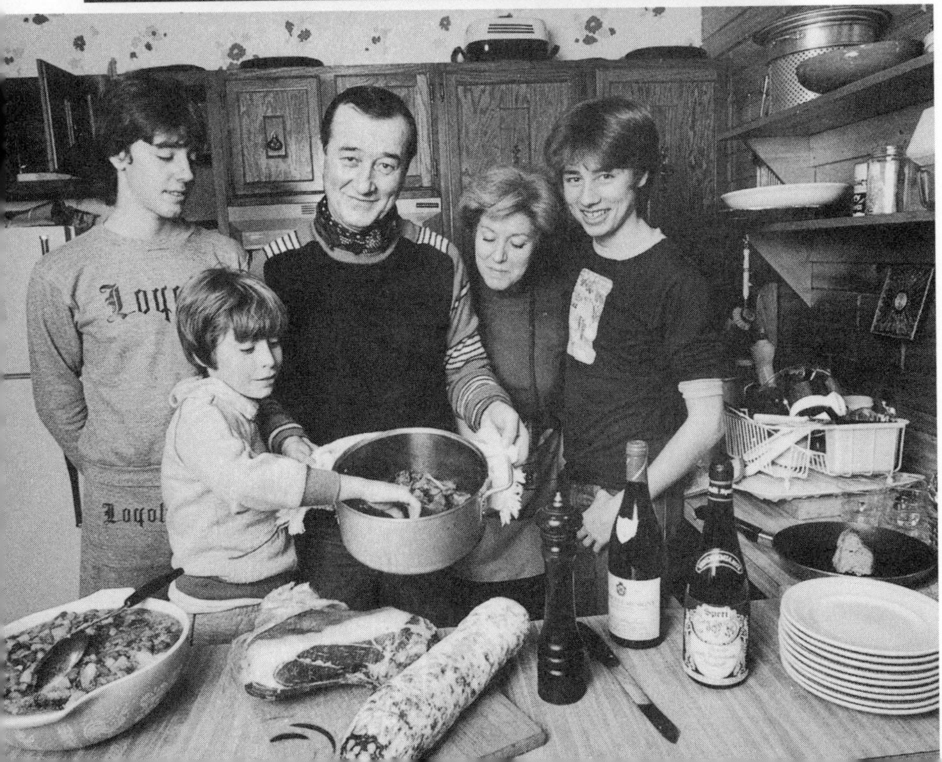

THIS PAGE

TOP:
Sirio and the chanteuse Egidiana Palmieri, Montecatini, 1957.

BOTTOM LEFT:
Sirio's first photograph as the sole owner of Le Cirque, 1978.

BOTTOM RIGHT:
From left to right: Renato Palmieri, Sirio, and Joe Garni, taking reservations, 1979.

FACING PAGE

TOP:
He takes your reservation and cooks too! Sirio serving Pasta Primavera, Le Cirque, 1978.

BOTTOM:
Sirio as maître d'hôtel, partner, and waiter at La Forét, "America's first disco." The Pierre Hotel, 1971.

RESTAURANT
REVOLUTIONARY

THE RESTAURATEUR

SIRIO

WHEN JEAN VERGNES AND I SPLIT UP I thought we respected each other and we did, but maybe I was a little naïve, since the respect didn't extend to everybody in the kitchen. The plan was that Michael Bourdeaux, who worked for Vergnes and Todeschini, and was really the person who did everything for them, would take over the kitchen. After the deal with Vergnes was done I went to Montecatini. In those days we had an arrangement: when we closed for a month in the summer, our clients would go to Lutèce, and the next month, when Lutèce closed, their clients would come to us.

Well, I don't think I even made it to Montecatini before I got a call from Frank saying that Bourdeaux had stopped by to say he was not coming to work anymore. And I say, "Stopped by? What do you mean he stopped by?" Frank was the most perfect man. I could run the whole world with just Frank and maybe a few others. He always spoke to me like I was sane, when everyone knew I was insane. He was very direct. And Frank just said to me, very level, very quiet, "He will not be cooking from the first of August, and you will need to find another chef." I remember thinking then that the life of a restaurateur means that you never sleep and that going on vacation is an invitation to the gods to make something bad happen.

I called André Soltner right away and he told me that Alain Sailhac was available. I knew that Sailhac had just received four stars at Le Cygne from *The New York Times,* but that there had been trouble. The day after the review, Sailhac took a vacation and asked for more money. Instead they fired him. Honestly, I didn't think Sailhac would want to work with me, but Soltner said call him, so I did. I told him what I wanted and he was very clear with me. He wasn't interested in pursuing the conversation unless I guaranteed him $750 per week, net. That was like $39,000 per year. I said yes, but that he had to come to Italy to talk. He came.

I'll never forget meeting in Florence. I hadn't really been there since I worked at the Otello during hotel school, and before with my grandfather. Sailhac drove into the Piazza della Signoria in one of those cars from Germany that looks like a bug. He parked the car and I was introduced to his wife, his first wife. We walked around the center of Florence and I heard her say to him in French, right in front of me, "I didn't know the Italians could be so civilized."

I wanted to yell at her right there standing in front of the Palazzo Vecchio, under the statue of David, that Catherine de Médicis had brought the first fork to France. But I didn't say anything. You know, it's like my whole life: I stand at the door and don't say what I really feel. Sailhac and his wife followed me to Montecatini and in the thirty minutes it took to get home I had decided that I would be the cook myself, that I couldn't hire Sailhac. Thank god I changed my mind. It was to be my first chef decision and I had to feel good about it. My wife can look at a person and know, better than me. You go with your sense, your sensibility, you just know, and I knew Sailhac was right, but when you take a chef you take his wife too.

I took him to the markets; I took him to the fields where my grandmother and I picked wild fennel and herbs. I took him to where the mushrooms grow. He'd never seen such things. I took him to my house, where Egidiana cooked dinner. Then to my sister Clara's and to the farmhouse where I was born. But I also took him to the restaurants, to the hotels, La Pace, which even then had good food—not great, but they knew how to please. I wanted the ingredients, but also the mentality. So we talked for days and days about the mentality. I knew that Sailhac understood what the customers wanted. He knew how to look into a face and see if they were happy or not. That's the most important thing. And of course, with the money I was going to pay him, I didn't want any more argument about the numbers. I would pay for the best ingredients—everything. But then we would make the food for as many people as we could—100, 200, 300. And he didn't flinch. It's about organization and mentality—and he had it.

> ALAIN SAILHAC *Working with Sirio is very intuitive. He's not a chef, but he knows like a chef. He describes to you what he wants, but he gets so excited sometimes it's hard to understand him. Even in French, he's the same way. You try, you go back, you try to please, you give it to him. He was the most generous person I'd ever worked for. I was younger, I knew what I wanted and I wasn't sure I wanted this big responsibility. He was talking about big numbers, big ideas. I was doing well, but I was used to making maybe 80 dinners a night while he was talking about impossible numbers. Somehow Sirio made it seem like the most exciting thing in the world. Like we could change the world from the kitchen.*

Sailhac was in the kitchen from the middle of July 1978. We talked on the phone but he put together a whole kitchen staff himself, because when he got there the old crew had all left—most to go work with my former partner.

> ALAIN SAILHAC *Finding staff in those days was not so easy. But I knew everyone, and I called everyone. Then I took the youngest people, because my inclination to teach was already very strong and I knew I could work with them. The first thing I did in the kitchen was just have it cleaned, and then I looked around and decided what I would need to make it work for what Sirio wanted to do and what I wanted to do.*

Not knowing the new staff made it easier to focus on the things that I wanted to do—repairs for the kitchen, work on the menu, those kind of things. I remembered all the times that I had been on the phone, dealing with a man from the union, or taking an order at the table and Vergnes would send someone out from the kitchen to say a lightbulb in some closet needed to be fixed. An army of people in the kitchen and not one with the sense to change a lightbulb! Now I had a man who didn't bother me with these stupidities. For the first time in my life I thought, "I am Sirio Maccioni, a restaurateur, who has the brains to hire a smart man who knows what he is doing!"

Right away Le Cirque started to explode. I tell you, there were days when sometimes I think the concrete underneath me started to shake. I asked for 500 dishes a night, and Sailhac gave me 700. I said I need this, and he gave me that. Nixon came in, and the rest of the world was there too, and I didn't have to say anything, Sailhac knew, he immediately came from the kitchen and took his order.

Was maybe the best thing ever happened to Le Cirque.

People, food, energy.

Was incredible. ⤜⤛

NOW THAT LE CIRQUE WAS HIS entirely, Sirio had a chance to prove his philosophy could make the most successful—and delicious—restaurant in the world. If he failed he would have only himself to blame. The first move had been to hire Alain Sailhac. The second was to allow his new chef a degree of control he would never have given his former partner. The particular balance Sirio was looking for in his restaurant's menu would become the hallmark of its cuisine: solid classic dishes such as flounder, dover sole, and grilled veal chops, the food of the Colony set and, if only they were prepared to admit it, of everyone else too; daily specials that reflected the seasons; and then what Sirio calls "the fantasy"—the experimental dishes, some of which, over time, might become classics. That meant fifty-five items on the menu, not including specials, or the almost daily moments when Sirio ran into the kitchen and asked for something entirely different.

At the rate Le Cirque produced food, the daily specials and fantasy dishes were enough to keep even the most energetic chef on his culinary toes. Instead of sequestering cooks, chefs, and service staff to the bowels of ships, he and Sailhac were raising them into the light, throwing at them managerial, culinary, and financial control beyond their wildest dreams. As Sirio had long proclaimed, it was about "the mentality": invest in your staff and they will invest in you.

Sirio's willingness to spend meant that Le Cirque's kitchen would become the best graduate school for chefs in the world. A generation of American chefs was educated under Sailhac over the next eight years. Where Vergnes and Maccioni had fought bitterly over every additional staff member, there was no one Sirio wouldn't approve for Sailhac. Eventually the tiny kitchen had twenty-four full-time cooks. They included Geoffrey Zakarian, who would become the first chef at Patroon, then at his own restaurant, Town; Terrance Brennan, later of Picholine and Artisanal; Rick Moonen, of Oceana and later his own restaurant, rm; Michael Lomonaco, of Windows on the World; and David Bouley, who went on to his own eponymous restaurant.

Then there was the food and its ingredients. Gone were the fights about risotto, extra glasses of champagne, and free desserts. Gone were the complaints about the food costs. Gone was the secret bottle of olive oil tucked into Sirio's station. So long as it was controlled by Frank, no food product was outside the range of Sirio and Alain's approval. Not only had Sirio elevated his staff to expect only the best, his purveyors started to fall over themselves to provide him with the best. He was not just their best customer, he was forging for them an entirely new market. Who else would pay for raspberries shipped from the first harvest in Provence? Who else would have a truffle flown over first-class? Sirio wanted the best food, prepared perfectly—the cuisine of a French or Italian household raised to restaurant standards. He also wanted the pizzazz of fireworks ricocheting from every table—a feature you might not expect from even the finest home-cooked meal. That part was pure, unadulterated Sirio.

There was another change in the restaurant having to do with Sirio's appearance. In the first few years of Le Cirque, Sirio had opted for what he considered radically casual attire for a maître d'hôtel—a perfectly cut, but sober, usually Italian suit, but only and strictly at lunch. Every evening had seen him in one of twenty-five various handmade tuxedos with starched white shirts that Egidiana kept stocked at home and at the restaurant. With full ownership, however, the "perfect robot with a smile" began to let his clothes loosen up. Daytime suits became more racy. The dark blues and grays weren't banished, but they were now in patterns, or in different cuts, or in luxurious fabrics; linens in summer, cashmere in winter, a collection of velvet jackets in blood-red crimson, deep green, and his favorite, royal blue with hand-carved bone buttons, lacquered blue in the middle; gold would have been too ostentatious. The silk pocket squares became more fluorescent, and the first-interview ties gave way to conservative but always chic designs from his favorite Italian designers.

At night, during the week, Sirio might even forgo the black tie in favor of one of his new suits, though over the weekend or at any special event it was always back to the tuxedo. Still, even there, the traditional waiter's garb suddenly included velvet or silk moiré lapels, or came in windowpane checks. In summer it could be a white dinner jacket with white satin collars. Sirio was defining his own style and the style of his restaurant.

Why not just change the name of the restaurant to Sirio?

SIRIO

MY GOD, that would be so presumptuous. Throughout the story of Le Cirque, we have never said, "We are the best restaurant." I want many more things than just to be the best restaurant. After all my years in the business, getting the best restaurant was easy. Hard work, but easy. It's everything else that's hard. Training the people to have the right mentality, making a future for my family, building something more than just a restaurant. If you have the right mentality, then getting people to come and giving them what they want, making them happy, is also easy.

What we have always been able to say is this: "We are the restaurant where everybody wants to go."

Sailhac's coming was the real beginning. I was no longer so insecure, and Sailhac came into his own too. What made Sailhac a great chef was that he was a teacher. People like Moonen and others became what they became because Sailhac had a fundamental understanding about food. He was a classical chef who knew he had the obligation to teach the people who worked with him. He was not a schizophrenic young chef screaming, "Do this, do that!" like most of them. A great chef has to create his own people. He was firm, but he had the best quality a teacher can have—he was never afraid to learn himself.

I don't care what people say—I brought the first white truffles to New York. Agnelli once said to me, "I am from Turin and I can't get white truffles! But I come to New York and you have the best." I knew how to get them, I know which ones were the best, and Sailhac had the courage to learn.

ALAIN SAILHAC *The legend about Sirio and the truffles is true. None of us, not Vergé, not Bocuse or Ducasse, even knew what a white truffle was. Sirio also knew about ovoli mushrooms and porcini. Maybe some chef in the east of France knew of these things, but not me! The Ovoli are shaped like eggs, faintly pink. Sirio would slice them and throw them on a salad with a little avocado—the pink and the green—then add just a little olive oil, and it was perfect. But the cost was outrageous! Those mushrooms cost $60 a pound back then! It was amazing to watch him eat them—whole, just like that! Sirio never questioned the price. If raspberries were $5 or $6 a pint, so be it. Our bill for truffles in my first year alone was $75,000. I was amazed. I had never known anyone I'd worked with to be like that. People talk about Le Pavillon, or restaurants in the old days, but no one even knew about these kind of ingredients—and if they did, they weren't prepared to pay for them. I worked out from him how to cook the risotto, how to incorporate the flavors. I didn't know about pasta, or carpaccio or the wines. I had to learn all over again.*

You know, if you talk to a real man, not a phony, they tell you where and how they learn things. It's part of history. So many of the chefs I know just pretend to know things. I know how to play that game. I got by with very little English or, when I was young, very little French, because I didn't have the education. I had to fake things to get by, but I always felt dirty, not right about it. Instead of feeling phony, I decided to learn so I didn't have to feel that way. I learned to speak French, not just good French, but excellent. I was ashamed not to know, but I didn't lie. Many times in the kitchen they don't want to learn anything at all, especially not from an owner who is usually a tired person who doesn't really care or who is pushing something or is bored.

I would call Egidiana at home and she would send over her ravioli, which she made with a special machine we got in Viareggio, ricotta and spinach, the most perfect things, and Sailhac didn't say, "Oh, he's good, but he's Italian." It was a pleasure to give him great ingredients. You'd see his eyes open wide, like this, like a kid. Then he took that information and taught it to people, honestly, without being phony.

You know I would always joke with Sailhac that maybe it took a stupid Italian to teach one Frenchman about nouvelle cuisine. The best ingredients done simply, prepared in an honest way, according to the season. We tried everything. We had everything flown over. The mushrooms. We started to order all types of fish. Fish from France and Italy, *loup de mer,* Mediterranean sea bass. We even tried the original bouillabaisse from Marseille, with the fish flown over in little plastic pouches so it was fresh when it got to us. So fresh it was getting to Vergé's restaurant, up in the mountains in Provence, almost at the same time!

GEOFFREY ZAKARIAN *Sirio was always bringing stuff back from Italy—sausages, cheeses, mushrooms, and equipment. I could never work out how he did it! But it was amazing to see and then watch what they were turned into. He taught Bocuse about soft-shell crabs. There were these huge Italian influences. Learning to make white truffle sauce, Sirio in the kitchen in his Brioni suits getting pasta right. Italian pot-au-feu with pigs' feet, and the best floun-*

der I've ever had in any restaurant anywhere. It was the dish I think that kept the restaurant alive! Lightly breaded ... perfection. And ingredients like none of us had ever seen. He kept hammering home the idea of the high-end bistro. It worked.

I loved the bouillabaisse. The only way to get real bouillabaisse is to get real fish, but those fish have bones. Americans won't eat a fish unless it looks like a white square. Fifty percent of the people who ordered the dish sent it back saying, "There's a bone, there's a bone!" I tried to explain to customers that fish have bones just like people have bones, but still they sent it back. So we took it back and looked at the recipe and Alain made the changes. Egidiana tested every recipe from every chef at Le Cirque; her version is still the best. I think she almost cried when I told her we were going to change the bouillabaisse. But she worked on it too—she added the things Americans like—lobster and shrimp. They worked to get the changes right but to keep the essence. Is the bouillabaisse as authentic Marseilles as I would like? No. Did we make the right decision to change it? Yes!

DAVID BOULEY *French food then was heavy. So heavy people thought they would have to exercise afterward! It was killing the cuisine and it killed the restaurants. Sirio has the power to make a chef bend to his will and let go of all the givens. He knows that, if you don't alter the cuisine, it dies.*

And this is the point—that Alain was willing to take a dish that was so famous in France and work with it so that it became palatable to American tastes. And that's why today it is on so many menus in America. That's what the Le Cirque philosophy is. I am here to prevent the chef from murdering the waiter who brings back the bouillabaisse. The tradition had always been that the chef was right no matter what. When people sent food back the chef would say, "Why did they send it back? This is perfect! My dish!" Instead of making a change, he chose to create a drama or to kill the waiter. "No, I won't prepare it again—this has never happened in any restaurant! Tell the waiter not to come in the kitchen again!" Sailhac never did this. He would take the dish, fix it, send it out, and have someone take it off the bill. Later we would go back and look at the menu. And because we changed the mentality in the kitchen, we started to change the world.

> ALAIN DUCASSE *Sirio is a revolutionary. He, Craig Claiborne, and Pierre Franey are the people who really changed food in America. American chefs would not exist without Sirio. Why? Because the food of today is the food of the customer first, and the food of a country second. Sirio was the first person to do that.*

Changing the mentality, breaking down the wall between the kitchen and the dining room, has always been the biggest obstacle. Changing the mentality of the dining room staff had to be part of that. Joe Garni, who had worked with me at the Colony, came to Le Cirque to manage the waiters so he was maybe what people of the old school would call a captain, but I hate using that term to explain who he was. At Le Cirque you have waiters. Joe came to Le Cirque and I had great respect for him, he was very popular, but sometimes he spent too much time with people, either when they came in and were waiting or just at the table. That was the old way. Finally, I said to him, "Joseph, you cannot stay at a table that long. Never mind five minutes—two minutes is a long time when everybody's looking at you."

You have to open your eyes, you have to be great with people. There's Renato, Egidiana's uncle. You know I think he has been in this country forty-five years and he still knows very little English. But he was great at the door. People loved him because he was real. Of course, Renato is Renato, and he loved gambling! He couldn't speak any English and he wouldn't remember what someone ate the day before, but he knew the name of the mother of some horse that ran at Belmont, and the grandmother too! Sometimes I think the secret to the success of Le Cirque was that every Whitney and Payne came in to Renato for advice on the horses!

Sometimes a customer would say to me, "Isn't it funny that you have a man who speaks no English but knows all about the races?" and I would just say, "The important thing here is he *wins* the races! That's why he works at Le Cirque." ◄◄

KIDS, WINE, AND
CRÈME BRÛLÉE

SIRIO HAD PLANNED on paying off his debt to Jean Vergnes within three years but worried that it might take him much longer. Instead, within two years of taking on Le Cirque on his own he cleared his debt to Vergnes and paid off the original note from 1973. For the Maccionis it was an enormous step. On their annual trips home to Montecatini, Sirio and family had squeezed into the apartment he had bought in the 1960s or used friends' houses. Alberto and Guido continued to live in the original family home and the two had offered to sell Sirio their shares of it to modernize it for his own brood.

Sirio and Egi had something else in mind. They bought a nineteenth-century villa facing the town's central park—the swankiest address in town—and proceeded to employ every master stonemason and architect in Italy to make it a Maccioni showplace. The house, traditional on the outside, is a tour de force of modern engineering on the inside. The building was virtually dismantled and lifted to make room for an underground world of wine cellars, garages, storage rooms—and the foundations necessary to allow the house above to have two rooms with no internal support columns. The result was a room with a giant wall that is closed most of the time to create a formal dining room, but can be opened to include the professional kitchen—a functional showplace for Egidiana's cooking. When Sirio's dinner parties swell, as they always do, the house can easily feed 100 for dinner. If guests need accommodations as well, both La Pace and the Croce di Malta are a few minutes walk away and function as the Maccioni family guesthouses.

The subterranean work also included construction of a sixty-foot swimming pool that forms the villa's front yard. Also included in the substructure are the pumps to keep the thermal waters of Montecatini at bay. From the pool you can see the Palladian red tile arches that form the roof of the Torretta Spa popping over the tall hedges and you can hear the orchestras that entertain the spa patrons, still sipping the waters. Sirio often calls the mayor to ask him to turn down the volume.

In New York, the Maccionis moved to a modern apartment building on East Sixty-fourth Street, where they bought two apartments, one on top of the other, and had them arranged so that Egi could cook there either for herself and their three children, or for thirty. Sirio's room was placed downstairs and in the back to accommodate his unusual schedule.

While Sirio remained more proud than he'd ever care to admit that he now had the physical symbols of wealth and privilege—houses, cars, and wines—it was in his children that he and Egi invested the most. Sirio insisted on sending them to the best private schools: Mario to a program for gifted children at Hunter College High School, Marco and Mauro to Loyola, in the hope that they would all do the one thing a Maccioni had not yet done: go to college.

W HEN WE WERE ON SIXTY-SECOND STREET, there was a synagogue nearby that had a preschool, and so when Mario was four
or five years old he went to the synagogue. One day I was at home in the
afternoon trying to sleep and Mario came in with a little hat on his head
and I suddenly realized I was sending my son to a Jewish school. I said to
Egidiana, "Let's start over, we are Catholic; he should go to a Catholic
school." She got very angry at me and told me it wasn't a Jewish school but
nonsectarian. So I went to the restaurant and asked what "nonsectarian"
meant, and someone told it meant that my son would be around many different people with different religions, and I thought this was very good. I
think it also maybe saved my marriage!

MICHAEL LOMONACO *They were normal, what I'd call New York
City kids. Mario would come to Brooklyn and we'd do stupid things
kids do, play ball in the street. I guess the only real difference was
that Egi would come out with the kids and hang out with the
Palmieris and cook and do everything like our mothers did, but her
kids spoke Italian—I mean, like Italians—and then go back to
sounding like American kids.*

Mario went to St. David's School after the synagogue and it was nonsectarian too. There were people there of every religion and that is my
philosophy—you are what you are. Later on he married a Jewish girl, who
I think I love more than him! I told my son, "You want to marry Lauren—
fine—she is a good girl. You know my grandmother may be turning in her
grave in Italy, because she would like you to have a nice Tuscan girl, but
they are terrible—so sarcastic, like men!" I mean, we Tuscans are the
worst race in Italy—but when we want to do something we do it. I wanted
my sons to be educated, to have everything, but to be nice people. Maybe
they are too nice! I mean look. The Borgias and the Medicis created the
Renaissance, but they were *not* nice people! ◄◄

TERRANCE BRENNAN *What I remember about Sirio's children was that they were just good kids. Their parents were very strict and they'd come to the restaurant when they were young, but I think the only thing that made you think they were any different was that when they came they had perfect suits, velvet jackets, and expensive ties ... just like their father.*

WITH THE KITCHEN producing food close to how Sirio dreamed it could be, it was time to turn his attention to something that had bothered him since he'd arrived in America—dessert. Even in the relative poverty of Sirio's upbringing, dessert was a feature of daily life. While American dessert culture celebrated domesticity—freshly baked chocolate chip cookies and apple pies baked by rosy-cheeked mothers in farmhouse kitchens—European households, even in the most remote areas, celebrated dessert as the one thing that was done mostly out of the home. In some areas of New York City, immigrants had brought with them the idea of the pastry shop, but by the time Le Cirque had opened in 1974, it was already in its dying phase. Sirio was baffled that there wasn't a pastry shop at every corner, and even more baffled by the strange conglomeration of dessert concepts in American restaurants.

At the time, pastry chefs in New York restaurants were a rare breed. Like *sauciers,* they worked whenever the restaurant didn't, arriving in the wee hours of the morning, or during the day, and leaving, usually for another restaurant, during service hours. For its first five years Le Cirque shared the same pastry chef as all New York restaurants of note. He or she would come to the restaurant, make desserts that tended to run in the same range, and lay them all out on a dessert cart to be rolled through the restaurant.

In the Vergnes years, Sirio's partner budged on the pastry issue only, according to Sirio, when Sirio threatened to use his own money to hire one and have the pastry made in his apartment. They settled on a part-time person who could at least make decent soufflés and sorbets. With Sailhac, reluctance to having a pastry chef evaporated, but still there was no space in the kitchen to employ one. Whoever made the desserts would have to work in the restaurant when the rest of the kitchen staff wasn't there.

SIRIO

I T'S THE THING I REMEMBER MOST with my father and my grand-mother. On Sunday my grandmother would go to church very early, so she could come home to make Sunday lunch. When I woke up she'd be cooking, we'd go to church and come back home. Sunday was the day I got to eat more than what I could have during the week. Now I wish I could have more of what then I didn't want so much. *Bollito misto,* fried rabbit, the pig pounded very thin, with wild sage. Then we'd walk to town and go to the pastry shop. On that day we no longer had to just look at the tourists or rich people eating their ice cream or buying a pastry—on that day my sister and I got to pick a pastry ourselves and my father or my grand-mother would pay. Compared to what I know now, I think that maybe the pastry wasn't so good, but then … my god, was it good!

We were not at a very high level with the pastry at Le Cirque. Chefs then and now say, "People don't like dessert." That is absolutely not true. They love it. You finish a good meal with a great dessert and you're happy. You finish a great dinner with a mediocre dessert, you are not happy.

When we opened on Sixty-fifth Street, every restaurant had a dessert cart. It was a game, to see which one was better—the one with three layers or the one with two layers? The silver tray, or a glass lid? I think it was the most disgusting thing that you could do in a restaurant because only the first two people saw everything. There was the *mille-feuille,* the chocolate cake, the fruit tart, the *mousse au chocolat,* the fruit salad with the orange cleaned and cooked in Grand Marnier—very fash-ionable. They were either good or not good, but my point is that, after you started to serve and cut and then you had to look at what was left, you wouldn't want to eat it.

Sailhac had mentioned that he had worked with a German pastry chef called Dieter Schorner whom he liked. I invited him to Le Cirque and offered him a job on the spot but he told me that he couldn't work in the kitchen—there was no space for him. He said, "Build me a space, and you'll have a pastry chef!" And I did. It took two years, but I carved out a space to have a very small pastry department and I called Schorner to have him come back. I think he was a little shocked that I had honored my side of the deal.

Maybe the best thing about Schorner was that he never went anywhere without Francisco Gutierrez, who was his dishwasher—really his assistant. Sailhac wasn't pleased—a pastry chef who had to have his own dishwasher? But I wanted Dieter to have whatever he needed and the deal was, Francisco came with Dieter. The funny thing was, when they both got to Le Cirque, I don't think Francisco ever washed a dish again—we had plenty of people to do that. Francisco is still here—he is the longest-serving Le Cirque employee!

Of course, everybody was in love with Dieter Schorner. He gave me all the things I had wanted, soufflés in every flavor, and instead of the chocolate mousse, a cake made from it, which we served with a pot of whipped cream, just a little stiff so you could eat it with a fork. He did one that was white chocolate, which can be too sweet, almost too greasy, and layered it with dark chocolate. And tarts, just perfect tarts, lemon meringue and one with pine nuts, caramelized. But like all chefs, he was a schizophrenic, too! You know, the sugar gets into the brain!

DIETER SCHORNER *I was amazed that a restaurateur would go through the trouble to create a space for the pastry. Especially for Sirio, where every inch counted. I used to joke with him that I thought when he took out the dessert cart that the space in the dining room would go to make a bigger pastry department, but instead it went to put in more tables.*

Dieter got the basic things I wanted—good cakes, tarts, and pastry—very quickly. In pastry, maybe it's the other way around—80 percent fantasy, 20 percent reality—but no matter what you do, it makes people happy. He would do *oeufs à la neige,* meringues really, but so simple and so easy to make dramatic. To me the most perfect dessert is maybe a pear poached in red wine with spices and cream. Dieter did a poached pear, but filled with raspberries, very simple, resting in a bowl with a shell of praline and instead of the wine it was an Armagnac sauce. You brought it to a table and people gasped. You have to remember, my whole life as a waiter in this country, you could do a flambé of anything and people would say, "My god, this is good." But you could flambé their handkerchief and they would say the same thing. ◄◄

SIRIO'S NOW CAREFULLY CRAFTED RELATIONSHIP with the press had directed attention toward the latest development at Le Cirque, and within weeks of Schorner's arrival, his creations were beginning to get almost as much attention from diners and the media as from the restaurant's famous clientele. Every competitive restaurant went through hoops to find its own pastry chef and there was a run on the market. By hiring and giving free reign to Schorner, Sirio redefined the role of the pastry chef in American restaurants. What had been an afterthought became a legitimate culinary profession.

The most important dessert of the Schorner period was crème brûlée. Schorner, who went on to become a senior professor at the Culinary Institute of America, was not, however, the person credited with creating—or rather re-creating—it. Sirio makes no claim to having invented the custard crème with a crunchy, not-too-thick, not-too-thin caramelized top. He does, however, take credit where credit is due, for reintroducing the dessert, hiring the most talented man of the era to refine it, and making it the most famous and by far the most popular dessert in restaurants from Paris to Peoria. Restaurants around the world still list the dessert on their menus as Crème Brûlée à la Sirio Maccioni or Crème Brûlée Le Cirque.

T HAT SUMMER I went back to Italy as usual. But it was an unusual summer because Italy was in the World Cup that was being held in Spain. We were all on vacation in the south of France and my sons were driving me crazy to get tickets for the World Cup. I knew it was impossible; besides we were on vacation. But the Italians kept moving up and it looked like they were in a position to win and even I was getting excited. So I called friends in Italy to get tickets, but I failed. And the boys kept saying to me, "Babbo, Babbo, please, don't you know anyone in Spain?" They kept begging so much that finally I called Juan Carlos, very embarrassed. And before I even opened my mouth, his assistant, Christina Barrios, said, "Forget it. Everyone in Italy is calling me!"

So that was that and we put everyone into the car and drove to Vergé's restaurant, Moulin de Mougins. Vergé was having a dinner for me, very nice, very grand, and in the middle of it Roger came up to me, maybe a little annoyed, "Don't try to impress me, there's a man on the phone says he's the King of Spain." And I really don't think he believed it because he brought the phone to the table!

When I picked up the phone, everyone was looking and I thought maybe this was a joke and I said, in my very best tones, "Your Majesty," and Juan Carlos said back to me, "What, are you with some woman? Who are you trying impress? Why don't you call me by my name?" I thought, my god, I've just insulted my friend, so I explained that I was standing in the middle of the room at Moulin de Mougins and that no one believed I was on the phone with him. So he said, "Well, let me speak to them!" And he did.

ROGER VERGÉ *I knew these things about Sirio, but honestly I didn't believe him! And sure enough, there I was speaking to the King of Spain on the telephone inviting him to come for dinner. You learn not to question these things about Sirio.*

When I finally got to speak to Christina again, she said she would get me five tickets to the World Cup match and that there would be rooms waiting for us at the Princess Sofia in Barcelona. The only condition was that we had to come immediately—the match was the next day—and we had to be the guests of the King and come to dinner. It was at the dinner in Barcelona that I first tasted the crème Catalan. I brought it back first to my wife, who did a lot of work on it, and then to Dieter and Francisco. They worked with it, and that became the Crème Brûlée we use to this day. ◂┼▸

DIETER SCHORNER *It was very similar to what I used to make at the Savoy in London, which they called crème reversé. The English used double cream, which had a fat content of up to 45 percent and it was too thick, too rich, in a very shallow dish. A version of the dessert existed actually in the American South, in New Orleans, where you'd get a cup with a crisp top, a petit pot, cooked on the outside but not really on the inside. It was simple, really: the American cream, at 36 percent butterfat, produced a much lighter version of the same dessert. Then I just added a little light brown sugar on top, of excellent quality, and we had it—crème brûlée.*

JACQUES TORRES *[later, Le Cirque pastry chef] When I was learning, we learned about it as "Crème Brûlée à la Sirio Maccioni." When I came to work with him and saw the recipe, he never said that he invented Crème Brûlée. He didn't take the eggs and the sugar and say "Voilà," but in our world you don't need to. He found it, saw how it worked, hired the best person in the world to adjust it the right way—and made it the most popular dessert in the world. To me it is Sirio's dessert because it symbolizes everything about him—how he knows what to look for and how to make it work on the table, not just on the page. He sees food both like a chef and like a waiter.*

ANOTHER AREA IN WHICH Sirio staked out new territory was wine. From the moment he arrived in New York, it was one of the skills that separated him from his colleagues. The standard for all wines purchased in restaurants was automatically French. As part of his training at the Plaza-Athénée, which had one of the world's great wine cellars, he had to have a mastery of the major regions of wine production in France—Bordeaux and Burgundy. When he opened his own restaurant, he championed Italian wine and wine makers. It was an uphill battle, since the popular image of Italian wines was either sickly sweet Asti spumante or pallid Chiantis in bottles that came in baskets. Most of the good Italian wine stayed in Italy.

The wine cellar at Le Cirque was part of the building's prior life as an apartment hotel. There had been not only a 25,000-bottle wine cellar for the hotel, locked like a bank vault, but individual cellars for the larger apartments in the building. Sirio was able to take over these spaces as the units became unoccupied and proceeded to fill them up. By 1980, Sirio had enough wine cellar space for 65,000 bottles. He also had the acumen and clout to cultivate wineries not just in Italy but around the world, mostly by taking large quantities of their wine and selling it at, usually, more moderate prices than their French competitors.

When Antinori brought out its now fabled Tignello in 1979, the entire first vintage, from 1971, was sent to Le Cirque—and Sirio, ever faithful, always managed to have a bottle somewhere in the background when photographs were being taken in the restaurant. At the same time, Sirio also cultivated lesser-known and less expensive wines from other regions in France. As with the regular menu, Sirio was adamant that the wine menu should have the best, most expensive wines as well as the best, most affordable ones. Sirio was not only the gatekeeper and visionary at his restaurant, he was also its sommelier. If he wasn't there, there were only a few senior waiters who could offer advice. Only Sirio and Frank knew the combination to the wine vault.

Knowing that he knows more about wine, especially Italian wine, gives Sirio more pleasure than actually drinking it. On the rare occasions when he does drink he, like many Italians, takes a sip, then either adds water, or nurses the glass all evening.

W HEN I FIRST CAME TO AMERICA I was very grateful for the "three martini lunch": by the time they ordered wine they couldn't taste anything anyway. What amazed me was that everyone asked for these very old, very expensive bottles, which many times were not good. Wine is all in the mind. I hate wine snobs. I'm a wine snob, but in a good way. I crushed grapes with my feet when I was a child. We didn't have great wine at our house, but we knew how to make it, which wine was good and which was bad, which wine you kept, and which you sold.

Wine in Tuscany is part of life. Even when you're a little baby, you have wine sometimes instead of water, which maybe explains some things about me. When you live on a farm, you get used to using every part of the grapes. We used the skin of the grapes to make grappa, we put the must into barrels and aged it the way my grandfather learned from his grandfather. A bottle of wine was something that came from the farm, like everything else.

So my view of wine is very simple, and very complex. All the great Italians who make wine—Antinori, Frescobaldi, Gaja, many others—are farmers first, then wine makers. It's hard work. Maybe I like wine because to make it you have to be more like an artist, you have to open yourself to the weather, the soil, the air. You have to be a great artist and I could never be so free. Everything else about wine, which is really the marketing of the wine, I have a great distaste for.

Why does everyone only concentrate on what wine costs, instead of what it tastes like? Like truffles, everyone always asks me, "How much are the truffles?" and I always say, "Priceless." It's the same with wine, "What is the most expensive bottle of wine that you have?" I always say, "The one that is in front of you." If you don't look at the price, then you open your mind to the taste, and the smell of great wine and food.

MARCHESE FRESCOBALDI *Without Sirio I don't know that we would have had a market to sell Italian wines to America.*

When I go to the wine shows, I'm always happy to taste the Petrus, but—honestly?—one Petrus tastes very much like another. Only a few people really know the difference. I want to try what is new, what is different. But when you look at something new you also have to know whether it will be around six months from now.

ANGELO GAJA *When I met Sirio, people didn't know Gaja. People in Italy would say, "No you can't make this wine this way," but Sirio would say, "Try it, and I'll take all the production." The wines were fantastic and he got them all! For a while, Le Cirque was the only place where you could find them.*

What we did in the 1980s really, with the help of Marvin Shanken, who had started the *Wine Spectator,* was to tell people that wine had changed. For $500 you could buy the greatest wine. I mean really—the greatest. So you say, "Ah, $500, that is expensive!" but in those days a bottle of '47 Cheval-Blanc, probably kept badly in someone's closet, or a '29 Lafitte, would sell for $1000 or more, and were very rare, and not always so good. There was an emphasis on age at a time when the technology made many great wines available at a much better price. And then there were the much, much less expensive wines. The original Chianti was all one grape, but they knew that to sell it to Americans it had to be smoother, so they added cabernet to the blend. It changed, but it was still very good. Really, very quickly, you could get a very good wine, from almost anywhere—France, Italy, Spain, Chile, Australia, and California—and know it would be very drinkable, and pay not so much money. ⤛⤙

THE LADIES AND MEN
OF LE CIRQUE

Y THE FALL OF 1981 Le Cirque was the most famous restaurant in the world. Some even thought it the most delicious. One critic in particular, *The New York Times*'s Mimi Sheraton, still felt otherwise.

Alain Sailhac had been at the stove almost two years before Sheraton, who had awarded him four stars while he was at Le Cygne in 1977, decided it was time to revisit Le Cirque. Her critique of Sailhac at Le Cirque, published in May 1980, read like a frustrated schoolmarm who can only concentrate on her pet student's failure to learn his multiplication tables fast enough. While praising some dishes—the bouillabaisse, for example ("beautiful ... with generous amounts of fish ... raised to sublime heights by a hefty, garlic-perfumed rouille")—she couldn't resist a critical barb when discussing nearly every dish. For instance, in talking about a *ris de veau cevennois*—sweetbreads with sliced cèpes and chestnuts—she wrote that it "illustrates Alain Sailhac's tendency to overdo his creations. The sweetbreads and wild mushrooms complimented each other perfectly, but the chestnuts added an unnecessary, cloying sweetness." In the end she raised Le Cirque's rating from one star to two. Her student's previously perfect instincts, she seemed to be arguing, were being clouded by the owner. Whether Sailhac's failure to raise Le Cirque's star status "has to do with the increased number of customers he cooks for, the particular style and size of the menu demanded by the owner, or the clientele," she insinuated, "is a question too complicated to answer here." Sheraton saved only a paragraph to describe her distaste for a restaurant that, she said, had a "tendency to fawn over celebrities and regulars, while giving unknowns the cold shoulder." Sirio thought this comment in particular was rich, given that she was one of the ones being fawned over. Still, this time he kept his mouth pretty much shut. Sheraton may have won a small battle. Sirio knew he was winning the war.

Nancy Reagan was already a Le Cirque regular by the time her husband became president. She had been brought to the restaurant originally by society figure Jerome Zipkin, who ate there as often as three or four times a week. Zipkin was legendarily disagreeable, although at Sirio's he was—more or less—as tame as a lion. To Sirio, Zipkin's frequently caustic comments were a breath of fresh air in the normally polite social repartee of the restaurant, even when Sirio himself was the subject under attack. Zipkin, along with about 250 other regulars, still kept private accounts with Sirio, although Zipkin had a little routine about the state of his expenditures. According to columnist Liz Smith, he would rage about the cost of the truffles or whatever treat Sirio had sent out, until the owner came by, whereupon the two would engage in some old-fashioned horse trading, which usually ended with Sirio offering to reduce the price of the offending item, or taking it off the bill. In fact, Sirio never reduced anything and never took anything off the bills, and they were always paid immediately. It was just part of Sirio and Zipkin's shtick.

Zipkin brought many more of the Reagans' inner circle—Mrs. Reagan's friends Betsy Bloomingdale and Claudette Colbert, for example—to Le Cirque. He also helped solidify Sirio's relationships with friends of the Reagans' who had been coming to Le Cirque from the beginning, such as Mr. and Mrs. Walter Annenberg and the Forbes family. In the almost imperial Reagan era, New Yorkers were shocked when the President decided to come to dinner, like a normal person, with his wife, at Le Cirque. The evening, shortly after his first inauguration on March 14, 1981, finally pushed Le Cirque over the edge in terms of hype. It was the new society's equivalent of Truman Capote's 1966 Black and White Ball at the Plaza.

SIRIO

WHEN I SAW REAGAN at his inaugural ball, he screamed across the room that he was going to come for dinner, but I don't think anyone paid attention. But then he must have thought I didn't hear him, so one of his people brought me over to him—and everyone saw that—and he told me again he was coming for dinner but that I must keep it a secret. And I said, "Mr. President, you just told everybody!"

Of course, everyone knew he was coming to see his son's last performance at the Joffrey Ballet, and since everyone knew the date, they started begging me for invitations. Everyone wanted the table right next to them. People came to the restaurant to talk to me about it, to try to offer me money, some very important people even tried to threaten me! All this for a dinner at 10:30 at night!

PAMELA FIORI *[editor, **Town and Country** magazine] There was something very Republican about Le Cirque in the 1980s. The money was big, the hair was big, and the jewels were big. It was ironic that in an era where everything was so big, America's elite chose to eat in a place so small—but that was part of the fun of it.*

Days before, the First Lady stopped in to select a menu and choose the wine. It wasn't expensive. They didn't eat big. She ate salad and asparagus, and chicken with nothing on it and he liked fish, usually flounder or sole, with a very little crust. It was the wines I remember. They chose a very inexpensive white Italian wine, Galestro, a new style from Tuscany, because she knew I was from there. And they had a little champagne to start, and nothing more.

I had had to deal with security before. Every president from almost every country it seems had been there, but it was nothing like this. The hotel was checked, every room, and the entire block was closed. You couldn't walk down the street without being checked. Everyone's limousines were parked along the whole block, row after row of them. I remember Mauro, who I don't think was even ten years old yet, saying that the street looked black. The funny thing was, Reagan himself only had two bodyguards. Niarchos used to have more than that! And [Ferdinand] Marcos came with eight and [Anastasia] Somoza with twelve! They brought Reagan through the front entrance, but security needed to check the room again, so he was in the back near the kitchen where I had my three sons waiting to greet him. Reagan, always very kind, said to me, "Sirio, your boys should be in school in the morning. Let's take a picture together before all this starts." So we did—it was very nice, they always thought of the family first.

While we were there, a waiter dropped a tray of glasses. It sounded like a bomb or a gunshot, and all the security people went into positions to prevent an attack. Mrs. Reagan just laughed and said to everyone, "That's the problem with all this security! They don't know the difference between a shot and a tray of glasses at Le Cirque! Sirio is the best security we could ever have!" It was funny—and very sad in a way, because a few weeks later Reagan was shot outside that hotel in Washington. After that he sent me the photograph, and wrote, "I'm sincerely sorry it took so long to send these but in the meantime somebody shot me!" ⫷

THE FIRST REAGAN PRESIDENTIAL DINNER at Le Cirque became part of American social history. Sirio had placed the Italian actress and princess, Ira Von Fürstenberg at the coveted table next to the Reagans and Cristina Ferrare, the former model and wife of John Z. DeLorean, directly in front of them. The Reagans dined with their friends Mr. and Mrs. Alfred Bloomingdale, Claudette Colbert, and Jerry Zipkin. To the left, Sirio sat Mr. and Mrs. William F. Buckley. Andy Warhol, who sat three tables away, recorded the event in his diaries. Throughout the room he placed the scions of fashion, art, politics, and finance. Unarguably Le Cirque was a veritable slice of the best of New York life. And New York being the center of an increasingly inter-national world, Sirio became its de facto social arbiter.

If it had been difficult to obtain a reservation at Le Cirque without knowing Sirio, now it required having his home phone number. When Mimi Sheraton's third *Times* review finally raised Le Cirque's rating to three stars in December 1981, it only made the situation worse. She described being in the restaurant when Governor Hugh Carey and his wife dropped in at 8:30 without a reservation and how all of the other swells had to adjust to make room. "It is understandable, then, why the occasional customer is relegated to the back of the room and why those who spend a great deal of money at Le Cirque several times a week get the best tables. But it is still too bad that some of the most crammed-in tables exist at all."

The issue of the numbers of tables in the tiny space had haunted Sirio from the beginning. A space designed for twenty tables was now regularly using forty. Sirio's team didn't have to worry about taking them away. They were always full. His own desire to see lots of powerful, beautiful, and interesting people bouncing about a tiny room could be read as electric and fun, or it could be read—as some critics continued to imply—as greedy. The advent of the Reagan years made Le Cirque so popular and so famous that soon the restaurant's tiny size became a virtue, although naysayers refused to be silenced.

T HE DIFFERENCE BETWEEN Americans and Europeans is that
  Europeans go to a restaurant because they don't want to cook at
home and they want to have fun, while Americans see dining as entertainment. And because they see dining as entertainment, having the best seat
is very important to them, like when they go to a football match. The person with the most money, the best connection, the best access, gets the
best seat. But in Europe no one applies the same theory to a restaurant. A
restaurant is a restaurant. But from my first days at Delmonico's it was
always, "This is my table, this is my table." The truth is that even back then,
none of us ever thought of a table as someone's property. Tables are just
numbers. Did we think, Table 2, Mr. Niarchos? Not really. That came from
the customer, not us.

I never saved tables for specific people. Not for one person, nobody.
And I got into lots of trouble because I didn't. Of course I saved groups of
tables when I knew I was going to have our people, or famous people, or
people I decided I liked on a particular night, to dress the room. It was the
patrons, not me, who decided this table was good, that one was bad, that
the back was bad—some people liked the back! It was a tiny room, and
you could see everyone anyway. It was all so silly. Really, the only "bad"
tables were behind the three columns in the middle of the room. To be
behind them was not so good and I'd do my best to move people.

Still, some people thought they had a table. There were Mr. and Mrs.
Schneider, who came to the restaurant every night for twenty-two years.
And everyone said, "Oh, that's the table of Mr. and Mrs. Schneider." They
were great. They were like part of the staff. If I wasn't there, they'd give
me a report when I came back of who was there, what had gone wrong,
what people were saying. But Mr. and Mrs. Schneider came to dinner at
5:30, they were gone by 7:30 and then it became someone else's table. If
Mr. Zeckendorf was coming, I tried to save him the table he liked—but
come on, he helped put me in business, and if anyone could say he "has a
table" at Le Cirque, it would be him and him alone! And yet he's a businessman, and if for some reason he walked by and the table wasn't there

for him, I don't think for a moment that he'd be angry that he didn't get his table. He's too smart.

We do what we can. But when people begin to think they have a particular table, I change it. The only time I remember promising a table got me into a lot of trouble. Swifty Lazar, the famous Hollywood agent, said to me he was having a very important lunch and had to have the table in the corner. So I said yes. A few days later, I got a call from John Fairchild, who was the publisher of *Women's Wear Daily* and *W*—and who only came to lunch at Le Cirque. He said *he* was having a very important lunch, and could I save the corner table? I said I'd be delighted to take his reservation, but that I would not promise a particular table. He threatened me, saying he would never come back to the restaurant. I said, "I'm very sorry to hear that." The next day at lunch, I seated Swifty Lazar at the corner table he had requested, and when I got back to door, Fairchild was standing there. He had come to have lunch with Mr. Lazar. They had both called about the same table, and I'd given it to one, and not the other, and Fairchild knew. Bad. Very, very bad. I wished I could have disappeared.

I never, never did it again. Unless of course for security for a president and even then I just showed them a part of the room and said, "Here." ◄◄

AT WHICH TABLE to place which president? And what to feed them? A poor farm boy from Montecatini should only have such problems. Sirio had come a long way. Slim Aarons, who'd captured many of the century's most interesting, powerful, or beautiful people on film, staged the perfect Sirio shot—the image that captured Sirio's essence forever. Under the caption "Host at High Noon, Sirio of Le Cirque," *Town and Country,* September 1981, put its selection of the world's most beautiful and powerful women seated in a row along a banquette in Le Cirque, with Sirio lying on the table in front of them. They were Mrs. Lauren Peltz, Mrs. Frank Gifford, Mrs. Robert Fairchild, Mrs. Roger Penske, Mrs. Donald Trump, Muffie Bancroft, Mrs. Roone Arledge, Mrs. Robert Sarnoff (Anna Moffo), Mrs. John Z. DeLorean, Marie Kimberly, Mrs. John Kluge, Mrs. Pete Rozelle, and the Countess Enrico Carimati di Carimate.

If there could ever be said to be a moment when Sirio was at his happiest, and his handsomest, it was in this photo. His only complaints? The room wasn't large enough to contain all the women that Sirio had asked to sit in the photo, and that the published version did not include his wife or his three sons.

The women in the photograph were only representative of a far larger group, what Sirio calls lovingly, "the ladies of Le Cirque." They represented New York's, and to a large extent the world's, aristocracy. They were women with powerful husbands, ex-husbands, or deceased husbands. They were women who were powerful in their own right, working women who were conquering industries and breaking class boundaries. They were artists, writers, singers, dancers, and designers. They were women who were models or beauties, amongst them: Cindy Adams, Mrs. Vincent Astor (Brooke), Alexandra de Borchgrave, Christie Brinkley, Mrs. Clifton Daniel (Margaret Truman), Anne Eisenhower, Mrs. Ahmet (Mica) Ertegun, Anne Ford, Charlotte Ford, Mrs. Winston Guest (C. Z.), Mrs. Reinaldo Herrera (Caroline), Bianca Jagger, the Princess Yasmin Kahn, Mrs. Thomas Kempner (Nan), Mrs. Henry Kravis (Carolyn Roehm), Estée Lauder, Gina Lollobrigida, Sophia Loren, Elle Macpherson, Alice Mason, Princess Grace of Monaco, Jacqueline Onassis, Mrs. Milton Petrie (Carol), Paige Powell, Lee Radziwell, Mrs. Abe Ribicoff (Casey), Mrs. Cliff Robertson (Dina Merrill), Diana Ross, Beverly Sills, Liz Smith, Mrs. Carl Spielvogel (Barbaralee Diamonstein), Arianna Stassinopolous, Pauline Trigère, Mrs. Trump (Blaine), Gloria Vanderbilt, Barbara Walters, Raquel Welch, and Lynn Wyatt.

There was another group of women—ones who did not have famous names—who were in some ways even more powerful in the restaurant; they were women Sirio had known over a lifetime, who for some reason or another he had become fond of, listened to, or admired. They were the ones who, with an unseen cue from Sirio, were treated with the utmost care and discretion, and who were never sent a bill. Sirio loved all of these women with a kind of affection that was and remains unique to Sirio because a part of each and every one of them was a fantasy of a woman he barely remembered.

Le Cirque seemed to be equally as comfortable for men in politics. Richard Nixon lived down the street from the restaurant and used Le Cirque as a launching pad for his social and political rehabilitation. His later stature as a dignified elder statesmen and foreign policy expert was honed largely with the restaurant's regular clientele of influential politicians and their network of wealthy donors and media connections. It was not uncommon to see Nixon huddled in conversation with former members of his administration, including Henry Kissinger, or key figures in the administrations of almost every subsequent president. Gerald Ford was a regular guest, but in this apparent bastion of Republican power, Jimmy Carter also frequently ate, sometimes unannounced.

It wasn't just the American presidents. A slew of international politicians made Le Cirque their home away from home. Canadian Prime Minister Pierre Trudeau was a regular patron, as was his estranged wife, "always at separate ends of the restaurant," Sirio says. Later on Brian Mulroney dined at Le Cirque so often that he found it easier to have his personal mail sent there. Nancy Reagan brought British Prime Minister Margaret Thatcher, on her frequent jaunts to New York. Then there was Imelda Marcos— before, during, and after her husband's fall from power. In some ways more important were the policy advisors, campaign managers, and lawyers for all the politicians, such as Reagan's front man Charles Wick and Roy Cohn, who claimed not only his own table at Le Cirque, but his own jar of mayonnaise. Not to mention New York Governor Hugh Carey, Senator (and former Governor of Connecticut) Abe Ribicoff, and all the mayors of New York.

All were regular customers of Le Cirque, and by regular, at least to Sirio, that meant at least once a week, regardless of their status. Sirio's job was to coddle them without being sycophantic. For many of the most powerful people in the world he was the perfect confidant. Better than a hairdresser, because you didn't have that much time to speak with him. More fun, because you could eat and drink with him. Ideal, because he knew everyone they might be talking about—in most cases personally. It wasn't so much that the powerful could trust Sirio. They did, but the trust went both ways. It was a mutually beneficial relationship. It was more that in the whirlwind pace of modern life, Le Cirque and Sirio were somehow, inexplicably, safe.

SIRIO

I WORKED HARD to get where I got to, and maybe it's everything and maybe it's nothing, but it wasn't easy. And I try to play by the rules, but I'm not very good at rules. I think that people who get somewhere don't always play by the rules. If they are bad, I don't like it. But I always like people who have personality, a style, a sense of themselves, and don't lie. I like businessmen, but not the stuffy ones. I like when they laugh, when Reagan thumps me on the shoulder and says, "My boy, my boy." I like Trump, who was little, then big, then little again after making a big mistake, but never lost his style, and he told the truth. I like them when they are young and I like them when they are old. I like them when they're famous and I like them when they're not so famous. The ones I like best are troublemakers in some way. Maybe that's why all those ladies come to me for lunch. I think every single one is really a nice troublemaker. But always the best kind of trouble, the best kind of people!

BILL BLASS *At lunch, women went to Le Cirque and men went to the Four Seasons. It was really that simple. At dinner, everyone went to Le Cirque. The Le Cirque crowd was the dressy, fun crowd. They'd have a drink and a smoke. What was really critical was that the best of everybody from so many different worlds collided there. Business people, media people, fashion people, power people, society people. I went there because, frankly, who wants to spend all their time with people in their own industry? Women are my business. Norell wouldn't have given a shit whether Babe Paley was wearing one of his creations or not to lunch. I did. It's important if you're designing for women to see where women go.*

MRS. WILLIAM F. BUCKLEY *We were all very close friends: Claudette, Nancy, Betsy.... It was just that at that particular time all of our lives were more or less in one place, New York. We liked each other and we liked Le Cirque! So that's where we were.*

ALAIN SAILHAC *Saturday lunch, especially. I'd go out just to look at them. You've never seen so many beautiful women in one room. We'd do 175 lunches, on a Saturday in the summer! All those women! It was electric.*

I think, in my mind, I imagine myself with every one of them. I'm a Tuscan, can you blame me? You know, most of the time, the women go to the bathroom, or are late, or whatever, and I talk to the man. I never sit down. Never. Life is already too complicated. But many times we do get talking and I get very upset about politics. I am not a political man. Please. I know too much about politics to be political. And I know too much about history. So when I had these people in the restaurant many became friends. Nixon, Carter, Kissinger, and, later, Giuliani.

When the Slim Aarons picture came out in *Town and Country* Nixon sent me a note, saying, "You will find that the most truly 'beautiful people' are those who are your friends, not just because you're on top, but because of their loyal personal affection for you." I kept that letter in my wallet for a long time.

I helped Nixon because I liked him. I am Italian. Watergate was not good, but it was nothing like what we had in Italy. Seeing the Americans suffer so much was more difficult to watch. To me it was a small scandal in the scheme of things, perpetrated by someone insecure, but not evil. He started to come to the restaurant after he was president. I don't think I had met him before, although he once told me we had met at the Colony. I can only judge him from how I knew him, and what I knew of him was that he was a good man. He cared for his family, his daughters and his wife. These were the things I saw, and that is what's important. He knew the dates of my wife's, my children's birthdays, better than I did. He would stay, or come in early, and we would gossip about politics, the situation in the Middle East. I came to think that he was a very intelligent man, and that you have to learn not to believe everything the world tells you about some people, especially the press.

> PETER DUCHIN *Sirio would go for someone like Nixon. He has a natural attraction to the underdog, the socially or politically insecure. He doesn't want to cross the line and he knows exactly where the line is. Did Nixon like him? Of course, but Nixon also wanted a table. Kissinger likes him too, but he also likes that kind of attention. If you're one of those guys, who wouldn't? Those guys felt comfortable because Sirio knew how to make them feel comfortable.*

> BILL BLASS *Those guys loved him. He spoke their language. And Sirio loved them. What restaurateur wouldn't want the president, every president, to come to their restaurant?*

I helped arrange the first public reunion of President Nixon with Kissinger. I said to Nixon, "Invite him for lunch," and he looked at me with this face. I told him, "You want to do something, you need a little help, you pick up the phone, and you call him." It was a great feeling to see these two men come together again, in a place I created. It's what I do. You have to have a little part of each world. Politics, fashion, sex, arts, and something a little rough. You can't have a party of all white people, or all black people, all the same people. It's putting different people together that's fun. And I never introduce people, I never say, "Oh, here is someone you should meet." You put everyone next to each other and there's an energy.

> HENRY KISSINGER *Nixon and I had spoken over the years, but we went to the restaurant separately. He had a special place when he came in, just to the right, so I was seated further down the wall. Then once, Nixon suggested we have lunch together and go to Le Cirque because he wanted to be seen by a lot of people having that lunch. He also knew that, while it would attract attention, people would leave us alone. The meal was all very carefully arranged, so that we would be seen in the restaurant, and walking out together. Sirio handled it perfectly.*

Sometimes when you get more successful or more famous, the people who work with you don't understand your real mentality. They read the papers and they have an image of who you are, and they execute decisions they think are yours. They protect you too much. One time when I wasn't there, my staff turned away Woody Allen for not having a jacket and it wound up on the front page of the *New York Post*!

Another time, I came in to work and a waiter told me that the hotel had tried to send in a guest but he was not allowed into the restaurant because he was not dressed properly. I looked in the book, saw the name Cappa, then went into the hotel and asked at the desk who Mr. Cappa was. The girl pointed into the lobby at a very rough-looking tall man who was sitting with a beautiful woman and these children. He didn't look so bad. So I went over to introduce myself and he said, "So you're the guy who won't let me in?" We talked for a minute, and I thought he was interesting. He was a musician from Los Angeles, and he had very long hair. I apologized for the problem with the jackets and he said, "So let me get this right, I have to put on a jacket and a tie to try this crème brûlée?" I told him to make another reservation, thinking, honestly, that he wouldn't and sent up four crèmes brûlées to his room.

The next day his wife comes to make a reservation. I said to the staff, "Oh my god, I don't want another scene, just let him in and put him somewhere where people can't see." But he came in looking very elegant, with a beautiful suit and a tie that we gave him. He said to me, "This better be the best fucking meal of my life—I've toured the Kremlin, met the Pope, and I've never needed a suit. If I don't like this meal, you're paying for the suit!" Of course he liked the meal, and we got to talking about everything—politics mostly, communism. He'd been on several trips to Russia, he'd been everywhere. Everywhere except Italy!

When I got home that night I asked my sons if they had ever heard of a singer called Cappa who had long hair and was a bit like a revolutionary and very funny. I thought my sons were going to throw me out the window. His name wasn't Cappa, it was Zappa, with a Z, Frank Zappa, and although I still didn't recognize the name, he was very famous. I just thought he was very intelligent. My sons told me his kids had funny names and that they were waiting to see him that same night on a television show.

When he came on, he was wearing the same suit and the tie, and the interviewer, Mr. Letterman, said, "Nice tie," and Mr. Zappa told the whole story of how he had gone to Le Cirque and I made him wear the suit and tie. At the end he said, "The best thing about this restaurant is that they let you keep the tie!" I laughed and laughed. He became, really, my best friend. He came to the house on Sunday with his children who had those funny names I can't remember. And he sent me all his records. I tried to listen to them, but the words didn't make sense to me. I had my sons read me the lyrics, but I still didn't really get them, except for "Catholic girls, with the tiny little mustache."

After that I always called him Mr. Frank Zappa, because he thought it was so funny. I tell you, he was a great American. I don't think I ever laughed so hard as when we were together. He always told me about the trouble he got into with everyone—the music people, the media, politics. Yes, I think I liked him because he was always in trouble! ◄◄

LIKE MOST THINGS having to do with Sirio, his relations with his clients and employees are based mostly on his concept of family. Allowing a cook time off for a personal problem or getting him the best ingredients money could buy are both part of creating a giant family in Sirio's mind.

Sirio's brand of paternalism is also fiercely competitive. One day a notice went up in the Le Cirque kitchen inviting a group of the kitchen staff to compete against their colleagues from Lutèce in a ski race at Hunter Mountain in the Catskills, where both Sirio and André Soltner had chalets. A few weeks before, Sirio had bragged to Soltner that he had learned to ski from none other than Zeno Colo. As a boy growing up in the mountains of Alsace, a good part of it on skis, Soltner was suitably impressed. The men agreed to race, one on one. Soltner tells the story that Sirio called the night before their duel to say he was stuck in the restaurant, that he was tired, that he'd had a bad weekend and certainly wouldn't be up to his top form. In fact Sirio had been up at Hunter for days practicing. Soltner went to

Hunter late that Saturday and when he woke up the next morning, the first call he got was from Egidiana. Sirio had torn his shoulder practicing. Instead of competing, André wound up driving a very humbled Sirio to the hospital. Still, Sirio wouldn't give up. If he couldn't ski, his kitchen crew would. He posted the notice in the kitchen, hired coaches to help train the cooks, and promised them a week off if they won. It was a replay of Sestriere. The Le Cirque team lost the race.

Sirio's method of running a business has enormous benefits and enormous pitfalls. Kitchen staff, from dishwashers to *sous*-chefs, were invited to his home some Sundays for a dose of Mama Egi's cooking. Anyone single, anyone unhappy, anyone who just didn't want to go home, or more likely those who didn't really have homes, were invited to Sirio's. Many of his staff bought into the idea of Sirio's extended family. Some merely felt obligated to show up. The latter tended to leave quickly and the former stayed, remaining friends of the family once they went on eventually to other restaurants and other families. In fact, Sirio always falls for the talented ones who dream, as Sirio did, of moving onto their own restaurants or businesses. The problem is that Sirio always wants to go on shepherding them through their careers. It can sometimes make for confusing relationships.

Dieter Schorner was one of the first to go. Schorner credits Sirio not only for the most famous dessert and most famous period of his career, but also with finding him a wife. When a partnership deal came up that Schorner wanted to pursue, he went to Sirio and told him about it. Sirio felt betrayed, even though he knew Schorner would have to leave. Sirio just wanted to avert the unhappiness he knew his charge would suffer from the deal he was pursuing. The two split company and Schorner went to Quo Vadis, which, Schorner says, did turn out to be a mistake. Schorner's pride, though, wouldn't allow him to go back to work for Sirio, although the two did eventually make up, and they remain professional friends.

Sailhac's staff were growing up and going onto ventures of their own. After eight years at the helm and tens of thousands of meals, Sailhac, himself, wanted to pursue his dream of teaching. A painful divorce didn't help. Although Sirio always says a change in command is a good thing, when Sailhac said he wanted to leave, Sirio reflexively tried everything to get him to stay, including an all-expense-paid trip around the world and arranging for the best marriage counselors that could be found. Sailhac knew that even Sirio couldn't fix his situation, but he utilized Sirio's skills and influence in the restaurant community to help pave the way for his next moves—a stint at the "21" Club, then as executive chef at the Plaza Hotel when it was run by Ivana Trump whose husband, Donald, had purchased it. Eventually he became the first dean of the French Culinary Institute in New York City. Each step of the way, Sirio was either directly involved or informed. Sailhac was wise. He knew that you could leave Sirio's kitchen, but you could never leave Sirio.

THE TRIUMPH OF
SIMPLICITY

FINDING CANDIDATES TO REPLACE SAILHAC wasn't hard. Sirio knew everyone in the business, and everyone knew him. For the first time in his career he had the time, money, and prestige to find a person who would adhere to his culinary philosophy. Two candidates came to the front burner fairly quickly: Daniel Boulud, who was cooking at the restaurant at the Plaza-Athénée around the corner from Le Cirque (New York's Athénée was the sister of the Paris original), and Christian Delouvier of the restaurant at the new Parker Meridien Hotel on Fifty-sixth Street.

Boulud was just thirty-one years old, but he had a pedigree that included time with Sirio's friend Roger Vergé. Delouvier was what Sirio calls the "best classic French chef I ever met," as reliable as he could hope to get, and talented to boot. Sirio preferred Delouvier's food, but he felt Delouvier might be less pliable than Boulud, and he knew Delouvier would not be happy producing the kind of numbers Sirio expected. He wanted spark from the kitchen, and Boulud promised fireworks. Usually quick to make decisions in the kitchen, Sirio labored over this selection. Might Sailhac be persuaded to stay on? Should someone in Sailhac's kitchen be brought up? Was someone sturdy and dependable like Delouvier really the answer? Negotiations rambled on.

SIRIO

I DON'T HAVE TROUBLE letting go of my staff. They have trouble letting go of me. It's starting the relationship where I get nervous. Maybe I knew that it was time for Sailhac to move on, but I don't think so. I would have liked him to stay. He was the best thing that had happened to Le Cirque and it was hard to see him suffer. At first I really thought the solution was to give him the time off to find a new life and to see new food and new things, but he was smart and he left. I talked to Vergé and Bocuse and Soltner, who are very close to my food philosophy. I always want the simple, which is the most difficult and costly thing to achieve. The food has to be lighter—classic and theatrical all at once. What I really wanted was a cook, not a chef. You want someone who will listen, who knows how to execute, who can manage a kitchen and produce in big numbers. But then, there was lots of new competition and I could get anyone in the world I wanted. Why not reach for the stars? ◀◀

BY THE SPRING OF 1986, "new American cuisine" had arrived. Chefs like Jeremiah Tower at Stars in San Francisco, Larry Forgione at An American Place in New York, and Jonathan Waxman at Jams, also in New York, had triumphed using indigenous American ingredients, with solidly American interpretations: lobster and brioche, red pepper latkes, and pan-seared buffalo steaks, all washed down with bottles of hearty cabernets from the Napa Valley. Barry Wine, the chef at the The Quilted Giraffe in the new pink limestone AT&T Building on Madison Avenue and Fifty-fifth Street, was the epitome of the new style. Arbitrageurs popped the restaurant's signature purses of caviar, wrapped with a hint of gold leaf, into their mouths by the dozen. David Bouley was wowing them with his own version of modernized French cuisine and restaurateur Drew Nieporent had Montrachet, both in the rapidly gentrifying industrial area known as TriBeCa.

Casual American cuisine, with an emphasis on relaxed but professional service, was the mission of Danny Meyer, who had opened Union Square Café. Not far away, at the Gotham Bar & Grill on East Twelfth Street, Alfred Portale was starting to make food that was piled up high on the plate to look like little towers. Drama in food was the new rage, and restaurants as entertainment were a market none of these chefs or entrepreneurs was prepared to leave to Sirio Maccioni alone. Still, no one knew how to produce drama on the plate and in the restaurant better than Sirio Maccioni. He selected Daniel Boulud to be his new executive chef.

When Daniel had arrived from Lyon a few years earlier, he was the chef at the Polo Lounge at the Westbury Hotel, on Madison Avenue. The manager, already taking a cue from Sirio's management style, sent his young chef on a tour of the city's best restaurants. He was told to pay special attention to Sirio. Boulud did, and was impressed. Unlike other figures in the restaurant world, Sirio had a name, a face, something tangible that the young Frenchman found mesmerizing. By the time he was hired by Sirio, Daniel had already spent more than half his life working in the kitchen but he longed to understand the restaurateur's craft. Sirio had already spent more years in restaurants than Daniel had been alive. It was perfect timing for both of them.

While Sirio set about indoctrinating Boulud in the Maccioni philosophy of food and service, Bryan Miller, the new *New York Times* food critic, published his first review of Le Cirque, even though the new chef had not yet started. In his review of September 19, 1986, Miller broke from his predecessors' style by focusing on the restaurant and its owner, as much as the food. Miller wrote, "Le Cirque is something much grander than the sum of its parts. When the world is gray and somber outside, it is still bright and filled with possibilities inside Le Cirque," confirming and celebrating the impossible standard Sirio had set for himself and his restaurant.

ONE OF MANY THINGS I LIKED about Daniel was that he reminded me a little bit of myself when I was young. He was skinny, attractive, talented, ambitious.

Every time you start with a new chef, you have an opportunity to change everything around. With Sailhac we were on top of New York. With Daniel, I wanted to be on top of the world. Really, Daniel was more than just his talent. He had more. I knew he would go wherever I took him.

DANIEL BOULUD *Sirio could have chosen anyone he wanted. It was the most sought after chef position in the world, and he chose me. He could have had much bigger, more famous, more accomplished names. I didn't have any ego, any reputation. I was working very hard to create a name for myself, but it was tough! For him to bring in somebody else with a preconceived idea of being a chef, or worse, being the chef at Le Cirque, with all the ego, would never have worked. I wanted to work for Sirio and let him mold me.*

Daniel came with two very good people, Sottha Kuhn and Marc Poidevan. At the level we're talking about, executive chef, you have to know that the chef cultivates people to do the real work. And much of what made Daniel attractive as a chef came from Sottha. When Daniel cooked a dish, he cooked it with confidence, but he looked to Sottha for approval, because it was Sottha who would execute it. When I hired Daniel I brought them all to Montecatini and we went everywhere: Tuscany, Piemonte. We even cooked a party at Vergé's house in France. Daniel had to go take care of something in France, and while he was there, Mark and Sottha went back to Le Cirque and started to work in the kitchen—long before Daniel even got there. I wanted them both to spend time with Sailhac.

When all this was going on we got the review from Bryan Miller in *The New York Times*. I had explained to Miller that Sailhac was still cooking and that Daniel wasn't even there, but he still wrote the review, which was very good. And I remember talking to Daniel in Paris, who kept saying he would change it—he would get four stars—and I said, let's not change anything for the press, let's change for ourselves and our customers first, and the press last. Of course I encouraged him—I wanted the four stars too—but I thought that Miller's review was the best. ⤛

DANIEL BOULUD *Sirio knows everybody. Le Cirque was famous because Sirio made Le Cirque famous. Sailhac was an accomplished, great chef, but for whatever reason he could not bring the four stars he had got at Le Cygne. I wanted to give that gift to Sirio, and I knew I could.*

GEOFFREY ZAKARIAN *Daniel had an obsession about the stars— like he was going to improve the food. And he did, he's an amazing chef. But there had been nothing wrong with the food before. It's perfectly plausible that there was something wrong with the critic. Sailhac was just a little more conservative and Daniel more cutting-edge. That the* Times *should give Le Cirque one more star for a room you couldn't get into anyway was hardly Sirio's top priority. Sirio was playing with fire and he must have known it. Right away it set up a kind of weird dynamic between the two.*

TO ACHIEVE HIS CULINARY PHILOSOPHY, Sirio had agreed to give Daniel not just Sottha and Marc, the two *sous*-chefs who came with the deal, but two additional *sous*-chefs as well. All were in place before Daniel's actual arrival in the kitchen and all had been taken on the Sirio tour and were indoctrinated in large daily doses in the restaurant. One of Sirio's favorite things to do is to wander into the kitchen before service—or even during service—and ask for something, anything, to eat. It was up to the chefs to dare to try to please their patron. From Sottha's chicken and ginger, to

Marc's plate of baked egg and tomato, Sirio knew that he was finally close to achieving his dream.

Sirio's culinary philosophy—simplicity with theatrical flair—was in fact the most difficult and costly thing to achieve. After a rough few weeks, Daniel delivered in spades. Daniel had been crafting his new menu for months. When he landed in New York, his team hit the ground running. For their first New Year's dinner, Daniel and Sottha created what they called Maine Sea Scallops in Black Tie: plump sea scallops with diamond black truffles from Perigord, which were sliced thin and layered into the scallop like a black-and-white line drawing. The whole concoction was then encased in spinach and surrounded in a light-as-air puff pastry. The dish looked amazingly complicated, but could be prepared hours in advance and baked to order just before serving, with just a hint of a light sauce of butter, vermouth, and truffle juice.

Daniel matched Sirio's hours, changed something when his master yelled, hung on to his every word, and studied as best he could the person he wanted to emulate professionally in every way. The problem from the start was that Sirio had proved the plausibility of the non-chef-driven restaurant, yet had just hired someone determined to be a star chef in his own right. To Daniel's mind, Sirio was famous. Le Cirque was not yet famous for food. The gauge he used was Le Cirque's failure to gain the four-star rating from *The New York Times*. All he had to do was deliver to his master the four stars and together they would create the best restaurant in the world. Sirio was happy to see that his new chef was so ambitious, but certainly didn't agree that his restaurant had been anything less before he arrived.

One of the new team's more famous dishes was the Bass in Barolo, a roasted black sea bass wrapped in paper-thin slices of potato that had been burnished golden brown, the whole dish set in a concentrated Barolo wine sauce with just a hint of thyme and shallots. The dish came as close as possible to Sirio's idea of perfection. When he had taken Daniel to Barolo a few months earlier, the two men had eaten grilled fish with the thin potato laid on top, brushed with butter, and accompanied by the Barolo sauce. Boulud had learned of a similar preparation from Sirio's friend Roger Vergé while working with him. The dish was part French, part Italian, and as Sirio likes to say, "part God."

For almost every preparation that Daniel and Sottha created, there was a Sirio variation. A lightly grilled fish with a sprig of rosemary would do just fine if you didn't want the more formal potato-covered dish. You could have your scallops black tie sans its protective pastry shell. Boulud, while not the first chef in America to use foie gras, was one of the first to put it to such a wide and varied use in the restaurant—no fewer than twenty-four different preparations of foie gras lay in his repertoire. Yet even here Sirio had his own ideas: while foie gras cooked to a molten perfection was a restaurant hallmark, Sirio's idea of heaven was a cold *torchon* of foie gras, cut off the round and laid on a plate with a clear aspic and fresh haricots verts. And then there were the dishes Sirio liked to create in the kitchen for passing around while guests waited: breadsticks wrapped in the best, thinnest prosciutto, focaccia made from his grandmother's recipe, even the capers at the bar had to be perfection.

SIRIO

DANIEL WAS BECOMING a good chef. The first time he told me the day's special, a *carré de veau,* I said, "You know, I saw this thirty years ago in France. I don't need it to do in here anymore. Here I want a mentality of simplicity. Olive oil, salt, pepper. This is the way it is."

After I hired Daniel, Christian Millau came to Le Cirque for lunch. We already had a rating of 19 out of 20 from Gault Millau, the highest in America, and I wasn't sure if he was here to really have lunch or he was coming to see Daniel's cooking. But Daniel was not cooking yet. Monsieur Millau had the table in the corner, table six, and I thought, Maybe he's reviewing, but I didn't know. We made him lunch and after he had been eating and smoking for a while we started talking and I told him that

Daniel's people were in the kitchen but that we were still developing ideas for the menu. I told him I craved a perfect roast chicken. He said, "*Mais, vous savez* ... you cannot have *poulet rôti* in high-class restaurant."

This is stupid. I judge a chef from how he makes an omelette and a good roast chicken. People go to the restaurant—not for the food or the chef. They go because they hear that other people want to go to that restaurant. Only a very small percentage go to restaurants just for the food. I'm all for it—I go to restaurants just for the food. And I'm all for doing new things. I'm usually the one who goes into the kitchen and says, "Have you seen this, have you seen that?" But I also know too much, so I try not to be stupid. Sottha's tuna tartare with curry is a great dish. Would I have eaten it in Montecatini? No. Does it have the simplicity of Italian food? Yes. You have to be alive to things, you have to give your staff the power to create, but you don't have to be stupid. I don't want any food piled high up on the plate that looks like anything other than what it is.

MICHAEL BATTERBERRY *Sirio brings the power of a great vision-ary. He talks about food in these great shifts, but it's all filtered through the idea of the stylish bistro. As a result, it's still the only place where you get a sense of shifting fashion in food, even when it is rooted in the inflexible traditions of Le Cirque's clients.*

Chefs, especially the ones who come up through the French system, and now more and more the ones who go to cooking schools, don't feel anything. When I get them here, we have to teach them all over again. The really talented ones get through, and those are the ones I like. I support them. I send them to tastings, I bring them to Italy, I have them come to my house to cook with my wife. My job is to make the chef the most important, the best, the most respected, the most famous. ◄✦►

ANDRÉ SOLTNER *Sirio is the best friend any chef ever had. He never says no. He becomes their number-one fan, public relations person, father, banker, advisor—everything. Not just the big ones, but the **sous-chefs**, the ones underneath trying to work up. Maybe he encourages them even more.*

DANIEL BOULUD *There's no question Sirio is the best owner to work for if you are a chef. Never in all the years I worked there did he ever question an expense. If it went toward creating the best, he trusted me to buy it. It was amazing. All the things chefs complain about, he took away! I couldn't argue about the money, and I couldn't argue he didn't let me have what I wanted. He never bitched about how many cooks were in the kitchen. Maybe he made even less money with me in the kitchen than with Alain, but he still didn't complain.*

ONE YEAR INTO DANIEL'S RUN, on October 9, 1987, Bryan Miller reviewed Le Cirque again, raising it at long last to four stars. Sirio, one of the few restaurateurs to have experienced a bad review from *The New York Times* and survived to tell the story, was begrudgingly prepared to accept that the *Times* was the highest standard by which restaurants in New York were judged. He, his chef, their staff, and the restaurant celebrated with bottles of vintage Dom Perignon and a night on the town at Sirio's favorite Italian restaurant, Nanni. A few waiters actually reported seeing a smile from the maestro and attempts to read the fine print of the review when he thought no one was looking.

A new media circus had begun. One of Daniel's many attributes was that he was media savvy. Sirio, always the consummate protector of Le Cirque's image and a master at attracting attention from the press (a very different concept from receiving a review), suddenly had a star on his hands. It was Sirio's theater and now, for the first time, the chef's name was on the marquee.

Even before Daniel's arrival, Le Cirque had become a kind of national standard. "As expensive as Le Cirque," "as elegant as Le Cirque," or "as famous as Le Cirque" were some of the superlative phrases to be found regularly in newspapers and magazines around the world. The 1987 film "Wall Street," starring Michael Douglas, reiterated the most enduring element of Le Cirque's success—simply getting a table. Getting one, the film suggested, meant you had reached the top and that you had access mere mortals didn't have. More press ink was spent on Le Cirque and on Sirio than any other modern restaurant. After Daniel's arrival, there was even more, this time with more of an emphasis on the food rather than on who sat at which tables. *Town and Country* published "The Making of a Gourmet Dynasty," a lavish article featuring all of the chefs who had come through Le Cirque's "graduate school" and a witty account of a day in the life of the restaurant. *Wine Spectator* couldn't find enough good to say about the comprehensive wine list and its selection of inexpensive and astounding Italian wines.

Now people *did* want to talk to the chef. They wanted to know about the food, what was in it, where the recipes came from, the ingredients they included, and the people who served them. When *Food & Wine* named Daniel its "rising star of the year," Sirio flew him to the magazine's annual festival in Aspen, Colorado, to present him to a curious and hungry press. At the top of the wave, Sirio and Daniel were riding it for all it was worth.

SIRIO

MY GOD, IT WAS CRAZY—but it was a good crazy, at least in the front of the house. In the back of the house we had some problems but we worked them out. The restaurant was already too small and the kitchen, which was never very big, was hard to use. Everything with the hotel, the union, was an issue. We had party rooms and we did lots and lots of parties, all from the same kitchen. To produce 500 covers was crazy, but we worked very hard. I don't care what anyone says—we're the hardest-working restaurant anywhere.

DANIEL BOULUD *We were always full, lunch and dinner, twelve to fourteen hours a day. With a better kitchen, more organization, we could have done even more! It's a good thing I lived around the corner, or there would have been days when they would have had to carry me home!*

It's always about the organization and the mentality. People always say to me, "Daniel was cooking better when he was with you." Well, of course he was. I did all the things that made it possible for him to be great in the kitchen. I dealt with the union, the waiters, the business. He got to cook and come out to the dining room, which he did very well. We were so cramped in that space and I always wanted to do more. But more wasn't easy. I wanted a bigger, better pastry department. It was the same story as with Dieter all over again. I went to Monte Carlo, where I met Alain Ducasse. We knew of each other, but we had never met. I was in the hotel to meet a journalist, I think. I presumed he wasn't there, but he was and he came out and said, "But you have to stay for dinner." I wasn't dressed correctly—me, can you imagine?—and so I had to take a tie from the hotel! Then we went into the kitchen and ate there and talked all night.

ALAIN DUCASSE *When I started in this business, I always heard there was this big restaurateur in New York. I always say: restaurateuring, he invented it—the mix of the cocktails, the cuisine, the people, the movies. The* cirque à l'italienne. *The culture of Italy, hospitality, welcoming, generosity, drama. It pleases people. And there he is in my kitchen and maybe he's a little more relaxed, or maybe it's something else, but we don't talk about business at all. He told us about his life, his childhood—it was incredible, passionate. The little boy from Tuscany who goes to Paris to eat, to live. Because he's young, and his life started there. An Italian in Paris.*

It was one of those moments. He has a Mediterranean mentality, especially in the kitchen, but his organization is almost like the Germans. Maybe that's why I feel very comfortable with him. He's nothing if not French, but he has the ability to see many things in a different way. When I was back in New York and asked him if he knew a great pastry chef, he sent me Jacques Torres. But when Torres came here and saw the space, he said he couldn't do what I asked him to do. I promised him space and we came to an arrangement. I wanted every meal to end with an explosion. Jacques knew how to do it.

JACQUES TORRES *I was in Atlanta. It was warm, and my girl-friend, Kris, and I were happy, and I got this call from Daniel. I hadn't heard of Daniel, but I had heard all about Sirio. Daniel said Sirio was looking for something big. I told him, I don't want to work in big cities, even for Sirio Maccioni. Daniel called back and offered me more money, but I still didn't want to go. Then I got the call from Ducasse, "Number one: If you want to do something in that country, it's not in Atlanta, it's not in Boston, it's in New York. Number two: When Sirio Maccioni calls you, you don't say no. You go and see him, you sit with him, you talk to him. If you don't like it, you say, 'No, I don't want to do it.' But you cannot just say no with-out going to see the man."*

I don't know how I knew that he was very close to his girlfriend, who is American. But you know, they are always more important than the man. I knew she would know what was smart for him, so I insisted that she come to New York for a holiday.

JACQUES TORRES *I remember going to meet him on Thanksgiving Day, and you know it was very strange. I'm French talking to this famous Italian who speaks perfect French, even kind of thinks French, but doesn't behave that way at all. The first thing he said was that money was not an issue. That's not French! They were numbers I couldn't even imagine. He just said, "Be reasonable and I will pay. Five, ten, twenty thousand dollars, I'm not going to argue." This just doesn't happen in the restaurant world, certainly not to a pastry chef. And I looked at the space, which was tiny, but I knew I could work with it. He said he'd take space from the ban-queting room. A restaurateur willing to take floor space for the pastry man? Still, when I left, I told Kris, "I don't want this job, but he is very impressive." And then we were talking later and I thought of all the things I wanted to do in this world and here was a man offering to help me do them. I said to myself, "What can happen to me if I work for that man?" And when I looked at it that way, suddenly it was very easy.*

Jacques understood what I wanted. We had to dazzle them, almost overwhelm them. They ask for one, give them three. They ask for three, give them six, and put the most amazing thing—a dome, a sculpture—in the middle of the table for them to talk about. You see it in people's eyes. All you have to do is look into their eyes and you know what they want. ⤛

WHERE SCHORNER HAD DWELLED within the realm of pastry as art, Torres made pastry as if by magic. His creations weren't just adaptations of classic pastry tastes or shapes, they leapt over the old ways and left them far behind. To Jacques, making crème brûlée was like riding a bicycle when you could just as easily sit behind the wheel of a Ferrari. Why have just cake, when you could have a tower of different kinds of cakes that looked like a build-ing? For Pierre Franey's sixty-fifth birthday party, Jacques built a life-size, edible stove. Covered in solid white and dark chocolate, its core was a classic L'Opéra cake: layers of cake, coffee butter-cream, and chocolate ganache. The pans were made of chocolate filled with fruit sauces. Franey and Sirio were ecstatic. It took fewer than thirty-six hours for Torres to reduce the life-size stove to a dessert-plate-size version and teach the wait staff to present the stove, lift off its covering to reveal the multilayered cake underneath, and, as a final flourish, pour the sauces over the plate.

With Sirio's blessing there was nothing Torres wouldn't try to execute in Le Cirque's tiny kitchen, often to the dismay and amazement of his co-workers in the crowded space. The first major piece about Torres wasn't in the pages of a newspaper or food magazine, but in *Scientific American,* which made Jacques seem more like a mad scientist than a pastry chef.

Torres's knack for creating new, usually extravagant desserts didn't stop him from making the classics that he and Sirio loved, from *bombolini* to biscotti. However, he couldn't resist tinkering. Even Le Cirque classics like crème brûlée might come out of the kitchen surrounded in one of Torres's spun domes of colored sugar. It depended on his mood—or the mood of his master.

I ALWAYS SAY that I do everything I do for my three sons. I do. But if I were to really admit why I come into the restaurant day after day, when I'm tired, when I would like to sleep—it's because I still love the excitement.

> DANIEL BOULUD *We were spinning Le Cirque up, up, up! It was incredible. Sirio would come in at ten o'clock in the evening and say, "I forgot to say fifteen friends have just arrived, let's whip up a menu." We did it, not so much to impress the guests, but to impress Sirio, to see if we could get him to fall on his butt. It was so exciting. It wasn't drudgery. I wish we could have recorded those moments so I could replay them over and over. He had the crowd, I had the food, Jacques was doing the pastry. Sirio would go to the cellar and get the big bottles. We were all at our very best.*

Success means I stay in the dining room. I become friendly with all these people, and you have to go to some parties, but you can't go to every party because if you do the same people that invite you start to say, "Why is this guy always at a party instead of at his restaurant?" So you stay at your restaurant. I still really believe in my heart that the best restaurant is one run by one person in one space and no more. ◂┿

> DANIEL BOULUD *Sirio's genius is how he behaves in the dining room. There's no one like him and never will be. He always has the right word for everyone, for every situation. He knows how to detach himself so that the business doesn't eat him up. It's something I still don't know how to do. When I arrived in New York City, Sirio was the first thing I heard about. He was the example of success. But the people who told me didn't really know. They thought it was about the people who went there or the money he was making. For me, the excitement was that Sirio makes the greatest restaurant experience the most simple, least pretentious one. Serve the*

King of Spain and make him feel like he's not the King of Spain—
you know what I mean? They didn't understand, but I did. It was
like that to work with him, every day.

HAL RUBENSTEIN wrote in Malcolm Forbes's *Egg* magazine that becoming so closely aligned with Nancy Reagan and her friends was either the best or the worst thing to happen to Le Cirque. No review or comment about Le Cirque ever started without mentioning the ladies of Le Cirque and very often the men. A front-page story in *USA Today* in 1989 featured Sirio with supermodel Elle Macpherson, opera diva Beverly Sills, and statesman Henry Kissinger. In that one photo Le Cirque managed to represent everything sexy, artsy, and powerful.

SIRIO

I T WAS A VERY EXCITING TIME—maybe the best time—but it was still hard work. Malcolm Forbes had invited me to his seventieth birthday party in Morocco and he'd also asked that we make the food for all the other people whom he was flying over for the party. We stayed up all night, me, Egidiana, Daniel, the boys, making cold roast poussin, hard-boiled eggs and caviar, and mini crème brûlées, all wrapped up and put in Le Cirque shopping bags. Mario and Marco took a refrigerated truck to Newark Airport and I followed in a regular car with my luggage. I checked in and then went to find the boys. The security people said that we could not bring the truck to the airplane and that we needed to go through different procedures. The flight was leaving in an hour. We had no choice. We just ran for it and got to the airplane in the nick of time. We started to load up the plane while the security forces came from everywhere! Forbes's people smoothed over everything and I didn't get arrested and I was very glad to see the door on the plane close. It wasn't until the 747 pulled back and proceeded toward the runway that I suddenly remembered I was supposed to be on the airplane. I was so exhausted, I just went home and went to sleep for a few days! When the party was over, Mr. Forbes returned my luggage. ◄–

LIZ SMITH *Malcolm died less than a year after his big party in Morocco. The memorial service was at St. Bartholomew's on Park Avenue. When I got there, there was Sirio standing at the front door. He was the maître d' at Malcolm's memorial! He brought me down the aisle, straight to the second pew, and seated me behind Brooke Astor, Elizabeth Taylor, and President Nixon. I couldn't believe it—there I was sharing the same pew with David Rockefeller, Katharine Graham, and Lee Iacocca. Soon we were all chatting politely and making friends. Even at his friend's memorial, Sirio was designing the room, which is really how Malcolm would have wanted it to be.*

THE NEXT DAY, a front-page article in the *Wall Street Journal* about the future of the Forbes empire began by describing Sirio's role in managing the Forbes's service. While solidifying his reputation, it exposed Sirio, yet again, to charges of favoritism, which sent him into a tailspin of helpless rage. He was damned if he did, and out of business if he didn't.

In the restaurant, to the dismay of his chefs and his waiters, Sirio would regularly keep the entire restaurant on overtime for one table of strangers, without a reservation, who arrived at 10:30, a time when most of the supposedly favored were well tucked into their beds. If Sirio found out that in his absence a guest had not been treated to the same privileges, staff and union meetings would be called and holidays canceled to enforce the idea that hospitality must be paid, at any price. Telling Sirio that a customer, new or old, famous or anonymous, was turned away has always been like telling him that his bank account had just been accidentally emptied. The lifeblood of the restaurant depended on newcomers, and they had to be treated like Kissingers and Trumps and Jaggers. Did it always work that way? No. Did kitchen and dining room staff look up blearily at 10:30 and suggest to a customer standing at the door that they ought to find a local diner instead of offering them a plate of cheese and a glass of wine? Yes. But only if Sirio was not nearby or, preferably, out of the country. If Sirio was there, a latecomer would become his new best friend and would often be treated to a small tin of caviar over baked potato, or a plate of prosciutto and melon: late-night food, Maccioni style.

SIRIO

YOU KNOW, I HAVE A PAPER a professor in Italy wrote about Le Cirque. Tuscany was the center of the world for a long time. All the roads went through it, and Montecatini, where I come from, was where they would stop and rest. They were called hospices, which became the word for "hospital"—where you take care of people. This feeling of taking care of people I think comes from the land. But after a thousand years, I don't talk about it, I don't write about it, it's not a manifesto—it's a feeling. To a Tuscan to be presumptuous is the worst thing you can be. And the people who accuse me of being a snob know nothing. I am who I am. That is smart, that is not "snob." I have fought my whole life so that someone can come in off the street and have a little saucisson and cheese before dinner. Not just my so-called friends, or the famous people who come to Le Cirque. Fame doesn't do anything for me. Even now I would never be so presumptuous as to say, "Bianca Jagger is my friend, or Henry Kissinger is my friend." Woody Allen come to my house in Montecatini and spent three days just cooking with my wife. Tony Bennett, whose real name is Antonio di Benedetto, came all the time because he was comfortable in my house. Tony Quinn too. They are good clients. We have a relationship. But we do what we do. I know they grow older, they move, they change their minds. You can't build a business around them, or invest too much of yourself. I call, I ask them to come to lunch, they come or they don't come. That I know how to dress, that I have been successful, comes from hard work, not from being a snob. All I ask is that people look nice and to look nice doesn't mean you have to look like one of the Hilton girls! Beauty is the way you carry yourself, it's an attitude. These people who think that it's phony are just phony themselves. Why is it so wrong to get dressed up to look nice, to feel good? Ugliness ruins it for everyone. Maria Callas was not a beautiful woman, but somehow she would put it all together and, my god, she would walk into a room and you would say, "She's beautiful."

LIZ SMITH *This is the role he feels comfortable with: he doesn't want to be one of his clients, yet he is the closest a lot of them have to a friend, or a shrink. In public though, outside of the restaurant, he's not comfortable sitting at their tables, or hanging out with them. He's really only comfortable with his family. He likes to take care of his clients, but he knows exactly what it is and where it is.*

HENRY KISSINGER *Sirio doesn't make you feel like you're doing him a favor to come to his restaurant. It's really that simple. Sirio is sort of deferential but informal, and keeps his own dignity. You don't feel as if somebody is making a huge fuss because you're famous, but you get the attention you need. You feel you are a part of something—his boys, his wife, his family. He might have been a great politician, his views are interesting because they come from a place I understand, maybe more conservative than the current generation. But in truth, what we talk about mostly is soccer! He knows I'm a huge fan and he has the game put on in the bar so I can keep score.*

MRS. WILLIAM F. BUCKLEY *Sirio is a great gentleman and makes damn good food. I've known him since the Colony. That's real history. I like that someone cares enough to call: "Why don't you come for lunch?" I say, "Maybe next week," thinking I won't, and usually do. Then there are those boys. I saw them in the restaurant growing up, I see what he's enabled them to do, and what they've become. He's the best example of a classic Italian family that I know, and I think that ought to be encouraged!*

I like the feeling of family and I really like when a restaurant can make you feel like you're coming home after a long day, after you've had trouble, when you're late, whatever it is, there has to be a kind of spontaneity. This is why I like to take tables late at night. The people who look after the money always tell me this is the surest way to lose money in the restaurant business, but I don't care. I always argue with the accountants and with my chefs—it's not losing money, it's investing money. The table that comes in at 11:00 is gone before the table that you sat at 9:30. People who want to eat late, eat simply, and they are so grateful that you cooked for them that they will never leave you as a customer. It takes a few minutes and you have a customer for life.

I remember that once Zubin Mehta, the conductor of the New York Philharmonic, came in late in white tie and tails. He always liked the same thing—lobster salad, baby lamb chops, and then *mousse au chocolat*. Daniel didn't want to reopen the kitchen, so I was standing there fighting with him. So what if everyone had to clean up again? You don't need a whole kitchen to make a lamb chop. And Daniel said, "No, no," and he did that thing that all chefs do, standing there with his arms crossed. I said, "Let's do it." And he said, "But … ?" I said, "What do you mean, 'but'? Imagine you are home, or in your own restaurant someday and somebody comes in, a friend, a customer doesn't matter—you don't think enough to take care of them? My god—you'd rather die. You cook something! You do anything." And Mehta came in for his lamb chops and was very happy. But I knew it was difficult to keep the kitchen open late.

> DANIEL BOULUD *Then, it wasn't my money, but you try to operate the restaurant as if it were. And yes, sometimes I wished Sirio would say, "Mr. Mehta, how about we open some caviar and toast for you and your wife, on the house," and not reopen the whole kitchen for one cover. But we did, and now in my own restaurant I wind up having to do it too.*

The lesson is, you never hesitate. A guest arrives at the door and you don't put a stupid look on your face that tells them they have to go back onto the street. You never give away that you are about to keep open a whole restaurant, or fight with your chef who is tired and wants to see his wife. You loosen your tie and make him feel like he's just come from a long trip and needs attention.

You have to make quick calls, and maybe sometimes you make the wrong call. That look in the eye, you can lose it in a second. Like on the phone. You never hesitate one second when dealing with a reservation. No maybes, no suggestion to please call back in one hour, no long explanations. You make the decision instantly and just say "yes" or "no." When you hesitate you've got trouble. Same with the food. If Ron Perelman wants his flounder a certain way, that's how you do it.

DANIEL BOULUD *Of course I always dreamed of making better food on Sixty-fifth Street but when Sirio would come in and tell me I had to cook this flounder for Ronald Perelman burnt, black, totally black, dry, overdone, killed, carbonized, not to the point of cremated but basically toast, I had to do it. Of course I grumbled. Of course I said things I shouldn't have, but I had to do it and I learned to do it with pride—Ronald Perelman's flounder, burnt to perfection. It was part of many things we had to do here, many unusual things we were asked. But that was part of the package.*

REMI LAUVAND [**sous-chef**] *Daniel really pushed his agenda. And Sirio was thrilled. He really was. Sirio would come back and say such-and-such person was there and to make something in a particular way. At the beginning Daniel was not thrilled about doing it, but he worked it to his advantage and just wound up building Le Cirque in a new way.*

When I see young waiters, I say, "If you keep looking up at the ceiling, you're going to break your neck." You need to look at customers, to understand what they need. And you learn to let go very quickly, no matter what it is. Maybe it's because of the war—we had so little and lost so much that I can't get concerned over a dinner or a glass of champagne or something going wrong. Otherwise I would have to kill myself. Maybe that's why I wasn't good with a partner and thank god I don't have another.

CINDY ADAMS *There's the side of Sirio that is nurturing and the side of Sirio that's brittle and witty. But you never doubt that it is all about business. And it isn't because I am useful to him. Of course I am useful to him. That's hardly the point. If he were just a sycophantic waiter it would all be easy, but we have a relationship. It's a bizarre relationship, but a real relationship. We also go way back. We know too much. But ultimately, he's ruthless about the business and that's where he's at his best. No one can match him, simply because no one else has eyes in the back of their head, or a nose as tuned in to bullshit as he does. I was once at a restaurant with Barbara Walters where they were doing the fussing and fawn-*

ing, the whole routine. There was the wait, the arrogance, some roadkill I didn't even recognize and then we ordered some wine and what do we know about wine? They never asked, they never offered. It turned out it was a $900 bottle, and it was Barbara's turn to pay, and she did. That's the kind of stupid thing Sirio would never do. He's just very, very savvy.

RUTH REICHL *[editor, **Gourmet**] I remember reading a piece about Sirio and one of these women said, "You know, Sirio was the sexiest man in New York." And they had a picture of him, and you know, goddamn, if he wasn't the most fabulous-looking guy you ever saw in your life. I think those women saw him as this absolutely gorgeous, suave guy who flirted with all of them. And there was always this little bit of sex hanging over that room. And, when you add to that his way of packing the room in the right way and filling it with enough glitz and enough money and enough glamour to make it always vibrate a little, and add onto that a real commitment to serving good food, you end up with this sort of heady mix that is New York. This is a restaurant that for a really long time sort of was New York, to not only New Yorkers but also out-of-towners. And that, by default, makes him the most impor-tant restaurateur of the era. I didn't like it, it had never worked for me, but you had to respect it and you had to respect him.*

I don't think I *have* anything, I just open my eyes and I try the best I can to please. And I've lived long enough and worked so hard for so long that I know more. It isn't much more than that. I think that if I don't please I might die. Is that so strange? Maybe it is. I just think it's where I come from, what my father taught me, what my mother taught me, what my grandmother and grandfather taught me. And I know the older I get, the more everything they did and said rings in my head. I'm not a saint. Sometimes I don't get it right with everybody but I try. We try. My sons try. I tell them all, Please, if you start to think that you are too smart, that you are somehow touched by God with some gift no one else has, then you are the stupidest person there is. ◄◄•

THE PRODIGAL SON

IKE THE RINGMASTER AT A CIRCUS, Sirio sees himself as the father of his entire kitchen, managerial, and wait staff. In 1991 that consisted of sixty-five employees. The signs of his affection are relayed unlike anyone else's. Not "hello" or "good-bye," but more likely a grumble and a wave of his hand, or the question "Are you a pain in the neck?"—sometimes with a gentle poke and a devilish smile that reveals his delight at seeing you.

An employee of Sirio has to believe that all of the buzz and chaos surrounding Sirio is not going to hurt you and that he has only your best intentions at heart. You either trust him or you don't. Employees who expect contracts, times, hours, straight answers, or even the same answer find Sirio exasperating; Daniel and Sirio would go for days, even weeks without actually talking.

As the restaurant Sirio had built reached its zenith in 1991, the ugly black and white of life started to intrude on the magic. The Mayfair Hotel was getting old. Sirio and his chef had long since outgrown their space. Banquets were being catered from a three-and-a-half-foot range and a refrigerator that might work in a bar in a small home. Meanwhile the fame of the restaurant had long since made it a potentially lucrative commodity to a host of hoteliers, financiers, and restaurateurs. With a proven brand name and established managerial skill there was no telling where Sirio—and potentially Daniel—could take Le Cirque. The choice deals, the conversation, and the possibilities of—and, of course, the fantasies about where—Le Cirque could go were all directed at Sirio. There was no shortage of offers, and Sirio listened to them all. His preference, however, was to make a deal with the hotel and the hotel union, in order to expand and stay where they were.

Meanwhile, Boulud was chomping at the bit. Although the restaurant world was changing rapidly, Le Cirque was still Le Cirque and Sirio still Sirio. As Daniel became stronger and more independent, there were more differences of opinion—although they were never discussed. The question was when and how Daniel would leave. Sirio demanded not only to be kept informed, as one would expect of an employer, but to have his advice followed, something only a father would expect. Sirio was desperate to prevent his own children—and his chef—from having the life he had led. You didn't need to ask a shrink what it was all about. Sirio and Daniel had connected on a deep level, and separation was not going to be easy.

Emotional, painful, and fruitful as the family structure of Le Cirque was, it had a basic legal structure. While Sailhac was still cooking, Sirio had established a policy that employment for any chef at Le Cirque was to be renegotiated at the five-year mark. Sirio was against putting anything in writing, since an employment contract could cut both ways. His lawyer, Victor Jacobs, had crafted a contract that compelled a chef to stay in the restaurant at least five years, but gave management the right to cancel at any time. Sailhac never signed an employment contract as such with Sirio, although he did sign a document forbidding him to work as a chef for two years after he left Le Cirque, a clause Sirio willingly waived for his departing chef. Daniel was the first chef to actually sign the agreement.

As it happened, Daniel didn't want to leave within the first five years anyway. Fame had made Daniel desirable, if not as desirable as Le Cirque, and he was flooded secretly with offers, the most lucrative of which was from Smith & Wollensky, a large, profitable steakhouse just opening its first non-steak restaurant, Park Avenue Café. Although he turned it down, Daniel, at thirty-six (late middle age for a chef), knew that if he didn't make a move to create his own restaurant, he would never have the energy to try again later.

And then there were Sirio's sons to consider. Mario, Marco, and Mauro were as photographed and profiled as their father, and very much a part of the Le Cirque magic. When Sirio's beam, inadvertent or deliberate, failed to shine, even the prickliest client was bound to fall for one of his handsome boys. Although Sirio told the press he expected his sons, each of them with impressive culinary resumes, to follow in his footsteps, privately he was in no way convinced that they would or should.

Meanwhile, issues more pressing than assuaging his talented and ambitious chef came to bear on Sirio. By 1991 the Reagan years were officially over, the country was preparing for war against Iraq, and the nation was mired in a recession. Sirio's mind focused on keeping his business robust in the face of continuing competition from other restaurants, and on dealing with increasing problems from the union and the hotel management, which had changed for the third time in Sirio's tenure at the Mayfair. He also had a lease that was coming to an end in the not too distant future. Things were going to have to change. Sirio shared some of the thoughts, ideas, and dreams about the future Le Cirque with his chef. It was clear Sirio was contemplating projects away from East Sixty-fifth Street. The timing, however, was not right for Daniel to have a piece of the action. So Daniel quietly and almost heroically started to extract himself, to protect himself and his interests, while telling himself all along that he would never betray or hurt the person who had made so much of his future possible: Sirio. And, of course, he wound up doing exactly that.

➤➤

I WAS A FOOL. The last years Daniel wasn't cooking, he was just handing out business cards. You have to know when to let people go, and it was time for Daniel to go. But there was so much else happening—problems with the hotel, the union, our future. The world was changing fast, people stopped coming for lunch so much, the limousines started to disappear, there was a new "politically correct" era, which seemed to mean mostly that no one eats right. These were the things I had to deal with while Daniel was out making the best deal for himself with Le Cirque's name.

> DANIEL BOULUD *Sirio was the generation of my father. I'd never worked with someone who gave me so much respect, especially in the kitchen. I did wish that someone could have tapped him on the shoulder and said to him, "You have an incredible name and an incredible reputation. Let's go for the next step. Let's do the next big thing." And, god, I wanted to … I would have … I'm sure I could have been included in that.*

Everything that was being discussed, every project and idea, I discussed with Daniel, but Daniel wanted to be a restaurateur *and* a chef and I don't think that is possible. When you have a chef who wants to be a restaurateur, you have a mediocre chef and a worse restaurateur. He wanted all the things that I wanted, but these things don't happen overnight. It wasn't my space. We had to fight for everything. I thought he was working with me, so I looked the other way when he started to do his newsletter and his cookbook—all of which was done in the kitchens of Le Cirque, all of which was produced with the people of Le Cirque and with the clients of Le Cirque.

> DANIEL BOULUD *We spoke about projects, but nothing concrete. There was nothing put down. Just lots of talk. I could not wait for things to come up. I could not ask Sirio if he wanted to be my partner in a future restaurant. He might have thought my new restaurant would cannibalize his. And at the time there was no*

structure like what he or I have now. It was just Sirio and his employees and I was just an employee. It's a big jump—employee to partner—and he had three children, a wife. Where could I go?

I knew Daniel was going to leave. I just didn't want to be used without my knowledge. He used the name of Le Cirque to get what he wanted and he lied to me. He told me directly to my face that he would tell me six months before what he would do, so that we could plan together for the restaurant, our clients, the press.

DANIEL BOULUD *We discussed the fact that I was going to leave. I knew that the minute I told him, it would be over. Better for a restaurateur to give a chef six months' severance than have him around your kitchens for six months with his head in his next idea. So instead I kept my search a big secret. I sent friends of mine to see locations. It was not easy looking for money, because Sirio knew everyone who has money. Even the business plan and pitches to investors did not have my name on them. I did it this way because a lot of people promise you everything when you seem to be successful, but when you come back to ask for the cash, they say, "Circumstances have changed." I'd seen it happen too many times.*

The reasons for a marriage breaking up are always the same as the reasons for its coming together. I knew why Daniel wanted me in the first place, and I knew why he would leave. What I didn't expect was that he would be so duplicitous. People say to me, "Ah, but you were young and ambitious too," and I say, "Yes, I was very ambitious, but I had integrity and respect. I worked five years for Oscar Tucci because he helped me get a green card. Did I talk bad about it? Yes, but not for thirty years, not until he was dead."

DANIEL BOULUD *I didn't know what Sirio's plans were. Either he didn't have any, or he had some he didn't want to share, or he felt that changing chefs would be a good thing. I believe that change is good. I'd only signed on for five years, after that it was all guesswork.*

I did what I had to do. For me. For my family. If the guy who was going to give me the money for my new restaurant pulled out, I would have been flat. I had nothing, so I could not afford to risk it. Maybe I would still be with Le Cirque if I hadn't raised the money and made that particular deal. As much as I had the ambition and the wish to make my own business, there's a little bit of luck in all this. Sirio came into business on Sixty-fifth Street because he had a little bit of luck with the Zeckendorfs.

There's a game in the restaurant world. Chefs and *sous*-chefs, dish-washers, managers, maître d's, go back and forth. I hear everything, I know them all. Benito went away for a few years, Bruno Dussin went to work for Cipriani's. We all know who's where, why they're there, how much they're paid, and when they go. I am not stupid. I know it's good for everyone to move on. What is not right is not to be honest about it. ◄✦

EVER SINCE *FOOD AND WINE* MAGAZINE had featured him and pasta primavera on the cover of its 1978 inaugural issue, Sirio had always felt a certain loyalty to its founding editor Michael Batterberry and his wife, Ariane. Ariane's mother, Francis Ruskin, had been one of the original ladies who lived at the Mayfair. During the summer of 1992, Sirio had let himself be talked into attending the magazine's annual conference—by the editors who had succeeded the Batterberrys, by his children, and by his chef, all of whom knew that the magazine was preparing to do a piece on Daniel and Le Cirque for its August issue. Even though it inter-fered with his annual trip home to Montecatini, Sirio had acceded to the combined pressure—someone from the family should be there. However, as soon as he landed in the snow-covered peaks of Colorado, his usual feeling of foreboding became intense.

The minute he had settled into his hotel suite, the phone rang. It was Marco calling from New York to tell him that moments after he had left for the airport, Daniel had presented a letter of resignation to Egidiana. Inadvertent or not, the timing— with most of the food media world less than a stone's throw from his window—evoked maximum hysteria from Sirio. In the twelve hours it took to arrange for his flight away from Aspen, Sirio vented his rage by grabbing people on the streets and holding court in restaurants. He had been caught completely off guard.

SIRIO

W E USED TO CLOSE for the first three weeks in July, but everyone told me I had to go to this thing in Aspen. Before leaving I said, "Daniel, I'm going to Aspen and Montecatini, I need to know what's going on." And he said, "Oh, no problem, I would never do this, I would never do that." The point is that he told me, over and over, "You will know six months before anybody if I'm really doing something. Of course there are a lot of rumors. I'm looking, because of my age, and everything.... But you will know six months before anybody." And so I left thinking that maybe for once in my life I could have a vacation. And the next day my son called to tell me that Daniel had given my wife his letter of resignation. Why? I never understood why he had to involve my wife and my children.

The minute I spoke to my wife I told her and my sons to tell him never to come back to the restaurant. They told me he had offered to stay to September but I said, "No, tell him he is finished now." ◄◄

DANIEL BOULUD *I had investors. It all had to be so quiet and there was a problem with the lease. It just happened that the day I wrote to Sirio was the day that it was all settled. I couldn't tell him even a minute before and it was just bad timing that it was the day he was leaving. It's never easy to say that you are leaving and I think I did it the safest way for me, and to not have words going around town beforehand that would hurt Sirio.*

WHEN CHEFS LEAVE RESTAURANTS, taking along their inner circle is usually de rigueur. As Sirio flew back east, the question that ran most through his head was whether Daniel's departure meant the departure of Daniel's aide-de-camp, Sottha Kuhn. Although

Sottha had already said he would stay when Daniel left, now all bets were off. Would Sirio walk into an empty restaurant when he got back to Le Cirque that night? No, he discovered when he opened the door. The clientele were blissfully unaware that anything had happened in the kitchen.

Sirio gets emotional to the point of tears when he is angry, frustrated, or hurt concerning matters of global importance. But if you ask him if he cried when his grandmother died, or when he thought his son might have a fatal illness, he'll deny it utterly. Just as he denies that he lifted his hand up behind his glasses to wipe away a tear when he ran into the kitchen and saw that Sottha was still behind the stove.

The food world, however, was abuzz with gossip about the departure of Daniel Boulud: the world's most famous restaurateur had lost his star chef, clearly by surprise. Who would Sirio find to replace Daniel? Could anyone match Daniel's ability in the kitchen? Was this the end of Le Cirque, now that Daniel intended to open his own restaurant? Who was the more injured party in the divorce, and which of Sirio's pampered platoon of regulars would break ranks to dine at his ex-chef's restaurant? Newspapers ran the story, magazines scrambled for answers. *New York* magazine's Gael Greene put the drama into some perspective: "It's not as big a shake-up as when the Communists took over China … besides, every time he changes chefs it just gets better!"

SIRIO

W⁹HEN I GOT BACK and saw that Sottha was there, I went around the room and everything seemed fine. I thought, "Things are different now, the chef is in the magazine, but the cook is in the kitchen, doing what he always did." It was the last night before we closed for July. We agreed that Sottha would come to Italy with me to work things out.

BILL BLASS *I happened to be in the restaurant the night Sirio came back from Aspen and it was probably the only time I ever saw him looking a little undone—I think maybe his pocket square was hanging out, which would be my definition of Sirio being undone. He told me he had a great secret. You know a secret with Sirio is something he only tells his hundred closest clients! He already knew Sottha was in the kitchen, so I told him to relax. He was always so obsessed with who was in the kitchen when in fact none of us really cared. And he was so angry. Angry like a father gets at his kid. I mean he was just a fucking cook. I told him, "Get another one!"*

I wasn't angry, angry is what stupid people do. I was hurt. When Daniel came to New York he was nothing, but he was a good cook. I was hard on him, but he was becoming a better cook.

DANIEL BOULUD *My relationship with Sirio didn't just stretch, it snapped completely. Leaving the most important person of your career was never going to be easy. I did it the safest and the most proper way I could under the circumstances. Did Sirio get hurt? Yes, he was furious. I swear you could hear the screams all the way from Aspen. He was so dramatic. But it's not like I just said, "See you, I'm out of here," I knew I had a whole year to work if he wanted me.*

It was a great time at Le Cirque when Daniel was cooking. Of course it was. But it was not an easy time in the kitchen while he was there. My relationship with people in the kitchen had changed. When Sailhac left, I helped him find work, I took him to see Mrs. Trump. I would have taken a dishwasher over if I liked him. That's my point. I'm not saying I'm easy. I'm difficult, but I don't lie and I'm not a phony. I was just upset and offended.

DANIEL BOULUD *How do you leave Sirio Maccioni? He was like a father to me. He spoke the language of food to me in a way my own father never could or would. Sirio is the greatest restaurateur that ever lived. He knows I know that. But Sirio was not ready. I dreamed at night that we could have thought big thoughts together. Was I too young to be trusted? No, the truth is, in 1992, there was nothing big coming to Sirio either.*

It was really more what Daniel wanted to do, what he wanted to show and that friction between Daniel and Sirio was part of what made them the most amazing team. Sirio had created a genius, he'd finally found someone who absorbed his very-forward-thinking mentality and then came back for more! Sirio began to realize that Le Cirque was as much Daniel's as Sirio's. What was most interesting to me was that Sottha was the mediator between everybody.

What I hate the most are the people who are now in the middle. Clients who go to his place and mine, even my sons, come to me: "Why don't you speak to Daniel?" He should call me, not send me flowers, or chocolates, or talk to me through friends. If you want my benediction, ask me for it. Later, when he was moving to Sixty-fifth Street, he could have called me to ask my opinion. I could have helped him like I did all the others.

DANIEL BOULUD *It's very rare that someone has the patience to try to understand Sirio. And in that way it was also tough to work with him. I remember once going to see the house where he was born in Montecatini. We stood in front of it. He was going to tell me something, but he didn't. I always wanted to know what he was going to say. His heart is in that house, in that land, but he doesn't get along with it so well. You know? That's why in his partnerships he has a hard time believing, trusting. Maybe he believed in me and trusted me too much?*

SOTTHA KUHN *Daniel's mistake was that you can't know what it's like to grow up being afraid for your life all the time, to have lost everything, to want so much to hang on to everything that you've fought for. Sirio and I share that. Daniel could never know what that feels like—nor should he.*

You don't come to the world the way I do and not be strong. I have lived too long and done too much not to know exactly what is the right thing to do. I like what I like and I don't like what I don't like. I want Zagat to know that I don't like his guide. And I want Daniel to know that if he wants to fix this thing, he should come and talk to me. ◄◄─

DANIEL BOULUD *I would never be Daniel Boulud without Sirio, without Le Cirque. I keep thinking that one day it will be okay again, like those magic days. I keep thinking I'll throw him a really big party, do something he likes. Pick up the phone? I can't. I just can't. I'd have to feel good about it, and he'd have to feel good about it. Maybe someday. I don't want him to misunderstand me. I invite him all the time but he never comes. Sending a letter or a note for the holiday is easy. But talking to him on the telephone? I never did. But not a day goes by here when I don't think of something he taught me, when I don't tell our staff something we all learned from him. I even tell them to go work for him. And anyone who comes to my office can see that there are pictures of him all around my desk. We both know in our souls, it was where we were happiest and at our very best. We were at the top of the world.*

LOSING AND
WINNING

DANIEL'S DEPARTURE would have been far less dramatic had it not come with the delicious puzzle of why his top aide, Sottha Kuhn, chose to stay at Le Cirque. Was it possible that Daniel wasn't as impish as he appeared? That Sottha preferred Sirio, mercurial as he might be? Or was it just that he dared not defy the most influential man in the restaurant business? Rumors flew that Sirio had paid him handsomely to remain, or that he had offered him the partnership role Daniel had so coveted, just to spite him.

The answer was in fact very simple: there was no guarantee that Boulud, for all his talent and potential, would survive as a restaurateur. The security of the Le Cirque family was far stronger. The odds may have been in Daniel's favor, but thousands of restaurants have opened with better odds and failed anyway. Boulud knew he could not expect Sottha to risk his own career on such a venture.

In Italy Sirio asked Sottha whether he would like to become the executive chef, knowing before he had even asked that the answer would be no. Sottha wasn't interested in stardom—Sirio's brand or Daniel's brand. He didn't want publicity or cookbooks; he just wanted to cook. If nothing else, Sirio had just learned the hard way that for the kind of restaurant he ran it was better to have a great cook than a great chef. However, he was torn because a restaurant of Le Cirque's stature needed a great, public, noticeable executive chef. With Sottha's silent blessing Sirio began his search, but it was evident to anyone who knew Sirio and Le Cirque that Sottha was the de facto executive chef of the restaurant.

According to a 2001 *New Yorker* profile of Sottha by Molly O'Neill, Sottha was the eldest son of wealthy Cambodian rice farmers around Siem Reap, 110 miles north of Phnom Penh. He went to Paris in 1974 to obtain his graduate degree in economics just as the Khmer Rouge were gaining strength. By the time his father died of a heart attack a year later, it was already too dangerous for Sottha to return home for the funeral. In the spring of 1975 the Khmer Rouge overthrew Cambodia's royalist government and Sottha's family disappeared without a trace. Penniless, he started to work in kitchens. "What else could I do?" he told O'Neill. Like Sirio, his talent is genuine, but his course was forced upon him by circumstances he could not control. Cooking seemed at least one way to maintain order.

Sottha worked first at Maison Prunier as an apprentice, then for Alain Senderens at L'Archestrate and finally at Troisgros, in Roanne. During the first five years of his career in kitchens, Sottha assumed his family members were all dead. However in 1980 a letter from Sottha's mother, slipped to an American journalist, found its way to Sottha. His entire family had been marched north into the jungle, where his grandparents and uncles had all died. O'Neill wrote that his eighteen-year-old brother, caught foraging for a yam, killed himself rather than face the typical punishment for "greed"—evisceration. His mother, two younger sisters, and two younger brothers had survived, though their house in Siem Reap had been flattened.

How do you explain Sottha? Sottha was, I think, my best friend, but we never spoke. I didn't know anyone else, except my wife, who ever understood me the same way—who could just look at me and know things. I would walk into the kitchen and without asking he knew to make the best things—a cup of coffee, eggs, anything. He just had the feeling in his heart, great intuition. Not like Sailhac, who also had it, but different. Sailhac was a salesman, in a good way. He would go to Nixon's table and take his order, and make very nice. Sottha would rather die than walk into the dining room, but he knew what Nixon wanted anyway. He remembered everything. He would do it for Kissinger too. What he thought about Kissinger and Nixon? My god, let's not get into that! ◄◄

REMI LAUVAND *Sirio may look like he favors the glamour of Daniel, but he invested most of his energy in Sottha because Sottha executed everything. Daniel was out front and Sottha was in back. That's not a bad thing. It's a great thing. Daniel and Sirio would come back from the dining room and communicate with Sottha or me, it was a kind of telepathy that exists only between them.*

GEOFFREY ZAKARIAN *It was obvious from the start, before Daniel even got there, that Sirio favored Sottha. If you didn't know them, you'd think they were in love with each other—and maybe, in a way, Sottha was in love with Sirio.*

WHILE SOTTHA WAS WORKING IN PARIS for Alain Passard, where he was named executive *sous*-chef in 1981, he met Daniel Boulud, then a rising star on the French cooking scene. The two became fast friends. When Boulud was offered an opportunity in 1984 to open the restaurant at the recently refurbished Plaza-Athénée in New York, he and Sottha went together, so when Daniel moved to Le Cirque in 1986, the deal was on the condition that the two come as a pair.

Sottha and Daniel remained, and are still, close. Yet Sirio and Sottha also developed a strong bond from the very beginning, though an unusual one. They shared almost nothing in the specifics of their histories. Sirio was poor and Sottha was rich. Sirio was tall and Sottha short. Sirio was ying to Sottha's yang. Since Sirio's English was only rudimentary and Sottha's practically nonexistent, they spoke in French.

What they shared was the language of survival. Sirio's path to safety is festooned with as much color and drama as possible. Sottha lives like a monk, surrounding himself with only bare essentials: music and his dog. The verb "to be" doesn't exist in Sottha's world. He winces when you mention Sirio or Daniel by name, as if by saying the words out loud you will cause them to cease existing. He'll say, "Sirio has the quality of being pleased," but never "Sirio was pleased." Sirio became to Sottha like Buddha, a contradictory if beneficent deity on earth.

SIRIO

S OTTHA WAS MY BEST, most dedicated, most conscientious cook. People think he is so quiet, so shy, but he is not. He is shy like I am shy. I understand him because he is a very emotional man, when he's mad, he speaks French, Cambodian. Like a shy person he overreacts to everything.

SOTTHA KUHN *When the arrival at Le Cirque happened, I was with Daniel. He was everything to me. You can never forget the kindness. Daniel is my friend. Things happen but that doesn't take away what was. We are all just parts of history and Daniel is history. When I met Sirio, it was very different. We heard of him in France. Working in the kitchen, people said that he made the best restaurant in the world in New York. He represented freedom to me, everything. Before anything you have to believe. Like people believe in God, I believe in Sirio. He has this ability to look into your face and know what you want, like a doctor knows if he should give you one aspirin or two. He doesn't need to ask you, he knows. There are no words.*

Each chef worked with me in a different way. Sottha saw one thing and he could make it better. I don't think we ever really became known for good pasta, the way an Italian makes pasta, until Sottha. He accepted the idea of it, he took his time in Italy to see how it is done. I could hire an Italian to learn that and he would not learn. I brought Sottha, he learned and made it better. He enjoyed cooking and reflected on cooking—he didn't just do it. He has this Asiatic way; a complexity that is very subtle. Sottha was a great cook. He never wanted to be a chef and there's a difference. ◄◄

JULIA CHILD *You couldn't run a great New York restaurant without an important chef. But I could see why Sirio almost didn't. He just knows so much more than other restaurateurs. So the person working with him would have to be very much under his control.*

THERE HAD NEVER REALLY been any question that Le Cirque would have a new executive chef. If Sirio couldn't have Sottha as his executive chef, he would set out to find the world's best, brightest, youngest Sirio protégé, and the world was going to know about it. No journalist was safe from Sirio's tirades on what he wanted in a chef and where he might find it. Sirio even briefly entertained the idea of interviewing American chefs, but decided it would be too radical a departure from his haute bistro philosophy. For all the public drama of the search, Sirio's ultimate choice was conservative. Sirio was not going to take a risk on someone who didn't have the gold stamp of world approval and the only approval that really mattered to him, his clients. He had called Alain Ducasse early in his search and Ducasse had suggested Sylvain Portay, the *chef de cuisine* at Le Louis XV in Monaco, Ducasse's most famous restaurant. It had been Portay who had been cooking the night his boss and Sirio had finally met. It was an illustrious choice.

Sirio was eager to break the connection that the world had made between Daniel and Le Cirque. The thirty-one-year-old Portay had started his career with Jean-Louis Palladin, an idol of the American food set for his irascible, gutsy, nicotine-infused charm, and his innovative take on French food, particularly the cuisine of his native Gascony. Only afterward had Portay trained with Ducasse and delivered for Le Louis XV three Michelin stars—a rating that Sirio felt was more honest and infinitely less corruptible than the *New York Times*'s stars.

But Portay was delayed by immigration troubles. The lag time allowed Sirio to build up his new culinary find to the media, to his clients, and to himself. Even if the building were on fire, he'd stay to answer the phones and would still tell callers that everything was fine and to come to lunch (which actually happened in 2002). He wouldn't admit that his restaurant was operating without an executive chef. From Daniel's departure in 1992 to February 1993, Sottha ran the kitchen as before. Once the new sensation finally arrived, Portay barely had time to unpack his bags or draft a menu before he had to deal with the most unpleasant welcome that ever greeted a new chef.

GAEL GREENE CAME IN and she wrote an article, saying I had made a mistake, that the new chef was not a star. Sottha was still cooking and Portay was barely there. We had to arrange for Sylvain's visa, which became very difficult, so he could not start until almost nine months after Daniel left. She wrote that I walked around the tables saying, "Daniel wasn't always a star." I did say that, and he wasn't. Great chefs don't happen overnight, they have to get used to the mentality of the restaurant. So while Sylvain got started, I worked extra hard to be positive. And maybe it made me like Sylvain even more, because everyone attacked him right away.

SYLVAIN PORTAY *Sirio protects you from these things like a father. Even if you did steal the candy bar he says "No, my son didn't do it." He's the best PR person a chef ever had. He called the critics, he called the customers. He makes you feel so good that I didn't take the criticism too personally. I was much more concerned for him. He was so upset—how could I be upset? And I was so busy. I was working at double the capacity and the way to do food at Le Cirque was very different from what I was used to.*

Good food is important, but it's more important that it's the kind of food people want to eat again and again. I could tell people weren't so happy. Maybe it was the times that were changing. The companies were telling their people they couldn't have lunch anymore. Iacocca got chased with "Chrysler CEO Fights with Union for Pay Cuts but Eats at Le Cirque." Ron Perelman was chairman of Revlon and could not even have a car. The glamour was starting to die out. If they wanted a salad, you had to give them a salad, but you made it the best salad. So we had to change. New York is the hardest place to have a restaurant because people expect so much and it changes so fast. Sylvain had trouble adjusting to New York mentally.

MIREILLE GIULIANO *[Veuve Cliquot, Inc.] I've seen a lot of companies and brands fail because they think they've made it. He's got a group of people—me, chefs, critics, maybe thousands of people. You are his friend, but he tests you. I call it the Sirio Test. He looks at who you've brought to the restaurant and you can tell, if you know him well, if he likes them or not by the way he tosses out a comment or how he is at the table when he comes by. If he sees he isn't interrupting or you get him alone, he's going to use you to "improve" himself and his restaurant. You think he isn't listening, but he soaks it up.*

JEREMIAH TOWER *[chef of Stars; author] The first time I ever met Sirio we were at a benefit. We spoke for maybe a minute and the next thing you know he keeps saying, "come here, come here, I need to talk to you." Suddenly I am in one of the coolers at the hotel restaurant where we were having this benefit, and I thought, "So, the famous Sirio Maccioni really likes boys, not girls!" But he just wanted to talk about Sylvain, how I thought he was doing. He absolutely needs confirmation of his success.*

We were busier than ever but there were more problems. The space at the Mayfair was getting ridiculous. I hired Adam Tihany, the architect who had worked on my New York City apartment, and we did as much work as we could to create more space in the dining room, to make it easier for people. He made the columns smaller and took out the ones we didn't need. We made lots of changes, but I couldn't change the hotel. It was getting very run-down and there was nobody to talk to. The union used to be supportive, but now we had troubles with them that were getting worse. Another guy and I were the oldest in the union, but now we were "Le Cirque" and they always tried to stop anyone from succeeding. I didn't want to see Le Cirque dragged down like the Colony. And, over my head, the lease was coming to an end. Not then, in the future, but not so far in the future: March 1998. I could never be sure that I would be able to stay in that space and succeed for the future—I had to think about my sons and my wife. So Adam and I started to look at spaces. ◄◄

ADAM TIHANY *Working with him on the Sixty-fifth Street space was a nightmare. He was intimately involved with every centimeter of it. But I survived. I fixed up the space, modified it. Then he came to me to tell me he wanted to design a restaurant from the ground up. Just like that. All I knew was that the concept would more than likely be Italian, that he refused to take in any investors, so that any design would come from Sirio's pockets, and that he hoped his sons would play an active role in whatever the restaurant grew up to be. As a restaurant architect, this just doesn't happen very often. I'd met him like everyone else, at the restaurant, and I guess I passed the test because we're still screaming at each other twenty years later. He simply won't take anything lying down.*

ONE OF THE CHANGES was happening at *The New York Times*. The dining pages of the paper now warranted their own section. New restaurants, food news, star chefs, recipes, and ingredients were the new fashion. Bryan Miller, who'd been the paper's restaurant critic for one whole phase in the American food revolution, was succeeded by the former food editor of the *Los Angeles Times,* Ruth Reichl. With her very first review, of Colors on Park Avenue, Reichl set herself apart from previous *New York Times* critics and food critics in general. Miller and his predecessor, Mimi Sheraton, were, at least on a culinary level, conservative Francophiles, and awarded their stars accordingly. Reichl made no bones about her disdain for the star system. She considered the experience of eating food to be almost as important as, if not more important than, the food itself. Her tastes were also more international. The combination was electric. Readers used to blow-by-blow descriptions of sauces and the food it accompanied were stunned to read Reichl's novelistic prose, quoting guests in the restaurant as she eavesdropped on their conversations, entwining daily life with her critique of the restaurant's food.

Reichl had grown up in New York City, the child of a professorial German Jew—a bookbinder by trade—and a mother hell-bent on poisoning her children with week-old leftovers from Horn and Hardart. Reichl's reaction had been to flee to Berkeley, California, where she lived a communal life, soaking beans and baking bread. She cofounded a cooperative restaurant called The Swallow and, like her mentor Alice Waters, was almost psychopathically drawn to good food and ingredients. If Sirio represented the culmination of the art of fine dining in the French manner, Reichl was the poster child for the new American food movement. Not that Reichl didn't appreciate French food; she just saw it from a different, more casual angle—partly as a result of the very food revolution fostered by the likes of Julia Child, Craig Claiborne, Pierre Franey, and Sirio Maccioni.

Had they met under different circumstances, Sirio and Reichl would probably have been attracted to each other on a purely intellectual basis. As it was, Sirio was about to be blindsided by a woman who he had never met, knew very little about, and was completely outside of his control.

On October 29, 1993, after six reviews for *The New York Times,* Ruth Reichl turned to Le Cirque. The review dropped two stars, and made one—its author, who became a celebrity and, overnight, the most powerful person in the food industry. The "two part" Le Cirque review remains probably the most talked about restaurant review ever written, and although the review may have hurt the feelings of its owner and his staff, it only cemented Le Cirque's position as the most important restaurant in the world.

Reichl's article was written like a play in two acts, complete with a prologue. Reichl describes herself as remaining mostly unknown to New York's restaurateurs. As a result, she could frequently dine incognito. She explained that, of her six meals at Le Cirque sampling the cooking of Sylvain Portay, it wasn't until the fourth meal that her identity was discovered by Sirio, and that this discovery made the two groups of dining experiences like night and day. While she ate incognito, she wrote, her meal was an ordinary "parade of brown food" and the service "brusque to the point of rudeness." At the end of a first act filled with humiliation, snobbery, and mediocre food, she wrote, "as I pay the bill I find myself wishing that when I walked in and the maître d' asked did I have a reservation, I had just said no and left."

The beginning of Act Two finds Reichl, now discovered, arriving early for a 9:45 reservation. The room is packed, but she quotes Sirio as saying, "The King of Spain is waiting at the bar, but your table is ready." Reichl has the meal of a lifetime. Without any further reference to the ugliness of her first visits, she lulled the reader into remembering what Le Cirque does best. After a few more meals as "a favored guest," she wrote, "I walk reluctantly out into the cool evening air, sorry to leave this fabulous circus. Life in the real world has never been this good."

Reichl wasn't the first to point out that being known to Sirio and the staff at Le Cirque made all the difference. Both Canaday and Sheraton had complained of the same treatment. In fact both had written similarly styled reviews. Canaday was unknown but didn't matter, and Sheraton, despite her best efforts to disguise herself, never walked into the restaurant without being recognized. Miller and Greene made no attempt to dine at Le Cirque incognito. Reichl's stinging success came in communicating to her readers what it felt like to be unrecognized in a restaurant where being recognized, especially by Sirio, meant everything in the world.

By contrasting the two experiences so brilliantly, and portraying herself as being treated well only because she had borrowed someone else's power—that of *The New York Times*—Reichl connected her to thousands of disgruntled patrons the world over who have felt mistreated by haughty maîtres d'hôtel.

Sirio, who can tell you the table numbers of certain parties thirty years ago and the date of every review ever written about his restaurant, has no memory at all of when Reichl's review was printed, or how he reacted. He succumbed to a blind rage that lasted for more than four years.

I LIKE MANY FOOD CRITICS. I think it is an important profession. What I don't like is that there is no way one person can know everything there is to know about food, French, Japanese, Italian, Chinese, and have an opinion about it, and then expect people to follow blindly what they write. So because they don't and can't know everything—about food, about people, about the business, or about the mentality of a restaurant— they reduce everything to the lowest level. They think this helps people, but what it really does is keep the critics employed, and reduce everything and everybody to nothing, to where everyone is the same, and boring.

When Ruth Reichl came it was a game. It was harder to see, and I didn't like it, but maybe it was at least honest. The part about hypocrisy was not honest. Some people keep on crying about hypocrisy in a restaurant when there is no such thing. I have the editors, the managing editors, the owners, and the investors of these papers and magazines all here for dinner. All of them want "their" tables held. Then their critic comes in and they never tell her that this is how they expect to be treated. They say they are fair, but they are not fair. They say they are liberal, but they behave liked Conservatives. It's good to be liberal, it's good to be socialist, it's good to be anything you want, as long as you're honest. But don't preach one thing—like most of the time the critics—and come in under disguise and then if you don't get recognized, get upset about it.

FLORENCE FABRICANT *It hurt him so much because it remains, probably, the most accurate portrayal of the dining experience at Le Cirque then, and of Sirio. Was it unfair? Yes and no. It just cut a little too deep. Because it was accurate, and because to the extent a critic can be, she was genuinely removed from the structure of the* **Times.**

RUTH REICHL *I was still in Los Angeles and I was coming to New York on the weekends to do reviews, I really wasn't known in New York a lot of that summer—when I was eating those meals it was very easy to be unknown. It was kind of a great period. The Le Cirque review came up early and there was a lot of pressure on that review. I knew that I was speaking to power in that one. I did not sleep for three nights before it came out. I knew that if there was one mistake, I was in terrible trouble. The publisher of* **The New York Times**—*Punch Sulzberger—liked that restaurant a lot. That was something that can't not be in your mind. My editors were nervous. I don't think they read any of my other reviews at as high a level before they went to print. That one was read at the very top of the paper.*

In a sense, it was a very good review. She came in from Los Angeles and didn't know anything about New York, about New York people or the people of Le Cirque. Maybe she was nervous when she came—I mean can you see me go to someone I'm supposedly pretending not to know, and say, "I give you the table of the King of Spain." The King of Spain was already sitting there. Maybe I joked with her ... that sounds more like me, and she took the sentence and made this thing of it that I still have to hear every day. I don't mind so much with her because she's an intelligent person and it was a good line. But let's call it what it is—a game. ◄◄

AT A RESTAURANT LIKE LE CIRQUE, the range of opinions has always been extreme because the expectation has always been so high. A freelance food writer named Regina Schrambling had had the same experience as Reichl at Le Cirque, but in reverse: she'd been once with a friend of the restaurant and had one of the best meals of her life, only to come back a week later expecting to be treated like royalty and finding they didn't remember her at all: "They were vacuuming the room, putting up chairs, the waiter literally demanded that we order, and Sirio turned his back on us."

Something had gone unnoticed and unfixed at the Schrambling table and a decade later she still has nothing nice to say about Sirio. No matter how successful, every restaurant finds a customer somehow, somewhere, who feels as enraged as Schrambling. The difference between Reichl's review and the many other reviews that had pointed out similar inconsistencies was that now more people cared. More people had been treated badly at restaurants, not necessarily at Le Cirque. Le Cirque was just the best-known, most international and recognizable brand name. In a world that was still without Mario's, Emeril's, Daniel's, or Wolfgang's, who else to cast the blame upon? In the post-Reagan world, Le Cirque fit the bill perfectly, and Sirio in particular. Where Mimi Sheraton had just sounded bitchy, Reichl sounded a call to battle.

SIRIO

S HE WROTE A STORY that worked for her and she became famous because of it. She doesn't know that I sleep on the banquette, that I have to smile and try not to complain when the wife of her boss comes, when I want to scream? She doesn't know that I am trying to make things better, but there's the union and the managers and the hotel people who never answer the phone, and all these things I have to do. I am on the stage fighting all the time.

RUTH REICHL *I think of restaurants as a kind of public theater. You know I think a place that aspires to this kind of four-star glory, which he does, pretty much promises anybody who is willing to plunk down that kind of money a really magical experience. And that means being well taken care of. I think that's in the contract. And I really felt that contract was not honored. As a restaurant critic I could not honestly say to, you know, Joe Sidewalk, you come in here and you're going to have a great experience. I think people go to those types of restaurants expecting to be treated—if only for a few hours—as if they are rich people who have servants and are being showered with that old English royalty kind of service. And I think those restaurants owe us that.*

JACQUES TORRES *Everyone always had an opinion about that review. But we went on. We were in many ways stronger than before. We came together. I always thought that after Sirio was finished screaming, that all he really cared about was losing the star. Not because I think he cares so much about the stars—Le Cirque is Le Cirque and Sirio is Sirio—but just because he is so competitive. He hates losing. Anything!*

ALAIN DUCASSE *When he gets attacked, he calls me. "C'est des cons! The worst paper." I tell him, "Laissez passer. This will pass." Sirio is too sensitive to criticism. I tell him, you're Le Cirque, you're Maccioni, don't worry about it! You're an institution. Critics will pass, positive or negative, and you continue on your route. You have no worries. You have three stars, four stars, you're Le Cirque. You're in the race. Let them talk. But I know he doesn't hear me.*

RUTH REICHL *I knew he was pissed. He attacked me for years in the press. I mean I would open these things, letters from Le Cirque's people, and they'd be like "Aaaah … !" And you sort of love him for being that out there—for caring that much, you know? Clearly it wounded him in some place that matters to him. So, I don't think it was just the stars. I think it was more than that because I would think economically my review was probably good for him, because it brought so much support from all those people who went and said, "What does that idiot know? She doesn't know anything."*

FOR ALL THE FURY, Sirio had to accept that Reichl had touched on the key element that he knew in his heart he would have to change if the restaurant were to survive another twenty years. Like the Colony before him, Sirio had survived so long and so well, he was now seen as the establishment, not as the champion of a very well dressed, but still aspiring, "Joe Sidewalk." It became clear that he needed a larger platform, a bigger stage, and a circus that traveled, possibly without him and his beloved ladies.

SIRIO

I TALKED ALL THE TIME to Frank Zappa. He had prostate cancer and was very sick. He was very brave. He was very matter-of-fact, very honest. The most honest American I ever met. We had done a TV show, he made fun of the ladies of Le Cirque with their big hair. He could make fun and not hurt. There just wasn't anyone like him, and I kept saying to him, "This talk is very bad, very bad, you must want to live. I'll see you next week in Los Angeles," And he would say, "Sirio, let's not play games, okay?" I sent Francisco out to Los Angeles to make him Crème Brûlée. I'm not stupid, I didn't think it would save him, but, you know, I wanted to make him comfortable, happy, something. We had always talked about traveling together. He wanted me to come to Moscow and I wanted him to come to Montecatini. We agreed we would, but of course it never happened. Very close to the end, we talked on the phone and he made me stop trying to pretend he wasn't going away. It was very hard. I never had this conversation with anyone else. When I finally gave in he said, "Good, good for you, you'll feel better. But I guess this means we're not going to get to Moscow or Montecatini." He died a few days later, on December 4, 1993.

It was the third death of a friend in three years: Victor Jacobs had died the year before, and Frank (Dilia) the year before that. Frank was so honest, so trustworthy: he did everything for me. He was a policeman back in Italy and even did part-time work for them in New York. Maybe it's why I get along well with policemen: I see Frank in all of them. And Victor, my god, I can't speak of it. I think I talked to him every day for my whole life. When he died, you know, I really felt like I was orphaned all over again. ⤛⤙

SIRIO MEANS IT when he says he does not go to funerals. After his parent's deaths, he never went to another, not even for his beloved grandmother, Annunciata, in 1971, or his uncles, Alberto and Guido, who died within a year of each other in 1996 and 1997. Superstitious as any Italian grandmother, he makes the sign of the cross every time he passes the cemetery in Montecatini where everyone in his family is buried—a main road that he uses several times a day when he is in residence. He knows they are there, but he doesn't go to see them. Many Italian families place their ancestors' remains in elaborate chapels, with statues and fig-urines, laden with fresh flowers that are changed daily. The Maccionis lie behind the smallest graves, their names clearly marked, with one small photograph each, a small vase of plastic flowers, and a votive candle. His parents and grandparents lie in separate vaults, together in the farthest reaches of the cemetery. Sirio likes it that way. No journalist or food critic or head of state has ever been there. Even though Sirio himself doesn't know exactly where they are in the cemetery, he knows that his parents and grandparents are there in death as they were in life—poor, dignified, proud, and terribly private.

Magret de Canard au Gingembre et Cassis Serves 4

When Alain Sailhac started cooking at Le Cirque he noticed that anything he cooked that had a bone attached to it—a leg of duck confit, a lamb chop, a chicken drumstick—was likely to get swiped off a cooking station by Sirio. Even a finished plate coming back from the dining room would get waylaid by the maestro, eager for a middle-of-service nibble. Sailhac also noticed that if there was anything sweet or tart nearby, Sirio would spread it on whatever he had salvaged—or dunk the meat in it. These days Sirio does sit down to eat—although at the height of service sometimes he still can't resist an impromptu dunk.

This recipe serves the duck off the bone. Sirio insists that the sauce be served on the side, as well as with the duck (a customer should never have to ask). It's great served with cooked wild rice and blanched snow peas.

- 1 orange
- 1 lemon
- ¼ cup sugar
- 1 cup Madeira
- 2 tablespoons minced or shredded fresh ginger
- 1 shallot, minced
- 4 tablespoons black currant jelly
- 1 tablespoon green peppercorns, rinsed
- ¼ cup demi-glace (or 1 cup chicken stock reduced to ¼ cup)
- 4 tablespoons preserved black currant berries (optional)
  Salt
- 2 duck breasts, halved

Take the zest off the orange and off half of the lemon. Juice the fruit. Mince the zests. Set aside.

Caramelize the sugar in a heavy saucepan over medium-low heat, being careful not to let it burn, about 4 minutes. Add the zests and cook for 2 minutes more, stirring constantly.

Add the citrus juices and Madeira—don't worry if the caramel seizes; it will melt as the liquid heats up—and cook, stirring constantly, for 10 minutes over high heat, reducing by almost half. Reduce the heat to medium and add the ginger, shallot, black currant jelly, peppercorns, and demi-glace (or stock). Simmer for 15 minutes more, stirring occasionally, to reduce the sauce considerably, so that it is thick but pourable.

Add the preserved black currants (if using), salt to taste, and reserve. This sauce can be made up to a week in advance and kept in a tightly covered container in the refrigerator.

When you're ready to finish the dish, set your broiling pan 6 inches from the heating element and preheat the broiler. Score the breasts' skin and the underlying layer of fat in a crisscross pattern, being careful not to cut through to the meat. Salt liberally on both sides. Arrange the breasts skin side down on the pan and broil for 5 minutes. Flip and cook for another 5 minutes. If the skin is not browned and crisped at this point, broil up to 1 or 2 more minutes, making sure not to let the breasts burn or blacken.

Warm the sauce while you let the breasts rest a few minutes before slicing them thinly on the bias.

TO SERVE Serve 1 breast half per person with 2 to 3 tablespoons of the sauce.

BOUILLABAISSE, MARSEILLES STYLE

SERVES 4 TO 6

AT THE RESTAURANT, the chefs adapted an authentic Provençal dish from the way it might be prepared on a seaside quay to the professional kitchen—and you can do something similar at home.

You should make the stock and rouille the night before you plan to serve the soup. And, as you assemble the bouillabaisee, make sure that the liquid returns to a rolling boil between batches of seafood. Sirio suggests, "There really is no recipe for bouillabaisse. This is what we do in the restaurant; at home, you just relax, make it with what you have, and serve with lots of toasted bread with garlic!"

BOUILLABAISSE

1 red snapper (about 2 to 3 pounds)

¾ pound medium shrimp (16/20 count)

1 pound monkfish filet, cut into 1½-inch pieces

2 cloves garlic, peeled and minced

½ cup plus 2 tablespoons olive oil

Pinch of saffron

2 ounces Ricard or Pernod

2 fennel bulbs, cleaned and cut into ½-inch slices

2 large tomatoes, peeled and diced

2 pounds littleneck or other small clams, scrubbed

2 tablespoons small leaf-Italian basil

FISH STOCK

¼ cup olive oil

1 pound lobster bodies, cut into small pieces

1 onion, finely chopped

1 small fennel bulb, finely chopped

1 leek, white part and half of green part, cleaned and finely chopped

1 head garlic, unpeeled and cut in half

6 ripe tomatoes, cut into large chunks

1 crushed star anise

2 quarts fish stock (or water)

Salt and pepper

4 *small new potatoes, peeled and cut in half*

4 *egg yolks*

6 *large cloves garlic, peeled, crushed, and chopped*

Pinch of saffron

½ *cup olive oil*

Salt and black pepper

Cayenne

Baguette, sliced and toasted

BEGIN THE BOUILLABAISSE AND FISH STOCK

Cut off the head of the red snapper and remove and discard the gills and eyes. Cut the fish into 1½-inch pieces, keeping the skin on (this should yield about 1 pound), and chill until ready to cook. Clean the head and the bones thoroughly in cold water.

Shell and devein the shrimp, reserving heads and shells. Chill the shrimp until ready to cook.

FISH STOCK

Heat the oil in a pan large enough to hold all the recipe's ingredients. Add the red snapper bones, shrimp heads and shells, and lobster bodies. Cook for about 5 minutes, until they begin to break down and the lobster bodies start to change color. Add the onion, fennel, leek, and garlic and simmer until the vegetables have softened, about 5 minutes. Add the tomatoes and star anise, cook for 3 minutes more, then add the fish stock (or water) and bring the pot to a boil. Keep it at a gentle boil for 10 minutes.

Strain the stock, pressing well on the solids to extract as much liquid as possible before discarding them. Season with salt and pepper to taste. Reserve in the refrigerator until needed, up to 2 days.

BOUILLABAISSE

Marinate the reserved snapper pieces and the monkfish pieces in a large bowl with 2 cloves of minced garlic, ½ cup of the olive oil, a pinch of saffron, and the Ricard or Pernod. Keep in the refrigerator until needed, up to 1 hour.

Heat the remaining 2 tablespoons olive oil in a 6-quart pot over high heat and add the sliced fennel. Cook the fennel until it begins to caramelize around the edges, about 5 to 7 minutes. Add 2 quarts of the fish stock and the potatoes (for the rouille) and bring to a boil. Boil until the potatoes are tender, about 10 minutes. Remove the potatoes to the bowl you'll make the rouille in and keep the fennel warm on the side. Turn the heat under the stock to low.

ROUILLE

Add the egg yolks, chopped garlic, pinch of saffron, and 1 tablespoonful of fish stock to the bowl with the potatoes. Purée using an immersion blender or pound to a smooth paste with a pestle. Slowly whisk in the ½ cup olive oil until the mixture is creamy and season with salt, black pepper, and cayenne to taste. Set aside.

TO FINISH AND SERVE

Add the tomatoes to the pan with the broth and bring to a boil. Add the clams, cover the pot, and cook them until they open, about 3 to 5 minutes. Discard any clams that don't open and divide the cooked clams among the warmed serving bowls. Add the reserved shrimp to the pot, cover it, and cook them until they've lost their raw gray color, about 2 minutes. Divide the shrimp among the warmed serving bowls, adding 1 tablespoonful of broth to each bowl to keep them warm. Salt the fish and add with the marinade to the pot, cooking it just a few moments after it turns opaque. If it looks like the fish will crowd the pot, cook in two batches. Portion the cooked fish among the serving dishes.

Ladle broth over the fish and shellfish, garnish with slices of cooked fennel and sprigs of small-leaf Italian basil, and serve the toasts topped with the rouille on the side.

BASS IN BAROLO SERVES 4

THIS LE CIRQUE FAVORITE was served to the Pope when the restaurant cooked for him in 1995. Browning the paupiettes, mounting the sauce, and warming the leeks à la minute is a tall order for many home cooks. So, if the recipe looks intimidating, cook it for two the first time (don't cut the sauce in half, however—it's hard to make less than the amount specified). Like many of the dishes prepared in the restaurant, a deconstructed version will work fine at home: Sirio just slices the potatoes very thin, cooks them until they're golden, lays them on top of the cooked fish, and then tosses on the leeks and sauce.

BAROLO SAUCE

1 tablespoon olive oil

4 shallots, roughly chopped (about 1 cup)

2 thyme branches

1 cup Barolo (or another dark, rich red wine)

½ cup ruby port

1 teaspoon cassis puree (or cassis jam)

1 stick butter, chopped and chilled

Salt and black pepper

BRAISED LEEKS

3 tablespoons olive oil

6 leeks, whites only, cut into a matchstick julienne

Salt

PAUPIETTES

2 or 3 very large baking potatoes, peeled

¾ cup clarified butter or more as needed

Four 4 x 2-inch sea bass filets

Salt and white pepper

BAROLO SAUCE

Heat the olive oil in a small saucepan over high heat, add the shallots and thyme, and sauté for about 2 minutes, until the shallots begin to color.

Add the Barolo and port and reduce until "dry"—there should be only a few tablespoons of liquid left in the pan. Strain the sauce, making sure to extract as much liquid as possible from the shallots before discarding, and return it to the pan. The sauce can be prepared through this step up to 1 day in advance.

BRAISED LEEKS

Heat the olive oil in a medium sauté pan over medium-high heat, add the leeks, and cook, stirring and tossing frequently until the leeks are soft but have not taken on any color, about 10 minutes. The leeks can be made a few hours ahead of time; warm over low heat and salt to taste before serving.

PAUPIETTES

Thinly slice the potatoes on a mandoline into 1½ x 4-inch rectangles. Toss the sliced potatoes with 1 or 2 tablespoons of clarified butter to keep them from discoloring. Dry the sea bass filets completely with paper towels and season liberally with salt and white pepper.

Lay a potato rectangle on the lower left-hand side of a clean, dry cutting board with the narrow end facing you. Arrange another piece of potato next to it, overlapping them by about ½ inch. Repeat twice more, so you have four pieces of potato shingled across the board in front of you. Now repeat the process, overlapping the bottoms of the next four potato slices by 1½ inches with the tops of the first potatoes you laid out. Set one filet in the center of the rectangle, over the section in the middle where the potatoes overlap. Fold the far side up over the fish, then the near side over those potatoes, and press gently to seal the paupiette. Turn the paupiette over and brush it with clarified butter. Repeat with each filet. Hold paupiettes in the refrigerator for at least 10 minutes, or until ready to cook.

Preheat the oven to 400°F.

Heat ¼ cup of clarified butter in each of two large sauté pans over medium-high heat until very hot (a drop of water should sizzle), then slide 2 paupiettes into each pan. Cook for 3 minutes on each side, or until the potatoes have browned and crisped. Set the pans in the oven for 1 or 2 minutes to finish cooking while you finish the sauce.

TO FINISH AND SERVE

Bring the sauce to a boil, remove from the heat, add the cassis, and whisk in the butter a few pieces at a time, adding more after each addition has been fully incorporated. Season with salt and black pepper and use immediately (the sauce cannot be reheated after the butter has been added.)

Make a bed of leeks just smaller than the paupiettes in the center of each plate, spoon the Barolo sauce in a ring around the leeks, then retrieve the paupiettes from the oven and set them on top of the leeks. Serve immediately.

BLACK TIE SCALLOPS SERVES 4

THE VERSION SERVED at Le Cirque 2000, called Maine Sea Scallops in Black Tie, is a signature dish. While it looks complicated, it's actually a study in kitchen preparation: once the spinach is blanched, the puff pastry is cut, and the sauce ingredients are prepared, it's just assembly-line preparation.

Out of the restaurant, Sirio simplifies the dish. He leaves out the pastry or makes it smaller. Without the pastry, it's an easy entrée—scallops, a shaving of black truffle, a hint of spinach, and the juice poured over just before serving.

> 1 black truffle, weighing a little over 1 ounce
> Flour, for dusting
> ½ pound puff pastry, defrosted if frozen
> 1 cup loosely packed large spinach leaves, stemmed
> Salt
> 8 sea scallops (1¼-inch diameter), tough muscle removed
> Pepper
> 1 egg
> 1 tablespoon olive oil
> 3 tablespoons ruby port
> 2 tablespoons demi-glace (or ¼ cup chicken stock reduced to 2 tablespoons)
> 2 tablespoons butter, at room temperature

Using a mandoline or truffle slicer, thinly slice the truffle and set aside. Reserve any trimmings.

Dust your work surface with flour and roll the puff pastry out as thin as possible, about ⅛-inch thick. Using a pastry cutter, cut out 16 circles of pastry just slightly larger than the scallops, approximately 1½ inches in diameter, and eight 1½ x 4-inch rectangles. Transfer to a lightly floured baking sheet and chill until ready to use.

Blanch the spinach leaves in boiling salted water for 1 to 2 minutes, until soft. Plunge the blanched leaves into a bowl of cold water, then drain, shaking off as much of the water as possible. Line a baking sheet with a kitchen towel and carefully unfurl each leaf onto the towel, arranging them so they don't overlap. Blot with paper towels if the spinach is wet. Reserve.

Make two parallel horizontal cuts into each scallop, cutting almost but not all the way through, so they remain attached on one side. Salt and pepper each cut lightly as you go and stuff with a slice or two of truffle. Place the stuffed scallop on a blanched spinach leaf and fold the spinach up over the scallop, using additional leaves as necessary to completely envelop the scallop. Set aside any remaining truffle slices with the reserved trimmings.

Make an egg wash: beat together the egg with 1 teaspoon water and set aside. Retrieve the pastry from the refrigerator. Brush one narrow end of a pastry rectangle with the egg wash, set the wrapped scallop on its side at the opposite end, and wrap the pastry around the scallop, sealing it with the egg wash. Trim to size if the pastry overlaps significantly. Brush the edges of 2 pastry rounds with egg wash and firmly affix them to the top and bottom of the pastry-wrapped scallop. Repeat with the remaining scallops. Chill for at least 15 minutes and up to 6 hours. Reserve the egg wash, in the refrigerator.

Preheat the oven to 450°F. Brush the scallop rounds with the egg wash, transfer to a parchment-lined baking sheet, and bake for 7 to 10 minutes, until puffed and golden brown. Rest for 3 minutes before plating.

To make the sauce, finely chop all reserved truffle pieces. Heat the olive oil in a sauté pan over high heat and sweat the truffle until fragrant, about 2 minutes. Add the ruby port and demi-glace (or stock) and reduce by half. Just before serving, beat the butter in off the heat. (The sauce cannot be reheated after the butter has been added or it will break.)

TO SERVE Cut each scallop round in half (vertically) with a serrated knife. Spoon a pool of sauce onto the center of the plates, arrange four scallop halves with their layered interiors facing outward per plate, and serve immediately.

Napoleon Le Cirque SERVES 4

THE FRUIT GARNISH and fruit purée for this dessert change with the seasons. In winter the fruit on the plate might be kiwis and blood oranges; in the summer, mixed berries and stone fruits. So follow the spirit of the kitchen at Le Cirque and use a mixture of the best fruits available to you.

> 1 pound package frozen puff pastry, defrosted
>
> Flour, for dusting
>
> ½ cup corn syrup thinned with 1 or 2 tablespoons water
>
> 2 cups pastry cream (page 100)
>
> ½ cup heavy cream, whipped
>
> Confectioners' sugar, for dusting
>
> 3 cups sliced mixed ripe fruit (mango, raspberry, kiwis, blood oranges, etc.)
>
> Granulated sugar (optional)

Preheat the oven to 375°F.

To prepare the pastry, line a baking sheet with parchment. On a lightly floured surface, roll out the puff pastry to the size of the baking sheet, place on the lined sheet, and cover with another layer of parchment paper. Weight the puff pastry with another baking sheet and bake for 6 minutes.

Lower the heat to 325°F and take the weighted pastry out of the oven. Remove the top baking sheet and parchment (don't discard the parchment) and brush a thin coat of the corn syrup mixture over the surface of the puff pastry. Lay the parchment back over the glazed dough, and flip the dough over. Remove the parchment from what was the bottom side of the dough (discard this piece) and brush a thin coat of the corn syrup mixture over the second side. Cut the pastry lengthwise into thirds and return to the oven uncovered. Bake until doubled in height, about 15 minutes.

Transfer the pastry to a rack to cool. Once the pastry is cool, cut each strip into into 4 even pieces.

To make the fruit purée, purée 2 cups of the ripe fruit in a blender or food processor, then pass it through a fine mesh strainer. Taste and correct for sweetness with additional sugar if necessary. Transfer to a squeeze bottle and reserve.

To assemble the napoleon, place a layer of puff pastry in the center of a large dessert plate, slather it with a ¼-inch thick layer of pastry cream, stack another piece of puff pastry on top off the cream layer, then follow with another layer of pastry cream and a layer of whipped cream. Dust a third puff pastry square with powder sugar and place on top.

TO SERVE Arrange one quarter of the remaining 1 cup of sliced fruit around the base of the napoleon and garnish the plate with 2 or 3 rings of fruit purée. Repeat for the other three portions and serve.

CRÈME BRÛLÉE LE CIRQUE   SERVES 8

WHILE FOOD HISTORIANS ARGUE about who "invented" crème brûlée, two decades and several pastry chefs later, Francisco Gutierrez, the restaurant's longest-serving employee, is still making it quietly in Le Cirque's kitchens—often 300 times a day. This recipe is his, with two minor alterations for the home kitchen: at the restaurant they bake the custards at a lower temperature (if you have a convection oven you can do the same) and, working with the even, high heat of a restaurant salamander, they use brown sugar for the caramelized crust.

To make this at home, you'll need eight 1-inch-tall-x-4-inch-long ovular ramekins (7 ounces) and a kitchen blowtorch.

  1 *quart heavy cream*
  1 *Tahitian vanilla bean, halved and scraped*
  ¾ *cup plus 8 tablespoons granulated sugar*
  8 *egg yolks, in a bowl large enough to hold all the recipe's ingredients*

Preheat the oven to 300°F.

Combine the cream, vanilla, and ¾ cup sugar in a saucepan, warming the mixture over low heat until hot to the touch (about 110°F), stirring occasionally.

Temper the egg yolks with 1 or 2 spoonfuls or two of the warmed cream mixture by stirring the cream together with the yolks to warm them through. Pour the remainder of the cream into the bowl with the yolks and stir to blend.

Pass the mixture through a chinois or a fine mesh strainer into a clean bowl or back into the pan the cream mixture was warmed in, using the back of a spoon to make sure as much of the scraped vanilla as possible passes through the strainer.

Split the eight ramekins between two rimmed baking sheets or roasting pans (or set them in one if you have one large enough to accommodate them all). Ladle the cream mixture into the ramekins, filling each one ladleful at a time to ensure that the vanilla is evenly distributed. Create a water bath for the custards by pouring enough hot tap water into the baking sheet (it's easiest if you use a teakettle) to come halfway up the ramekins.

Cover the sheet(s) with aluminum foil and bake for 1 hour 15 minutes. The custards are finished when they look firm and tremble just slightly in the center. Chill for at least 3 hours and up to 3 days.

TO SERVE Just before serving, sprinkle each custard with 1 tablespoon of granulated sugar and "brûlée" with a kitchen torch on full power from about 1½ inches away, browning but not burning the sugar. Serve immediately.

THIS PAGE
TOP:
A Maccioni and Palmieri family reunion in front of Sirio's birthplace, Summer 1983.

BOTTOM LEFT:
Richard Nixon and Henry Kissinger exiting Le Cirque after their "reunion" lunch, 1985.

BOTTOM RIGHT:
Bill Blass, Sirio, and John Fairchild outside Le Cirque, 1992.

FACING PAGE
TOP:
Sirio and Sofia Loren at Le Cirque, 1981.

BOTTOM LEFT:
Mrs. Jaqueline Kennedy Onassis and Sirio at Le Cirque

BOTTOM RIGHT:
Four Stars! Daniel Boulud, Dr. Bernard Kruger, Sirio, Egidiana, and Sottha Kuhn, 1987.

THIS PAGE

TOP LEFT:
Sirio with Andy
Warhol, at
"The Studio"
New York, 1985.

TOP RIGHT:
Barbara Walters,
Beverly Sills, and
Sirio, Le Cirque,
1983.

BOTTOM:
President Reagan
comes to dinner like
any "normal" person,
March 1981.

FACING PAGE

TOP:
Sirio in his kitchen
in Montecatini,
wearing only "an
apron, out of respect
for the white
truffles!," 1982.

BOTTOM LEFT:
Liz Smith and Sirio
at his apartment on
64th Street, 1983.

BOTTOM RIGHT:
Frank Sinatra at Le
Cirque, 1980.
Donald and Ivana
Trump are reflected
in the mirror.

THREE-RING
CIRCUS

SINATRA

ONE OF SIRIO'S most important maxims is that a restaurateur or a waiter must never cross the line between client and friend. Yet much of Sirio's success has come from knowing when it is advantageous to step over the line, and to pay for its consequences.

Sirio's relationship with Frank Sinatra had only continued to deepen. By the time the two found themselves sitting at President Ronald Wilson Reagan's first inauguration in January 1981, they had been friendly for thirty years. Sinatra had been "Chairman of the Board" for as long as Sirio had been working his way up through the restaurant trade. Just because Sirio had arrived at the pinnacle of his success as a restaurateur didn't stop Sinatra from treating Sirio as his protégé. And Sirio, ever careful of the role he had to play, trod carefully.

SIRIO

S INATRA LOVED TO TALK ABOUT FOOD. He thought he knew
everything. He was always telling me that he would show me what
"real" Italian food was all about. I couldn't say to him I was from Tuscany
and knew more about food than he would ever know, so I kept my mouth
shut. Somehow I gave him some connection to the old country ...
although the old country wasn't so fond of him. The one time he went to
Italy he got booed. But he was very nice to me, very nice, and I learned a
lot from him—but not about food!

We had this problem. He was always asking me to call him by his
name, Frank. And I always told him, "Mr. Sinatra, I cannot." But he did not
accept that this was how it had to be, and he did not like to be contradicted.
In my head I could not even say the name "Frank," so I said to him, "Outside
the restaurant, I will call you Francis." He liked that—although every time
I saw him it was in the restaurant, so I still always called him Mr. Sinatra,
and he got angry and said, "Francis!" and I said, "Yes, Mr. Sinatra, Francis."

He was very good to me, very generous. He would hand out hun-
dred-dollar bills to us for nothing. But maybe I could say we had a special
relationship. When my son Mario was born he sat much of the morning
downstairs in his white limousine before going right up to the floor with
an engraved silver brush from Cartier inscribed "To Mario from Francis."

He could also be a pain in the neck. Right from the beginning he
would leave me these notes. If he liked his meal, he'd leave a note that said
on it, "Yes." And if he didn't like it, he'd leave a note that just said "No."
Nothing else. And I knew that if it said no, I had to talk to him. He would
ask me to call him very early at the Waldorf Towers, where he stayed when
he was in New York. He couldn't sleep at that time of day, but for me, it
was the only time I ever got to sleep. Still sometimes I had to go to the
Waldorf, and I waited in the lobby and he would come down and we
would have coffee and he would go through every detail of what was
wrong in the restaurant. I have overworked my whole life so I don't have
to hear the criticism of so-called food critics—but I had to listen to Sinatra
tell me what makes a good restaurant and what makes good food.

After I left the Colony, I went back to Europe with the idea that maybe I would stay there for good. I was in Paris and he rang up to tell me to come to his birthday party in Biarritz, as his guest. I don't know how he knew I was in Paris, but he always seemed to know when I was looking into a deal. Mauro had just been born and I explained to him that he didn't want a whole family at his party. "Just come, bring the whole family."

So we went. It was a horrible drive over the mountains across France. All of Sinatra's gang was at this party and it was fun. Sinatra had taken all the cabanas around the famous pool by the ocean at the Hôtel du Palais in Biarritz. Egidiana did the walk, you know, like women do, coming down the stone stairs to the pool. She looked great, but then she slipped and nearly broke her neck and my god, afterward he treated her like the Empress of Persia. It was almost too much. He showered the boys with presents and mostly with affection. He really liked them, though he also didn't hesitate to give me a warning. Marco had taped my wife's falling and Sinatra's fussing—the whole scene—with a small camera. Sinatra said that if the tape ever fell into the hands of the paparazzi, who were everywhere in the hotel, he would kill either me or them. Other than that, we talked about business and I told him that maybe if the deals in Paris didn't work out that I was going to start my own restaurant. He was very supportive. But he kept saying that when we got back to New York he would show me this "real" Italian food.

So when we got back to New York he wanted to be very involved in the food at Le Cirque and he took me out to a place where he always ordered the veal milanese. I went into shock. I couldn't believe it, they dropped this barely pounded-out veal into oil ... I swear to you it was the same oil they used for the *fritto misto,* the fish, and probably the dishes too. It was disgusting. It wasn't food, it was garbage, but the people came out and smiled at him with stupid faces, and he ate it and said, "Now, this is food!" And he kept taking me to places, every time, for months, and I couldn't say anything to him, and he came to Le Cirque and only ate the Italian dishes and left the notes with the "no" written on them. One night I even had Edigiana come to the kitchen to cook—he didn't know—and he still left the "no" note. She was very upset!

By the time we were together at the inauguration of Reagan in 1981, we had known each other—my god—thirty years. He did not invite me to the inauguration—Reagan did—but he invited me to a party he was having. Every one of his people were there—Johnny Carson, Sammy Davis Jr., Peter Lawford—and they had a white actor put on black face. To me, an Italian, that was bad enough, but then this same actor presented an act about Miss Lillian Carter, the mother of the president, which was very mean. Now I didn't know Miss Lillian. But I had spoken many times to Carter, and I thought him the most intelligent man, the only one who had the decency to try to look at the world in a right way—and here they were making fun of his mother.

We left and went back to the Fairfax, where Sinatra was also staying, and I wrote a quick note to Sinatra.

The next morning at 6:00 A.M. the phone starts ringing and it's Sinatra screaming into the phone, "*No?* You leave a note that says *No!* You son of a bitch, How *dare* you come to *my* party and criticize me." He demanded that I come down to the lobby to meet him for coffee. I said, "*No,* Mr. Sinatra." He screamed back, "Are you refusing to talk to me?"

I got angry and said, "*Yes,* Mr. Sinatra," and he said that if I called him Mr. Sinatra one more time that he was going to kill me, but I hung up the phone and went back to bed.

We didn't speak for a very long time, and I really missed him. His wife always came to Le Cirque, but he wouldn't. He would sit outside on Sixty-fifth Street in a limousine waiting for his wife and I would send food or sandwiches out to the car—and the driver would bring back the plate empty.

Many years went by. We still didn't talk. But we both got older, and when the old restaurant was closing, he came in for lunch. I didn't make a big deal of it. He came in. It was very tense at first. Things got even more tense when he sat down at a table, took his hand and wiped everything off—the flowers, the knife and the fork, the glasses, everything—in a big crash.

All the staff looked at me, but I signaled to them that it was "Okay," and he took out a pen and on the tablecloth he starting drawing a portrait of my three boys. He drew it from memory. It was perfect, and he signed it, "Francis." Later I told him about what we were doing, ideas I had to maybe open a new restaurant for my sons, or to move Le Cirque entirely—and I showed him the designs. When he left he came up to me like he always had, patted me on the shoulder and said, "Nice job, kid."

I took his hand, and said, "Thank you, Francis." ◄┿

TWENTIETH ANNIVERSARY

L E CIRQUE CELEBRATED its twentieth anniversary in the spring of 1994 with an extravaganza that outdid all of Sirio's previous parties. The maestro himself, though, was in no mood for celebrating. Although to the outside world Le Cirque remained at the height of its success, Sirio knew better. Dining habits in America were changing. Sirio had no fear that he could change or adapt again. He had a problem, however, with the Le Cirque space itself—and what to do for his three handsome, privileged, and ambitious sons, all of whom were leaning toward careers in the restaurant business.

The space in the Mayfair was always larger than the sum of its parts. When you took it all apart, it was a small, undistinguished, leased room with fewer than seventy employees, in a run-down but handsome hotel. To the outside world it was Le Cirque. One part of Sirio liked the intimate scale of the restaurant—he could control, he thought, every single element of what went on in the space. The other part of Sirio wanted Le Cirque to become everything the outside world associated with it—physically and visually larger than life, an international brand name that stood for Sirio's ideas on food, service, and fashion. On his more demure days, Sirio favored trying to find a solution at the Mayfair. The hotel had been outdated when Sirio moved into the space in 1973. A few minor alterations over the years had kept the hotel's status afloat—but only barely. Having put Sixty-fifth Street and the hotel on the map, Sirio felt that the hotel itself would now drag Le Cirque down. It was the Colony all over again. Sirio's dream was to gut the original space, expand into the rest of the hotel, even take it over if necessary. The problem was, Sirio had little real influence over the hotel. The Zeckendorfs had sold their interest in 1979, and the hotel had had a succession of absentee owners. To them Sirio's relationship with the hotel existed on paper only, and the details of the contract were simple: Sirio had to be out March 1, 1998. (Although by fighting the clauses he claimed were guaranteed him in court, he could have remained to 2005 or beyond.) Sirio was forced to work with what he had.

Sirio insisted that his original deal with the Zeckendorfs included promises to pay for a new kitchen fifteen years into the lease and to maintain the public spaces of the building in a manner worthy of Le Cirque. The clause about the kitchen existed, but couldn't be implemented since the hotel itself wasn't making enough money to pay for them. Sirio wished he had taken the leap as a hotelier and a restaurateur back when he was offered the opportunity. He also screamed tirelessly to anyone he thought could fix the problem that investing in the hotel would ultimately make it successful and profitable. The hotel owners merely pointed out that the costs to rehabilitate the hotel were substantially more than the cost of a free dessert and a glass of champagne.

The problems with the hotel, in Sirio's mind, could be worked out. He'd buy the hotel, he'd find a friend to buy the hotel; there were no shortage of people who had offered him the opportunity. Even if he could pull it off, he would still have to deal with the union. Since Le Cirque operated within a hotel, all of Le

Cirque's waiters, dishwashers, and kitchen staff belonged to Local Union 6, the hotel union, not the restaurant union. Almost half of them had been with Sirio since the restaurant opened. To compete in the new world of restaurants, he needed more precision, more commitment, and more work from all of his staff. Instead, the union and its workers wanted less time and more money. Negotiations dragged on, petty scandals would disrupt the camaraderie of Sirio's carefully constructed core of waiters, and more and more rules and regulations constricted his ability to manage his restaurant effectively. All that was bad enough, but what really bothered Sirio was that he was still a card-carrying member of the same union that was causing him such grief. Just as Sirio sees a direct line from the food critic of *The New York Times* to its publishers and owners, Sirio sees a direct line from his waiters, dishwashers, and kitchen staff to the person who signed him up in 1956 and later became a head of the union. That this person should now view him as the enemy incensed him.

SIRIO

I WAS THE FIRST PERSON to open an independently owned restaurant in a hotel and get great staff to work in it, *with* the union. But then the waiters and other staff working for me got older and it became the same thing. When people get to a certain age, they don't want to work hard anymore and they like the union because of job protection. To me seniority too often means people don't want to work, but Le Cirque needs people who want to work. I believe in the union, okay? But it doesn't work anymore. The union needs to be a partner in your business, because in the restaurant business things change every day. You have to adapt and if they don't adapt, that can kill any restaurant. I run a restaurant that has a hotel union that is impossible. I would give an arm or maybe a leg to have the restaurant union, which is just difficult! How can you have a hotel and a hotel union making decisions in your business when they know nothing about how to run a restaurant? It's crazy.

WILLIAM LIE ZECKENDORF *Sirio isn't exaggerating when he says he was the first person to operate a successful restaurant in a hotel. His genius was to have it be part of the hotel but give it a separate identity. First he put the restaurant on the map, then the hotel, and then the whole neighborhood. He created the whole market for synergy between hotels and restaurants.*

I made it so that everyone got something from the deal: the owners, the hotel, the neighbors, but most of all the people in the union. It worked very, very, well for a long time because whatever someone said, they did. We didn't talk about contracts, we talked about what I do for you and you do for me. We didn't have problems because everyone was honest and, no matter what anyone says, not greedy. Everyone wanted to make it work and so it worked. A man's word is his everything. If you say something to me, I remember and I believe you. I don't need lawyers and diplomats and people. You say you do something, you do it, and if you can't, you say you can't. I understand that. I hold people to it and they should hold me to it. Is this wrong?

WILLIAM LIE ZECKENDORF *The thing about Sirio is that in this world where everything is finessed by lawyers he remembers everything and never forgets a favor. My family did him a favor and although our interest in the hotel ceased, he never forgot it. My father continued to go to the restaurant, Sirio continued to treat him like a king and extends the same courtesy to me, and I'm the third generation!*

DAVID TELL *[Sirio's lawyer] Sirio believes that if you say it, you mean it. If I weren't there to stop him, Sirio would probably do multimillion-dollar deals on a handshake. When something goes wrong, he never wants to know the legal issues—he wants to talk to whoever is in charge. He holds them responsible. And so he gets hurt, because he is a little too trusting. It's very charming sometimes, and sometimes very naïve.*

I had all these problems going on with the hotel and with the union, so what did we do? We had a party! If I didn't know better I'd say I was a crazy. It was Nixon's idea to hold a twentieth-anniversary party. I didn't want to have it, but he said to me I was stupid not to, and when I thought about it I agreed that these kinds of events are good for the restaurant. But I only wanted to do a party if the focus was on the new, not the old. Who wants to celebrate being old? I just like to celebrate. Every year I give a party in Montecatini and my wife says every year if I do it again she will leave me.

> ALAIN DUCASSE *Sirio can't help himself. You go to his house in Montecatini and he says dinner is for ten, maybe fifteen people. You get there and he's got the mayor, celebrities, and every chef in Europe—literally a hundred people all in one house, packed in like an Italian wedding. He has to have his audience.*

The twentieth-anniversary party was incredible—fifteen hundred people! We took over the restaurant, the lobby of the hotel, the party rooms, everything. They closed the street because there were too many people and cars, and traffic was all backed up! It was like the Academy Awards, with the cameras, the photographers, the red carpet—but better because we had more important people, famous people. Nixon called the day before to say he couldn't come because he didn't feel well. I told him I was going to cancel the party, but he insisted we go on. I found out that he was taken to the hospital that morning. Thank god they didn't tell me until after the party that he had died. So it really was the farewell party for Nixon. You know, he was a good man. He wanted to be part of a family. It was very strange to have Nixon die and then be on the phone again, arranging for his memorial service the next day. You have the party, you celebrate, you have fun, and then it's over. ◄◄

> FLORENCE FABRICANT *The thing about Sirio is that even when he's upset he loves to have fun. There's an energy—always chairs, tables going over your head, always someone you have never seen in person before.*

PAMELA FIORI *Everywhere else in the world you sit in a restaurant and when someone comes in you say, "They look just like So-and-so." At Le Cirque, it really is So-and-so! So when you go to one of his parties—which always seem to be held when Sirio is complaining the most, the most tired, the most impossible—there's always some fabulous-looking person that you can't believe you're really seeing in the flesh.*

Osteria del Circo:

A FAMILY RESTAURANT?

S IRIO SAYS choosing to work in restaurants is a question of lifestyle. You have to accept that you will never live like other people, never again have Christmas or New Year's or weekends at home like others. When Sirio and Egi got married, the arrangement they forged worked because it was classically Italian. As Egi says, "He takes care of everything outside of the house and I take care of everything inside of the house." Sirio took care of the restaurant. Egi took care of the children. And the line was rarely crossed. Egi never once saw the inside of the Colony in the entire decade Sirio worked there. When Le Cirque opened, Egi was the unseen power behind her husband. She was rarely at the restaurant, but every cook knew that his recipes were being tested at home and if they didn't past muster there, they would be pulled off the menu immediately. Mario, Marco, and Mauro, depending on their ages—and their homework—came to help out in the restaurant, but only if they wanted to.

Sirio was adamant that they should never be asked, and he got no argument from Egi. It wasn't until the late 1980s that each boy started to show his own interest in food and in restaurants. Mario started to work in the restaurant and would spend time with Sirio's legion of friends in the restaurant and wine industry from around the world. Eventually he enrolled at Cornell University's Hotel and Restaurant Management School. Marco took his summers off from New York University to work with French hotelier and restaurateur Gerard Boyer. Mauro, the youngest, chose a degree in economics at Columbia University.

Sirio had always been content to think that whatever empire he would build would be contained within the walls of the Mayfair Hotel, even as he conducted negotiations with Pierre Cardin to run Maxim's in Paris in the early 1990s, or a restaurant in Monaco owned by the royal family with negotiations conducted by none other than Princess Grace in the early 1980s. Although the newspapers faithfully reported on these and many other possible ventures, he had always thought of himself as a consummate restaurateur—not an entrepreneur. Sirio was well aware of the alternative career path. Tony May had started one of the best Italian restaurants in New York, San Domenico, during the 1980s. The Mays lived in the same apartment building as the Maccionis, and their children grew up together. "Tony May," Sirio says without being snide, in the way only Italians can talk about each other, "is an entrepreneur, not a restaurateur. Tony is smart. He's on a golf course while someone else stands at the door." Sirio would entertain any number of potentially profitable ideas put forward by hundreds of wealthy or connected clients sitting on his plush banquettes, some of which even went into the contract stage, but his innate sense of caution prevented him from doing much more than talk about them. Sirio's style in business was the reverse of his menu theory—in business it was 80 percent fantasy, 20 percent reality. He would enter into any idea with enthusiasm and intent, talk about it endlessly, but never fully commit himself.

By the time his restaurant turned twenty Sirio started to look actively at restaurant spaces and entertain ideas. His friend the restaurant architect Adam Tihany had opened a restaurant on West Fifty-third Street called Remi and in the process had convinced Sirio that a clean start, in a new space and a different neighborhood, could be a solution to his problems on Sixty-fifth Street. In early 1994 he signed a letter of intent for a space on Fifty-fifth Street just west of Sixth Avenue.

SIRIO

PROBLEMS ON SIXTY-FIFTH STREET were getting worse, not better. I couldn't come to any agreement at all with the hotel to improve things. My god, I couldn't even get them to pick up the phone. The economy was bad. I thought, "What if the boys want to come into the business with me? How do I make a business for myself and my sons when these ladies come in and have a glass of water and nothing else?" When I made my first money, I bought two apartments in Montecatini. Real estate, you know, just in case? It made me feel safe. So I went out to look for a space, a place to go if things didn't work out well at Sixty-fifth Street. We had the big party for the twentieth anniversary, then there was the memorial for Nixon, then right away we had a trip on the *Queen Elizabeth II* with people from *Food Arts.* I didn't want to go, but Egidiana was cooking on board, so we went.

MICHAEL BATTERBERRY *I remember the entire five-day crossing as an intense exposition on the subject of My Three Sons! I'd been to the restaurant thousands of times and was used to Sirio's shtick: "I work for my three sons ... would you like to adopt them? ... Would you like to buy a restaurant?" On the ship he emerged as an even more lovable figure, because I saw that his passion for his boys surpassed his passion for his restaurant. It wasn't the usual jock thing—my boys scored a touchdown, or made the team—it was really his burning concern that they receive the best education and the best preparation for life, that they have the best lives.*

I had no choice. My father had no choice. I'm in love with my sons and I wanted them to have a choice. But I didn't do all that I did just so they could become a waiter like me. I believe that children should be allowed to have the time to make mistakes. I never could afford it and it made me unhappy. I decided on the boat with Egidiana that if the boys wanted to take on restaurants, it would be on the understanding that they were allowed to fail.

BARBARA WALTERS *Sirio's crowning achievement is those boys. I can remember them as teenagers, walking around the restaurant, asking if there was anything they could do. Sirio's very strict and very loving. It's wonderful to watch how they interact together, how they tease him ... how marvelous they are when he's not there.*

My sons are the greatest thing about me. They are better-looking, smarter, and have more possibility than I ever had and that is what I want for them. Of course, you come to our house and you think we are all going to kill each other. How anyone would think we are normal is a miracle. Mario decided he wanted to get married very young, much younger than me. I had never heard of her before, but he came to me before we all went on a vacation and said, "Papa, I want to bring this girl on vacation with us." I think he thought we'd say no. So we went to Casa de Campo and this girl, Lauren, came to me and said she wanted to marry my son. She was so correct, how could I say no? I think they think I am conservative, like my uncles or my grandmother, but I am the opposite. So they got married, at the restaurant, on New Year's Day 1993. Maybe the thing that makes me happiest, like any Italian? Lauren had a baby girl, Olivia, on the first of July, 1995.

Now Marco. I wish Marco would get married, but instead he has a dog. I like the dog, sometimes, and he said to me, "If you keep talking bad about my dog, I'll get another." And he got another.

Mauro. Now Mauro is too smart for his own good. He went to Columbia and the first thing he decided was that he wants to go into the restaurant business, so maybe he's not so smart. ◄✦

MAURO *Growing up there were always people in the house, food people, wine people. We would come home and my mother and Danny Kaye would be cooking. I knew we were from a foodie family, but when you're a kid it's just kind of normal. I remember once my father had Dieter Schorner make a cake for a birthday party at school and this triple-layered dark chocolate cake arrived, covered with chocolate fondant. It was so embarrassing. We wound up ordering a cake from Carvel.*

MARCO *The restaurant business is what I knew. I tried to think about other things, but it's where we grew up. When you're a kid and you think about what you want to be when you grow up, you look at your parents. I admire them—bang, you're in the restaurant business. My father. He thought a lot about us being in the business—or not.*

MARIO *I'm the oldest. The big difference between me and my other brothers is that they grew up at Le Cirque. I was nine already when Le Cirque opened. I had a great childhood, but it wasn't like a glamorous childhood. I remember the apartment beside Lutèce, walking up a million flights of stairs, not going to the Colony because we weren't allowed to go to the Colony, and never really seeing my father unless we were in Italy. So I didn't feel an immediate desire to go into the business. And god knows he didn't push us to do it. But when I was at college I found myself drifting toward it. You know the way these things happen: "Here's an opportunity, it's right in front of me and I should at least try it." So I did. But I wanted to do it differently. I went to Cornell. I wanted to know about the nuts and bolts. And that, my family and my history, made it inevitable that I'd go into the business.*

EGIDIANA *I cook. I like to cook and I love being a housewife. Sirio makes so much of my singing, but I never wanted anything other than to be a housewife and mother. I picked up the restaurant busi-*

ness the way you pick up cooking. You see the ingredients that go into making something and you make sure the ingredients are the best and you do as little to them as possible. So my boys wanted to go into the restaurant industry—no, I can't say it's what I wanted for them, but I can't say either that I wanted them to be doctors or lawyers. I wanted them to be happy. Even now if they came to me and said they didn't want it, that would be fine. And you know what else? If they went to Sirio, he'd say the same thing.

ALTHOUGH EGI HAD BEEN the de facto consulting chef since Le Cirque opened, it took the cruise aboard the *QEII* for Sirio to realize that she commanded the respect of her colleagues in a professional kitchen. He had no question that she could direct the cuisine at an Italian restaurant owned and operated by the whole family. It had taken a lifetime, but suddenly Sirio realized that he should ask his family for the support that he needed to realize his dreams as a restaurateur.

When Egi and Sirio returned from their trip, he made his sons an offer that was hard to refuse: he would pay for the construction and allow them to develop and operate the space so long as they would bear the brunt of the daily work that running the restaurant would entail and become partners in any other ventures. Mama would oversee the menu, acting as the consulting chef. He would promise, more or less, not to interfere.

Sirio envisioned his role as chief executive parent. He'd done everything in the restaurant business, but he'd never had to manage a start-up with his own family. Sirio's insistence that everything come out of his own pocket financially meant that for as long as the Maccionis held the lease, the space could be a laboratory for Sirio's sons to tinker and play with as they matured, as Edigiana became a professional cook and restaurateur, and as Sirio grew from restaurateur to entrepreneur.

B Y THE TIME WE STARTED CIRCO everything had changed. When we opened Le Cirque in 1974, if there was a problem, I called Mr. Zeckendorf and the problem got fixed. Lots of things went wrong, but compared to Circo it was easy. We learned many lessons building Circo—things that were stupid and maybe wrong and that I would never do again. But if we hadn't done them, the rest would not have been possible. The first problem was the location and the space. Everyone told me, "It's on the West Side, no one will go to the West Side." I said, "People change, areas change, people go where the food is good and they get treated well." I knew. We did it before and I knew we would do it again.

> ADAM TIHANY *It was a very interesting process. Like watching a family grow up before your eyes. It was a very difficult build-out, putting a restaurant into an office space. And it was all Sirio's money. So at first it was very much Sirio. Sirio wanted this, Sirio wanted that. Looking, needling, arguing. Then I think he realized either his wife or his kids were going to kill him and he started to pull back—but only when he saw that Egi and Mario really did have skills he didn't. Of course, in the meanwhile, you'd think you'd landed on some explosion or something!*

When we started to think about Circo, I said to Egidiana, "If this is what they want, if they really want to be in this business, than I want a letter from each of them explaining to me why they want to be in this business and promising that they will not leave me as the one always standing at the door." I didn't want any investors. I didn't want to go through pleasing other people, other chefs. At least with my family we fight—my god, we fight!—but if we want to make a change, we make a change, we don't have to ask some chef or some investor. All the best trattorias are run by families, usually with a woman in the kitchen, who is always much more intelligent than a man. With Circo I asked myself, "What if I had to do it all again?" If I knew then what I know now, I'd have gone into my own business years before, when I was twenty-five or thirty, not forty. The truth is, it was only when we built Circo that I realized I had the confidence to jump over the old and try the new. Its success was all due to Mario, who is very strong and knew what he wanted. We almost never agreed. But he fought and he prevailed. ◄←

THE MACCIONI FAMILY'S version of an Italian trattoria, depending on whom you talk to, cost somewhere between five and seven million dollars to create. The name of the restaurant, Circo—an Italian circus instead of a French one—dictated Tihany's design. A giant red-and-yellow circus tent was pitched on the inside of the soaring, almost vertical space. The tent turned, whimsical animals were perched on hidden shelves, and mechanical acrobats soared through the air. Tihany designed everything: the glasses, plates, and flatware, the fabric for the seats, even the light fixtures. It was an explosion of almost fluorescent color.

SIRIO

→→

M Y FATHER DIDN'T WANT me to go into hotels, he wanted more for me. But my sons wanted to go into restaurants too. You know if I had to go back, I would have spent more time with them outside of the restaurant, but they grew up in the restaurant. At least they see that it's hard work and if they chose this, then god help them.

MARIO *Customers and the press presented Circo as the creation of this dynasty. Maybe that's what it is, but when we were in it, it didn't feel any different from the way we were when I was ten, or fifteen or twenty. What was different wasn't us—what was different was my dad, trying really hard to execute his ideas, while trying to be respectful of us and Mom.*

MARCO *You know some kids go to the park and bat balls around with their father. We did that, but not with him. With him we saw food, service, people, that kind of thing. Suddenly here was this chance for him to show us what to do.*

EGIDIANA *Sirio is Sirio. They boys do the best they can and Sirio does the best he can. I am in the middle. I keep their fights from becoming bad fights.*

Edigiana is a miracle. She's always been a miracle, but in a restaurant she's even more so. She was just going to consult, look at the menu, do a little this and a little that, and then she was hiring the staff! Her instincts for that are much better than mine. She looks at someone, tastes the food, and somehow she knows. She'll say, "Yes, he's good," or "He's good, but he won't last," or "Don't even try." I should listen to her more.

MARCO *The day we opened, January 8, 1996, was probably the defining moment of my relationship with my father. There's a saying in Italian, "Di venere e di marte non si viene e non si parte." Basically, it means don't start anything new, have a baby, or open a restaurant on a Friday or a Tuesday. So we decided to open on the Monday. But Sunday night, while we were in the restaurant, it started to snow—I mean, really snow. My mother was in the kitchen making sauce and pasta for everyone and at some stage we realized the snow was getting serious. My father was out on the street getting taxis and paying for the dishwashers and everyone to get home, because he was afraid we'd have an army of people sleeping in the restaurant or at home. But we were all so tired, we just hoped we'd wake up in the morning and it would all be gone. When I woke up the next morning, I rushed to the restaurant at 7 A.M. but the doors to the restaurant were blocked because of the snow. I had to go around to the main part of the building and use an entrance from the lobby just to get in. There were no deliveries, there wasn't even any food in the restaurant. I didn't know what to do. I figured, go to a deli— hope they had some tomatoes or something and just wing it.*

MARIO *We had to make a decision. My father was screaming, "It's your first day in business and you want to close? You never close, never. Work it out!" But we explained we couldn't even get in the front door, there was no food. He went into one of his speeches, "You should always be prepared!"—but we stuck to our guns and decided to close. "Fine, it's your damned restaurant, do what you want!" he screamed and slammed down the phone. Then ten seconds later he called back to ask for the list of reservations and phone numbers so he could start calling to explain. Except we didn't have a very good list—just some phone numbers and some names, but not always together—so we all got screamed at again for not taking reservations and phone numbers right. It was a long day.*

MARCO *Mario and Lauren were already married and had Olivia, I was living downtown and Mauro was at home, but we were on the phone with each other all day long, working out what to do. Finally Mom got overruled and we decided to open the following day, even though it was a Tuesday. I remember walking up the middle of Park Avenue that night because the snow was so thick, and walking into Le Cirque. If we weren't going to open Circo, he needed us to fill in for waiters who couldn't make it in to Le Cirque. I couldn't believe it, I walked in over these planks they'd put up to get across the snowbanks and the puddles, thinking the place would be empty, and it was packed to the roof. There were piles of coats and boots. It was like everyone had dressed up just for the occasion and there's my dad passing around cups of Paul Bocuse's consommé. Jacques Torres, who had never seen snow before, had invented a new dessert for the occasion, a snowman made of meringue, filled with lemon curd and chocolate. Don Chaney, then coach of the Knicks, showed up without a reservation in a sweat suit. My dad was about to toss him out, but I told him he couldn't and explained who he was. My dad put a tie over Chaney's sweat suit and became an instant expert on New York basketball—as if suddenly it's his idea that Don Chaney should be the only person allowed into Le Cirque not dressed properly!*

You have to be ready for anything. The secret is never to make too much of anything. A customer complains, you fix the problem quickly, but you don't announce it to the world, or reach too much, or too little. In the kitchen you always have to be prepared. The night we opened Circo wasn't the first storm or problem we'd ever had. Maybe it's Le Cirque's customers, but I swear that when the weather's the worst they dress up the most. The coats came out, they sit at the bar taking off their boots and showing their legs and taking their high heels out of shopping bags! It was a fashion show, not a blizzard.

MARCO *We did open Circo the next day, but it was a nightmare. Someone had the bright idea to have John Mariani follow us around on our first day in business for an article in the* **Wine Spectator** *and everything went wrong. Everyone from Monday had been pushed to Tuesday. We were triple-booked and of course my father had probably invited a hundred of his best clients and among the three of us, we'd probably all said to someone, "Just come!" Ruth Reichl was there, in disguise, but we were so crazy I never got time to tell anyone she was there. Gael Greene had written a piece in* **New York** *magazine saying Circo was the hottest ticket in town, and so all those people were trying to get in, and everyone had on these giant coats, so there wasn't enough room in the coatroom, and it wasn't like Le Cirque, where we could put them all somewhere else. I couldn't believe it. All these people were backing up into the doorway, the bar was packed, Mariani was following me around, and I was trying to look cool, but kept thinking, "I can't believe that after all this time and money we're going to get killed because the coatroom isn't big enough." Benito had to come from Le Cirque to separate out the Le Cirque customers from the new customers, Sottha was in the kitchen, and Jacques was making the desserts. We had Michael Cimanusti and Sandro Giuntoli cooking with Sottha! These are guys you don't want to mess with. They're the terminators of the Italian restaurant business. It was totally insane, but I guess if I was ever trained at anything, it was to look calm when everything is falling apart.*

JOHN MARIANI *I'd known Sirio and his family a long time. It was great just to watch. This posse of angry clients was blocking up the front door, the kitchen was getting behind, but food was coming out, and at least the people at the tables were happy. I remember Pino Luongo, who runs some very successful Italian restaurants, just taking in the whole scene. By 8:30 almost anyone sane would have just crawled under the table. It was bedlam. But somehow the boys did okay. It wasn't until they realized that one of the people trying to push his way through the crowd at the door was their father that I saw a look of terror in their eyes.*

Why should they be scared? I didn't sleep for three months before the opening of Le Cirque, and opening day was a nightmare. But they were managing, in their own way. I found a place to sit at the bar with Mariani and I just watched my sons. Maybe it wasn't right, but they were doing it. My wife was on the phone, trying to keep everyone calm and I thought, "Hah! Now she will know why I don't want to talk sometimes when I come home, I just want to go under the bed and sleep forever." Lauren came in with Olivia and we walked around the restaurant and the baby was so innocent and Mario was so proud. I thought it was a great night. Everyone said it was chaos. I don't remember chaos, I remember happy times. ◄✦

THE FOOD AT OSTERIA DEL CIRCO represented the four parts of Egidiana's life: the food she ate or cooked as a child, the food that she cooks for Sirio, the food that she took from Italy and adjusted to accommodate American ingredients (as well as the tastes of her children), and the food that she cooked for Le Cirque and now for Circo. From her childhood came dishes like *ribollita,* the Tuscan bread soup that she had learned to make from her grandmother, using bread from her father's bakery. From the same front came her experience with pizzas and fried dough. When Sirio is in Montecatini, not a week goes by that Egi doesn't make *tonno e fagioli,* tuna and beans with red onion, or little white onions sautéed with balsamic vinegar. Perhaps his favorite, though, is Annunciata's sausage stew with white beans.

The press was generally kind about the food, but vacillated over Tihany's design for Circo, some calling it modern, avant-garde, and unusual, while others questioned why it didn't look or feel more like an "Italian restaurant." It never occurred to any of the Maccionis that Tuscany should be represented by dusty Chianti bottles and pictures of crumbling towers. Tuscany to the Maccionis means tanned women and shopping at midnight on the streets of Forte di Marmi in the latest summer fashions from Milan. Only the food had to remain rooted in tradition.

It was Sirio's wish that the customers of Le Cirque and Circo be interchangeable, with each restaurant catering to a different mood. Nothing pleased Sirio more than to see Lee Radziwell and other clients at Le Cirque dressed in some chic couture gowns on one night and the next at Circo, in something a little more casual, but nevertheless elegant. Sirio felt the same way about the food.

SIRIO

WITH ALL DUE RESPECT to the great chefs, why is it always that my wife's cooking is the best? Italian food is the best way to cook. This doesn't mean I don't like French food. I love it. When it's cooked right, without the schizophrenic chef, it's still the best food to be served in a restaurant. But the mentality has to be the same, at Circo or Le Cirque—food that I recognize, food that the people like. Le Cirque is the food I have spent my whole life getting right—the quenelles as light as air, the potato so thin around the sea bass that it almost looks like the fish still has scales. I can taste the food of any great chef—of Bocuse, of Ducasse, of any of the chefs who work for me—and tell you what is right and what is wrong for our customers. The food of Italy is more accessible, more spontaneous. That is the food I grew up with, and the food I love. ◄◄

SOTTHA KUHN *Sirio is a man of fashion. He made a line of food for casual wear that is Circo, and a haute couture line that is Le Cirque.*

THE
PALACE

LMOST EVERY FRIEND that Sirio has made and every deal that he has done have started at Le Cirque. In 1993 Richard Cotter, a longtime regular who also had experience in hotel management, was placed in a position few people can even imagine: he became responsible for spending hundreds of millions of dollars belonging to the Sultan of Brunei, at the time, the world's richest man. The Sultan's brother, Prince Jefri, had created an investment arm called the Amedeo Group and had hired Michael Salbi and Cotter to create a hotel chain that would outdo all others in exclusivity, glamour, architectural perfection, and profits.

The group had scooped up some of the choicest hotel real estate in the world: the Dorchester in London, the Beverly Hills Hotel in Los Angeles, and the Plaza-Athénée and the Meurice in Paris. Equivalent real estate in New York was not for sale. Fortune presented them with an unusual solution: the Helmsley Palace Hotel on Madison Avenue. The Palace did not have the cachet of the Beverly Hills Hotel or the Plaza-Athénée, but it had several assets not shared by those hotels—namely, a location just behind St. Patrick's Cathedral, and including the landmarked late-nineteenth-century Villard Houses that formed the hotel's formal entrance. The Helmsley Palace was the single most interesting piece of hotel real estate available in the world, but it also carried some unusual baggage. That's where Sirio came in.

The Palace had been the brainchild of New York City developer Harry Helmsley and his wife, Leona. Helmsley had used all of his skill as a developer to gain valuable concessions from the city to build the fifty-story tower behind the landmarked McKim, Meade, and White town houses. In exchange for permission to build, the Helmsleys had agreed to preserve the unified, neo-Renaissance façade of the cluster and two of the houses in their entirety, including the jewel of the complex, the Villard Mansion at the corner of fiftieth and Madison. By the time representatives of Amedeo Group met Sirio, Harry Helmsley was on his deathbed. His wife, who had just been released from prison for a tax evasion scheme —which led to the media's turning her formerly catchy moniker "The Queen of the Palace," into the even more catchy "The Queen of Mean"—immediately put the hotel on the market. Amedeo bought it, and quickly replaced the "Helmsley" with "New York," to rechristen the hotel, "the New York Palace," and started a two-year-long top-to-bottom renovation.

Cotter and Salbi had known from the beginning that the hotel itself was never going to be able to compete architecturally with the likes of its neighbors, the St. Regis or the Plaza. What made the Palace unique was the Villard Mansion. It remained exactly what it had been when the hotel opened in 1977: a non-functional, ornate appendage to a modern tower. The Sultan's people needed someone who could tame these vast and ornate nineteenth-century spaces—and who had a brand name that would forever eradicate the memory of Leona Helmsley from the complex. The restaurant that would occupy Henry Villard's Mansion would have to be the main attraction for the rest of the hotel. The Sultan of Brunei told Cotter personally there was only one restaurant that would fit the bill: Le Cirque.

In late 1994, in between courses of white truffle risotto, Cotter and Sarbi gently presented the idea to Sirio—after all, for all they knew, Sirio was committed to the space at Sixty-fifth Street and had no particular reason to consider a move. To Sirio, concerned about the union and about the future of his children, the deal turned out to be not unlike that which the Zeckendorfs had presented him twenty years earlier.

Sirio played it cool, but his boyish curiosity was spinning out of control. He called every friend and client who could keep a secret to look at the baronial space. Architect I. M. Pei, Henry Kissinger, the Zeckendorfs, society decorator Mark Hampton, and his own architect, Adam Tihany, all went to examine what could possibly be the next Le Cirque. Sirio was intrigued, but the Villard Mansion space was riddled with difficulties. It was one of the few designated interior landmarks in America. Not a light sconce could be removed, not a thumbtack could penetrate a wooden panel. Another drawback was that, instead of one large dining room, the Villard Mansion had two, each separated by a central foyer as large as the space he was contemplating leaving. Could Sirio project his magic over such a large space? An even more serious problem was the kitchen. When the hotel had been constructed in 1977, it had been placed along the back of the modern tower, a full 200 feet from the original drawing room of the mansion, which would be the most logical space for a dining room. Navigating stairs, another dining room, a bar, and the entrance foyer to serve a meal, presumably now cold, to a patron was out of the question. The kitchen would have to be moved—a multimillion-dollar proposition. To top it off, there was the union. Should he move to the Palace, he would still have to deal with the same union as on Sixty-fifth Street.

On the plus side, the Sultan was prepared to offer minimal rent and pay all build-out costs, including renovating the mansion and constructing the kitchen of Sirio's dreams. The party rooms were the best in Manhattan, ideally suited for people coming from uptown or downtown—an important factor in the new world of New York restaurants, where the party business often had to pay for excesses of the restaurant. Sirio in particular adored the fact that the Catholic church was the ultimate landlord of the space, since it owned the land underneath the complex. If he chose to go through with the deal, he would at least have God as his partner.

What Tihany liked most about touring the space, he said later, was that the sixty-three-year-old Sirio lit up from head to toe.

SIRIO

THERE WAS INCREDIBLE POSSIBILITY in the space. I could see how it could have been almost anything. But first I had to look at how it could function as a restaurant and that wasn't so good. The kitchen was practically on Park Avenue and the dining rooms were on Madison Avenue. The rooms in the mansion couldn't be altered. I told Cotter and Salbi that nobody, not even me, could make this space work unless they did something about the kitchen. I told him, if the Sultan moves the kitchen, I will move my restaurant. Cotter and Salbi agreed to my request. They said they would do anything. So I thought, "My god, if I can do anything, what do I want to do here?"

> ADAM TIHANY *The thing people don't understand about Sirio is that he's not this imperial Tuscan aristocrat, he's a playful and devilish and very avant-garde little boy. Sirio didn't want to do anything … appropriate. He wanted to fly.*

I kept bringing people to see the space, which was incredible, but was dark and very serious. A part of me really thought that the thing to do was to fix it up and make it a very grand restaurant like in Monaco or in Paris. But I thought to myself, the restaurants that are grand in New York don't work, like at the Plaza or the St. Regis. People don't feel comfortable in those rooms. They like them for weddings but I'm not in the wedding business. When I buy my house in Montecatini, everyone said, "Oh, Sirio, you have to fix it up and make it the perfect nineteenth-century villa," but I didn't want a perfect nineteenth-century villa. It was a nice house, but let's not get carried away, okay? And everyone in New York kept talking about the Villard Mansion in the same way, like it was sacred. I grew up in Tuscany: we all think we are the descendants of Michelangelo and da Vinci. Surely no one serious could take this Beaux-Arts mimicking of the Italian Renaissance as something sacred? It didn't work as a house, it didn't work as offices, and it didn't work when they built the hotel. A space has to breathe, it has to live, and you have to use it. Adam said we should do what we do in Italy with an ancient palazzo, preserve it perfectly, then park a Ferrari in the middle. At first I thought maybe a little more conservative, but the more I thought about it, the more I realized that something modern, radical, was the right thing to do. But the space wasn't mine. ◄┼►

TWO WEEKS AFTER CONSTRUCTION on Circo started in January 1995, Sirio signed a letter of commitment to take the space at the New York Palace and commissioned Tihany to draw up the plans for a restaurant in the Villard Mansion. Everyone involved in the project was sworn to secrecy. At least in Sirio's mind, the signing of the papers did not mean that Le Cirque would necessarily be moving there. Like his negotiations for Circo, the space was both a bargaining chip and a vehicle for Sirio's fantasies, not necessarily a solution for his problems at Le Cirque on Sixty-fifth Street.

With renewed vigor, Sirio set out to see if the space at the Mayfair might yet contain his dreams for a reborn Le Cirque. Sirio had Adam draw up plans for a new Le Cirque in the Mayfair. The cost of a new kitchen alone was estimated at $1.5 million, which Sirio offered to bear, in exchange for a significant extension on similar terms of the original Zeckendorf lease. The hotel refused. It offered no new lease to Sirio, and the union offered him no new contracts. The developer Tom Barrack had started negotiations to buy the entire Mayfair Hotel, and he pledged to give Sirio better terms than the Zeckendorfs had granted him originally. The timing, though, was shaky. The Sultan and his people started restoration of the mansion's delicate woodwork, gold leaf, and mosaics, and had started to install the kitchen that Sirio had asked for and, miraculously, kept hoping Le Cirque would utilize. Meanwhile, Sirio hoped Barrack's deal would come through before he had to make any commitment to the Sultan.

SIRIO

W E WERE HAVING A GREAT TIME. The restaurant was busier than ever at dinner. Lunch was still very busy—if not as busy as it was in the 1970s and '80s. What we always have and had very strong then was the Europeans, the South Americans, and even some of the Russians. I liked the new energy very much. Liz Smith hosted a very chic party for Barbara Walters. She invited men only and came dressed as a man. Something about it was very sexy and wonderful. She danced with Oscar de la Renta, who is a very good dancer. You know, usually it's the job of the man to make a woman feel special, but I am now at an age where it's very nice to have a woman make so many of us feel good. It was one of my favorite nights because maybe for the first time in my life I felt like I wasn't there just because it was my restaurant, but because she liked me being there.

> LIZ SMITH *I thought, What could I do for Barbara that would make her feel great? What better than to surround her with the most intelligent, handsomest men in the world, men she loved and who loved her? Sirio was a dream, putting it together and keeping it mostly a secret! If I'd gone anywhere else, they'd have thought I'd lost my mind, but he just bought right into it ... none of this politically correct stuff.*

I hate politically correct. I am not politically correct. I hate it when someone talks bad about his country when he's not in it, but good when he is. I always talk bad. People talk bad about Ivana Trump, who was divorced then from Mr. Trump. Both were coming to the restaurant, both were very nice, and the press said they were fighting all the time but in fact he came and she came and it was fine. They were stupid to pick on her: Ivana is everything that's great about this country. Sarah Ferguson too—in New York, she can live.

My grandmother would say people don't like women who do what they like. They are smart, sexy, rich, and mostly they are free. Mrs. Trump says to me, "I'm not going to stop coming to lunch just because people don't do it anymore. I like to get dressed up, I like to eat." She is great. A beautiful woman is like nothing else in the world, when she walks in everyone's eyes go... ah, ah.... It makes life exciting. Why does the so-called intelligentsia make fun of Ivana Trump, George Hamilton? It's so stupid. Don't they know that the people of this country admire Mrs. Trump, George Hamilton, Sarah Ferguson, people out there doing things, not just talking about things?

And why is everyone so quick to judge? Woody Allen came to the restaurant with Soon-Yi Previn and said to me, "Please, make her feel at home," and I did. He is so direct, so honest. We did the best to make him feel comfortable at a terrible time.

WOODY ALLEN *There are so few places left in New York that feel like New York. In the old place and in the new place you really get a slice of what makes New York great. He's the master of the circus, always all these balls up in the air, but what makes him the consummate host is that with all the stuff going on he always has time for a friend or a patron. It seems unlikely that a place with that kind of energy could be so enveloping. It's like a cocoon.*

One of my favorite times was when Ron Perelman was here for lunch with his wife and not one but two of his previous wives were in the restaurant too. I don't think he even noticed, but one of them came up to me and told me never to let such a thing happen again. I said, "I can't stop the wives of Ron Perelman from coming to lunch." Later when he left, he looked at me with a smile as he leaned toward the tables with the ex-wives, and left.

RON PERELMAN *Did I? I honestly don't remember, but it sounds like me! I've been going to Le Cirque since I moved up from Philadelphia, but my first wife's family knew Sirio all the way back to the Colony. One of the things I like about him is you can be up or you can be down and you're always the same guy. In a world where I have to take the rough with the smooth, I always feel safe with Sirio. That's probably more valuable to me than the restaurant itself.*

We were doing lots of events in those years. Once we gave a party with all the best French chefs in the world together—Paul Bocuse, Alain Ducasse, Roger Vergé, Gerard Boyer. The party was called the Dinner of the Millennium. Marvin Shanken, the man who owns the *Wine Spectator,* decided to put together the best meal of the century, and it was. None of these people had ever cooked together before. He is really a great man. Without him no one would do these things. Ducasse decided that he was going to prepare the famous ortolan. It was illegal to bring in ortolans, but somehow he got them into the diplomatic pouch. The problem was that the day before someone found out and, my god, the next thing I heard was that the dinner was going to have to be canceled and they wanted to inspect the restaurant for anything else illegal. Every journalist everywhere was calling me! Pamela Harriman, who was then ambassador to France, helped fix the problem—they brought in monitors from the government to stand over and watch while the famous chefs made dinner. The dinner was a great success—and the people from the USDA learned about good food! ◄◄◄-

FLORENCE FABRICANT *The ortolan debacle was a great example of how he turned the greatest piece of negative publicity to his advantage. Before you knew it, stories about the ortolan and the French dinner at Le Cirque were in every paper in the world!*

SIRIO HAS ALWAYS maintained a relationship with the Catholic church in New York. His children attended Mass every week and more often than not, Sirio would join them. If nothing else, it was good for business. The highest-ranking clergymen frequented Le Cirque as often as propriety would allow. Archbishop Renato Martino had been a client and friend of Sirio since Le Cirque's opening and by the early 1990s had been elevated to ambassador from the Holy See to the United Nations. Over the years he had introduced Sirio to Cardinal John O'Connor, who selected Le Cirque as the most appropriate restaurant for His Holiness to visit on his trip to New York in October 1995. When Pope John Paul II arrived in New York, it was decided that for security reasons the Holy Father should not dine publicly. Martino and O'Connor arranged instead for Le Cirque to come to the Pope.

C OOKING FOR THE POPE was a very big event for me, as a Catholic and someone who tries to be a good person. And not just for me. The Pope changed the lives of many people on my staff. What he did for Jacques and for Sottha, for everybody in the restaurant, was very important.

They couldn't have him come to the restaurant, so we prepared a lunch at the residence of the Holy See on the Upper East Side. They asked us not to have so many staff, so we did everything ourselves—Mario, Marco, and Mauro worked in the kitchen with Sottha, Sylvain, Jacques, and a few others to produce the lunch. Jacques went really crazy—he made a white chocolate copy of the whole of St. Peter's Basillica. When the Pope saw it he gasped, touching it like it was real marble. And then like a little boy, he just took his finger and poked a hole in it to taste the cake underneath!

JACQUES TORRES *I'm a good Catholic boy! It was one of the great moments of my life. He came into the kitchens of the residence and talked with us all individually and gave us rosary beads, which I sent back to my mother in France. What was great was before the lunch I looked into the room where he was going to be eating and saw no one was in there, no security or anything. So Sottha and I snuck in with a*

The person most affected was Sottha. He was the only one who got on his knees when he was presented to the Pope. And when the Pope leaned down to ask Sottha to rise, I could hear him say in French, "I'd like to speak with you in your language, but my Cambodian is a little rusty. ... We can talk in Thai though, can't we?" and they did. They had a private conference. Sottha wept. He was shaking all over for days afterward, I don't think he was ever the same. The Pope is Polish but speaks Italian perfectly, like a Tuscan.

SOTTHA KUHN *I never saw such an incredible man. The Holy Father spoke to me in my language. He moved me very much. I can't speak of it.*

I was standing with a group of cardinals and bishops who were talking with the Pope and Martino, who is a very serious but very playful man, said that their jobs would all be a lot easier if there was a very good restaurant in Heaven. The Holy Father asked me if it was true that you couldn't get a reservation at Le Cirque. I said, "I'm sure that if you call we can find you a table," and Martino carried the idea further and said maybe having a reservation system to get into the restaurant in heaven would be a good idea. The Pope looked very serious and scolded, "Are you so sure that we are all going to go up?" It was all very light, very funny, but Cardinal O'Conner got very nervous. We talked seriously and the Pope asked me if I was a good Catholic or just one who showed up when I needed it. I said I thought I was a very good Catholic, and then he tricked me, saying "So I will see you tomorrow at Mass." And I said, "But Holy Father, it's Saturday night and we work very late and your Mass is very early...." He just reminded me of what I had just said and asked the cardinal to save a seat for me where the Pope could see me. And so on Sunday morning I went to Central Park for the Mass and I sat in the front row and when he came to the altar, I thought I saw him tip his hand to me. ◄◄-

BY JANUARY 1996, construction at the Villard Mansion was finally reaching a critical stage. The setbacks and delays that accompany the reconstruction of a hundred-year-old landmark had so far played right into Sirio's hands. Two years had gone by, the work was almost done, and now the Sultan and his team were asking to complete the deal by having Le Cirque move to the New York Palace. Sirio couldn't demur any longer. Barrack's plan to buy the Mayfair was still not signed and the Sultan's terms were ultimately more attractive. On March 24, 1996, Sirio finally made the decision to close Le Cirque as quickly and as delicately as possible and move to the Palace. He signed the contract. It was twenty-two years to the day after he had opened at the Mayfair.

SIRIO

T HE DAY I SIGNED the contract to go to the Palace was the day that marked the real end of Sixty-fifth Street for me. It was the hardest day. It was sad because I had wanted to make the space work and moving is never easy. I knew it was going to make my life more difficult. Everyone else my age was retiring, going away, living a very luxurious life—and I could have done that as well. No one believes me when I say I did it for my sons. My sons and my wife gave me the energy to take the biggest jump.

> TOM BARRACK *They [Amedeo and the people in charge of construction at the hotel] were saying to him, "use it, or lose it." As a businessman, I knew that what the Sultan was offering him was unlike any deal ever done in the world. There was no way I could compete with it. As a friend, I also knew he was making the right choice—at least the right choice at the time. He was very attached to that space and being free of it was bound to do all the things he wanted it to do, for him, for his family, for his business.*

And once the decision was made, running Le Cirque became very easy. My future was somewhere else. Maybe it was why, when I was introduced to the painter Robert Cenedella, I agreed to a portrait of everyone who came to Le Cirque—everyone. He said he could get maybe 200 people into the painting and he did. I think he wanted to paint the new space, which is so much more dramatic, but I wanted the painting to have the people in the old space. I wanted something physical but very abstract of the old space to come with us to the new. What I wanted to do would come with me because it's me, my sons, my philosophy. The problem was the space. Now I could afford to be less attached to a space. I'm attached to my family house in Montecatini, where I was born, where I lived, and where I suffered. Sometimes I wish it were not so, but it is. My sister and I keep it, without living in it. It sits there, weeds growing around it. Everything else, I try not to be so attached. ◄◄

MARCO *We were at the restaurant with our lawyers, who were telling us that there was really no point in continuing negotiations with the Mayfair Hotel or the union. I don't remember exactly what happened that made us realize it was over, but both my dad and I felt it at the same time. This warm feeling all over and then just a fuzziness. The colors of the room, the drapes, and carpets—it was the private dining room on the Park Avenue side of the hotel—all seemed really important. I remember looking over at my father, who was white as a ghost, and quiet for the first time in his life. He was standing up and I thought if I coughed he might have fallen over.*

SIRIO WAS DETERMINED to close the old restaurant and reopen as quickly as possible in the new space, to keep Le Cirque's name in circulation and avoid his competitors' grabbing the limelight. Journalist Peter Kaminsky was hired by *New York* magazine to chronicle the transition to the new restaurant, to be called Le Cirque 2000—to emphasize Le Cirque's place in the future instead of the past. For the first time Sirio hired an outsider— Fern Berman, a publicist who had been hired initially to work just with Osteria del Circo—to keep the hype about the new Le Cirque at fever pitch. Nevertheless, every word had to be cleared through Sirio.

With a plan in place, invitations went out to a few carefully selected regulars for the final dinner at Le Cirque, June 29, 1996. Otherwise, it was a normal night at the restaurant. Sirio wanted it to be a fairly low-key affair by Le Cirque standards—he didn't want the closing to be publicized so much that it would frighten away either his regulars or his potential newcomers. Though few had been formally notified, the room soon grew full of devotees. There was Ivana Trump, Gérard Depardieu, former mayor Ed Koch, and radio host Bill O'Shaugnessy. As always the Schneiders, who'd passed almost every night of the previous twenty-two years in the restaurant, guarded the door at table 12b. A parade of regulars stopped in to say farewell—Mayor Rudy Giuliani, Warner LeRoy, and Ron Perelman. Sirio's family sat at table 27 by the kitchen door and tried to have a family dinner, while Sirio continued to chat with guests and answer phones: business, almost as usual. Champagne was poured freely, thirty pounds of caviar were consumed, and Torres pulled out all the stops to give the Le Cirque of old one more blast of sugar. Every table was served crème brûlée, and every employee had his or her share of champagne. One by one, the family slowly left the restaurant: Egi and Marco back to Circo to deal with their own restaurant, which was operating as usual, Mario home to his wife and their child, and Mauro went to meet up with some friends for a late-night game of basketball.

The last tables were cleared around 12:30 and Sirio waved them off at the door as if nothing were happening. The kitchen crew celebrated with Sottha and Sylvain, then cleaned up, put everything away as usual, and walked out the doors around two.

Normally Sirio might have left the physical closing up of the restaurant to Benito and his staff so that he could go to Circo or home. On this night he stayed behind, as in the old days. He checked the night's numbers and tabs as usual. He complained about the usual things to Benito: Why hadn't someone called to find out why some customer hadn't come? Why didn't someone think to have taxis waiting to take the dishwashers home? He went searching around the space for things to fix—stuck in a routine he had performed in this space a million times.

T O MOVE WAS EITHER genius or totally crazy. I don't like to get too attached to spaces, but this was sad. We had twenty-two years of the greatest success there. We left behind a very good lease, and we didn't have to. Everyone said to me, "Why are you closing a restaurant that people can't get into?" It was true. We were doing better in 1996 than ever before. In a way I liked it better than the early days, because it was the success we deserved, success without the permission of the press.

MARCO *It was really much sadder for our clients than it was for us. We already knew where we would be going, and at Circo we were already doing very, very well.*

PETER KAMINSKY *That last night he tried to speak to every table but couldn't really manage to say anything. He was all choked up. He says he hasn't got any emotions, but in fact he's one of the most emotional people I know. His business side wants to connect to every table to make sure they would be there at the next restaurant, but his human side betrayed him.*

EDWARD HELMORE *[journalist] We came in very late, and the restaurant seemed to be operating normally but as the last people started to leave, Sirio looked more and more lost. Waiters were telling stories about serving the Pope, some of the great moments in their lives there. Another was crying because he wasn't going to be taken to the new restaurant. As the night got longer, the stories got a little bawdier. One waiter was telling me about a night they realized that a woman was masturbating a man under the table, and how they did their best to shield the scene and, when it was over, brought a bowl of water with rose petals in it and a hand towel!*

BENITO SEVARIN *I'd been working with Sirio a long time, on and off since the beginning. Working in a restaurant, giving the kind of service, meeting the kind of expectations that people have for us, is very intense, and I spent all that time—twelve, fourteen, sometimes sixteen hours a day—with Sirio six, sometimes seven days a week. You get to know someone as intimately as if ... well, very intimately. All the screaming he does has nothing to do with him being upset. When he's upset he gets very quiet. He does this thing with the back of his hand, you know? He lifts it up behind his glasses to rub his eyes but makes it look like it's because he's tired, when he's really wiping away a tear.*

I don't like when people point out the obvious. Okay? Of course I was upset. It was a stupidity that we had to leave that space. Years to go on a good lease, the union, the people in the hotel—and none of them would lift a finger to make something good continue. It was a tragedy.

TOM BARRACK *By the time of the closing night, I had signed the deal. I owned the hotel and was totally prepared to give it to him. The whole thing. On better terms than the Zeckendorfs had given him—which was basically free! That night I was begging him to stay; I could have got him out of the Palace contract. He was determined, now that the deal had been signed, to move on. He was already gone.*

I love parties. I always have and I always throw the best parties. They are fun. But you know the secret to a great party? Knowing when it is over. I don't like the parties where people sneak away because they have somewhere else to go. You come to a party, you have a good time, you leave when you leave. Sometimes I call drivers for everyone and I say, "Now the party is over," and whoever wants to stay behind to have a drink in the kitchen does so. When I make a decision it's the same way. I made a decision to move. And so I left. I can't go back. I love the fig tree in my old house. I don't have to see it to know that it is there and if someday someone comes and chops it down, I won't be sad, because I know exactly what it looks like. ◄◄

BENITO SEVARIN *Sirio never says "Good night" or "Good morning" like a normal person. Not to the people he loves, or the people he works with. The last night he walked around and I kept gently trying to tell him that everything was okay and that he should go home, but he stayed, yelled, checked on the day's receipts as usual, then just walked out the door.*

RUDY GIULIANI *Sirio can seem bleak sometimes. He's never happy, even when it looks like the whole world is going in his direction. I'll tell you though, it's a great strength. It probably protected him, and all Italians. It's probably the reason why he's successful. Sirio has never seen himself as a victim. The minute you see yourself as a victim, you start acting like one.*

THE ARRANGEMENTS FOR CLOSING the old space had happened with such stealth that on June 30, 1996, the morning after the closing dinner, New York's social and culinary worlds were stunned. Word had leaked out that the restaurant had closed, that it would reopen at an as yet unnamed space in midtown (although many restaurant insiders knew), and that Sylvain Portay would not stay on as executive chef. Many suspected that Sottha would now rise to the position, but no one knew for sure. Sirio had arranged it so that as New Yorkers woke up to the news, he was bound for Montecatini to escape what he knew would be a barrage of questions from the press, clients, colleagues, and business associates. Sirio insisted that Le Cirque's phones be answered as always, although instead of accepting reservations they were told just to say that the restaurant was not *closing,* but *moving*—a distinct difference to Sirio, who hated to give even the faintest impression that he wouldn't be back standing at the door in a few weeks. Anyone who pressed for more information was told to ring Fern Berman or Sirio directly.

Sirio, however, was nowhere to be found.

LE CIRQUE 2000

S IRIO MACCIONI HAS ALWAYS loved gadgets. The first (Sony) Walkman, the first mobile telephone, the first digital camera—if it is new, and expensive, Sirio has it six months before anyone else has one. A guest on the way to Sirio's house in Italy encounters first "the car": a subdued-looking gray Lancia that, at the touch of a button, sprouts spoilers and ailerons; the only hint of the Ferrari engine growling underneath comes from the yellow and black horse sewed discreetly into the brushed suede interior and the feeling of rushing by lesser cars on the *autostrada*.

The gadgets that were about to sprout within the Villard Mansion's landmarked interiors went a long way to soothing the shock of the move from Sixty-fifth Street. Adding the kind of infrastructure that a restaurant needs within interiors so heavily protected that not even an extra nail or extension cord could be used was an engineering nightmare. Everything—from how the bar could function as a totally independent entity working off of one household electrical outlet, to drainage and electric facilities

for cappuccino and espresso makers in the front dining room—
had to be rethought and reengineered.

The New York Palace Hotel originally allocated more than
$7 million to the project just for the infrastructure, not including
restoration of the interiors or whatever Adam Tihany would ultimately design to fill the space.

Adam's translation of the "Ferrari parked in the middle of
the *palazzo*" was literally a stage set. Like the tents for a wander-
ing circus troupe, all of the interior features that would make the
restaurant "Le Cirque" could be placed into a box and removed
within 24 hours. To Sirio the essence of hospitality is the ability to
move and, of course, think fast. Since the walls couldn't be
touched, lighting fixtures were designed to fit into the chairs and
banquettes, and self-supporting steel frames were created that
could support acres of colored silks.

As politicians have headquarters for election campaigns, so
the staff of 455 Restaurant Corp., soon to be known as Le Cirque
2000, were using the former offices of the Archdiocese of New
York. There, on the fourth floor of the Villard Mansion, Sirio,
Benito, and Sottha worked at desks, for the first time in their
careers. Months earlier, Sottha had finally accepted Sirio's offer to
become executive chef, while Benito, in addition to his duties at
the door, took on the job of Le Cirque's general manager.

While Benito concentrated on construction details and hiring dining room staff, Sottha worked on finalizing his new
kitchen, putting his stamp on the Le Cirque menu and hiring his
kitchen crew. Sirio supervised both but upon his return from
Montecatini in mid-July 1996 he also spent much of his time
working up a marketing strategy. The centerpiece of that strategy
was to do what a real circus troupe does: hit the road.

Sirio's idea was that he and his whole troupe—Sottha,
Jacques, and key *sous*-chefs, managers, and support staff—would
leave in September for a world tour and arrive back in New York
at Christmas, just in time for the opening of the new Le Cirque.
Sirio wanted to show off Sottha and draw worldwide attention to

Le Cirque, as well as give his hardworking crew an adventure and rattle their ossified routines. By August it was clear that the restaurant would not open at Christmas and March was looking more likely. Sirio decided the world tour should go on in any case. The spots on the tour followed the path of Sirio's career: Montecatini, Paris, Germany (both Munich and Frankfurt, though not Hamburg), with London added.

At the beginning of September, just as the chattering classes were returning to New York from their summer holidays, Sirio revealed publicly that the institution known as Le Cirque was moving "downtown" to the Villard Mansion and that, after twenty-one years in the shadows of other chefs, Sottha Kuhn would be executive chef. He also released a menu and the world tour itinerary. The menu showed the first hint of the Asiatic touches Sottha would bring to Le Cirque's French and Italian menu. Chilled oyster soup with caviar and lemongrass stood alongside Le Cirque classics like Bass in Barolo. A space on the menu was left for a "fantasy of the pastry chef."

The phones rang off the hook with journalists calling from all over the world. Restaurant staff and Fern Berman were instructed to tell as much and as little as they could while still telling the truth, which had the effect of whipping up even more curiosity. One repeated question, which threw Sirio into a rage, was "How could someone as shy as Sottha handle such a position?" Was he making another mistake as some of the media had suggested when he hired Sylvain Portay? Wasn't moving to Fiftieth Street tantamount to abandoning New York society? Had the ringmaster gone mad?

SIRIO

EVERYONE ALWAYS SAYS Sylvain was a mistake. Sylvain was not a mistake. Maybe Sylvain was not right for Le Cirque, but he was right for the company, right for Sottha, and right for me. Jeffrey Steingarten, *Vogue*'s food writer, who is a very intelligent man, says Le Cirque under

Sylvain was one of the three most important restaurants in America. So why does everyone say bad things about Sylvain?

> SYLVAIN PORTAY *People talk, but in the kitchen we know what's real and what's not real. I would be nowhere without Sirio. Working for Sirio gave me a position in the world I would never have had. Yes, it was hard at first, but I stuck with him because he's the best. He turns you into gold.*

Perhaps the most important thing about Sylvain was that he was very influential in the design of the new kitchen. Even more important: without his and Jacques's support, I don't know if Sottha would have finally made the decision to become the chef of the new Le Cirque.

> SOTTHA KUHN *Everyone in life is ready for the big thing only at the right time. It was a very big thing to me to become the executive chef. I prepared a long time. Before this, it wasn't my time.*

Sottha was ready. We were talking about big numbers. The new space has three big party rooms. We were planning on a staff that could make 500, sometimes 700 meals and more. Every day, seven days a week. Staff went from sixty or so to 170. That takes incredible organization, and Sottha knew how to do it. Finally, he had all the equipment, the staff, the Bonnet ranges. And not just the kitchen, but the kitchen between the kitchen, the garde-manger—a whole area just to assemble salads, first courses. Benito worked to design areas that would really function. We looked at everything, how coffee is poured, toast is made. We even made sure that a waiter could plate simple things like focaccia or soup to bring out quickly. I wanted to take down the wall between the kitchen and the dining room in every way. There's no reason why great food can't be made very fast for a lot of people.

> DANIEL BOULUD *Doing numbers is only a matter of organization. The food quality shouldn't suffer at all. It's a chef's dream to have all the tools to produce quality and quantity. If Sirio had done the deal at the Palace in 1992, I'd have never left!*

Everyone says Sottha is so shy. Sottha is like a boxer. He knows exactly how to get what he wants, especially in the kitchen. No one else could have done what he did to get the kitchen up and running.

LIZ SMITH *Sirio was very mischievous. Anyone who knew him could have worked out that he wasn't just going to do the usual thing. But none of us had any idea. He would just sit there and his eyes would sparkle and he'd go on about what he was doing but leave out all the details. It really built up a sense of suspense—which is really unusual for Sirio. When it comes to his own life, he can't keep a secret for five seconds.*

MICHAEL BATTERBERRY *The period in between the close of the old Le Cirque and the new one was very telling about who Sirio is. He casts himself as the ringmaster. He says he doesn't like it, but he created it. He has to be in control. Look at the clothes, the shoulders, the bulletproof jackets, the sequined waistcoats. It's his armor. It was extraordinary to see him during that time on the street— dressed for work even when he was just stopping by Circo, or going to check on the construction at the Villard Mansion as if he were going to work, or he might find his missing flock out there and set up an impromptu meal right on the street. And you know what? He'd do it. Very Fellini.*

Maybe it was my revenge against some of the critics, the press, and, yes, maybe the man at Ciga, and the girls who wouldn't go with me in Montecatini, the waiter who looks like Charlie Chaplin. I knew I was doing something big. A big risk and a big reward. Normally in life nothing is worth it. ... If you don't do something that gives you back at least 10 percent it isn't worth it. With the move, I knew I would get maybe 11 or 12 percent. My lawyers and the accountants yelled at me, but I always say, if one year you have 20 percent don't get stupid because you should plan everything much lower. Maybe it's because I remember the shoes my grandmother painted, or my sister waiting a year to get a dress. In life I try to plan everything lower. Then when you have a big success, it is so much bigger.

I worried a lot, but I always worry. I worried that I spent my whole life building a business that was perfect and then threw it all away. I know it was not perfect, that food had changed, that people had changed. I had to change too, a big change, or the business would die.

CINDY ADAMS *When he was feeling rough in that period, I would talk to him more than usual. He's obsessed with himself, like all men! And I came to understand his obsessions better. I mean, I may have a relentless pace to my life, but it's at my own speed. Being a restaurateur is not at your own speed, it's at everyone else's. So here's this guy who's all about control, but really doesn't have any.*

Sometime after Thanksgiving I went to Dr. Kruger for a checkup. Thank god he is a smart man, because he let me have the first Christmas and New Year with my family in my whole life—the restaurant was closed. Afterward he told me that the tests that had come back showed I had cancer.

I thought, My god, it's all over for me! But with the help of Dr. Kruger, I then realized—I have a great family, I have a great wife, my business is going to be okay, and I know all the right people to help make the decisions. I decided then and there that I was going to fight. ◄◄

MOST PEOPLE SEE THEIR DOCTORS only when they have a regular checkup or when something goes wrong. Coming from a town where health and medicine were as ingrained into his psyche as how to serve at the table, Sirio has a far more personal relationship with his two primary physicians, Dr. Bernard Kruger in New York, and Dr. D'Alpino in Montecatini. Rarely a week goes by when he doesn't speak to either or both of them. Whereas other people might use the Internet to do research, Sirio has but to stand at his front door to get the best information on every facet of politics, art, finance, and in this case, medicine. Within a week he was an expert on prostate cancer and presented his doctors with the treatment options he had learned about.

His doctors knew better than to be surprised.

His decision came down to a choice between having a radical prostatectomy or using chemotherapy to reduce the tumor. There were strong pros and cons associated with both approaches. Surgery, if successful, would improve Sirio's chances for a normal life, sexually as well as otherwise. If not successful it could result in impotence, incontinence, even death. In any event it would need to be done immediately and recovery, unfortunately, would require two to three months of nursing care and probably six months without work. Thus having surgery not only entailed physical risk, it also probably meant missing the opening of his new restaurant. If Sirio chose chemotherapy instead, he could continue working (though he would suffer illness and nausea), but the same physical risks applied—and there was no guarantee that the chemotherapy would reduce the tumor.

Sirio's friend Warner LeRoy had been forced to confront the same dilemma, and he tried to persuade Sirio to take the more radical approach. LeRoy frequently argued that Sirio was altogether too conservative in his business, with his clothes, and now with his health. Sirio was mesmerized that his friend could appear publicly, dressed from head to toe in crimson velvet, with oversized epaulettes and a magic wand, or that he would festoon his restaurant, the Tavern on the Green, in millions of Christmas lights—but he wasn't sure that LeRoy's flamboyant tendencies should be applied to his health.

Sirio put off a decision and tried to turn his attention to the Palace and Le Cirque 2000. There, as bits of Adam's stage set began to appear, Sirio was more prickly than ever. One night he and Egi went to see the bar that had just been installed. He hated it and immediately ordered it carted off. Luckily it was a Friday. Over the weekend Egi persuaded him to go look at it again, and by Monday he was convinced the bar was the best part of the restaurant.

By the third week of January almost all of the interiors were finished, and the only large task remaining was to lay the carpets. It looked like Sirio could start accepting reservations for March 1.

Then, when the old carpeting was pulled up, the parquet floors—as much under protection as everything else—came up with it. The Landmarks Commission insisted on a full restoration. Sirio organized workmen from Italy to be flown in to do the job. The opening was delayed until May 1.

With three months available, Sirio decided it was now or never: he would have the operation as soon as possible. He had already driven down twice to Baltimore with Dr. Kruger to meet Dr. Patrick Walsh, a professor of urology at Johns Hopkins University and his surgeon, and now he scheduled his surgery for February 8, 1997. Though he would likely still miss the opening, there was a slim chance he wouldn't.

SIRIO

WARNER LeROY was a great man. He arranged for everything—a limousine came to pick up Mario and me and and take us to Baltimore. The car was full of things that Warner knew I liked—caviar, good bread, olive oil, my favorite water, truffles. I went straight in for surgery and when I woke up from the anesthesia, Dr. Walsh said it was 100 percent successful. I was supposed to be in the hospital a long time, but Dr. Walsh said do what you feel, and I felt better, so after a few days they said I could go home. Warner sent the car again, and this time it was full of silk pillows, so that I didn't feel the bumps in the car.

> EGIDIANA *It was a very difficult time for us. Sirio came to where we were staying, an apartment on Fifty-fifth Street—we had sold the apartment on Sixty-fourth Street to be closer to the new Le Cirque and to help pay for Circo. The new place was dark and gloomy and not a very happy place. Sirio did not want a nurse, but he required constant care. I was at Circo, the phone would be ringing in the apartment, Sirio was having meetings on the telephone, getting upset about the contractors, the hotel, the union. I worried that he was not going to get better.*

MARCO *Everyone always says, "Your mother is a saint." I think if there was ever a time when we realized why everyone calls her that, it was when my dad had the operation. It was probably the first time in his life he was ever at home during the day. My dad always has to be in control. But at home Mom is in control. She was mother, nurse, restaurateur, diplomat, bodyguard, cook, prison warden, you name it. We all had to stand back and see what would happen.*

Tuscans come in two kinds: very serious ones, like my grandmother, who think that as long as you keep working you keep living; and storytellers, like my grandfather, who would invite everybody over to the farm and talk and sing all day. I think I am the worst of both and so I don't think I've ever had a tranquil moment in my life. When I lie down, I think about how not to lie down!

I thought about everything I did wrong. I wondered if I deserved to have all the things that I had. And I have a lot. I have the best wife and three sons I'm in love with. The rest is all nonsense. But the worst part was I really thought that I was going to die—there were the tubes, there was the pain, I thought I would never be a man again. It was terrible, terrible. And construction on the restaurant went on, with all the problems and the dishonesty. The promises not kept. I think the pain made it more real. I didn't want to be in a situation like Sixty-fifth Street again, where there's nobody in the hotel to talk to, where the union keeps asking for more. Finally, the head of the union and the hotel management came to my house and told me that everything would be okay, that I would not have the same problems I had on Sixty-fifth Street, that all the details would be worked out. So I said okay, I believed them. Then I started to look to the future and I started to feel better.

They had told me to use the tubes and not to touch, but one day it felt as if I could go to the bathroom—and I did. My wife went back to Circo more and left me alone. So I started to move around the apartment. They had said to move only when I felt okay, that when I felt pain to do nothing. Then one day I went down and I walked around the block, looking at people. You know, I never thought I was going to look at people again. When I did that, I realized I was going to live.

EGIDIANA *It was a terrible time. I try to forget it. I try to block it out of my mind because it was the worst thing that could happen. In a marriage your relationship changes. The love you have at the beginning is different from the love you have later. It's the same love, just different. To me there could be nothing worse in the world than to lose my sons or Sirio. To see him so vulnerable and scared makes you have to go deep inside to find all the strength to hold everything together. You cannot show your husband that you are scared, even when you are. We don't talk of these things. I had to be strong so that he could use my strength when he had none.*

I think I'm a very strong person, but in a different way. With Egidiana it's different. I think she called the contractors, management, Cotter, the head of the union, and said, "Come to my house, tell my husband it will be okay. If you upset him one more time, I will kill you." Like that. I'm sure they would be much more afraid of her than me. To me she just said, "Don't worry, the doctor said this or that, and business is good." She's that type of person. After the surgery I was not strong enough to lie and hide the pain. My wife was so sure of herself that she could lie very easily. She makes it so you want to believe her. She was so good that I told myself, "If I get through this, I will be a better husband and a better father, maybe take more time to be with my family." After we get the restaurant open.

It was only three weeks later that I went back to the restaurant and started to work again. From being away, I remembered that work is the discipline I was born with. I'm not a natural performer or showman, like Warner, but I am naturally very disciplined. Maybe it's my only real skill. I am always fifteen minutes early, always ready to move quickly. I am always prepared to work harder than everyone else.

The first day at the Palace I started taking phone calls again. Ninety-nine percent of success is picking up the telephone. By April 15 we had three thousand reservations! It was crazy, out of control—but I had learned that I was strong enough, my family was strong enough, that we could go through anything and still be okay. I do not have to be in control of everything.

Just never remind me I said that. ◄◄

ON SIRIO'S FIRST DAY back on the job, he walked through his new restaurant with his usual mixture of pride and rage. Critical details in the kitchen were still unfinished; a wall had been constructed too quickly and had collapsed, the garde-manger area had yet to be enclosed. There were a hundred details that needed attending to in the dining rooms, foyer, and bar. *New York* magazine was scheduled to take top-secret photographs for their all-important cover story on the new restaurant—the first glimpse of what Sirio was doing to the space and the initial salvo across the bows of his critics. Security guards were hired to keep prying eyes from seeing the space before the magazine was released. The most prominent feature of the entrance, a steel cage on which sheets of multicolored silk were to be hanging, stood naked. He toured the space with I. M. Pei, who said the new carpets looked more appropriate for a bordello than a restaurant. Sirio had them ripped up and replaced with something subtler.

Overall, Sirio was more pleased than his demeanor would allow. The original drawing room—Stanford White's palatial salon, dotted with green tinged marble columns, two onyx fireplaces, and a triple-paneled gold leaf ceiling—now played host to Adam's swooping purple velvet banquettes, high-backed velvet chairs with clown-button spines, and futuristic lights hanging from the ends of giant steel wands.

Sirio played with every single table—each was designed to be transformed in size at the flick of a lever. Unlike the old space, the purple room had four corner banquettes that could transform in seconds from four-tops to ten-tops. A table in the center could grow as well. He loved the technology of them.

The mansion's former dining room, once a long, narrow, dark wooded space, now was iridescently red and yellow. Sirio loved how the light towers with their horizontal stripes, and the line of tables straight down the middle, gave the room the feel of the beloved French ocean liners, the Île de France and the Normandie; modern, slightly outré, and not at all politically correct—everything the stodgy red velvet room at the Colony wasn't. The element he liked best, of course, was that the entire eastern wall, as he had wanted, opened up to the kitchen.

The bar, the former music room of the Villard Mansion, was Adam's triumph. Its barrel-vaulted ceiling was domed twenty feet overhead and intricately paneled in gold. At each end were five plaster copies of Luca Della Robbia's 1431–1448 marble "Cantoria," or choir lofts, which were created as headpieces for the two sacristies in the Duomo in Florence (now in the Museum of the Opera del Duomo). Lunettes by the nineteenth-century American painter John La Farge representing music and drama were above the panels and tapered under the curved ceiling on both sides of the room. Inside all this neo-Florentine pizzazz, Sirio could imagine the pop of champagne bottles, bowls of perfectly cured Italian olives, and plates of foccacia. Three giant steel frames, each looking like an oversized cornetto, connected a trapeze of red and blue neon light. The bar was raised, slightly angled, and appeared to float on a bed of soft green light, which in fact hid the storage and drainage equipment that allowed it to operate. The solution to creating a bar without connecting it to any plumbing had been to treat it like a giant concession stand at a stadium. Twice a day the bar has to be restocked and cleaned, the intake and outake tubes snaked through the Red dining room and up the stairs to a special panel in the kitchen. Behind the bar, a flat panel television was hooked up to a set of cameras located throughout the kitchen and the dining rooms. Throughout the bar and the central foyer—in particular, on the landing at the bottom of the stairs, just beneath Augustus Saint-Gaudens's seminal inlaid bronze clock of the zodiac—were more velvet sofas, all in a multitude of colors, all too bright.

The staff that followed Benito and Sirio through the new space waited breathlessly for some kind of commentary. Little was forthcoming.

In the kitchen Sirio let go of his Tuscan reserve. Everything tickled him, from the Bonnet ranges, which he touched and stroked, and the garde-manger area, where he relived his youth chopping vegetables, to the pastry shop, where even he aped for the cameras. Sirio personally tested every cappuccino and espresso maker and opened every cabinet along the wall, pulling out cups and saucers to make sure the space worked well.

The change from invalid to superstar restaurateur happened at double speed. Gone were the days when Sirio would sleep on the banquettes to get through a shift. Now he had plenty of staff to take care of things—170 to be exact, plus 90 more at Osteria del Circo. Things were falling into place in an almost alarmingly controlled fashion. Sottha had been training the kitchen staff for months, waiters had been negotiating the spaces, practicing on groups of Sirio's friends and clients, like publicist Peggy Siegal, who reveled in wearing a hard hat as her party dined. For the first time in his restaurant life, Sirio felt totally secure about the kitchen. It was showtime.

The new Le Cirque 2000 was open for business first for an Alzheimer's Foundation of America benefit where First Lady Hillary Rodham Clinton was the guest of honor, then to the press, the food industry, and selected clients, culminating in a belated birthday party for Sirio. A week later, on May 1, 1997, Le Cirque opened to the public. Immediately it absorbed 500 covers a day, not including the party rooms upstairs and downstairs. The Food Network sent Bill Boggs to chronicle the opening, CNN did an hour-long documentary on a day in the life of the new restaurant, touching on Sirio's childhood in Italy. When the interviewer pressed Sirio for more information about his father (questions about his mother were off limits), he started to cry, very gently. She stopped the interview. Throughout his career he had made Le Cirque for other people. Now he was having Le Cirque for himself.

SIRIO

I KNEW THAT we had a big success. I loved that everyone talked about the new space. Of course, some people said we had desecrated it. We didn't desecrate it, we brought it alive for the first time—and we touched nothing! No one, not even now, understands that I could get my sons and a few strong men and move the whole thing out in a truck, overnight, and no one would ever know we had been there.

What I didn't like so much were the people who said I had ruined the social life of New York. This was a nonsense. The society people who like to live come to Le Cirque, no matter where we are. I wanted to prove that Le Cirque is for everyone who aspires to be something, somebody.

BARBARA FAIRCHILD *[editor,* **Bon Appetit***] Sirio really took New York by surprise. In a way Le Cirque had belonged to them, and suddenly he turned the tables and gave it to us. All the buzz was about the celebrities. Just off the top of my head I can still recall who was there the first weeks: Lou Dobbs, Larry King, Natasha Richardson, Ivana Trump. But there was also Mr. and Mrs. Everybody. I was there too, I wasn't editor yet, he didn't really "know me," and I wasn't part of the old club. Celebrities are fabulous and you want them to be there, but they weren't who mattered, either to Sirio or his team.*

BILL BLASS *The stuff about ruining society and the tables and destroying this sacred décor and the location was all just horseshit. I thought the move took a lot of courage, although I didn't like the design—it's a stage set. In truth, I don't think he liked it either, but it's a statement that screams "***not moldy***"—and that is fucking brilliant. Of course, I was sent almost at gunpoint to tell him to get rid of those damned chairs. You couldn't see anyone.*

The chairs were a problem. They had backs that were too high. I had said to Adam that I didn't like them. But to change the chairs was going to delay everything and cost a lot of money. We couldn't just take them down with a knife. So we opened with them and the only thing I heard about for weeks was the chairs! I went home at night and thought, "My god, if after all this all they have to complain about is the chairs, then we are a success!" After a few weeks I knew there were other problems but when you have a problem you turn it to your advantage. I had to be everywhere at once: upstairs, downstairs, the two dining rooms, the bar. So I started to stay in the middle, at the podium, where I could see everything.

BRYAN MILLER *I didn't like the new space myself, not because of the design so much but because I thought it limited Sirio's abilities. The space was so much larger that he couldn't do what he does best. The new space has a life of its own, not necessarily Sirio's. I knew that's what he wanted, though: to change the definition of what Le Cirque is. It was hugely successful, but lots of us missed that part which really was Sirio.*

When we opened the new Le Cirque I stopped hearing about whether Le Cirque is French or Italian. Le Cirque is Le Cirque, it's the food people want to eat, and I have the best people making it. It was really for them we moved: Sottha and his team. Sailhac would have killed to have that kitchen when he was cooking. You can feed the world with great skills, a great garde-manger, a great prep kitchen, and we finally have it. Of course, at the beginning, we did too much. Sottha finally came to me and said, "If you don't stop inviting people I am going to leave!" And so we started to be more sensible with the reservations. Well, at least on Friday and Saturday.

HENRY KISSINGER *I wasn't so sure about the room. At first I did think I'd prefer something more sedate. But you start to think, why do I go to a restaurant? I go there for the way I am treated, I go there because I am comfortable, I go there because the food is good and delivered without fuss.*

RUDY GIULIANI *I had met Sirio at the old place, but I thought the new place suited his personality better, which was quite different from what other people thought. It was a big, bold move. There's probably no one place that I've been to more often: charitable, political, social functions. For me it's just one of the great locations.*

BRYAN MILLER *It's not really about great dishes. Sirio already had the great dishes. What he finally had was the ability to deliver across a much wider spectrum to many more people. This business of rushing in to proclaim a new cuisine every time you open a restaurant is ridiculous, and that's part of Sirio's genius. You're just adapting the same food to a different time.*

BARBARA FAIRCHILD *Sirio's place in the history of restaurants— no, in the history of food—is that he educated his dining audience without the audience even knowing it.*

Sottha and Jacques really made it easy for me. Finally, after fifty years, I could walk into a kitchen and make a change and see it executed immediately. There are some things that only we do, like the way you lay out a salad so that when you lift with your fork it all stays together. Not that "silly food" all piled up on a plate so that after you touch it with your fork it looks disgusting. We still serve flounder, with the peas, separate, with the potatoes, perfect, on the side so it stays clean. There's a reason for these things. If you get too clever you ruin everything. I let Jacques go a little crazy with the desserts, but that's my weak spot. I like there to be a show at the end.

I was happy. I liked what we were doing in the kitchen. I liked what we were doing with the service. People were happy, I was tired. In the early days people still complained about the change, but people do that. But you know, I don't think we lost a single customer. They all came back. They came for lunch, or dinner, or for a party, or a drink. I wanted the new crowd but I also like the old, I'm old! Still, I always say, I should be the only thing old in my restaurant. The change was a trauma, but a good one. We pushed ahead to the future. ◄◄-

ALAIN DUCASSE *Sirio is one of the most modern men in the world! Everyone laughed at first. I was in L.A., Le Cirque had just opened, everyone was saying, "He will fail, you can't move an institution," but I said, "Just you wait, he will succeed."*

NEW DIRECTIONS

SIRIO MACCIONI AND SONS' all-new Le Cirque 2000 was everything he hoped it would be; delicious and scandalous all at the same time. Although he complained tirelessly about how tired he was, about how many more reservations he'd taken, about the constant sense of imminent failure, his eyes sparkled and he looked noticeably younger. The circus décor set in its Beaux-Arts container, the constant presence of celebrities, Sottha's Asian-inflected additions, and Jacques's fantastical pastry were the perfect fodder for television cameras, the media, and anyone with an opinion. To even the most cynical eye, Le Cirque 2000 was a hit—whether you liked it or not.

There was no shortage of drama behind the scenes. Getting the kitchen to produce upward of 1000 meals a day was a Herculean task that fell to Sottha and took a heavy toll on his kitchen staff. That the opening months appeared seamless to diners was entirely due to Sottha, who lived at the restaurant, personally filled in for worn-out *sous*-chefs, and executed every plate that left the kitchen. It was clear that even Sottha would burn out if he didn't find someone he could rely on in the kitchen, so Sirio and Sottha rehired Marc Poidevan, Sottha's colleague back in the Boulud days (Poidevan had left Le Cirque five years before to work as the chef at Tavern on the Green and Maxim's).

There was something else going on behind the scenes. Barely a month into his run, Sirio felt confident enough to sign a contract to open not one, but two new restaurants in Las Vegas, Nevada.

SIRIO

⊱

ALL THIS TIME we were building the new restaurant there was this pressure to commit to a deal in Las Vegas with Steve Wynn. He was a very good client. In the old Le Cirque, a long time ago, he told me about this place he wanted to build out in the desert. I said, "Yes, yes," but it was a long time before we went out there with my sons. I didn't see how Le Cirque could be a part of this hotel that he wanted to build. And we didn't have Circo then, which was maybe more casual, more appropriate for the hotel. It was Mario who opened my eyes to the possibility. ⊰⊹

ENTREPRENEUR STEVE WYNN envisioned a new kind of hotel project in Las Vegas—a scheme that would make the city a chic culinary destination, not just a gambling mecca. The hotel he imagined, he told Sirio and his sons over and over again, would be like a hotel on the shores of Lake Como, American style: acres of marble, fountains that could imitate the lakes of Italy, and the best restaurants in the west. The key to the Bellagio's success, as the new hotel was to be called, had to be a name that registered as the ne plus ultra of class in American society. Sirio entertained the idea—he liked Wynn, and Las Vegas had a certain arriviste appeal that attracted him. Still he kept the idea at Sirio-arm's length; close enough to keep Wynn interested and far enough not to have to sign anything.

It was Mario who became convinced that the future of Le Cirque—and Osteria del Circo—was in Las Vegas. On his first visit there in 1994, Mario saw that Wolfgang Puck's restaurant in the desert, at Caesar's Forum, had lines out the door. It was a market waiting to be tapped. As Wynn's project moved closer to reality, Mario proposed moving his family to Las Vegas to run both restaurants. Mario saw the move west as an opportunity to extend the family's brand name to the mass market and to make some money. Sirio, however, saw Mario's idea as a direct threat to the cohesion of both his family and his business, and he was vehemently opposed. Nonetheless, he opened an active line of negotiations with Wynn.

SIRIO

I DID NOT LIKE the deal we had going in Las Vegas. Mostly I didn't like that my son was going with his family. For twenty years we spent every Easter together at the Tavern on the Green, Warner LeRoy's restaurant. I like to be in one place with my family. And then he wanted to move everyone to Las Vegas. And I said to him, "You have opened one restaurant, one, with your brothers, with your mother, with me, it's not the same thing as dealing with these hotels on your own. You went to Cornell where they teach you things, but not the difference between an apple and a potato! Fine, I like Cornell, but you can't make a restaurant from a computer. These people will eat you alive! Stay in New York, work in your own restaurant, work in other restaurants. Get more experience." I said all these kind of things, but I think, really, I just didn't want him and Lauren and Olivia, who I'm in love with, to go away. ◄◄

ANDRÉ SOLTNER *Mario, in particular, needed to fly, to be away from his father. Under his father he was nervous, insecure. He had to find his own way in the business and he was very brave to fight for it with his father. And look at him now. You go to Las Vegas and he's maybe a smarter restaurateur than his father. Just don't tell either of them I said so.*

DESPITE HIS RESERVATIONS, something about Las Vegas appealed to Sirio's sense of glamour. He had always been somewhat drawn to the gangster life of 1950s Cuba, having served the likes of Lucky Luciano and Bugsy Siegel—outlaws, but with a certain style. To Mario, glamour was a game that came naturally to his father and his brothers. To him it was a concept, not necessarily a way to live. As the eldest child he was less taken with the fast life of New York and all that went with it. He preferred his father's family-oriented side, not his Le Cirque side. His family's two restaurants seemed in better hands with his two still unmarried brothers and his restaurant-obsessed father. Las Vegas would allow him to stay in the family business and manage his life and his own family not just in a simpler way, but in his own way. Mario now had the experience and the business acumen to manage all the details. Had he not been as adept at securing almost everything necessary to open both restaurants in the new Bellagio without ruffling his father's feathers, and had Sirio not taken a personal liking to The Mirage Group's point man, Bob Baldwin, the move might never have happened. Instead it was done so seamlessly that his father had to be impressed.

SIRIO

I WENT OUT to Las Vegas and saw where Mario wanted to live and I got scared. Not for me but for him. When I first made money, I put it into two apartments so I would have a place to live. Mario wanted a house with so many bedrooms that I couldn't find them and he had to have a car for the nanny, a car for his wife, a car for him, and a swimming pool bigger than the house. Though I suppose if you have kids in Las Vegas you have to have a pool or otherwise you have to put the children in the refrigerator. So I got scared. I hope I taught my children not to be afraid—but when I see things like that, I think I made them too soft. We fought a lot that year, but Mario was right. He is much better than me.

ANDRÉ SOLTNER *Sirio is part of the old world in the sense that, like me, he has to stay with his restaurant. The new guys—Danny Meyer, Drew Nieporent, and all the others, and Sirio's own sons— are smarter than we were. They manage their personal lives much better. They have them, and we did not. Sirio even less than me. Sirio will never let go, though he is very happy to know that his children can. He fights with Mario but it's a kind of jealousy that people outside of restaurants probably cannot understand. He wants him to be better, to show him, to raise his family, to have his time, because he could not. He will work until he gets sick or worse, so they never have to.*

MARK STECH-NOVAK *[kitchen designer] The building of Le Cirque Las Vegas actually came before the Palace in New York. I was working with Alain Ducasse, in the kitchen, as a cook, at the Dinner of the Millennium in 1995. I was fixing this rotisserie. If any inspector had seen the work I was doing, I would have been arrested, but something about Sirio made me want to do it. So there I was underneath this thing and he walked up with a phone and said, "Talk to this man." I was all covered in grease and it took me a while to realize I was in the middle of a board meeting with Steve Wynn and all the contractors and engineers for the Bellagio. Sirio made this leap that took me from "guy who fixes a rotisserie for Ducasse" to "guy who can design a multimillion-dollar kitchen for a 4000-bedroom hotel."*

I like to hire young people, to give people a chance, and mostly to give my sons a chance. Someone gave me a chance, right? And I like to explore ideas. I can now. I've worked my whole life to do so. Now I have the experience and, thank god, the courage still to try new ideas, even the bad ones, though not the stupid ones. You know when something is stupid. Agnelli used to say to me, "You look at a beautiful woman, you talk to her, you are happy when she says yes, and, when she does, you send for the driver!"

MARCO *My dad is a junkie for new ideas, new people, new gadgets—mostly new ideas. I'll be walking down the street and someone will come up to me and ask if it's true that we're opening a restaurant in Timbuktu or that Elle Macpherson is going to work at Le Cirque as a bartender and all I can say is "Probably...." You just never know with him. We think he tells us everything, but he's always got a trick up his sleeve.*

Restaurants, life, it's the same thing. Try things, *do* things. It's always the people too long in the business, any business, who want to say "No." The best always say "Yes." You want something done, ask the busiest man in the world, he will get it done for you. Or ask a woman, preferably Italian. Or ask someone young, give them a chance. We hired a wine man, Ralph Hersom, for the new Le Cirque. It was the first time we'd even had a sommelier. He was twenty-eight—not even old enough to drink—but he was smart, good with people and he knew his wine. I took a chance and it worked. Mario believed in Las Vegas and he stuck to what he wanted. I said, "Yes, he has a point," and I became his biggest supporter. ◄◄

SIRIO DIDN'T ALWAYS AGREE with Mario, but was prepared to put everything behind him. A boutique version of Le Cirque and a giant version of Circo would open in the Bellagio. The waiting had paid off. The new Le Cirque's media presence nationwide played no small part in persuading Steve Wynn to grant favorable financial terms to the Maccionis. The deal has remained a benchmark for subsequent restaurateurs eager to cash in on the Las Vegas restaurant phenomenon. Within weeks of signing the contracts, a plethora of other restaurants from across the country clamored to open in Las Vegas—on lesser terms.

Almost immediately Mario moved out west with his family. Mauro and Marco did double time working at Circo with their mother. The family took a new apartment equidistant from Circo and the new Le Cirque, so that one member of the family was almost always on one of the streets between Fifty-fifth Street and Fiftieth Street walking—or running—between home and Circo or Le Cirque.

Although he would never admit it to anyone, there was really only one critic whose opinion about the new Le Cirque he really cared about. And by that September she had already been to the restaurant eight times, in various disguises. Sirio, who prided himself on always knowing when a critic was there in disguise, genuinely didn't know Reichl had been to the new Le Cirque, except on her last visit just before publication of her review, when she came with her brother and effectively "outed" herself. On October 1, 1997, Ruth Reichl of *The New York Times* restored Le Cirque's four-star rating. Her review was so flattering, so directly opposite everything she had written four years earlier, that many wondered if she had lost her critical eye. To admire the glitz and fun of the place was one thing, but for the most important critic in the food business to declare it a serious restaurant in the same league as other four-star restaurants including that of his "ex-chef" Daniel Boulud, smacked of treason. The natives tittered that perhaps Reichl had fallen victim to some political force at the *Times,* or had spent too much time at the top of the mountain— or perhaps, it was just that she had succumbed, as all women eventually do, to the serpentine charms of Sirio Maccioni.

SIRIO

I T WAS THE BEST REVIEW of any restaurant ever written. Not just because it was about Le Cirque. It was intelligent. It would have been so easy to say it was all bad, that a great restaurant can't have fun or complain about the same things from the last time, like all the others do. She had the courage to see it clearly. I was happy for the stars, but I was happier that she had the courage to be different.

> RUTH REICHL *By the time I was doing the second review it was very elaborate doing these disguises. And it took a lot of energy managing to sneak in there. Makeup people, costumes, hair— everything. I was determined to be unrecognized. And, I admit, I was looking for a repeat of what had happened before, just in a different location. But it was completely different. I think one of the differences was that Sirio knew that he had a lot more seats to fill and that he was going to have to appeal to a lot more people.*

From the beginning it was always my idea that Le Cirque be fun. When we closed on Sixty-fifth Street, you still couldn't get a reservation.

If I had had more tables, more space, I would have taken in more people. It wasn't the concept that was constricted, it was the space. I don't think we changed the concept of Le Cirque one bit, we just changed the surroundings so that we could finally fill the space with our ambition and our idea—which is not the mentality of *The New York Times* or the food critics. I think that after her years in California and New York she started to see that I'm not so crazy, that a restaurant is food and theater. ◄◄

> RUTH REICHL *Unlike many people, I really admire his courage to take on this landmark of a place. He made it a much better, much larger space and invested in this amazing kitchen. He spent it all on a huge gesture—and you as a customer reaped the benefit. If you went in there, they treated you well and you got to eat in an amazing fantasy of a place with an extraordinary wine list and good service and fabulous food. With a real restaurateur standing at the door and moving through the room with his personal charm, spreading joy, and Jacques Torres sending out these absurd desserts—though there's something restaurant-wonderful about them. I thought he created a fabulous experience. If that's not four stars, I don't know what is.*

IN FACT, the number of seats in the dining rooms at the new Le Cirque had hardly changed. Officially it had gone up only two from Sixty-fifth Street, to 130 seats, spread between two dining rooms. It was rather that the physical space of the entire restaurant had expanded—more than fifteen-fold. The old Le Cirque dining room, including the bar, had measured barely 1400 square feet, about the size of what New York realtors call a "classic Six"—a generous two-bedroom apartment. The front dining room of the new Le Cirque 2000 alone measures 1800 square feet. Between the two dining rooms, three party rooms, office, and kitchen, the whole Le Cirque 2000 space occupied 25,000 square feet on three floors.

I LIKE THE NEW SPACE. It has a different energy. I like that there's lots going on in lots of different places. We knew when we moved to the Palace that there would be much more: Las Vegas, Circo, maybe Paris or London, and if you want the restaurant to come with you, you have to be able to promote people from within, to take people who can carry the mentality to other places, because that's really where the strength comes from. The design, the fuss, everything people talk about is really nothing. Being a great restaurant is not about luck, it's about hard work. And getting everyone to work very hard is the most difficult thing. People want to work here because they like to, and because they make money. Our costs at the new space were huge, we paid much more for labor, but less for the space, so it sometimes works out, as long as business is good. Still, to me it has always been about the experience and not about making money. If you make the restaurant and the experience good, the money comes. If I wanted to make money, I'd have opened Le Cirque to Go, or I'd have opened four pizzerias in four different parts of Manhattan. ◄◄

AS THE TWO NEW Las Vegas restaurants neared completion at the Bellagio in the summer of 1998, Sirio decided to combine the official announcement of their opening with Le Cirque's twenty-fifth anniversary. The party, held on September 25, 1998, was more spectacular and star-studded than any of his previous festivities. A stage was set up in the middle of Villard Houses' courtyard, a giant video screen forming its backdrop. Bill Cosby, who had taken refuge after his son's death in the still under construction kitchens of Le Cirque 2000, was the unofficial master of ceremonies. Mayor Giuliani proclaimed it "Le Cirque Day" and presented Sirio first with a key to the city and then to the waiting crowd. Sirio was overwhelmed by the elbow-to-elbow sea of well-wishers that stretched from the courtyard all the way into the restaurant. The master of the one-line quip, who usually thinks a minute is too long to spend with anyone, now started to address the audience as if rambling to his biographer. He had already covered topics as diverse as the importance of a restaurateur's living close to his work, to his childhood in Montecatini, to feelings about New York City's rent control laws and the Renaissance, before Fern Berman came from backstage to whisper in his ear that he had not yet made the announcement about Las Vegas that everyone had come for.

The following month, Circo and Le Cirque in Las Vegas opened. The spaces, designed by Adam Tihany, both carried the Le Cirque/Circo design aesthetic in a slightly more subdued manner. Sirio's only major fight with Mario had been on the size and scale of the new Le Cirque. Sirio insisted on keeping it smaller than the other restaurants planned in the mammoth Bellagio as a way of keeping quality under control and, by extension, preserving the Le Cirque brand name. On Sirio's orders, the 78-seat Le Cirque became a jewel box in the western dessert.

Egi, who has a minor penchant for gambling, took to Las Vegas. Lauren had also given birth to twins earlier that summer, Nicolas and Luca, and now Egi had three grandchildren to fawn over, cook for—and to teach Italian to. Sirio came out for the requisite opening phase and a series of opening parties that October, but was remarkably respectful of Mario's position in the Las Vegas marketplace. For the first time in his life he could sit back and look at what his son had done and fantasize about the opportunities his intelligence would afford the whole family. From being adamantly opposed to Las Vegas, now Sirio pinned all of Le Cirque's hopes and dreams on the kind of expansion that his son had wrought.

An ironic twist in one of Sirio's mentoring relationships happened almost as soon as Le Cirque 2000 celebrated its first anniversary. The old Mayfair Hotel was being converted into condominiums and the former Le Cirque space, as well as the original hotel lobby and bar, had been leased to none other than Daniel Boulud, who was going to unite them into one. It was the deal both men had dreamed about a decade before. The irony that Boulud should take over the old space was far less stinging to Sirio than the original insult of his leaving Le Cirque. The two had not spoken since Boulud's departure although they met at various culinary occasions, including some at Le Cirque 2000. Sirio refused to go to Daniel's restaurant until 2003. When he did go, it was for an event to benefit City Meals on Wheels, the charity founded by Gael Greene. Ironically, Greene was out of the country and did not attend the dinner. He attended the event almost as an afterthought, with Egi, on a Sunday night, as if they just happened to be walking down the street. What was the former Le Cirque space is now a faceless private party room that bears no resemblance to the original space except for the structural pillars Sirio spent so much time trying to hide. Daniel made a speech and the two smiled for the cameras.

Meanwhile, the cozy little restaurant that had been Le Cirque had spawned a mini-empire—Le Cirque 2000, Osteria del Circo, Le Cirque and Circo Las Vegas ... and, as always, deals elsewhere were being considered. While the hype and fame were fun and had taken on a new dimension, a part of Sirio lived in fear that it was all too good to be true.

Toward the end of 1999, the Amedeo Group declared bankruptcy. Although Sirio's deal at the Palace was unaffected—at least on paper—Sirio knew he would be heading into a duplication of his problems at the Mayfair: a stream of absentee owners who would install new management teams every other week and further complicate a deteriorating relationship with the union. Sirio felt betrayed by almost everyone.

The new millennium brought with it an appropriately spectacular New Year and a host of new challenges and difficulties. After eleven years at Le Cirque, Jacques Torres wanted to go into business for himself. He had already expanded his career with two cookbooks and a television series, and now he joined Alain Sailhac as a dean at the French Culinary Institute—all with Sirio's support and blessing. Jacques stayed to train his replacement, filled in on occasion, continued to use the Le Cirque name, and continues as Le Cirque's pastry godfather in absentia.

Sottha was a different story. He and Sirio became embroiled in a fight with the union over management of overtime wages and an incident between Sottha and a kitchen worker. Management and payment of the kitchen staff was technically the job of Sottha, the executive chef, even though the system of allowing extensive overtime to select employees had been Le Cirque practice for the previous twenty-five years, approved by Benito and by extension, Sirio. It was the Zubin Mehta story gone awry. Every executive chef knew there was no point in asking Benito for permission to keep a crew to cook one meal or to create a special menu. Now the union was demanding a standardized distribution of overtime pay. The union offered several impossible choices, the most expensive of which was a limit on all overtime worked in the restaurant, payment of back pay, fines, and Sottha's head. Sirio paid the fines, agreed to the limits on overtime for the kitchen staff, and offered a compromise. Sottha would officially accept responsibility and apologize to the union, instead of relinquishing his job. The union accepted. The case was settled, but at an enormous cost, emotionally and personally, particularly to the bonds connecting Sirio and Sottha. Both emerged, older, wiser, and a little more guarded. Sirio felt he was the beleaguered restaurateur, forced to make compromises that his employees didn't appreciate. In fact, they understood completely. They had just learned the hard way that Le Cirque might indeed be a big family, but that it was also a big business.

Not long after, Sottha let Sirio know that he wanted to leave Le Cirque. In 1998 he had returned to Cambodia for the first time in twenty-five years, in order to dedicate his father's grave. According to the 2001 *New Yorker* profile of Sottha, he saw his mother briefly but was so overwhelmed by the changes in the country that he took the next available flight back to New York. His middle brother was also killed in an accident the same year. By the time of the incident with the union, Sottha had been working in the kitchens of Le Cirque practically nonstop for fourteen years. The union debacle only underscored the need for him to move on.

Still, neither he nor Sirio wanted anyone in the restaurant world to get the impression that he was leaving because of the incident with the union. They agreed that Sottha would leave at the end of the year, once tempers had died down and Sottha had seamlessly designed his exit. During the summer, Sirio made the decision to promote Pierre Schaedelin, Sottha's assistant and friend, to the position of executive chef. The two had been working together since early 1999.

On Christmas 2000 Sottha had a quiet and emotional farewell dinner with the Maccioni family, and on New Year's Eve he cooked his last meal in the kitchens of Le Cirque. At midnight, the kitchen crew grabbed their diminutive and shy leader, hoisted him into one of Adam's velvet-covered chairs, and paraded him around the packed restaurant to the cheers of its patrons. Not sure whether to cry or to laugh, Sirio moved to the corner table in the kitchen, the "chef's table," where the original Le Cirque menu was framed along with the most cherished Le Cirque mementos—the Rauschenberg-like displays of old Le Cirque china, the most prominent awards, the *New York* magazine cover, and selected photos of Sirio's family. Then, when the chef was brought back to the kitchen, Sirio handed Pierre a hammer and a nail and together they placed above the door of the most sacred space in the restaurant, a hastily typed note, shoved into a cheap gold frame, that read simply "Chef Sottha Kuhn's Table."

Le Cirque is closed New Year's Day. Pierre started on January 2, 2001. That same day Sottha Kuhn took an airplane to Cambodia, this time vowing to stay for a long time. He has not worked in a professional kitchen since.

SIRIO

WHEN WE STARTED at the Palace I knew we had much more competition, and that some of our competitors were even smart, although not always so smart about food. Sottha was successful because he did not try to invent what cannot be invented. You should not manipulate. He knew that it had all been done already. Some restaurants started to put the steak over salad. I didn't get it—it just made the salad warm and the steak cold. Or they said, "Look at the combination—the green of the kiwi and the red of the passion fruit"—and the piece of lousy fish or chicken in the middle that does not have a past and will not have any future!

ANDRÉ SOLTNER *For all of his personality, Sirio truly under-stands that there is nothing new in food. That's a very smart message to get across to your staff. Let them experiment, let them master old dishes, but don't go around calling something new, because it isn't.*

MICHAEL BATTERBERRY *Sirio has an innate understanding of what people want to eat. He always has. It's from growing up in those great hotels and spas and serving that food. The rich ate bet-ter, but that didn't mean they were eating foie gras every night.*

Everyone is always telling me to cut down the menu. Wrong. If I cut down the menu, I cut down my business. A great kitchen should be able to produce anything. If one client comes in and asks for something they can't have, maybe she or he won't come back. A stupid restaurant is the one where you walk in and you ask for a glass of water, and the waiter asks the captain, who asks someone else, who calls the manager and fifteen min-utes later you get a glass of water. Probably in a dirty glass. Every busboy should know the menu too, so anyone can ask you anything. That is what a restaurant is.

FLORENCE FABRICANT *Sirio is smooth. There is no restaurateur with his eye, his ability to fine-tune. He has some blind spots. He's really a very, very solid professional, but from the old school. He can be childish and insecure, but he'd never be stupid.*

After fifty years I think I know what is right and what is wrong. I've seen it all happen not once, but twice before. Sottha was my best, most dedicated cook. He understood the mentality, and so do Pierre and Alain Allegretti. More than anything, it's the confidence. You can't stop to make decisions. You have to know. In your soul. Sottha was very loyal to me and to the family. What happened with him was terrible. I did not fire Sottha. He decided he didn't want to work as a chef in a restaurant anymore. The union took advantage of him and of me. Sottha had the most difficult job of any chef in the world: to reopen Le Cirque. He worked harder than anyone, harder than me. Maybe too hard. He worked seven days a week but the people who worked with him didn't appreciate him. And when they brought in the union, they attacked and would not let go. It was maybe the worst thing that ever happened to me in this business.

SOTTHA KUHN *The incident with the union was bad but I knew what I was doing and what Sirio was doing for me. I was fine. Sirio doesn't like to see anyone attacked and if you attack me, or the restaurant, he thinks you are attacking him and his family.*

PIERRE SCHAEDELIN *People say Sirio is very "old school." He is not, he is Sirio. Where he is very old school is he believes in honor. The issue in the end with the union wasn't about the money—Sirio gave them the money, we changed around forever how the kitchen works, just for them. No one can work more than thirty-five hours a week anymore in this kitchen, except for me and a few others. The issue was about honor. That Sottha's honor was compromised hurt them both very much.*

BENITO SEVARIN *You have to be very careful, very measured, with the union. And Sirio is not very good at that because he takes in everything with them as if it was war. In the restaurant we have everything pretty much to a state of controlled chaos, but Sirio can't control the union and the union can't really control Sirio.*

This "politically correct" is killing the world. It's what people do in history to control the people. They just want everyone to say yes to them. Unions are great so long as they are honest. There should be laws that protect people who work. You go to other parts of the world, you can have a restaurant in a hotel, but in New York we are all castrated by them. I try to work with them, but I lose my patience very quickly. The only way to be free of them is to close and I am not ready to do that. All I ask is that people tell the truth when they do business. You see a mistake, you fix it and you tell the truth. Too many people try to blame. Don't blame, fix. And don't lie about it. ◄◄‑

WHEN RUTH REICHL RESIGNED from *The New York Times* in 1999 to become the editor of *Gourmet* magazine and a new food critic came on board, Sirio knew he was ripe for yet another raking over the coals. The official announcement of Sottha's departure secured it. In May 2001, the *Times*'s new food critic, William Grimes, demoted Le Cirque to three stars. Sirio took particular umbrage at Grimes's jibe at the post–Jacques Torres pastry department and at his inference that Sirio's folding of napkins near his table was staged for his benefit.

The sting came not only because, in Sirio's opinion, Grimes's review had got it wrong, but because Sirio had started to sense a changing in the tide of the New York restaurant world. Le Cirque was in good financial shape, but by the last quarter of 2000, a recession had started to take hold in New York, resulting in a natural attrition from the restaurant boom, of which Le Cirque 2000 was one of the most prominent leaders.

SIRIO

→→

GRIMES ACCUSED *ME* of picking up a napkin just for *him*? Please. It makes me so mad. What really made me angry, where I think he was really just wrong, was to go and attack other people by name. Restaurant critics should leave their commentary to the food, the ambience. Fine, attack me, I'll scream, but don't attack my guests—not by name. It wasn't very nice. And then he attacked the people in my kitchen; he took three things he knew nothing about and wrote about them for fun. Please, let's talk about something else or I won't stop. ◄◄‑

ROGER YASEEN *Sirio gets so upset about these reviews when even a guy on the street would know not to waste a breath about it. Anyone who really counts to Sirio knows that all he really does is pick up napkins and, until it was outlawed, ashtrays. I've always thought that the increasingly draconian laws about not smoking are really a subversive attempt by politicians to get Sirio out of his restaurant.*

MIMI SHERATON *I've come to consider him a very, very shrewd restaurateur. One of things that makes me like Sirio very much is that he's very transparent, he wears all of his emotions on his sleeve. He still hasn't forgotten I took stars away. Years later we were at a roast at the FCI [French Culinary Institute] for André Soltner, and I said in my speech, "They never forget, these people, do they Sirio?" And he jumped up and started yelling like it had been yesterday.*

BRYAN MILLER *Sirio knew Claiborne. They were friends, they cooked together. It was a different world built on respect and an understanding that restaurants developed over time. Criticism wasn't a sport. Sirio knows that it's just a game and he plays it better than anyone. But he also craves approval. He gains it from thousands of people a week—but the one person who doesn't approve will always make him hysterical.*

PIERRE SCHAEDELIN *It's just a horrible feeling, like hell. But you know inside that all that it means is you didn't provide what one person liked. I know that Sirio produces what his customers like and that's all that's important. For four stars* The New York Times *wants that very formal kind of restaurant, and that's not Le Cirque. Do I wish he hadn't taken the star away? Yes. Did it hurt? Yes. Le Cirque is Le Cirque—when you look back at the history of Le Cirque you'll see that it was probably very good to have that review. Having a fourth star would probably hurt us these days!*

DON'T PLAY GAMES
WITH GOD

SIRIO IS DEEPLY SUPERSTITIOUS. He has always liked the number five. He likes that there are five members of his immediate family. With the birth of Mario and Lauren's twins, Nicholas and Luca, he liked that Mario's family now numbered five. And he felt that at five years, there should be a complete overhaul at his restaurant. Circo reached its five-year anniversary in 2001 and the family felt it was time for some changes. Circo was always billed as an "Italian" restaurant, with a Tuscan soul, and the menu items listed under Egidiana's name, by inference, the most Tuscan of all. Everyone in the family (and most critics) agreed that the most authentic and delicious items on Circo's menu belonged to Egi. Her ravioli, filled with bitter greens and sheep's milk ricotta, dressed in either a light tomato sauce or butter, her *cacciucco*—the Tuscan fish soup—and even her family recipe for *trippa gratinata alla Toscana* (tripe), were best sellers. That was proof positive that the menu should be reconstituted as almost entirely Tuscan. The restaurant could finally be billed as Tuscan first, Italian second.

Egi and the boys promoted a young Italian American from Staten Island, Alberto Di Meglio, rather than hire a new chef. Alessandro "Sandro" Giuntoli, Sirio's nephew-in-law, had decided to return with his family to Montecatini and open a restaurant of his own. Circo was closed for the summer, and Di Meglio and James Benson, the *chef de cuisine* at Le Cirque in Las Vegas, were flown to Italy to work in several Tuscan restaurants and then to cook for two weeks in Montecatini with Egi and as co-chefs for Sirio's summer fête.

At Osteria del Circo, the space was opened up to the kitchen, making the restaurant look even more circuslike, if such a thing was possible. They rehired an old Le Cirque hand, Bruno Dussin, to run the front of the house and act as general manager. A revitalized space, a new maître d'hôtel, and a young Italian-American chef in the kitchen would see Circo through its next five years. In a bid to crush the Italian superstition about Tuesday openings once and for all, they set a reopening date of Tuesday, September 11, 2001.

The wail of sirens that arose from the streets that morning propelled Sirio and Gillian Duffy, the culinary editor of *New York* magazine, who was at the family's apartment finishing up the photography for a Thanksgiving feature, to turn on the television. Egi, as always an early riser, had left to deal with the flowers for the reopening of Circo. Cocooned in the sleek midtown high-rise, Duffy, her crew, and Sirio were just in time to witness the second airplane hitting the World Trade Center, a few miles to the south. One of Duffy's reporters called in from the Trade Center, giving her and Sirio a second-by-second update. Egi rushed in, having heard the news on the street. She first made sure their children were safe—all three were in town—and then, like millions of Americans, they sat glued to the television. As they watched the first tower fall, Sirio's demeanor changed. He suggested they go to Circo, where they were sure to feel better, but the group did not take up the suggestion. While he screamed instructions at Egi, she showed Duffy and her crew to the door, saying, "It's just like the war, it's just like the war."

A part of him wanted to close the restaurants. The other part knew he would stay open no matter what. As he grappled with the decision, it didn't help that it had been on a September 11, fifty-seven years earlier, that his father had been hit by the bomb that killed him. A phone call from Tony Carbonetti, Mayor Giuliani's right-hand man, sealed his resolve. The mayor asked that Sirio stay open and carry on with the opening of Circo—although Giuliani and Carbonetti would not be able to attend. He also asked that food and drink be sent to the rescue crews working amid the wreckage created by the fallen towers. Giuliani wanted his friend to send a signal about the city's intentions in the face of catastrophe: Le Cirque represented New York, and New York would soldier on.

SIRIO

HE CALLED ME in the morning to say, "Please, Sirio, stay open. Please." He told me to get food down there, which we did, and not to talk about it, which we didn't. We took the Le Cirque bags and put stickers over them so people wouldn't see.

Sometimes it is better not to tell the truth.

On the way to Le Cirque, I could hear the sirens. There was so much confusion. In my head it was like that—the end of the world had come. It was just like when I was walking to school and the bombs were falling. Someone came into the restaurant and said, "What are you doing here, are you stupid?" But I had to be there. Where else could I go? It was terrible. I did what I always do, I worked. We tried to tell people we were still open, and that Circo was still going to open. We were putting on a big lunch that day for the Italian Trade Commission, for Lucio Caputo, who is a very good friend. I knew his offices were on a very high floor in the World Trade Tower but I couldn't remember which one. And, my god, at

12:30 he walked into the restaurant, covered in dust. The plane hit just above him. He was on the seventy-eighth floor and had just come down from breakfast at Windows on the World. They told him to stay, but he decided to leave. He got out of the building a few minutes before it came down and he walked straight here to lunch—what is that, five miles? He said he did it on purpose. Only two other people arrived who were supposed to come to the lunch, so they all sat down to have lunch at the same table. One person said that all this was happening because of the Europeans, most of all the French, who were protecting the Arabs. Another person said it was happening because of the Americans, who were protecting the Israelis. Finally Caputo said, "Do you mind? I'm supposed to be dead. Can we have lunch?"

Some people who worked in the kitchen either couldn't go home or didn't want to go home, so they stayed and worked with me. Everyone worked very hard. That night, we had 250 for dinner. They laughed and talked like normal, like before. There were New Yorkers, people who couldn't leave the city, people who were not from New York—everyone still had to eat, and we were open. Circo reopened on schedule and was full too. It was the last night the restaurant business in this city was like the old days. ◄┿

FOR THE NEXT WEEK Sirio remained pathologically attached to his restaurant. If you rang the main number, it was his voice that answered the phone, not his staff. His wife and children tried to persuade him to get some rest, but he would just turn on the radio, as he had when he was a child trying to find out about the war. He listened in Italian to the BBC from London, to American stations, and even tried to listen to Arabic stations.

Four days after the attacks on the Twin Towers, Rudy Giuliani walked into Le Cirque, to a standing ovation. He encouraged people to eat, drink, and live. Sirio, dressed in his finest black silk dinner jacket, did his best to maintain the joie de vivre. His bloated and puffy eyes and shaking hands betrayed him— underneath he felt as he had at his father's funeral.

A week after the attacks, on September 18, 2001, I sat down with him in his "official" office, a room separated from the main office (where he usually sits) by a narrow hallway that snakes its way through the labyrinth of little rooms that eventually connect the basement of the Villard Mansion to the Palace Hotel. The room is always locked, and only Sirio and his assistant have keys. It is so cramped with the detritus of Sirio's restaurant life—mementos, awards, unused furniture, books, china, Stefano Ricci ties—that he hates people to see it. Once in his chair, he started moving piles of paper around the desk. I asked if he and everyone in his family were fine. He answered, "More, or less. Probably a lot less," and was off on an uncontrolled, frustrated diatribe at the world.

SIRIO

WHAT HAPPENED TUESDAY was terrible. But America hasn't tasted an inch of what is terrible. The people who crashed into the Towers were crazy. Were they not able to judge what they were doing? Or maybe there's another reason. If there is, then we have to think about what it is.

I think I know what that kind of crazy is like. In Italy I grew up being taught that the French and the English were going to take away our way of life and that the Germans were good; but before that and after that it was the Germans who were bad. These people, they grow up poor and hungry, and when you are poor you are angry and very susceptible to what people tell you. Nobody wants to go back to the basis and see what made this happen and try to stop it there.

Instead it's always bombs, and they don't fix anything. I grew up with bombs falling on my head. I saw my father and so many other people killed. In the morning we woke up to see how many had died the night before.

What I know is that the bomb makes it worse. Vengeance might feel good now, but it never lasts. And it changes. It has consequences none of us can control, least of all governments.

My wife, my sons, everybody says to me, "Sirio, you are overreacting." Of course I overreact. I'm Italian. I overreact to everything, thank god! People tell me to go home and sleep, but if I go home I just hear a voice. People killing each other. The Red killing the Black. The Fascists killing the Communists. Please. You have to understand. I've lived through this. Don't you see? Whoever wins the war wins only the right to say they were right. I can hear Mussolini saying, *"Italiani faciant la guerra per avere il diritto di redere al tavolo di pace."* We fought to have the right to be at the table of peace. It didn't matter that he almost destroyed the country, that they almost destroyed the world. And it won't matter now.

In my life I tried to re-create a place that is home, a place I love, where I am comfortable, that I want to stay in and raise a family. I am proud to have brought my family to this country. And I'm proud even to try to make it so the people in the union can raise their families. No one makes it easy for me to do that, but I do it. This is what I thought I had done. Now I don't know, I don't know.

Doesn't anyone see that when you start a war you never know how it will come out, even if you know you're winning? What you do in war is destroy a piece of humanity or civilization. After a while you don't know anymore who is right and who is wrong. War is a terrible mistake.

That's why the best thing that has happened is Giuliani, who does not say, "Go to war," but "Hatred and prejudice is probably why this has happened and more of it won't help." He's not a saint. But he knows. ◄◄

THE EVENTS OF 9/11 contributed to the denouement of a nationwide recession that had started nine months before. The vigor that had brought Le Cirque 2000 to the Palace four years before was seeing its first real test. Who would be the winners and losers? To the outside world Sirio remained as confident as ever. To employees and friends he behaved as if it were 1973 all over again—and that nothing short of a full-scale revitalization of his business interests would guarantee that Le Cirque and Circo survive what he knew would be a lean few years.

In the months after 9/11, the high end of the restaurant business dropped by as much as 30 percent. The Europeans and South Americans who had kept late nights at Le Cirque ticking dropped to a trickle. Also gone were the American tourists who filled the restaurant evenings from 5:30 to 7:30. Over the next few months restaurateurs would start to change their schedules, dropping lunch services, shortening hours, or closing entirely. Daniel Boulud closed his restaurant for lunch. Warner LeRoy's Russian Tea Room closed for good—Warner himself had died in February 2001 after a long battle with lymphoma, leaving the operation of the Tea Room and the Tavern on the Green to his youngest daughter, Jennifer. Days before he died, he asked Sirio to guide her through the business. Warner had no way of knowing that 9/11 would destroy the Tea Room's already faltering business.

Sirio refused to make any changes whatsoever to Le Cirque's schedule. The numbers continued to be high, not like the first four years, but enough. Table turnover was lower, and people weren't spending as much. Sirio felt changes in the menu would help. He had Pierre put more comforting items on the menu— choucroute, stews, more salads, and the return of classic bistro dishes like roast chicken and onion soup. He insisted that the number of available dishes, not including specials, remain at 55. When times get tough, Sirio insisted, people want choice, "and don't kill them with the price."

Instead of contracting the Le Cirque brand name, Sirio decided to expand it. If the audience from Latin America wasn't coming to New York, he would go to them. Juan Pérez-Gómez, the president of Camino Real Hotels in Mexico City, had been trying to get Sirio to open a Le Cirque in one of their hotels for several years. He'd been to Mexico City several times to look at the space in the Camino Real Mexico hotel, designed in 1968 for the Olympics by Ricardo Legoretta, and had fallen in love with the bold colors and architecture of the hotel and the country. Mexico, Sirio declared, was the new frontier and the new frontier was exactly where Le Cirque should be. In New York, Egi and Marco could take care of Circo and Mauro would be the face of the Maccioni family in Mexico City.

Mauro spent the summer of 2002 in Spain working at Restaurant Arzak, in San Sebastian. He wanted to perfect his Spanish, and also to be at the forefront of the surge in avante-garde cuisine—led by Sirio's friend and contemporary, the Basque chef Juan Mari Arzak, his daughter Elena, and chefs like Ferran Adria—near Barcelona. Would a foam of spiced celeriac, or cellophane noodles that tasted of the sea, appear on Le Cirque's menus in the future? Sirio was, as always, suspicious of the new trend but quick to make sure he and his family understood it. Benito moved to Mexico City to oversee construction of the new Le Cirque and to manage the Maccioni family's new Latin American branch, including construction of an Osteria del Circo on the Gulf of Mexico at another Legoretta-designed Camino Real hotel in Cancun.

Le Cirque Mexico City opened officially in December of 2002 when King Juan Carlos came for a private reception. Adam's design, six years after Circo and five years after Le Cirque 2000, is more textural and more opulent. In addition to the main dining room, there are six velvet-clad private dining rooms, and another room that is effectively a climate-controlled glass cube inside the wine cellar. The main dining room, like all the Le Cirque and Circo designs, opens straight to the kitchen. Where the kitchen at the Palace had two standard Bonnet ranges, Sirio and Benito had Molteni hand-craft two giant ovens that quadrupled the capacity of the Bonnets. Mexico has almost twenty thousand square feet of cooking and prep space, compared to New York's eight thousand. To Benito, it made the New York kitchen, so modern only five years ago, an anachronism.

After a series of opening parties throughout February 2003, Le Cirque Mexico City settled into the kind of routine that Sirio loved best—tables of beautiful women who arrived at 3:00 in the afternoon for lunch and sometimes stayed until midnight, eating, drinking, smoking, and creating Le Cirque, Mexican style. Benito became adept at dealing with the flotilla of armed bodyguards his patrons frequently had in tow. Sirio feels the best way to deal with security is to get them to put their guns down and have a little something to eat, maybe give them their own room where they can watch their employers and relax. Benito held firm and the security teams now wait patiently outside the entrance to the restaurant, although Sirio frequently sends plates of prosciutto and bread out to them. The main dining room originally faced an eighty-foot-long internal piazza, surrounded by fifty-foot walls. The space was roofed over with glass, air conditioned, and planted to make a giant conservatory garden. Sirio had it decorated with eleven giant circus murals by his friend, graphic designer Milton Glaser, and it has become the scene for Mexico City's most chic Sunday brunch—a business Sirio swore he would never get into. Two hundred and fifty people, mostly women, "*c'etait comme en cirque!*" have a way of changing Sirio's mind. Le Cirque Mexico City, Sirio said, was even more fun than the original Le Cirque had been—and now he wants to do brunch at all of his restaurants.

Sirio continues to stay in the game. The ideas still swirl in his head, waiting for the place, time, and location to strike. He's got into the habit of keeping a lease or two in reserve. He developed plans for what he envisioned as a re-creation of the Colony, to be called the Colony Grill, at the world's most expensive corner, Fifth Avenue and Fifty-ninth Street, facing the Plaza in midtown Manhattan. He even hired architects to develop a massive glass staircase to solve the problem of how to get people to descend under the plaza in front of the General Motors Building. He continued to look for spaces for a new restaurant for his wife to, at last, serve the food Sirio really wanted to eat, although Egi says if it happens, Sirio is never allowed to come to the restaurant. Or perhaps a small restaurant to mimick the original Le Cirque in energy and feel, but with an entirely Italian bent, or maybe to pick up his tent and troupe and move Le Cirque out of the Palace entirely.

Robert De Niro, a client, friend, and fellow restaurateur, had his sixtieth birthday party at Le Cirque in New York in 2003 and, as a surprise, whisked Sirio to Italy on his private jet to continue the celebrations at Sirio's house in Montecatini. The Italian paparazzi, not for the first time, descended on the villa—but inside, Egi cooked as normal, tenor Andrea Bocelli crooned by the swimming pool, and Bob and Sirio fantasized about their futures in the restaurant business: the real estate, the philosophy— dreamers both. "Would the owner of Le Cirque and the owner of Nobu create a new restaurant together?" the European gossip magazines screamed. "Actually," Sirio told an Italian newspaper, "Mr. De Niro is a friend. Anything is possible but why complicate things? A restaurant would kill a perfectly good friendship and he has a nice time in my pool with his family. In truth, right now I think the new frontier—where I am really excited to be—is Shanghai."

SIRIO

I GET MAD when people tell me I am lucky. I worked very hard. For the first three months on Sixty-fifth Street I slept on a banquette because we had to do room service and open the kitchen at 6:30 A.M. It wasn't my great intelligence, it was not inspiration, it was desperation. The only person who ever really inspired me is my wife.

I try to forget but I can't forget, and the older I am the worse it gets. My wife, my sons, my grandchildren, good honest food, olive oil, salt, pepper, the fields around my house in Montecatini, my grandfather at the table, reading poetry. And God, dear God, my grandmother, who worked to give me everything I have, even now. And my Uncle Alberto and Guido, who gave their lives for me and for Clara. Once, in the early days, when we were on Sixty-fifth Street, Alberto came to Le Cirque. He was so proud of me. But he wouldn't eat anything. When he saw things being made with milk, he got a look of terror across his face—back home we were only given milk when someone was sick. He was afraid. When he left, we found an entire pile of biscotti amaretti wrappers. He must have lost ten pounds being with us. Every night I go back to that feeling that I had when I was six, seven years old, about war and the difficulty of finding food.

Leaving home was a tragedy that still goes on for me today. When I'm in a place that I like and tomorrow I have to think about closing my luggage to leave again, I get anxious, that feeling in the stomach, because

I remember when I closed my luggage the first time I went to Paris, with three big suitcases, no money, and I had to wait at the station. You don't feel handsome, you don't feel famous, you don't feel protected. You feel skinny and poor and lonely. And again when I went to Germany, and when I boarded the ship. I'm not good at letting go of the things I love. Why should I be? I just know I have to keep going with the *angoscia*.

I go back to the time of the war in Italy. The Allies were bombing every night but still we went out to dance. We had to press on, to dance, because we had to go on with life. Does any of all this I am saying, about food, about restaurants, about all that I have been through, mean anything? I want to stop war, I want to stop the bombs, but I just sell soup. I have to be happy to know that I did at least one thing right. And that isn't making a restaurant.

Peter, this is the point:

I think, I talk and I talk, and this is all I know. My life is not a tragedy. It's the life of so many Italians. I love Italy. I loved my house. I loved my mother and my father and my grandfather and my grandmother and they took it from me. It is where I was once happiest, but so long ago I don't even remember, I really just imagine how it must have felt. So I know I can never really go back. All I can do is make a home here, with my wife, and try to give whatever that feeling is to my children.

I never get to have that feeling again.

I think my father tried. I think he tried very hard to give it to me, to my sister.

He just didn't win the war.

I think that, maybe, I might have won the war. ◄◄◄

Sottha's Consommé with Foie Gras Ravioli SERVES 8

INTRODUCING FRENCH OR ITALIAN CHEFS to American markets by letting them cook at Le Cirque is one of Sirio's favorite strategies. Paul Bocuse's consommé, with its puff pastry top, was put on the menu in 1980 and remained until Sottha Kuhn created his own consommé, with a distinctly Asian touch, that has become famous in its own right. At home, the consommé can be made a day before and the foie gras ravioli in the morning—and you don't have to get the ravioli restaurant perfect.

CONSOMMÉ

- 5 pounds oxtail, trimmed of excess fat
- 1 tablespoon vegetable oil
- 3 onions, unpeeled, halved
- 1 cup chopped onion
- ½ cup chopped carrot
- ½ cup chopped celery
- 1 bunch parsley stems, leaves reserved for another use
- 1 tablespoon black peppercorns
- 3 plum or other red ripe tomatoes, crushed

  Salt

THE "RAFT"

- 8 egg whites
- 1 teaspoon salt
- 1 pound lean ground beef

RAVIOLI

- 1 pound foie gras terrine
- 48 wonton skins (2-inch squares)
- 1 egg beaten with 1 teaspoon water

TO MAKE THE CONSOMMÉ

Preheat the oven to 400°F.

Toss the trimmed oxtails with the vegetable oil, then spread them out in single layer on one or two baking sheets, making sure there's enough room between the pieces for the meat to brown instead of steam. Cook, turning occasionally, until the oxtail is deeply browned, about 40 minutes.

Meanwhile, "brûlée" the 3 halved onions: heat a large nonstick pan over high heat for 2 minutes, then add the halved onions cut-side down and cook, undisturbed, until blackened.

Put 6 quarts cold water into a large stockpot. Add the onions brûlée and all the remaining consommé ingredients and bring to a boil over high heat. As soon as the pot boils, reduce the heat to medium-low and cook at a bare simmer—you should see bubbles breaking the surface occasionally—for 2 to 3 hours. Skim the pot regularly, removing any scum or fat that rises to the top.

Strain the beef broth from the vegetables and meat, then pass through cheesecloth into a clean container, and store in the refrigerator overnight, discarding all solids.

Retrieve the beef broth from the refrigerator, remove any fat that's hardened on the top of the stock, and return it to a stockpot on the stove.

To Make the "Raft"

Beat the egg whites until frothy in a large bowl, add a pinch of salt, then stir in the ground meat, stirring or beating the two for a couple minutes, until well mixed. Bring the stock to a boil over high heat. As soon as it begins to boil, pour in the raft mixture and stir for a few seconds, until the raft starts to come together and float to the top. Reduce the heat to low so the broth slows to a simmer, and cut a small hole in the middle of your raft with a spoon (the hole allows the heat to escape without threatening to tip or break the raft.) Cook at a simmer for 40 minutes, basting the top of the raft occasionally.

Remove the raft from the top of the pot, but do it carefully—it's best to remove it in one piece, though if breaks into a couple of large chunks, the consommé will still be clear. Pass the consommé through a coffee filter, discarding all solids. You can use it immediately or store in an airtight container in the refrigerator for a day or two. If there is any fat on the consommé, remove it by dragging clean paper towels across the surface of the broth (meaning you should use a clean paper towel for each pass).

To Make the Ravioli

Cut the foie gras terrine into ½-inch cubes (you need 24; if it seems like your terrine won't yield that amount, adjust accordingly or serve 2 ravioli instead of 3 in each portion). Brush one side of a wonton skin lightly with the beaten egg and place a cube of foie gras in the middle of the square. Brush another wonton skin with the beaten egg and drape it egg-washed-side-down over the cube of foie gras. Gently press the 2 wonton skins together, expelling any air pockets, and set aside. Repeat with the remaining wonton skins and foie gras. When all the ravioli are made, cut them out with a fluted 1½-inch cookie cutter and keep them covered with plastic wrap on a baking sheet in the refrigerator until you're ready to cook.

To Finish

Bring a large pot of salted water to a boil, add a pinch of salt to the consommé and bring it to a simmer, and warm 8 small soup bowls. Boil the foie gras ravioli in batches, taking care not to crowd the pan, just until they float, 1 or 2 minutes at most. Drain them well and put 3 in each of the soup bowls. Ladle consommé into the soup bowls and serve immediately.

Chicken with Ginger   serves 4

A BUSY SATURDAY NIGHT was winding down when Sirio sent word to Sottha Kuhn that he was in the mood for "chicken, maybe sweet and sour." Sottha created the dish quickly, sent the plate out to Sirio, and promptly slipped, fell, broke his nose, and was rushed to the hospital. On Monday morning Sottha returned to the restaurant to find that Sirio wanted the dish on that night's menu. The chicken and vegetables are now cooked separately in the restaurant, but this all-in-one version is precisely how Sottha made it the night he broke his nose!

  1 chicken cut into 8 pieces (breast halved, legs separated, wings without tips)

  2 cloves garlic, minced

  1 cup roughly chopped ginger

     Salt and pepper

  1 tablespoon canola oil

  2 loosely packed cups shiitake mushroom caps, cut into ½-inch strips

  1 yellow bell pepper, peeled, cored, and cut into ½-inch strips

  ½ bunch scallions, cut into thirds

  1 large red onion, cut into ½-inch slices, rings separated

  2 tablespoons honey

  ¼ cup red wine vinegar

  1 to 2 tablespoons brandy or port (optional)

  1½ cups chicken stock or water

Combine the chicken, garlic, and ⅓ cup of the ginger in a large bowl. Season with salt and pepper, toss to ensure the ingredients are evenly distributed, and marinate for 20 minutes at room temperature.

Preheat the oven to 350°F.

On the stovetop, heat the canola oil in a large roasting pan over medium heat and cook the chicken, skin side down, until lightly browned and crisp, about 7 to 10 minutes. Flip the pieces and transfer the pan to the oven.

After 5 minutes, add all the vegetables and half the remaining ginger to the pan. Cook until the vegetables have begun to wilt and color slightly, about 30 minutes. Take the pan from the oven, brush the chicken with honey, then return the pan to oven and cook 5 minutes more.

Divide the chicken among four warmed plates, surround with the vegetables, and return the roasting pan to the stovetop. Deglaze the pan over high heat with the red wine vinegar and brandy or port, if using. Add the chicken stock or water and the remaining ginger and cook until reduced by just more than half. Salt and pepper to taste, spoon the sauce over the vegetables, and serve at once.

CURRIED TUNA TARTARE   SERVES 4

IF ONE DISH defines and represents both the move to the Villard Mansion and the particular style of Sottha Kuhn, this is it. You need a very, very sharp knife for this recipe. The vegetables for the tartare are prepared as a brunoise, which means an exact $1/16$-inch dice.

If you're adverse to the idea of making your own curried mayonnaise, use 1 cup of prepared mayonnaise with a scant tablespoon of curry powder stirred in.

CURRIED MAYONNAISE

1 *egg yolk*
   Salt
$1/2$ *cup lightly flavored oil, such as grapeseed, canola, or corn*
   Juice of $1/2$ lemon, plus additional for seasoning
1 *scant tablespoon curry powder*

TARTARE

12 *ounces sashimi-grade (#1) tuna, cut in $1/4$-inch dice, silver skin removed*
1 *tablespoon plus 1 teaspoon celery brunoise*
1 *tablespoon plus 1 teaspoon shallot brunoise*
1 *tablespoon plus 1 teaspoon radish brunoise*
   Salt
   Juice of $1/2$ lemon

4 *radishes, sliced as thin as possible on a mandoline*
   Celery leaves

CURRIED MAYONNISE

Whisk the egg yolk with a pinch of salt until it starts to thicken. Dribble in a few drops of oil, whisking all the while, and repeat, gradually increasing the amount of oil you're adding with each addition. Continue whisking until it's thicker than you want the mayonnaise to be, approaching a custardlike texture, and then stop adding the oil. Whisk in the lemon juice. Season with salt and additional lemon juice if necessary. Whisk in the scant tablespoon of curry powder and keep the mayonnaise in the refrigerator until ready to use.

TARTARE

Toss the diced tuna with the brunoise of vegetables in a medium bowl, then gently work in 4 tablespoons of the curried mayonnaise. Season with salt and freshly squeezed lemon juice to taste.

TO FINISH AND SERVE

Set a 2-inch ring mold in the center of a chilled dinner plate. Spoon a quarter of the tartare into the ring mold, remove the mold, and repeat with the three remaining plates. Apply the paper-thin radish slices to the walls of the tartare cylinders, decoratively overlapping them. Garnish the tops of the molded tartare with sprigs of celery leaves. Decorate the plate with dots of curried mayonnaise and serve immediately.

Pierre Schaedelin's Baeckaoffa

Traditionally, this dish was left at the *boulangerie* in terra-cotta pots and cooked while everyone worked in the field and then picked up at the end of the day. Sirio loves this as a dish for a big party. The pastry crust seals in the steam and makes for a dramatic presentation.

To make things easier on yourself, ask your butcher to cut the short ribs and the lamb shank across the bone into 2-inch sections.

- 3 chicken legs, split into thighs and drumsticks
- 4 beef short ribs (about 3 to 4 pounds), untrimmed, cut into 2-inch sections
- 1 lamb shank (about 1 pound) cut into 2-inch sections
- ½ bottle white wine, preferably an Alsatian pinot blanc or riesling
- 3 tablespoons olive oil
- Salt and pepper
- 1 quart chicken stock
- 1 cup beef stock (or additional chicken stock)
- 6 leeks, white and pale green parts only, cleaned and cut into ½-rounds
- 4 large carrots, peeled and cut into ½-inch rounds
- 3 large russet potatoes, peeled and cut into ½-inch rounds
- 2 tablespoons butter
- 8 cloves garlic, peeled
- 1 cup all-purpose flour

Combine the chicken, beef, lamb, and white wine in a large bowl or freezer bag and marinate in the refrigerator overnight. Dry the meat with paper towels before cooking and reserve the wine marinade.

Heat 2 tablespoons olive oil over high heat in a 3-quart (or larger) sauté pan and sear the meats. Working in batches, brown the chicken, then the beef, then the lamb, discarding excess fat from the pan between meats and taking the time to brown each piece well, approximately 30 to 35 minutes total. Season the meats lightly with salt and pepper as they finish browning and reserve.

Discard any fat left in the pan and deglaze with the reserved wine marinade and the chicken stock. Reduce slightly, about 10 minutes over high heat, then remove from the heat and add the beef stock (or additional chicken stock). Season the resulting broth to taste with salt and pepper.

Layer the ingredients in a large Dutch oven. Start with a layer of leeks, carrots, and potatoes, follow with a layer of chicken, beef, and lamb, and repeat as necessary until all the meat has been used, finishing with a layer of vegetables. Add the stock and wine reduction, making sure it covers ¾ of the mixture, adding water to make up the difference, if necessary. Dot the top with butter and the peeled garlic cloves.

Preheat the oven to 400°F.

To make the dough, combine the flour, the remaining 1 tablespoon olive oil, and as much water (approximately ½ cup) as necessary to make pliable dough. Roll it into a long snake shape and affix it to the rim of the Dutch oven—the dough is there to seal the lid to the pot and keep in the steam as the dish cooks. Moisten the top of the dough with a little water and nestle the pan's lid into it, making a tight seal.

Set the pot in the oven and bake for 2½ hours. Serve from the Dutch oven at the table, breaking the seal in front of your guests.

CHESTNUT DACQUOISE CAKE

SERVES 8 TO 12

CHESTNUTS ARE TO SIRIO what madeleines were to Proust. When he was a child, he would be sent out to forage for chestnuts and his grandmother would roast them and coat them in sugar—a commodity as rare as, if not rarer than, gold.

Over the years, Sirio's various pastry chefs have tried to concoct desserts to appease his chestnut cravings. This one requires hard-to-find chestnut ice cream; ask your local ice cream shop if they can make it for you, or you can make it yourself, or substitute chocolate or hazelnut.

MERINGUE

6 *egg whites*

1 *cup confectioners' sugar*

1 *cup granulated sugar*

¼ *cup pignoli*

1 cup chopped bittersweet chocolate

1 cup heavy cream

2 tablespoons butter, at room temperature

Chocolate Sauce

1 cup water

4 tablespoons granulated sugar

½ cup cocoa powder

2 scant tablespoons dry milk

1 pint chestnut ice cream

Candied chestnuts for garnish (optional)

Meringue

Preheat the oven to 300°F. Use an 8-inch springform pan as a template to trace 8-inch circles onto three sheets of parchment paper. Line three baking sheets with the parchment paper.

Beat the egg whites in the work bowl of a stand mixer fitted with the whisk attachment, on a low setting until they turn opaque, and then on a higher speed until they've begun forming stiff peaks. Gradually add the confectioners' sugar while still beating on high, until the sugar is incorporated and the peaks are stiff and shiny. Remove the bowl from the mixer and fold in the granulated sugar and pignoli with a spatula, deflating the whites as little as possible.

Transfer the meringue into a pastry bag fitted with a ½-inch tip and pipe out flat discs ½ inch smaller in diameter than the circles traced on the parchment.

Set the sheet pans in the oven and immediately turn the heat down to 200°F. After 20 minutes crack open the oven door for a few minutes to help reduce the temperature to 200°F, then cook at 200°F for 3 to 4 hours, until the meringue is dry all the way through. Turn the heat off and, once they've cooled, remove the meringues from the parchment and store in an airtight container for up to 2 days.

Ganache

Place the chopped bittersweet chocolate in a heatproof bowl and set aside. Bring the cream to a boil in a small saucepan over high heat. Pour the boiling cream over the chocolate and let the mixture stand for 30 seconds. Slowly stir the chocolate and cream together with a whisk. When the mixture looks almost homogenized, stir in the butter.

Continue to stir until the ganache is shiny and smooth. Cool to room temperature and reserve until ready to use.

CHOCOLATE SAUCE

Bring 1 cup water and the sugar to a boil in a small saucepan. Remove the pan from the heat to add the cocoa powder and dry milk, then return it to the flame and bring the sauce to a boil. The sauce can be made a few days in advance and kept covered in the refrigerator until ready to use.

TO ASSEMBLE

Set a meringue disk into the bottom of an 8-inch springform pan. Retrieve the ice cream from the freezer at this point—if it's too warm, it will dissolve the meringue—and spoon ice cream over and around the meringue. Set another disk on top of that ice cream layer, top with ice cream, and repeat once more—you should have 3 meringue disks and 3 layers of ice cream. Transfer the sheet immediately to the freezer and freeze for at least 3 hours or overnight.

To glaze (while keeping the chocolate off your counter), set the pan on a wire cooling rack over parchment, or any kind of paper. Pour the ganache over the top of the cake, spread it evenly with a spatula, and return the pan to the freezer as quickly as possible.

TO SERVE

Remove the sides of the pan (if they won't come off easily, briefly warm the sides of the pan with a hair dryer). Slice the cake with a serrated knife, wiping the blade clean between slices. Place slices on chilled dessert plates decorated with candied chestnuts (if using) and a drizzle of the chocolate sauce.

Caramel-Walnut Soufflé SERVES 8 TO 10

"A SOUFFLÉ IS THE EASIEST thing in the world to make and a great way to make a profit in a restaurant," Sirio says. This is one of his favorites. Once you master the basic recipe, soufflés—sweet or savory—can become a standard part of your home repertoire.

CARAMEL-WALNUT BASE

- 1 *cup sugar*
- ½ *cup heavy cream*
- ½ *cup whole milk*
- *About 1 ¾ cups walnuts, chopped*
- *Splash of rum (optional)*

SOUFFLÉ

- *Softened butter*
- 13 *large egg whites*
- ½ *cup meringue powder (optional)*
- *Juice of ½ lemon, strained*
- ¾ *cup plus 1 tablespoon sugar*
- ¼ *cup light corn syrup*

CARAMEL-WALNUT BASE

Pour the sugar into a 2-quart heavy-bottomed saucepan and place over medium-high heat. Cook, stirring occasionally with a wooden spoon, until the sugar melts and turns a light caramel color. Watch it carefully; once the sugar begins to caramelize, it can burn very quickly.

Once the sugar has melted and has turned the light golden brown color, slowly and carefully add the heavy cream. The addition of the cold cream to the hot caramel will cause the mixture to hiss and possibly splatter, so do not lean over the saucepan while you are adding to it. When all of the cream has been added, mix thoroughly with a wooden spoon. Add the milk and walnuts. Remember to mix into the edge of the saucepan and mix until well combined and the walnuts are evenly dispersed. Insert a candy thermometer and cook over medium-high heat until the mixture reaches 225°F.

At this point, the caramel will have thickened and darkened slightly. Remove the saucepan from the head and pour the filling into a heatproof bowl. Let cool. (This recipe amount yields more than what you need for the soufflés, so store the rest in the refrigerator, tightly covered with plastic wrap, for several weeks.)

TO BEGIN THE SOUFFLÉ

Preheat the oven to 375°F. Use a pastry brush to coat the inside of eight to ten 1-cup soufflé molds evenly with softened butter. Fill each mold with sugar, then pour out the excess. If you have properly buttered the molds, the sugar will stick to the bottom and side of them.

Place a 1-quart saucepan half filled with water over medium heat and bring it to a simmer. Make a double broiler by setting a large mixing bowl over the simmering water. Place 1½ cups of caramel-walnut base in the bowl and heat until warm. If the base is too thick, you can add a splash of rum to loosen it slightly. You'll know the base is too thick if its consistency is similar to that of peanut butter. The base will be easier to incorporate into the warm meringue if they are each about the same temperature.

TO BEGIN THE ITALIAN MERINGUE

Pour the egg whites, meringue powder, and lemon juice into a medium mixing bowl and whisk to combine. (Tip: Old egg whites whip better than fresh ones because some of the water has evaporated and the albumen is more concentrated. By adding meringue powder to fresh egg whites, you can get the same result.) The lemon juice keeps the egg whites from separating and having a crumbly texture.

While the base is heating, pour 2 tablespoons water, the ¾ cup and 1 tablespoon sugar, and the corn syrup into a 1-quart heavy-bottomed saucepan and place over medium-high heat. Insert a candy thermometer and cook the mixture until it reaches 250°F, or the soft ball stage as indicated on your candy thermometer. Remove the cooked sugar from the heat.

Use an electric mixer set on medium speed to whip the egg whites for about 5 seconds. Increase the mixer speed to medium-high and make an Italian meringue by pouring the hot sugar down the side of the mixing bowl into the whipping whites. Be careful not to pour the hot sugar directly on the beaters, or it will splatter. Adding the cooked sugar when starting to whip the meringue will give the meringue more strength and elasticity while making it heavier. This will help the soufflé hold up for 2 to 3 hours before being baked. Continue to whip the meringue until stiff and glossy, about 5 minutes.

To Finish the Soufflé

Combine about one-third of the meringue with the caramel-walnut mixture and use a rubber spatula to gently fold them together. Adding part of the meringue to the caramel-walnut mixture makes the two textures more similar, which helps them blend more evenly. Fold the remaining meringue into the mixture. Remember to fold to the bottom of the bowl to evenly distribute the walnut mixture.

Use a rubber spatula to fill the prepared soufflé molds. Rounding the tops will make the soufflé nicer when baked. Place the soufflés in the oven on the center rack. Remove the top oven rack if necessary to allow enough room for them to rise. If the soufflé is too close to the top of the oven or under a rack, it will stick when it rises. If the soufflé is too close to the bottom of the oven, the bottom of the soufflé will burn before the inside is properly baked. Bake until the soufflés have risen to about one and a half times their original height and start to brown on top, about 20 minutes. This will make the center of the soufflé soft and a little wet. If you like a drier soufflé, bake it a few minutes longer. Serve immediately.

From Dessert Circus at Home: Fun, Fanciful, and Easy-to-Make Desserts *(William Morrow and Company, New York, 1999) by Jacques Torres with Christina Wright and Kris Kruid.*

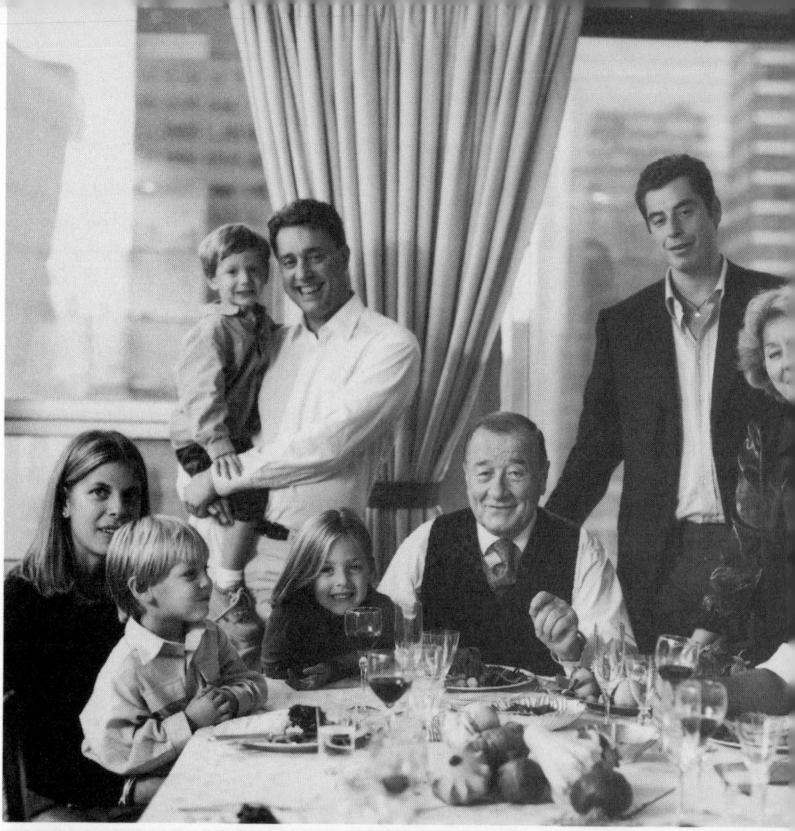

THIS PAGE

TOP:
The Maccioni family, September 10, 2001, for *New York* magazine's Thanksgiving issue: Lauren, Nicolas, Luca, Mario, Olivia, Sirio, Mauro, Egidiana, and Marco.

BOTTOM:
His Holiness Pope John Paul II, His Excellency Archbishop Renato Martino, Permanent Observer of the Holy See to the United Nations, giving advice to Sirio about reservations in heaven. October 1995.

FACING PAGE

TOP:
Sirio makes a point during one of President Bill Clinton's visits to Le Cirque 2000.

BOTTOM:
Chef Sottha Kuhn and Ivana Trump in the kitchen at the all-new Le Cirque 2000, May 1997.

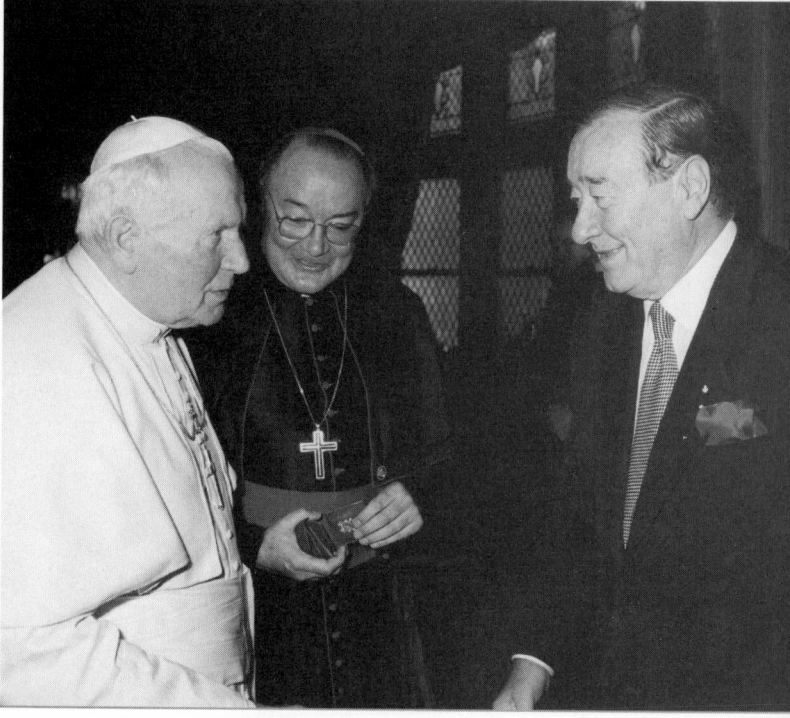

THIS PAGE
TOP:
The Maccioni family
in Stanford White's
"Living Hallway," Le
Cirque 2000, 1997.

BOTTOM:
Sirio with Julia Child
at Le Cirque,
September 2000.

FACING PAGE
TOP:
Woody Allen and
Soon-Yi Previn visit
Sirio in Montecatini,
1995.

BOTTOM:
"The love you have
when you are older
is different." Egidiana
and Sirio after their
35th anniversary
party, walking home
via the Tettucio Spa,
Montecatini, 1999.

BIBLIOGRAPHY

Agarossi, Elena. *A Nation Collapses, The Italian Surrender of September 1943*. Cambridge University Press, 2000.

Bacall, Lauren. *Lauren Bacall: By Myself*. Ballantine Books, 1985.

Batterberry, Michael and Ariane. *On The Town in New York: The Landmark History of Eating, Drinking, Dining and Entertainments from the American Revolution to the Food Revolution*. Routledge, 1973, 1999.

Beebe, Lucius. *Snoot if You Must*. Appleton Century, 1943.

Blass, Bill. *Bare Blass*. HarperCollins, 2002.

Boulud, Daniel. *Cooking with Daniel Boulud*. Random House, 1993.

Brenner, Leslie. *The Fourth Star*. Clarkson Potter, 2002.

———. *An American Appetite: The Coming of Age of a National Cuisine*. William Morrow, 1999.

Brody, Illes. *The Colony: Portrait of a Restaurant and Its Famous Recipes*. Greenberg Publishers, 1945.

Brooks, Thomas R. Foreword by Senator Bob Dole. *The War North of Rome: June 1944–May 1945*. Castle Books, 2001.

Calcocoressi, Peter, Guy Wint, and John Pritchard. *The Penguin History of the Second World War*. Penguin, 1972.

Cavallero, Jr., Gene, and Ted James. *The Colony Cookbook*. Bobbs-Merrill, 1972.

Chandler, Charlotte. *I Fellini*. Cooper Square Press, 2001, pp. 233, 340, 357.

Clarke, Gerald. *Capote: A Biography*. Simon and Schuster, 1988.

Dewey, Donald. *Marcello Mastroianni: His Life and Art*. Diane Publishing, 1993.

Duchin, Peter. *Peter Duchin; Ghost of a Chance, a Memoir*. Random House, 1996.

Duggan, Christopher. *A Concise History of Italy*. Cambridge University Press, 1994.

Escoffier, Auguste. *Memories of My Life*. Van Nostrand Reinhold, 1997.

Hamon, Hervé and Patrick Rotman. *You See I Haven't Forgotten*. Knopf, 1992.

Hayward, Brooke. *Haywire*. Alfred A Knopf, 1977.

Herausgeber. *Das Atlantique Hotel zu Hamburg, 1990–1999*. Hamburg, 1999.

Gentry, Curt. *J. Edgar Hoover, the Man and His Secrets*. Norton, 2001.

Giusti, Maria Adriana, editor. *Montecatini, Spa and Garden City*. Skira, 2002.

Greenspan, Dorie, and Pierre Herme. *Desserts by Pierre Herme*. Little Brown & Company, 1998.

Johnson, Hugh. *Hugh Johnson's Wine Companion*, 2nd ed. Mitchell Beazley Publishers, 1987.

Krantz, Judith. *Princess Daisy*. Random House, 1988.

Kuh, Patric. *The Last Days of Haute Cuisine, America's Culinary Revolution*. Viking, 2001.

Lang, George. *Nobody Knows the Truffles I've Seen*. Knopf, 1998.

Lowe, David Garrard. *Stanford White's New York*. Watson Guptill, 1999.

Pépin, Jacques. *La Technique*. Wallaby, 1978.

——. *An Apprentice, My Life in the Kitchen*. Houghton Mifflin, 2003.

Rondeau, Gerard. *Photographies*. Reflet, 1990.

Root, Waverly. *The Food of Italy*. Atheneum, 1971.

Schwartz, Arthur. *Naples at Table*. Harper Collins, 1998.

Shopsin, William A., and Mosette Glaser Broderick. *The Villard Houses: Life Story of a Landmark*. Viking, 1980.

Smith, Liz. *Natural Blonde*. Hyperion, 2001.

Smith, Sally Bedell. *Reflected Glory: The Life of Pamela Churchill Harriman*. Simon & Schuster, 1996.

Spang, Rebecca I. *The Invention of the Restaurant, Paris and Modern Gastronomic Culture*. Harvard, 2001.

Swanson, Gloria. *Swanson on Swanson*. Pantheon Books, 1984.

Trager, James. *Park Avenue, Street of Dreams*. Atheneum, 1990.

Tower, Jeremiah. *California Dish*. Simon & Schuster, 2003.

Vergnes, Jean. *A Seasoned Chef: Recipes and Remembrances from the Chef and Former Co-owner of New York's Famous Le Cirque*. Donald I Fine, Inc., 1987.

Villard de Borchgrave, Alexandra, and John Cullen. *Villard: The Life and Times of an American Titan*. Doubleday, 2001.

Wechsberg, Joseph. *Dining at Le Pavillon*. Little Brown & Company, 1962.

INDEX

Stewart, Martha, 173
Sulzberger, Mrs. Arthur Ochs, 172
Sulzberger, Arthur Ochs, Sr. (Punch), 281
Sulzberger, Iphigene Ochs, Mrs., 146
Surmain, Henri, 122

T

Tables:
 availability of, 79
 in Le Cirque 2000, 353
 patrons' attachment to, 227–228
Taillevent, 68
Tavern on the Green, 361
Taylor, Elizabeth, 130, 253
Tell, David, 311
Thatcher, Margaret, 230
Thomas, Michael, 128, 130
Tihany, Adam, 277, 316, 320, 329–331, 344,
 356, 368, 383
Todeschini, Jean-Louis, 176, 179
Torino, Albert, 129, 132
Torres, Jacques, 218, 248–250, 283, 323,
 324, 335–336, 339, 344, 346, 358, 359,
 369–370
Tour d'Argent, 68
Tower, Jeremiah, 239, 276
Town and Country, 171, 247
Trigère, Pauline, 229
Troisgros, Jean, 76
Troisgros, Pierre, 76, 77, 176
Trudeau, Pierre, 230
Truman, Margaret (Mrs. Clifton Daniel), 229
Trump, Blaine, 229
Trump, Donald, 231, 237, 301, 333
Trump, Ivana, 4, 228, 237, 301, 333, 339,
 356, 401
Tucci, Oscar, 112–115, 117, 118, 122, 123,
 143
Tuscan Red Sauce, 51
Twentieth anniversary party, 312–313
Twenty-fifth anniversary party, 367–368
"21" Club, 111, 112, 122

U

Umberto II, King of Italy, 118
Unions:
 at Hotel Atlantic, 84

incident with Sottha, 370, 373
and new location for Le Cirque, 351
as partners with owners, 310–311
Sirio's membership in, 112
USA Today, 252

V

Vanderbilt, Gloria, 229
Vanderbilt, Mrs. William K., 120–121, 128
Vaudables, Louis, 78–79, 150–151
Veal Milanese, 192–193
Vegetables:
 Frittata di Cipolle, 47
 Pasta Primavera, 186–187
Ventura, Lino, 61
Verdi, Guiseppe, 8
Vergé, Roger, 67–69, 73–77, 176, 217, 244,
 334
Vergnes, Pauline, 182
Vergnes, Jean, 155–157, 159, 161–162, 164,
 172–174, 176–179, 181–182, 200, 210,
 213–214
The Villa Pierre, 109
Villard Mansion, 328, 329, 331, 337. *See also*
 Le Cirque 2000
Villas, James, 90
Von Fürstenberg, Ira, 225

W

Wainer, Mario, 3
Waldorf-Astoria, 109–110
Wallace, Celestina, 123–124, 130, 135
Wall Street (film), 246–247
Wall Street Journal, 253
Walsh, Patrick, 350
Walters, Barbara, 229, 257–258, 300, 317, 332
Warhol, Andy, 226, 300
Waxman, Jonathan, 239
Wayne, John, 25, 41
Welch, Raquel, 229
Wick, Charles, 230
Windsor, Duke and Duchess of, 34, 39, 128,
 131–132, 151
Wine, Barry, 239–240
Wines, 218–221
Wine Spectator, 247, 324
W magazine, 171

Maybe for you always delicious food + thats mixture

À l'ami Sirio
Bonne cuisine
et accueil incomparable
Tous mes compliments
Paul Bocuse
21 Sept 1982

Pour Sirio Maccioni
et ce formidable déjeuner
A bientôt ; à Presto !..
" il francese-toscano " di Monsummano !....
Y. Montand
< IVO LIVI 7
Y. MONTAND
New York. Printemps 84

To Sirio —
Great ! Wonderful
food & Service —
J. Carter

Nice Souffle !
Love
Billy Joel

To Sirio — Keep Punching
out that great
food !

Arnold Schwarzenegger

Sylvester Stallone

*la meilleur de N.Y
Après le Cirque de Lola Montès
le cirque de la belle et grande Cuisine
Amitiés à Sirio Claude

To Sirio —
You're the very best!
And so is Le Cirque.
Love
Barbara Taylor Bradford

to be here for the
temps.
Steven Spielberg